'Getting it right'

Reimagining Ireland

Volume 131

Edited by Dr Eamon Maher,
Technological University Dublin – Tallaght Campus

PETER LANG
Oxford - Berlin - Bruxelles - Chennai - Lausanne - New York

'Getting the Words Right'

A *Festschrift* in Honour of ~~Eamon Maher~~
Eamon Maher (signature)

Grace Neville, Sarah Nolan and Eugene O'Brien (eds)

With my gratitude + deep affection.
Eamon xo

PETER LANG
Oxford · Berlin · Bruxelles · Chennai · Lausanne · New York

Bibliographic information published by the Deutsche Nationalbibliothek. The German National Library lists this publication in the German National Bibliography; detailed bibliographic data is available on the Internet at http://dnb.d-nb.de.

A catalogue record for this book is available from the British Library.

Library of Congress Cataloging-in-Publication Data

Names: Maher, Eamon, honouree. | Neville, Grace, editor. | Nolan, Sarah, 1980- editor. | O'Brien, Eugene, 1958- editor.
Title: 'Getting the words right': a festschrift in honour of Eamon Maher / Grace Neville, Sarah Nolan and Eugene O'Brien.
Description: Oxford; New York: Peter Lang, 2024. | Series: Reimagining Ireland, 1662-9094; 131 | Includes bibliographical references and index.
Identifiers: LCCN 2024016202 | ISBN 9781803741444 (paperback) | ISBN 9781803741482 (ebook) | ISBN 9781803741499 (epub)
Subjects: LCSH: English literature--Irish authors--History and criticism. | Irish philology. | Ireland--Civilization. | Ireland--Intellectual life. | LCGFT: Festschriften.
Classification: LCC PR8704. G48 2024 | DDC 820.9/9415--dc23/eng/20240506
LC record available at https://lccn.loc.gov/2024016202

Cover image: © Paul Butler.
Cover design by Peter Lang Group AG

ISSN 1662-9094
ISBN 978-1-80374-144-4 (print)
ISBN 978-1-80374-148-2 (ePDF)
ISBN 978-1-80374-149-9 (ePub)
DOI 10.3726/b20745

© 2024 Peter Lang Group AG, Lausanne
Published by Peter Lang Ltd, Oxford, United Kingdom
info@peterlang.com – www.peterlang.com

Grace Neville, Sarah Nolan and Eugene O'Brien have asserted their right under the Copyright, Designs and Patents Act, 1988, to be identified as Editors of this Work.

All rights reserved.
All parts of this publication are protected by copyright. Any utilisation outside the strict limits of the copyright law,
without the permission of the publisher, is forbidden and liable to prosecution. This applies in particular to reproductions, translations, microfilming,
and storage and processing in electronic retrieval systems.

This publication has been peer reviewed.

To Eamon Maher: il miglior fabbro

Contents

Acknowledgements — xi

GRACE NEVILLE, SARAH NOLAN AND EUGENE O'BRIEN
Introduction — 1

GRACE NEVILLE
1 *Une Femme Libre*: Edna O'Brien, A Wild Irish Girl in the French Media 1965–2023 — 5

ANDREW AUGE
2 Waking the Living and the Dead: The Revelatory Power of Funerary Rituals in John McGahern's Late Fiction — 19

BERTRAND CARDIN
3 An Intertextual Reading of John McGahern's Short Story 'Korea' — 33

ANNE GOARZIN
4 Friendship and Literature — 45

DEREK HAND
5 Elizabeth Bowen's 'The Good Earl': Escaping the Past — 57

PIERRE JOANNON
6 Reflections on the Relationship between Ireland and France — 71

ALEXANDRA MACLENNAN
7 The Importance of Being Eamon — 87

CATHERINE MAIGNANT
8 French Theory and the Academic Study of Religion in Ireland   99

PATRICIA MEDCALF
9 1960–1989: The Making of a Guinness Drinker   117

SYLVIE MIKOWSKI
10 Children in Recent Irish Fiction   129

MARISOL MORALES-LADRÓN
11 Nuala O'Connor's *Nora* and the Challenges of Biographical Fiction   145

MARY S. PIERSE
12 Judging George Moore's 'Wild Goose': The Case of Ned Carmady   159

MARÍA ELENA JAIME DE PABLOS
13 Trauma and Artistic Creation in *Another Alice* by Lia Mills   173

EAMONN WALL
14 He Lived among These Lanes: Bioregional John McGahern   185

HARRY WHITE
15 *Fifth Business*: George Moore and the Cultural History of Music in Ireland   197

PILAR VILLAR-ARGÁIZ
16 Transparency and Secrecy in the Poetry of Colette Bryce   209

Contents ix

BRIAN J. MURPHY AND MÁIRTÍN MAC CON IOMAIRE
17 Generous Curiosity: Connections, Community and
    Commensality in Research   229

EUGENE O'BRIEN
18 'To write poetry after Auschwitz is barbaric [...]': Micheal
    O'Siadhail's *The Gossamer Wall*   243

MICHAEL CRONIN
19 Is There a Translator in the Text? Language, Identity and
    Haunting   263

VIC MERRIMAN
20 At Someone's Expense: Nation, Fulfilment, and Betrayal in
    Irish Theatre   275

ANNE FOGARTY
21 Writing the Unspeakable in Irish Feminist Life-
    Writing: Emilie Pine's *Notes to Self* and Doireann Ní
    Ghríofa's *A Ghost in the Throat*   289

SARAH NOLAN
22 Re[p]laying Voices in Translation: Peter Sirr and the
    Troubadours of Twelfth-Century France   303

BARRY HOULIHAN
23 'The Fear of Speaking Plainly': Translating John McGahern
    and the Letters of Alain Delahaye   319

JOHN LITTLETON
24 The Changed Reality of Being a Catholic Priest in Today's
    Ireland   333

Notes on Contributors   345

Acknowledgements

The editors are infinitely grateful to all of the contributors for their timely and scholarly contributions – and for not letting the *Festschrift* cat out of the bag!

GRACE NEVILLE, SARAH NOLAN AND EUGENE O'BRIEN

Introduction

To mark the milestone 100th book in *Reimagining Ireland*, Peter Lang commissioned a special volume offering both a retrospective on what has been achieved to date in the series, and an outline of future possibilities. Clearly, Irish Studies is a discipline that has blossomed over the past number of decades. One hundred books in a series is a milestone in anyone's language and the series is now the largest and most significant one in the area of Irish Studies, with multidisciplinary and interdisciplinary focus that ranges across literature, literary and cultural theory, Francophone issues, socio-cultural and political topics and a range of new interactions and intersections across a range of genres.

While it is important to mark the series, we, his colleagues, feel that it is even more important to mark the career and intellectual history of its founding editor, Eamon Maher. The statistics of Eamon's career are impressive. As a research supervisor, he has graduated some nine PhD and seven Research MA students. He is the founding editor of two series with Peter Lang: Reimagining Ireland which is recognized as the largest Irish Studies series with 125 books in print, and Studies in Franco-Irish Relations which to date has 22 books in print. He has written four monographs and one translation:

The Prophetic Voice of Jean Sulivan (1913–1980) and His Ongoing Relevance in France and Ireland (Dublin: Veritas, 2024 forthcoming);

'*The Church and its Spire*': *John McGahern and the Catholic Question* (Dublin: The Columba Press, 2011);

Jean Sulivan: La Marginalité dans la vie et l'œuvre (Paris: L'Harmattan, 2008);

John McGahern: From the Local to the Universal (Dublin: The Liffey Press, 2003);

Crosscurrents and Confluences: Echoes of Religion in 20th-Century Fiction (Dublin: Veritas, 2000);

Anticipate Every Goodbye (trans.) (Dublin: Veritas, 2000).

He has edited or co-edited 27 books across a range of literary and socio-cultural topics, and has published some 167 journal articles, 48 book chapters and 63 newspaper articles.

He is a regular contributor of articles and reviews to *The Irish Times* and journals such as *Studies: An Irish Quarterly Review*; *Doctrine and Life*; *Irish Studies Review* and *New Hibernia Review*. He is also a newly appointed member of the Comité Scientifique of *Études Irlandaises*. His work on Franco-Irish academic relations has made him very popular in French diplomatic circles – and in France in general, where he has received the Palmes Académiques and was recently made honorary President of the French Society of Irish Studies (SOFEIR). Clearly, this is a career to be reckoned with and a number of his colleagues felt that it needed to be marked in some way, and for someone who is such a prolific writer and editor, what better way to mark it than with a *Festschrift*, written by friends and colleagues with whom he has worked across a range of projects over the years. As is clear from these outputs, Eamon has been a powerhouse in the field of Franco-Irish Studies, where he founded the National Centre for Franco-Irish Studies,[1] and the Association of Franco-Irish Studies,[2] both of which are thriving enterprises with very healthy memberships and a strong tradition of outputs and productions. He is also a world-ranked expert on the work of John McGahern, and he is one of the most knowledgeable contemporary thinkers about the Catholic novel. He also edited some seminal books on the rise and fall of the Celtic Tiger. His work also segues into contemporary culture, and he has written and edited books on the contemporary state of Catholicism in Ireland.

He is also the founder of the *Journal of Franco-Irish Studies*,[3] whose latest edition was published online in 2023. Impressive as these statistics are, they do not capture the drive, imagination and sheer intellectual ebullience

---

1 National Centre for Franco-Irish Studies, TU Dublin https://www.tudublin.ie/research-innovation/research/discover-our-research/research-centres/ncfis/ [accessed 9 December 2023].
2 Association of Franco-Irish Studies https://www.tudublin.ie/research-innovation/research/discover-our-research/research-centres/ncfis/about/afis/ [accessed 9 December 2023].
3 *Journal of Franco-Irish Studies* https://www.tudublin.ie/research-innovation/research/discover-our-research/research-centres/ncfis/about/jofis/ [accessed 9 December 2023].

that Eamon brings to every project in which he is a participant (or more usually, an instigator). The number of people with whom he has worked across a range of books is huge; their multidisciplinary and interdisciplinary nature is impressive; and the intellectual scope and range of his interests is daunting, as is his postgraduate supervision. As a supervisor, Eamon understands that life, and sometimes babies, can delay the final text production! But he embraces these realities and this allows the student, and research project, to develop. Eamon knows the importance of maintaining a focus on the projected plan, and does this expertly himself, often completing material ahead of time, but he also naturally encourages others to be unafraid to loosen the edges of a subject before pursuing their line of inquiry. The three editors have all worked with Eamon for a number of years and across a range of projects, and are proud to call him a friend. In our opinion, he is one of the pre-eminent figures in what has become a broader notion of Irish Studies, and the books that bear his name will stand the test of relevance and significance as we move through the twenty-first century.

The following chapters in this *Festschrift*, are all written by colleagues with whom Eamon has worked, and their scope and range is reflective of that broad intellectual sweep that is characteristic of Eamon. The book was written in a very busy semester and the fact that all of these very busy people were happy to be included speaks to the respect and affection in which Eamon is held by his colleagues.

As editors, we would like to thank all of the contributors who have been a joy to work with, and also to thank Eamon himself for his friendship, his kindness, his intellectual energy and his sense of an intellectual community into which he has brought us all in such a productive and enjoyable manner. May his work continue to inspire and elucidate: *ut ille vigemusque per plures annos* – 'may he thrive for many more years'.

GRACE NEVILLE

1 *Une Femme Libre*: Edna O'Brien, A Wild Irish Girl in the French Media 1965–2023

The story of the reception of Irish literature in translation in France is, overall, a remarkably happy one. In recent times, from the early twentieth century onwards, one is struck by the high esteem in which Irish writers are held in France, often more so than in their home country. Colum McCann has always acknowledged French support for him as a young writer just starting out, implying that without it he might have taken a different path and abandoned hopes of a career in literature forever. Even for established writers like Nuala O Faoláin, translations of whose books, especially of *Are You Somebody?*, became best sellers in France, French acclamation was an enormous boost even at an emotional level: according to her French publisher, Sabine Wespieser, O Faoláin had always dreamt of being published in France. More recently, the runaway success of Sally Rooney is arguably as significant in France as in Ireland, with her books on prominent display in bookshops right across the country.

The names of some Irish writers have overflowed the literary sphere and entered the public space. In *Le Monde*, a prestigious publication with a strong arts focus, the Irish writer most frequently referenced since its establishment in the 1940s is Oscar Wilde, with well over one thousand mentions. However, most of these allusions turn out to be fleeting ones – to Wilde's *bons mots* or to Wilde as icon. It is as if Wilde has become larger than the sum of his parts, certainly more than the sum of his writings. To date, James Joyce has garnered just over one thousand mentions in *Le Monde*. Here again, most are 'second-hand' ones, for instance, to James Joyce pubs; they surface fleetingly in articles on *inter alia* Leonard Cohen, Peggy Guggenheim, soccer, rugby and Apple. Similarly, the Frank McCourt most referenced is the billionaire Boston-born owner of OM

(Olympique de Marseille), not his Limerick namesake who penned the bestselling *Angela's Ashes*.

This is where Edna O'Brien comes in. There are no Edna O'Brien pubs, no ships have been named in her honour, she has no namesakes in the world of French sport! She enjoys fewer mentions, for instance, in *Le Monde* than Wilde and Joyce, both of whom arguably had an advantage over her in their proximity to the French public since, unlike O'Brien, they had actually lived in France. Nonetheless, from the range, depth and strength of the reception of her work in France, O'Brien emerges as the Irish writer with the consistently strongest presence in France since the 1960s: she is France's 'go-to' writer where Irish literature is concerned.[1] This chapter will explore the reception of O'Brien in France down to 2023 with particular emphasis on her latest novel, *Girl*, published in 2019. It will contend that French reaction to this short novel is significant as it crystallizes well over half a century of consistently positive French commentary on O'Brien. It will argue that from the time that O'Brien was a young writer, her concerns chimed with those of reviewers across the French media who welcomed her as a soulmate long years before her native country ever did.[2]

When investigating the reception of O'Brien in France, it is difficult to avoid French adulation for her especially over the past decade. On 7 March 2021, at a lavish ceremony organized *sous les ors de la République* and presided over by French Minister for Culture, Roselyne Bachelot, O'Brien was presented with France's highest cultural distinction, the rank

---

1 The 'wild Irish girl' in the title of this chapter refers, of course, to the trope of 'wildness' used by French visitors to Ireland from the early modern period onwards. The 'wild Irish' ('les Irlandois sauvages') were denigrated as being 'different', 'Other', ruled not by intellect but by emotions. Sydney Owenson's 1806 classic, *Wild Irish Girl*, provides a more nuanced and positive version of this trope; see Jean Brihault's numerous publications here.

2 A fascinating and highly original analysis of the reception of Edna O'Brien, Nuala O Faoláin and Jennifer Johnston in France by Université de Lyon 3 Professor, Jeanne-Marie Carton-Charon, in a recent addition to the Peter Lang Studies in Franco-Irish Relations series: *Réception d'Edna O'Brien, Jennifer Johnston et Nuala O Faoláin: Clubs de lecture, et forums en ligne* (Oxford: Peter Lang, 2023), focuses on the reception of these three Irish women writers in the wider French public, for instance, in book clubs and online fora.

of Commandeur de l'Ordre des Arts et des Lettres. Until then, only two Irish people had received this supreme distinction: Seamus Heaney in 1996 and Bono in 2013. The symbolism of the date for the ceremony, on the eve of International Women's Day, was lost on no one: 'La décoration a été remise à Edna O'Brien la veille de la Journée internationale des droits des femmes, comme un écho aux valeurs qui ont construit son oeuvre et accompagné tant de femmes.'[3] To quote the French Ambassador in Ireland, Monsieur Vincent Guérand: 'Les liens entre la France et l'Irlande sont très forts en particulier dans le domaine culturel et littéraire. Mme Edna O'Brien à travers sa vie, son oeuvre et ses engagements en est un magnifique exemple.'[4] In the summer of the previous year, 2020, O'Brien starred at the opening of France's leading annual theatre festival, Le Festival d'Avignon, organized in partnership with France Culture, when Maryam, *Girl*'s main character, was re-imagined by the iconic Barbara Hendricks. In 2019, *Girl* was shortlisted for no fewer than three prestigious prizes, the Prix Médicis, the Prix Fémina Etranger and the Prix du Roman FNAC. In the event, O'Brien became in that year the first non-French person ever to be awarded the Prix Fémina Etranger not for any one publication but for the totality of her *oeuvre*. In 2017, she received the Irish Francophone Ambassadors' Literary Award when the French translation of *The Little Red Chairs* was selected from a short-list of seven works by a jury of twenty-five ambassadors. At the award ceremony on 23 October 2017, organized in Dublin by the Embassy of Switzerland and the Embassy of Morocco, O'Brien 'went over her career in a passionate speech before a practically mesmerised audience', as reported by the French Embassy in Ireland. Nor were her translators forgotten: Aude de Saint-Loup and Pierre-Emmanuel Dauzat were awarded internships at the ceremony by Literature Ireland.

O'Brien is no newcomer on the French literary landscape, however. For well over sixty years now, 'Mlle Edna O'Brien' (as she was fetchingly called in *Le Monde*),[5] has been a constant on the French literary landscape. Her first novel was published by Julliard as early as 1960 when she was barely

3   *Le Petit Journal* https://lepetitjournal.com/ [accessed 12 September 2023].
4   *Le Petit Journal* https://lepetitjournal.com/ [accessed 12 September 2023].
5   *Le Monde*, 9 May 1965.

30 years old. *La Jeune Irlandaise* (later *Les Filles de la Campagne*) was highlighted as 'un ouvrage anticonformiste, irrévérencieux mais attirant [...] un style qui ne se réclamait pas de maîtres' in *Le Monde* as early as 9 May 1965.[6] Her later works were snapped up by leading publishers including Gallimard, Presses de la Cité, Fayard, Stock and, since 2010, by Sabine Wespieser. In fact, such is Wespieser's confidence in O'Brien that she republished her earlier books originally published by Fayard but which had become unavailable in French, including *La Maison du Splendide Isolement* (2013), *Dans la Forêt* (2017) and *Tu ne Tueras Pas* (2018).

Still now in 2023, O'Brien's power to captivate leading French reviewers endures. Her 2023 play, *Femmes de Joyce*, was reviewed on 29 June 2023 in *Le Monde* by its main editor of foreign fiction, Florence Noiville, as was her 2021 *James & Nora*, with Noiville going so far as to imply that O'Brien herself was in fact one of the *Femmes de Joyce*, O'Brien's great hero. Another reviewer even draws a parallel between Joyce's work and that of O'Brien: 'elle-même réputée pour son oeuvre abordant franchement la sexualité'.[7] O'Brien features in a recent *Le Monde* review of Nicole Flattery (born 1989, *Le Monde*, 25 June 2020) though she is a lifetime older than the young writer under discussion: throughout, she remains the touchstone, the reference point, the year zero, the *fons et origo*.

The publication in the 2019 *rentrée littéraire* of O'Brien's nineteenth and latest novel, *Girl*, was widely heralded as a major event across the French media. It tells the story of a young Nigerian girl, Maryam, one of several hundred girls kidnapped by Boko Haram in 2014 and subjected to unspeakable sexual, physical and mental violence. As preparation for this book, O'Brien made two research visits to Nigeria in 2016 and 2017, visits facilitated by the Irish Embassy in Nigeria and Médecins sans Frontières, and for which – as Andrew O'Hagan, who later interviewed O'Brien, recounts – 'she also confessed to having smuggled £15,000 into the country, wads of cash concealed in her sleeves and her underwear'.[8]

---

6   *Le Monde*, 9 May 1965.
7   *Le Monde*, 1 April 2021.
8   *The Observer*, 25 August 2019.

On 5 September 2019, O'Brien's French publisher, Sabine Wespieser, kindly agreed to meet me in her Paris office to discuss O'Brien and this new novel. The date in question, 5 September, was significant as it was the official launch date of both the English original and the French translation: a rare exploit. Wespieser told me that *Girl* is quite simply the most remarkable book she has ever dealt with. She said that one of its two translators, Pierre-Emmanuel Dauzat, was so struck by the original pre-published English version that he immediately set aside all other projects to prioritize translating *Girl*. Hence the *coup double* of the joint publication on the same day just a few months later of the English original with Faber and the French translation with Wespieser. For Sophie Creuz on the Belgian national TV and radio site, rtbf.be, this joint publication is much more than a question of the alignment of dates or of agendas: for her *Girl* is 'd'une telle urgence, d'une telle nécessité, d'une telle beauté aussi que ses éditeurs anglais et français ont décidé de le publier en même temps'. In conversation, Wespieser further explained to me that while most French translations are longer than their English originals, the translators of *Girl* succeeded in matching the English and French texts so closely that the original and its translation perfectly mirror each other length-wise.[9]

So how has *Girl* been received across the French-language media? As well as *Le Monde*, the very varied publications mined in this chapter include *Libération, Le Figaro, Lire, Le Canard Enchaîné, La Croix, Le Journal du Dimanche, Télérama, Femme Actuelle, Le Soir, La Déferlante, Axelle Magazine, Transfuge, Le Devoir, Les Echos weekend, Elle, Version Femina, La Vie, Le Matricule des Anges, Livres Hebdo* and *Pages des Libraires*. Though mainly French, some Québec and Belgium sources also figure. To these print sources can be added numerous reviews and discussions of *Girl* on French radio and television, for instance on France's leading television books programme, 'La Grande Librairie' (France 2, 27 October 2021), or the one-hour interview by France Culture's Marie Richeux with O'Brien in her London home (*Les Girls d'Edna O'Brien*, 5 November 2019). At another level, acclamation for *Girl* flows too from readers and booksellers

---

9   Interview with Sabine Wespieser, 5 September 2019.

in towns large and small across France and beyond: Lille, Saint-Etienne, Aurillac, Bordeaux, Yvetot, and Namur.[10]

A summary of this cornucopia of reviews would be that the best has just got better, with *Girl* hailed as surpassing six decades of O'Brien's superb writing. Superlatives abound:

'superbe et terrifiant [...] peut-être son roman le plus puissant'; [11]

'un roman ahurissant [...] le plus fort qu'elle ait jamais publié';[12]

'texte d'une effroyable splendeur [...] livre d'une radicalité extrême'; [13]

'éprouvant et extraordinaire'.[14]

One reviewer who chose *Girl* as a highlight of the literary *rentrée*, advises readers to wake up and hang on: 'Réveillez-vous et accrochez-vous'.[15] For a novel that is so intensely physical, with unspeakable descriptions of the extreme physical violence perpetrated on Maryam and on her fellow prisoners, it is interesting to see that some reviewers – perhaps unconsciously – using physical terms (emphasis added below) to describe it: thus, *Girl* is:

'saisissant de vérité, il empoigne aux tripes'; [16]

'ce livre coup de poing, puissant requiem pour une enfance assassinée'; [17]

'un roman dont on ressort cabossé mais pas sans voix';[18]

'250 pages pendant lesquelles le lecteur retient son souffle';[19]

---

10 See Sabine Wespieser's website, swespieser.fr.
11 *La Croix*, 12 September 2019.
12 *Télérama*, 18 September 2019.
13 *Page des Libraires*, rentrée littéraire 2019.
14 *Elle*, 27 September 2019.
15 *Femme Actuelle*, 2–8 Septembre 2019.
16 *Libération*, 4 October 2019.
17 *Bibliobs*, 19 September 2019.
18 *Lire*, 2019.
19 *Le Devoir*, 12–13 October 2019.

The experience of reading *Girl* is so terrifying for one reviewer that 'elle appelle une course effrénée pour sortir du cauchemar'.[20]

Perhaps as an unconscious homage to a writer who, one suspects, takes infinite care à *la Flaubert* over every handwritten word, every carefully crafted image, French reviews often contain clever plays upon words: 'Edna O'Brien, L'Eire et la Manière.'[21]

The quasi-assimilation of *Girl* into the French literary canon, into the very pantheon of French literature, is frequently implied by references in these review titles:

'Voyage au Bout de l'Enfer': a reference to Céline's Voyage au Bout de la Nuit;

'A l'Ombre des Jeunes Filles en Pleurs': a salute to Proust's very different A l'Ombre des Jeunes Filles en Fleurs.[22]

Of the opening sentence in *Girl* ('J'étais une fille autrefois, c'est fini. Je pue'), reviewer Jean-Michel Thénard comments: 'En une phrase, tout est dit, comme dans tous les grands livres dont la lecture vous bouleverse.'[23] Is he thinking of other killer sentences that open so many French classics: of 'Aujourd'hui, maman est morte, ou peut-être hier. Je ne sais pas' in Camus' *L'Etranger* or of Proust's 'Longtemps je m'étais couché de bonne heure' or even of 'Tout est dit', the abrupt opening to La Bruyère's *Des Ouvrages de l'Esprit* over three centuries earlier?

A similarly French-centred reading is offered by critic Olivia de Lamberterie: for her, Maryam's cry, 'je suis morte et pas morte', recalls recent history not in Africa but closer to home: 'on pense au silence des rescapés des camps d'extermination après la Seconde Guerre mondiale.'[24] France again emerges when, in an interview by Marine Landrot, O'Brien salutes Claude Levi-Strauss, 'expert de toutes formes d'oppression'.[25] And one is struck by the resonant and quintessentially French terms such as

20 *Télérama*, 21 September 2019.
21 Eire/air, *Libération*, 19 April 2013.
22 *Le Canard Enchaîné*, 11 Septembre 2019.
23 *Le Canard Enchaîné*, 11 September 2019.
24 *Elle*, 27 September 2019.
25 *Télérama*, 18 September 2019.

'lumière' and 'liberté' that pepper so many French reviews, with *Girl* being interpreted as a continuation of O'Brien's 'combat au nom des femmes et de leur liberté'.[26]

The sometimes differing approaches to O'Brien's work in the French and Anglophone worlds stem partly from the centrality of '*civilization*' or cultural studies in literary analysis in France, with O'Brien's publications often explored less for their literary value than as a living archive of versions of Ireland.[27] Again and again, French reviewers of *Girl* are clear: O'Brien is Maryam, Maryam is O'Brien, with one review title, 'Vaillante, résistante, survivante', referring both to Maryam and to O'Brien herself.[28] Thus:

> A 88 ans, Edna O'Brien continue de parler des jeunes filles qui se révoltent contre l'ordre des choses et conquièrent leur liberté sans faillir. Cela lui a valu, dans les années 60, de voir ses premiers romans interdits dans son Irlande natale. Aujourd'hui, *comme son héroïne*, elle n'a pas renoncé à se battre contre la connerie, dont le fanatisme, la religion et le conservatisme sont les premiers producteurs. (emphasis added)[29]

In such readings, Ireland – and specifically County Clare – in the 1950s becomes nothing less than Nigeria under Boko Haram:

> cette écrivaine irlandaise de 88 ans a dû se battre pour exister. Dans les années 50 en Irlande c'était encore à bien des égards l'obscurantisme, tout était 'Haram', 'péché'. Etre une femme libre de ses choix, indépendante, écrivain se payait au prix fort. Elle aussi a été mise au ban de sa société et de sa famille, lapidée symboliquement, jugée impure. Et c'est fantastique que cette vieille dame de lettres ne l'ait pas oublié et qu'elle mette toutes sa vigueur, son talent, sa notoriété, au service de ces jeunes femmes réduites su silence;[30]

> N'est-ce pas que le destin de l'une des filles enlevées, la jeune Maryam, lui rappelait, par certains aspects, ses premières années dans le comté de Clare, et son éducation par

---

26 *L'Obs*, 22 October 2020.
27 See Grace Neville, '"*I don't think I could have made a decent living without the French*": An Analysis of Reviews of Irish Literature in *Le Monde*, 1950–2017', in *Patrimoine / Cultural Heritage in France and Ireland*, edited by Eamon Maher and Eugene O'Brien (Oxford: Peter Lang, 2019), 237–256, especially 249.
28 *Livres Hebdo*, 12 June 2019.
29 *Le Canard Enchaîné*, 11 Septembre 2019.
30 rtbf.be.

les sœurs de la charité? Une jeunesse pieuse dont elle a toujours dit qu'elle avait été 'suffocante', dans un milieu replié sur lui-même, hostile au progrès et à la nouveauté.[31]

Other French reviewers take a more universalist approach: for them, O'Brien's focus is less on Irish than on universal issues, with O'Brien belonging ultimately not to Irish but to world literature, an interpretation reinforced by the decision to select the eve of International Women's Day in 2021 as the date on which she was to become a Commandeur de l'Ordre des Arts et des Lettres. O'Brien's move beyond the term 'girls' used in several earlier titles (*The Country Girls, Girls in their Married Bliss*) to *Girl* – as if to include all girls – is seen as significant. In such readings, Nigeria is not Ireland and Maryam is not some version of O'Brien herself or of one of her eponymous country girls. Instead, *Girl* is seen as a more focused, more intense and angrier take on what it can mean to be any girl anywhere in the world in this day and age. In fact, several French reviewers contend that in *Girl* O'Brien has created nothing less than an everywoman and a universal story, with Maryam transcending time and space to enter mythology: 'elle fait de Maryam une héroïne de mythologie. Son livre s'ouvre par ces mots d'Euripide: 'Voici le bandage pour fermer vos blessures'. C'est ce que réalise somptueusement Edna O'Brien.'[32]

Throughout, it is clear that O'Brien's reviewers know their subject: they can comment knowledgeably on O'Brien's entire *oeuvre* and thus put *Girl* in context: 'On est proprement estomaqué par la capacité qu'a Edna O'Brien à se renouveller tout en restant fidèle à elle-même, à écrire un roman à la fois d'apparence si différent des autres et si profondément pareil à eux.'[33] From this perspective, *Girl* is not just one more novel in an already impressive list but something quite different in its audacity and in its ambition: it confirms O'Brien's status as one of the greats: 'Et, une fois de plus, elle témoigne de sa profonde empathie pour un personnage pourtant si différent d'elle: c'est le propre des plus grands romanciers.'[34]

---

31 *Bibliobs*, 19 September 2019.
32 *Elle*, 27 September 2019.
33 *Le Figaro Littéraire*, 12 Septembre 2019.
34 *Le Figaro Littéraire*, 12 Septembre 2019.

France is arguably a country used to seeing women writers punch above their weight, writers like George Sand, Colette and Simone de Beauvoir down to the recent Nobel Laureate, Annie Ernaux – determined, disruptive women who commanded attention and respect. It is thus no surprise that in France O'Brien has always attracted both male and female reviewers: a reminder that for French audiences O'Brien was never strait-jacketed as a 'women's writer' dealing with 'women's issues'. However, even allowing for that, the unadulterated praise lavished on O'Brien in France from the beginning contrasts starkly with the very different reception long reserved for O'Brien and for other Irish writers in their home country. It is true that in recent years Ireland has belatedly opened its arms to its wild Irish girl, that – to quote *Guardian* critic, Ed Vulliamy – she has gone 'from Ireland's cultural outcast to literary darling'.[35] This tardy validation includes honorary doctorates, adjunct professorships, the staging of her plays in the Abbey national theatre, her election to the highest rank (that of Saoí) in Aosdána, along with praise, thanks and even apologies showered on her by Michael D. Higgins and Mary Robinson. However, it is easy to forget that this was not always so, that the blanket positivity that has greeted her work in France from the 1960s was all too often cruelly absent in Ireland. Julia Carlson's 1990 study, *Banned in Ireland: Censorship and the Irish Writer*, contains a nine-page interview with O'Brien whom Carlson describes, along with John McGahern, as the most controversial writers of the 1960s in Ireland, a judgement reprised by Maurice Leitch: when asked by Carlson how aware he was of Irish literary censorship as a writer living in the North, he is unambiguous: 'I knew about it and there was always talk. The most notorious cases were John McGahern and Edna O'Brien.'[36]

35   *The Guardian*, 10 October 2015.
36   Julia Carlson, *Banned in Ireland: Censorship and the Irish Writer* (London: Routledge, 1990), 99. See also Maureen O'Connor, 'Girl Trouble', *DRB/ Dublin Review of Books* (May 2014). It is interesting and significant to see how very often O'Brien and McGahern are linked by literary critics and historians: see *inter alia* James M. Calahan, 'Female and Male Perspectives on Growing Up Irish in Edna O'Brien, John McGahern and Brian Moore', *Colby Quarterly*, 31 (March 1995), 55–73; Michael G. Cronin, 'Arrested Development: Sexuality, Trauma and History in Edna O'Brien and John McGahern', in *Impure Thoughts: Sexuality, Catholicism and Literature in Twentieth-Century Ireland* (Manchester: Manchester University

Anyone who remembers Ireland in the 1960s remembers the fate of censored writers like McGahern and O'Brien. Such opprobrium came at a heavy personal cost. In McGahern's case, in 1965 he lost his job as a primary school teacher, a highly desirable permanent pensionable post at a time when few similar alternatives were on offer. How many other writers lost their nerve or were paralysed into silence? How many had the self-belief or the thick skin to survive being lambasted by Archbishop McQuaid, as O'Brien was, as 'a smear on Irish womanhood', 'a renegade and a dirty one'.[37] To this could be added the animosity of the then Minister for Justice, Charles J. Haughey: '[L]ike so many decent men with growing families, he was just beaten by [O'Brien's] outlook and descriptions.'[38] With hindsight, it is difficult to know whether to laugh or cry. Throughout all this, O'Brien remained unapologetic, in the untranslatable French phrase she was first and foremost 'une femme libre': her own woman.

Still today, in the English-speaking world at least, O'Brien does not enjoy the blanket positivity that France continues to offer. In this context, a widely discussed article on O'Brien in the prestigious *New Yorker* magazine in February 2019 is relevant. This profile by long-standing *New Yorker* staff writer, Ian Parker, was damned as an 'astonishing hatchet job' by O'Brien specialist, UCC professor Maureen O'Connor.[39] Weighing in at around ten thousand words, it applies the kind of revisionist perspective to O'Brien's *oeuvre* that in recent decades has been applied largely to history. In particular, Parker suggests that O'Brien's family was not really poor, that her books, though banned, were never really unavailable. Parker clearly has no idea of how impossible it was to source O'Brien's books in the bookshops or libraries of Cork in the 1960s or 1970s.

Press, 2012); Laura C. Schluter, *Bodies of Shame and Shame of Bodies: Reading the Gendered Shame Complex in the Fiction of John McGahern and Edna O'Brien*, PhD thesis (University of Manchester, 2018). Similarly significant is the focus on O'Brien among McGahern specialists: see for instance Eamon Maher, 'Catholic Sensibility in the Early Fiction of Edna O'Brien', *Doctrine and Life* 64/8 (2014), 50–59.

37 *Irish Times*, 30 September 2019.
38 *Irish Times*, 20 November 2019.
39 *Irish Times*, 16 April 2020.

What O'Brien herself makes of this blanket French adulation is a matter for conjecture. That said, a short piece from her in *Le Monde* in 2017 allows us to glimpse what that newspaper means to her:

> Le Monde est une référence pour ceux d'entre nous qui vivent en dehors de la France [...] Il a conservé sa dignité culturelle et intellectuelle et, pour l'essentiel, sait faire la différence, dans la production littéraire contemporaine, entre ce qui est sérieux et ce qui est ouvertement vulgaire.[40]

Despite her now universal acclaim, O'Brien comes across as a solitary, private person, no longer interested in appearing in society as she once did. The impossibly glamourous, well-rehearsed list of *glitterati* who formed her 'tribe' in 1960s swinging London is now fading into a distant era: Marilyn Monroe, Marguerite Duras, Roger Vadim, Philip Roth, Princess Margaret, Jackie Onassis, Peter Brook, R. D. Laing, Jack Nicholson, Paul McCartney, Sean Connery, Marianne Faithfull, Gloria Steinem, Robert Mitchum, Samuel Beckett. Hence the surprise that O'Brien allows so many French journalists into her home in Chelsea, which they all agree is private, small, quiet, a nest, a cocoon. Even when a French reviewer does not explicitly say that s/he was one of the chosen few, the details supplied, such as the huge fig tree in O'Brien's small London garden, allow readers to conclude that the interviewer was indeed invited inside.[41]

By her own admission, Frédérique Roussel, like many French interviewers, is initially almost struck dumb by O'Brien's appearance: 'Edna apparaît, la chevelure flamboyante [...] extraordinairement belle, sorte de princesse celte matinée d'élégance british [...] Sa voix, profonde et sifflante, demeure rocailleuse et envoûtante.'[42] Such visual richness is often strengthened and complemented by haunting photos O'Brien taken by leading photographers including Jerome de Missolz and Sophia Spring. French journalists imply that being allowed to interview O'Brien *in situ* is a rare privilege; their nervousness at approaching the *grande dame* is clear. Hence,

---

40   *Le Monde*, 1 February 2017.
41   *Libération*, 21 June 2001.
42   *Libération*, 19 April 2013.

they repeatedly stress that their interview is something rare, exclusive, to be cherished. However, what is most striking and perhaps unexpected here is how open, confiding and even vulnerable O'Brien is with them, at pains to welcome them, to make tea for them, to ensure that they are comfortable. It is as if she is now at ease, surrounded by French soulmates, enjoying setting aside her *grande dame* persona. Florence Noiville's engrossing, lengthy account of her interview with O'Brien is a *morceau d'anthologie* its own right.[43] O'Brien playfully wrongfoots Noiville – surely a maker-and-breaker of literary careers – when, having frostily reprimanded Noiville for arriving late at the start of an interview that began badly and then slid steadily downhill, she is later full of solicitousness as Noiville heads out into the London rain, asking Noiville if she has an umbrella, if she knows her way to the nearest Underground station.[44] As she set out for home after an extensive interview, Marine Landrot was similarly love-bombed, with O'Brien handing her a going-home present as unforgettable as it was unexpected: a 'délicieux sponge cake à l'orange, dont elle tient à vous glisser une part dans votre sac, au moment de vous dire au revoir'.[45] In total control from beginning to end – sacrée Edna!

In conversation with me on the day that *Girl* was published in 2019, Sabine Wespieser gave me the best description of O'Brien that I have ever come across: she said that for her O'Brien is 'comme une flèche': like an arrow.[46] This image implies strength, focus, determination, sharpness and efficiency; but more than that, it suggests that from the outset O'Brien knew exactly what she was about and where she wanted to go; nothing and no one – no cleric, no judge, no censor, no politician, no partner, no former neighbour – had the power to knock this arrow off its course. It is now as if, after decades of silence, followed by devastating disclosures of all sorts, along with debates, controversies, referenda and people's fora, Ireland has finally caught up with its wild Irish girl, has finally understood that from the outset she was indeed, to quote her French publisher – 'comme une flèche' – speaking truth to power throughout all those years, opening up a

---

43 *Le Monde*, 27 March 2013.
44 *Le Monde*, 27 March 2013.
45 *Télérama*, 18 September 2019.
46 Interview with Sabine Wespieser, 5 September 2019.

space for the unsayable, for the silenced, for the dismissed, for the damned. For all the Maryams of the world.

This is an extensively reworked version of an unpublished paper, *Wild Irish Girl? Edna O'Brien in France*, presented on 12 November 2017 at a conference on the international reception of Irish literature held at the Université Jean Moulin – Lyon 3, with the support of the Embassy of Ireland in France, EFACIS, GIS / EIRE, IETT, the Université de Lyon and the Université Jean Moulin – Lyon 3.

ANDREW AUGE

2 Waking the Living and the Dead: The Revelatory Power of Funerary Rituals in John McGahern's Late Fiction

Death pervades John McGahern's fiction. His first novel, *The Barracks* (1963) centres upon Elizabeth Reegen's long, lonely death by breast cancer while his last one, *That They May Face The Rising Sun* (2002), concludes with the emigrant Johnnie Murphy's dying while on his annual summer visit to Ireland. Such a focus on human mortality is hardly unique. More distinctive is McGahern's extensive attention to the rituals surrounding death in rural twentieth-century Ireland. In contrast to the prevailing functionalist notion that such rituals only serve to maintain social cohesion and continuity, Kevin Schilbrack argues that they also constitute 'a form of metaphysical inquiry, that is, as a source of knowledge about the most general contexts of human existence'.[1] In *The Barracks*, McGahern emphasizes the exclusively Catholic aspects of the rituals associated with death and dying: the Sacrament of Extreme Unction, the deathbed confession to the priest, prayers soliciting the Blessed Virgin's merciful intervention. For the dying Elizabeth Reegen, these rituals are nugatory, more irritant than salve. As Eamon Maher indicates, what allows her 'to make some accommodation with her plight' is a revelation that emanates from her own idiosyncratic version of Catholicism:[2] the awareness that 'she had come to life out of mystery and would return, it surrounded her life'.[3] In his later fictional representations of these rituals, McGahern focuses less

---

1 Kevin Shilbrack, 'Ritual Metaphysics', *Journal of Ritual Studies*, 18/1 (2004), 77–90, 83.
2 Eamon Maher, *'The Church and Its Spire': John McGahern and the Catholic Question* (Dublin: The Columba Press, 2011), 45.
3 John McGahern, *The Barracks* (London: Faber & Faber, 1963), 211.

on those aspects of this process that arise directly from Catholic dogma and more on those that emanate from an amalgamation of Catholicism and indigenous folk tradition. This shift enables the profound metaphysical insight implicit in these customary rituals to be discerned more clearly. Both McGahern's late short story 'A Country Funeral' (1992) and his valedictory novel, *That They May Face the Rising Sun*, recount traditional Irish funerary practices in detail and invest them with a revelatory power that reaches back beyond the doctrines of Catholicism toward something more rudimentary. In each of these fictions, participation in these rituals elicits in central characters an intuition of a deeper mythic consciousness that supersedes the ravages of chronological time.

Ethnological reports differ in their presentation of the rituals associated with death in rural twentieth-century Ireland. Drawing upon responses to a survey from the Irish Department of Folklore in 1976, Patricia Lysaght's account highlights the centrality of Catholicism: sacraments, especially Extreme Unction; the Rosary and other prayers; accoutrements such as a scapular, candles, holy water, and crucifix.[4] Lawrence Taylor's description of these rituals is rooted in first-hand observations from his field work in 1980's Donegal and centres upon the wake, which lasts up to two days and takes place in the home of the dead person or their closest relatives. As friends and neighbours gather, they visit the room where the deceased lies to pay their last respects. Afterwards they gather elsewhere in the house to eat, drink, and converse about the dead person and share local gossip. For Taylor, the 'rural wake is [...] the quintessential expression of communal values and relations'.[5] Contrarily, the funeral confirms the authority of the Catholic Church. McGahern's later fictional descriptions of these rural funerary rituals interfuse features noted in both these ethnological accounts, but the sacerdotal elements – the sacraments, the funeral mass – fade to the background. Those distinctly Catholic elements that remain, such as the recitation of the Rosary, serve not to reinforce doctrinal precepts, but to bring the mourners together in act of solemnity.

4   Patricia Lysaght, 'Visible Death: Attitudes to the Dying in Ireland', *Merveilles & Contes*, 9/1 (May 1995), 27–60, 33–41.
5   Lawrence Taylor, 'Cultural Conceptions of Death in Ireland', *Anthropological Quarterly*, 62/4 (October 1989), 175–187.

It is ironic, then, that the story in which these funerary rites first evoke an intimation of some metaphysical insight, 'The Wine Breath' (1979), centres upon a priest. Like many of McGahern's later fictional works, this story is set in Co. Leitrim, near the village of Fenagh, by Laura Lake and Gloria Bog, where the author and his wife eventually relocated. The story borrows its title from W. B. Yeats' 'All Soul's Night',[6] where the poet summons the ghosts of his past to a gathering at which these spectres will partake only of the wine's aura, not its actuality. As this title implies, 'The Wine Breath' deals with an experience that is secondary or derivative, indirect rather than first-hand. Thus, the epiphany that animates the story arises from a distant event that the priest observed in childhood: the funeral cortege of a revered local man, winding through a snow-lined pathway toward the burial plot.

What elicits the priest's revelation is a Proustian involuntary memory. As he watches a parishioner sawing a beech log, the scattering of its white chips in the blazing sunlight triggers a childhood recollection of this burial procession in the winter of 1947 when deep snow abounded throughout Ireland. This visionary moment transfixes and enlivens the priest who had been reduced to a moribund condition in the aftermath of his mother's death: his life nothing more than 'dead days'.[7] Unsurprisingly, he interprets the epiphany in familiar religious terms. As he envisions the coffin's slow procession toward the graveyard, he feels himself in the grasp of 'the Mystery' that in its 'awesomeness' confirms 'everything we had been taught and told of the world of God'.[8] But this vision remains abstracted from his actual life. As he puts it:

> Never before though had he noticed anything like the beech chips. There was the joy of holding what had eluded him for so long, in its amazing simplicity; but mastered knowledge was no longer knowledge unless it opened, became part of a great knowledge, and what did the beech chips do but turn back to his own death?[9]

---

6 Richard Robinson calls attention to this allusion to Yeats, *John McGahern and Modernism*, 199.
7 John McGahern, *The Collected Stories* (New York: Vintage International, 1992), 182.
8 McGahern, *Collected Short Stories*, 179–180.
9 McGahern, *Collected Short Stories*, 183.

Among the many parallels between this story and James Joyce's 'The Dead' – the ubiquitous snow, the repeated evocation of death, its isolated protagonist – the most significant is the similarity between the priest's epiphany and that of Gabriel Conroy's. In each case, the potentially life-altering vision leads only to a sense of imminent death. 'The Wine Breath' concludes with the priest welcoming his own ghost while imagining a younger alternative version of himself meeting a lover and 'feeling himself immersed in time without end'.[10] As with the burial itself, the priest remains a spectator. Through his vision he glimpses the ritual's significance, its suspension of chronological time and evocation of a more primordial state of timelessness. But he is unable to incorporate this revelation into his own life.

That is not the case with Philly Ryan, the protagonist of 'The Country Funeral', whose participation in the funerary rituals occasioned by his uncle's death elicits a sudden transformation. Published shortly after McGahern's magisterial novel *Amongst Women* (1990), 'The Country Funeral' shares its precursor's setting in the McGahern heartland of rural Leitrim as well as its detailed recounting of the traditional rituals accompanying death. However, in *Amongst Women* (1990), the death and burial of Michael Moran, the bitter patriarch who dominates the novel, is not the centrepiece of the plot but its coda. For Moran's daughters, this experience triggers no epiphany, just a confirmation that their father's hold over them remains even in his absence. This makes McGahern's portrayal of what happens to Philly in the aftermath of his uncle's death even more noteworthy.

When their ailing mother learns of the passing of her brother, she insists that her three sons travel from Dublin to represent the family at the funeral. Philly, on holiday from his job in the oil fields of Saudi Arabia, is visiting his mother and his disabled younger brother, Fonsie, who lives with her. Their elder brother John, who is married and a teacher, has moved beyond his family's working-class background and is somewhat distanced from his brothers. When the request comes from their mother, Fonsie is adamantly opposed. The brothers had spent their childhood summers at their Uncle Peter's, and while all of them felt his sense of imposition, it was

---

10   McGahern, *Collected Short Stories*, 187.

the disabled Fonsie who registered their uncle's resentment most acutely. But Philly embraces the opportunity to escape from the Dublin neighbourhood where he feels like an outsider. Adrift in a place where he no longer seems to belong, he spends his time in local pubs buying rounds of drinks in a futile effort to establish communal ties. After the brothers' journey westward, the remainder of the story focuses on the events surrounding their uncle's wake and burial.

McGahern recounts this process in precise and extensive detail, a testament, as Eamon Maher notes, to the 'funerary rituals that have been observed for centuries' in rural Ireland.[11] Upon entering the dead man's cottage, the brothers are taken to the upper room where the clock has been stopped, as was the custom, and the body has been laid out in a traditional manner. The ensuing wake begins in the evening and lasts through the next day. Its pattern mirrors the wake that Lawrence Taylor describes in his anthropological account of funerary practices in rural Ireland. Visitors enter the upper room to pray for and take leave of the dead man after which they move downstairs to drink and eat and share stories of the deceased. The distinction and complementarity of these two stages is highlighted by McGahern:

> It was as if the house had been sundered into two distinct and separate elements; and yet each reflected and measured the other as much as the earth and the sky. In the upper room there was silence, the people there keeping vigil by the body where it lay in the stillness and awe of the last change; while in the lower room that life was being resurrected with more vividness than it could ever have had in the long days and years it had been given [...] The two rooms were joined as the Rosary was recited but as soon as the prayers ended each room took on again its separate entity.[12]

On the next evening the body is removed to the church where the accompanying mourners pray a Rosary over it. Of the funeral, McGahern notes nothing more than the relative paucity of its attendees.

In contrast to the neutral tone adopted by anthropologists, McGahern's account of these funerary rites shifts between two opposing partisan perspectives. From the outset, Fonsie distances himself from the process,

---

11   Maher, *The Church and Its Spire*, 119.
12   McGahern, *Collected Short Stories*, 392.

regarding it as 'barbaric, uncivilized, obscene' while Philly participates fully and enthusiastically, elevating the rural custom over its urban counterpart where 'the whole thing [is] swept under the carpet'.[13] This difference culminates in a heated disagreement on the journey back to Dublin, which centres on their divergent responses to the burial. Philly, who helped carry the casket up the hill to the grave, is deeply moved by the quiet beauty of the site and by the mourners 'gathered around' as 'the priest started to speak of the dead and the Mystery and the Resurrection'.[14] Fonsie, who observed the burial procession from a distance, scathingly mocks his brother's response, describing the pallbearers as being like 'a crowd of apes staggering up a hill with something they had just looted'. Ultimately, he casts the whole process as something 'out of the Dark Ages'.[15] Richard Robinson connects this opposition between Fonsie's scepticism and Philly's seemingly nostalgic embrace of tradition to Adorno and Horkheimer's dialectic of enlightenment in which rationality and myth mutually subvert one another.[16] The text, however, resists containment within this philosophical framework. The dominance of Philly's perspective, the contradiction between Fonsie's dismissal of the ritual and his sense of it as 'unbearably moving',[17] point to the story's endorsement of the mythological substrate of these funerary rituals.

On an overt level, Philly's participation in the wake and burial elicits a sense of community. In the stream of people that attend the wake, Philly encounters what had been missing from his lonely life in the oil fields and Dublin – the presence of a communal bond. This opportunity to abide in communion with his neighbours and with the local landscape lies at the heart of Philly's startling decision to buy his uncle's cottage and to live there when he next returns from the oil fields. But there is a deeper dimension to Philly's epiphany. On their long ride back to Dublin, his brother John, a mostly silent observer throughout the funeral and its aftermath, declares

---

13   McGahern, *Collected Short Stories*, 385.
14   McGahern, *Collected Short Stories*, 405.
15   McGahern, *Collected Short Stories*, 405.
16   Richard Robinson, *John McGahern and Modernism* (London: Bloomsbury, 2017), 183; 191.
17   McGahern, *Collected Short Stories*, 400.

with relief that what made the experience bearable is the awareness that 'it's over now [...] that everything we were doing was being done for the last time'.[18] Philly responds emphatically, declaring twice 'nothing is ever over'.[19] The repetition signals the statement's importance. The fact that it is expressed colloquially in a barroom conversation frees it from a false-sounding portentousness without diminishing its significance. One might be inclined to attribute this insight to the priest's brief words renewing Philly's faith in the Catholic doctrine of resurrection, but there is no evidence of that. Instead, it is the ongoing presence of nature at the grave site that animates him the most. The cumulative impact of the funerary rituals as a whole is what evokes Philly's revelation. According to Mircea Eliade, the renowned scholar of comparative religion, participants in traditional rites of passage 'emerge from their historical time – that is, from the time constituted by the sum total of profane personal and intrapersonal events – and recover primordial time, which is always the same, which belongs to eternity'.[20] Philly's plain-spoken, reiterated declaration that 'nothing is ever over' suggests that his participation in these long-standing Irish funerary rituals has triggered in him a vestige of this archaic experience. While his statement echoes the priest's more formal evocation in 'The Wine Breath' of 'being immersed in time without end', Philly breaks out of the paralysis in which the priest was entrapped. The epiphany that he experienced results in a life-altering transformation, the decision to return to his family's Leitrim homeland where he intends to live a simple life and then be buried, like his uncle and mother, in the local cemetery.

This idea of the return and its adjacent notion of circularity are identified by Eamon Maher as guiding principles of McGahern's fiction.[21] These themes have an ancient provenance as is evinced by the title of Eliade's famous analysis of the metaphysics of archaic rituals – *The Myth of the Eternal Return* (1954). It is in the last of McGahern's novels, *That They*

18 McGahern, *Collected Short Stories*, 406.
19 McGahern, *Collected Short Stories*, 406.
20 Mircea Eliade, *The Sacred and The Profane: The Nature of Religion* (New York: Harper & Row, 1959), 88.
21 Eamon Maher, 'Circles and Circularity in the Writings of John McGahern', *Nordic Irish Studies*. 4 (2005), 157–166, 159–161.

May Face the Rising Sun, that this motif of circularity evokes this mythic significance. According to Maher, *That They May Face the Rising Sun* has 'almost no plot'.[22] Its coherence derives instead from the natural cycle of the seasons and the human activities that occur in tandem with them, the most notable of which is the emigrant Johnny Murphy's annual summer visit to Ireland from England. The novel is bookended by his penultimate and last return home.

To the extent that there is a central character in the novel, it is Joe Ruttledge who with his wife has come back after decades in England to live in the countryside where he grew up. But the Ruttledges are not so much protagonists as magnets around which a cluster of local inhabitants gather. These are mostly residents of the area around the lake where the Ruttledge's cottage and small farm is located. Their most frequent visitors are Jamesie and Mary Murphy, the brother and sister-in-law of Johnny, who live across the lake. But other neighbours make regular appearances: Patrick Ryan, a bachelor who works as a handyman; Bill Evans, who survived the trauma of an orphanage only to be pawned off as a servant for a family of local gentry; John Quinn, whose unctuousness cloaks his sexual exploitation of women. Particularly noteworthy is Ruttledge's uncle, whose nickname, The Shah, indicates the elevated status that he earned through his business acumen despite his lack of formal education. The Shah's main enterprise is appropriately enough a salvage yard since the novel itself seeks to salvage the traditions of a rural society that are rapidly becoming outmoded.[23]

The typical novel imposes an overarching pattern upon a succession of incidents; it draws consequence from the sequence of action. As such, it relies upon chronological time, however much it may be bent or warped by the author's hand. *That They May Face the Rising Sun* signals its intent to move beyond the primacy of sequential temporality not just through its relative lack of a plot, but even more overtly through a seemingly arbitrary detail that resonates with symbolic significance. Jamesie's home is filled with pendulum clocks that he inherited from his father, but they

---

22 Maher, 'Circles and Circularity', 161.
23 See Eamon Maher, 'John McGahern and the Commemoration of Traditional Rural Ireland', *Studies: An Irish Quarterly*, 95 (Autumn 2006), 379, 279–290.

strike irregularly and inaccurately. Chronological time, the image suggests, is spurious. In lieu of it, the novel privileges the cyclical round of days and seasons. It follows the course of the year as it moves from one summer to the next, and as the seasons pass, the characters linger in the recurrent days, which are, as Kate Ruttledge suggests, 'all we have'.[24] While this attunement to a natural temporal rhythm evokes an aura of timelessness, the novel undercuts that with its persistent evocation of the ephemerality of human life. The folk wisdom dispensed by The Shah neatly encapsulates this point: 'The rain comes down. Grass grows. Children get old.'[25] The prospect of mortality hovers over the novel. Johnny's death at the end is foreshadowed in his first appearance when after a brief bout of dancing he 'looked distressed, sweating profusely'.[26] These intimations of mortality, according to Richard Robinson, curtail the cyclical temporality ascribed to the novel: the 'momentum is towards death, and in this sense the narrative, for all its circularity reveals itself to be end-directed'.[27] In other words, having purged itself of the illusion of circularity, the novel reverts to the commonplace notion that human temporality is ultimately linear and terminal. This reading is modified by a crucial passage near the novel's end where Ruttledge envisions human existence as ultimately being contained within an all-encompassing circle. This revelatory insight occurs after Ruttledge's participation in the funerary rituals associated with Johnny's death. The fact that it runs counter to the novel's prevailing atmosphere of unbelief highlights its significance.

That attitude is established at the novel's outset when Jamesie asks the Ruttledges why they don't go to Mass. Joe simply declares that he doesn't go because he doesn't believe. Kate elaborates on this by explaining how her atheist parents taught her 'that all that exists is what you see, all that you are is what you think and appear to be'.[28] Such scepticism might be

24 John McGahern, *That They May Face the Rising Sun* (London: Faber & Faber, 2002), 216.
25 McGahern, *That They May Face the Rising Sun*, 158.
26 McGahern, *That They May Face the Rising Sun*, 81.
27 Richard Robinson, *John McGahern and Modernism* (London: Bloomsbury, 2017), 225.
28 McGahern, *That They May Face the Rising Sun*, 2.

expected from the former inhabitants of the metropolis, where religious faith was an anachronism and rampant materialism eclipsed the spiritual. But surprisingly, this disbelief is shared by their rural neighbours. In response to Ruttledge's comment, Jamesie proclaims 'none of us believes'.[29] Even The Shah who attends Mass regularly follows his contrast of nature's perdurance and human ephemerality by asserting the finality of death:[30] 'That's it. We all know that. We all know full well and can't even whisper it out loud'.[31]

Like most of the novel's other characters, The Shah finds the stability that is no longer provided by religious faith through immersing himself in 'the familiar and habitual'.[32] His days are spent working at the salvage yard while every Sunday he goes to Ruttledge's for dinner. Other characters follow their own routines. Joe Ruttledge devotes himself to the everyday chores of a small farm. Jamesie regularly visits the Ruttledges to share and gather gossip. His brother Johnny returns from England at the beginning of each summer as if he were a migratory bird. Bill Evans, the ageing servant, comes down every morning from the Big House on the hill to collect water from the lake. The notorious John Quinn's life is given over to the serial pursuit of sexual conquest. Routines, such as these, are the profane counterpart of ritual. Both involve reiterative actions, but otherwise, they are divergent. Routines are idiosyncratic, rooted in the ordinary, devoid of larger significance; rituals, on the other hand, are communal and traditional, focused on liminal events, resonant with meaning. These distinctions are not hard-and-fast. It is possible for routines to elevate gradually to the level of rituals, but it is far more common, especially in an age of depersonalizing technological advancements, for rituals to lose their heightened status and fall into the profane realm of the routine.

---

29 McGahern, *That They May Face the Rising Sun*, 2.
30 In *The Church and Its Spire*, McGahern reports that when he returned to live in rural Ireland, he discovered 'that most of the people there had no belief'. He also recounts a conversation with a neighbour about why he didn't go to Mass that is quoted verbatim at the outset of *That They May Face the Rising Sun*. John McGahern, *Love of the World*: Essays (London: Faber and Faber, 2009), 146–147.
31 McGahern, *That They May Face the Rising Sun*, 158.
32 McGahern, *That They May Face the Rising Sun*, 38.

As *That They May Face the Rising Sun* reveals, this is precisely what was happening with traditional funerary rituals in late twentieth-century Ireland. Early in the novel, Ruttledge and Patrick Ryan visit Patrick's terminally ill brother Edmund in the hospital where he lies among rows of sick men on the cusp of death. There is no communication between the brothers since disease and medication have rendered Edmund virtually comatose. We learn later that after Edmund died in the hospital, he received no wake, but 'went straight from the hospital to the church'.[33] The funeral itself is distinguished only by Patrick's effort to ingratiate himself with former and prospective clients. In this brief episode, McGahern exposes the antiseptic and perfunctory nature of the more modern treatment of death. The contrast with the traditional funerary rituals that accompany the death of another bachelor, Johnny Murphy, is exemplifying. The extensive description of these rituals dominates the last part of the novel. In his final act as a fiction writer, McGahern seeks to preserve this rapidly disappearing tradition, arguably the most significant of the rural customs that he commemorated. Perhaps that is why his recounting of the rituals associated with Johnny's death emphasizes crucial aspects of this process that were left out of 'The Country Funeral' – specifically, the preparing of the body of the deceased and the digging of the grave. Each of these actions affects Ruttledge significantly and lays the groundwork for his culminating revelation about death.

In the absence of Patrick Ryan, whose myriad skills include the preparation of the corpse for the wake and funeral, this difficult task falls to Ruttledge, who is assisted by Tom Kelly, a hairdresser in Dublin back home for a visit. The procedure is described with exacting precision. After the clothes have been removed, the body's orifices are sealed with cotton wool. This act, especially the insertion of the cotton into the rectum, induces in Ruttledge a sense of intimacy as intense as the act of sex and elicits a recognition of 'the innate sacredness of each single life'.[34] When Kate asks him later about the experience of preparing the body, he replies that 'it made death and the fear of death more natural, more ordinary'.[35] Taken together,

---

33   McGahern, *That They May Face the Rising Sun*, 98.
34   McGahern, *That They May Face the Rising Sun*, 288.
35   McGahern, *That They May Face the Rising Sun*, 294.

these insights identify human death as both sacred and natural. This nexus deepens during the digging of Johnny's grave.

After the wake, which follows a similar course to the one in 'The Country Funeral', and before the removal of the body to the church, the grave is dug. Ruttledge is joined by several neighbours in this task, including Jamesie and Patrick Ryan. Near the end of the process, Patrick Ryan notices that the grave's layout is reversed so that it would be the feet rather than the head that is facing east. When Ruttledge asks whether it makes a difference, Patrick responds: 'He sleeps with his head in the west […] so that when he wakes he may face the rising sun' (ellipsis in the original). He follows this by dramatically motioning towards the east and proclaiming, 'we look to the resurrection of the dead'.[36] The theatricality with which this last statement is rendered prevents it from being an authentic declaration of faith. But even though this crucial Catholic doctrine about the afterlife is not affirmed, the traditional positioning of the grave manifests something more than just superstition. The alignment of the dead and the rising sun reflects a more ancient belief that incorporates death within the natural cycle and envisions it as a return to a point of origin.[37]

Ruttledge expands upon this point when Jamesie questions him several days after the funeral. The clocks in Jamesie's house have been restored to working order. Before his conversation with Ruttledge, Jamesie humorously translates the message conveyed by the clocks: 'Tick-tock. Pass no heed. Tick-tock. Say no bad. Tick-tock. Turn a blind eye. Tick-tock. Get into no trouble. Tick-tock. Put the hand over. Tick-tock. Don't press too hard. Tick-tock. Ask why not but never why.'[38] In Jamesie's rendition, the imperatives implicit in the clock's ticking counsel passivity. There is an incipient awareness in his comment of human impotence in the face of chronological time's inexorable movement. This, together with his brother's recent death, leads Jamesie to question Ruttledge about the possibility of

---

36   McGahern, *That They May Face the Rising Sun*, 297.
37   Stanley van der Zeil identifies the positioning of Johnny's body in the grave as 'a Celtic burial rite' in his article 'The Aesthetics of Redemption: John McGahern's *That They May Face the Rising Sun*', *Studies: An Irish Quarterly*, 93 (Winter 2004), 272, 481.
38   McGahern, *That They May Face the Rising Sun*, 309.

an afterlife. When Ruttledge tempers his negative response with an acknowledgement of the limits of his knowledge, Jamesie presses the matter by asking Ruttledge if he believes that our deaths are as final as those of animals and other natural entities. In response, Ruttledge cautiously conveys his intimation of post-mortem existence:

> More or less, Routledge answered carefully. I don't know from what source life comes, other than out of nature, or for what purpose. I suppose it's not unreasonable to think that we go back into whatever meaning we came from.[39]

What scant critical attention this passage has received treats it as further evidence of McGahern's rejection of Catholic doctrine. Such a reading is supported by Ruttledge's subsequent comment that orthodox Catholic conceptions of the afterlife – hell, heaven, purgatory, eternity – are simply projections of aspects of human experience. Ruttledge's enigmatic concluding statement is largely ignored. What is most striking is its use of the word 'meaning' to designate the primordial condition to which humans return after death. 'Emptiness' or some other word denoting vacuity would have seemed preferable to the non-believer Ruttledge. But instead, he identifies this ultimate source as a site of inscrutable significance. Equally surprising is the extent to which this passage from McGahern's last novel echoes one from his first. Quoted as the outset of this essay, Elizabeth Reegan's insight arises, Eamon Maher suggests, from her own unorthodox version of Catholicism.[40] There is less evidence of that in Ruttledge's outlook. Instead, his revelation emerges from traditional funerary rituals that imparted a sacrality to nature. What both passages share is a vision of human existence incorporated within a cosmic circle. In that, they reflect the deep-rooted mythological thinking encapsulated by Mircea Eliade for whom archaic rites of passage elicit a return to *in illo tempore* – 'the atemporal instant of primordial plenitude'.[41] In *That They May Face The Rising Sun*, if not in *The Barracks*, this revelation effects a subtle shift in the novel's perspective. When Patrick Ryan comes in the

---

39   McGahern, *That They May Face the Rising Sun*, 310.
40   Maher, *The Church and Its Spire*, 45.
41   Eliade, *The Myth of the Eternal Return*, 82.

aftermath of Johnny's death to finish constructing the shed in Ruttledge's farmyard, he interfuses the sacred and mundane by playfully referring to the building as a 'cathedral'. In the novel's poignant final sentence, the Ruttledges 'look back across the lake, even though they knew that both Jamesie and Mary had long since disappeared from the sky'.[42] The foreboding tenor of this conclusion is tempered by the belief that they will return, not just to the Ruttledge's, but eventually to the resonant mystery from which they emerged.

---

42   McGahern, *That They May Face the Rising Sun*, 314.

BERTRAND CARDIN

3 An Intertextual Reading of John McGahern's Short Story 'Korea'

'Korea' is a short story by John McGahern, taken from the collection *Nightlines*, published in 1970. It is a minimalist text centred on one event, one emotion and two anonymous characters. The plot could be summed up as follows: in the early 1950s, during a night fishing scene on the river at Oakport (Co. Roscommon, Ireland), a widowed father tells his son about his memories of the War of Independence. From his prison cell, he witnessed executions in Mountjoy. The image of the executed boy's buttons being thrown in the air by the impact of the bullets left an indelible mark on him. Many years later, during his honeymoon, the sight of furze pods bursting rekindled memories of the execution and ruined his day. More interested in the present, the father suggests to his son, whose studies are coming to an end, that he should leave Ireland, a country he feels has no future, and emigrate to America, the land of opportunity. The son is surprised by this proposal, especially as the father agrees to finance the trip, when he is usually so stingy. But the son promises to think about it. Incidentally, the next day, he overhears a conversation between his father and a cattle-dealer, Farrell, about the Moran family, whose son, Luke, enlisted in the US Army, was killed on the battlefields of Korea for which they received substantial allowances, sheltering them from want for the rest of their lives. Light is shed in the son's mind. The father's supposedly generous intention in fact conceals a highly venal motivation. As the son puts it: 'He'd scrape the fare, I'd be conscripted there, each month he'd get so many dollars while I served, and he'd get ten thousand if I was killed.'[1] The young man feels a real shock. The following night, on the boat, when his father asks him if he has made up his mind, the son replies:

---

1   John McGahern, 'Korea', *The Collected Stories* (London: Faber & Faber, 1992), 57.

'No, I'm not going.'

'It'll be your own funeral', rants the father, sarcastically.

'It'll be my own funeral', his son repeats, watching each move the old man made, 'as closely as if I too had to prepare myself to murder'.[2]

This article aims to illustrate the intertextual aspect of 'Korea' by linking it to writings both before and after its publication. Although, unlike some other McGahern short stories, 'Korea' does not contain any quotations or specific references to other texts, the reader is allowed to establish intertextual relationships, considering that 'any text is the absorption and transformation of another'.[3]

The general theme of the story – a father sending his son to death in order to live a better life – brings back to the reader's memory ancient texts recounting sacrifices. To kill in order to live could be the profound reason for sacrifice. According to primitive religions, for humanity to survive and life to be assured, it is necessary to spill blood and, in particular, to sacrifice human beings. This practice is justified in different ways in every culture and on all continents. In Western culture, Greek mythology and the Bible narrate quite a few human sacrifices. The biblical story in which God tests Abraham[4] is mobilized by the reading of 'Korea', for it is more or less the same story that is reformulated. Abraham, etymologically the father of a host of nations, is the emblem of fatherhood. In the biblical episode and the Irish short story, the father is a man who has fought and suffered, yet is prepared to cut the thread of his lineage and offer his son as a holocaust. In both texts, he dodges embarrassing questions from his child, to whom he cannot confess his secret and divulge his true intention:

'Why should you scrape for me to go to America if I can get a job here?

I feel I'd be giving you a chance I never got.'[5]

---

2 McGahern, *The Collected Stories*, 58.
3 Julia Kristeva, *Desire in Language*: *A Semiotic Approach to Literature and Art* (New York: Columbia University Press, 1980), 66.
4 *Genesis*, chapter 22, v. 1–24.
5 McGahern, *The Collected Stories*, 56.

'Where is the young beast for the sacrifice?'

Abraham answered, 'God will provide himself with a young beast for a sacrifice, my son.'[6]

Abraham reveals the spiritual dimension of the sacrifice. He testifies to his fear of God by doing His will, for it was God who asked him to sacrifice his son. In the short story, on the other hand, the sacrifice is not spiritualized but, on the contrary, motivated by venal instincts, perverse and selfish desires. Whereas Abraham, torn between faith and absolute justice, shows man's anguish in the face of God, the father in 'Korea' shows only concern for his personal comfort and the material conditions of his existence. He sends his son to his death with indifference, unlike the father in the biblical story. The magnanimity of the one is matched by the pusillanimity of the other. Yet three days pass between the decision to carry out the sacrifice and its conclusion, leaving plenty of time to change their minds. Indeed, the journey from the point of departure, where God gives his recommendations, to the point of arrival, the land of Moriah, where Abraham offers the sacrifice, takes place over three days, a period that prefigures Jesus's passion and death on Mount Golgotha. McGahern's story is set over one night, one day and one night, so roughly speaking three days as well. Consequently, the fathers do not act spontaneously, but in full awareness and lucidity. They have time to think, to imagine the future while they work with their sons: in the short story, father and son sail and fish together. In the Bible, they are united in reaching the hill, building the altar, arranging the wood and the fire, as illustrated by the repetition of the adverb 'together',[7] which accentuates the dramatic intensity of the scene.

In both cases, the environment seems frozen; nothing moves except the eyes of the protagonists, who stare at each other in silence. Faced with their father's strange behaviour, the sons begin to guess, to understand on their own, and are then suddenly struck by the revelation that gives them access to knowledge when the obvious becomes clear to them. Just

---

6   *Genesis*, chapter 22, verse 8.
7   'The two of them went on together', *Genesis* (v. 6 & 8).

as Abraham binds his son to the altar of sacrifice, leaving him no choice but to die, the father in 'Korea' symbolically ties his son to the fatal destiny he imagines for him. The angel of God calls out to Abraham, who, knife in hand, suspends his gesture. This third character intervenes after the story had previously focused on the two protagonists, who were presented as alone in the world. This angelic creature is perhaps also present in McGahern's short story in the guise of Farrell, the evil angel who convinces the father to send his son off to war.

In the two texts, the sons escape the death to which their fathers lead them. Although one deliberately renounces being sacrificed and the other is saved by the intervention of a third party, both of them are survivors. Death is vanquished, fate revoked. At the last minute, they escape their status as scapegoats. However, the sacrifice is no less consummated: through a process of substitution, a ram is offered in the holy text, and other young men are sacrificed on the altar of the Korean War.

The entire biblical tradition sees in the interruption of Abraham's gesture by a divine creature the prohibition of human sacrifice. The Jewish religion has thus undergone a major transformation in the history of religions. Nevertheless, doesn't the hecatomb of war represent the perpetuation of human sacrifice, of the mechanisms of death that gnaw at humanity? These texts illustrate truths: a father is not free to dispose of his son as he sees fit, since the latter is not his property. They also have allegorical significance: the story of Abraham contains the whole Jewish destiny. It incorporates all the great themes, passions and obsessions of Judaism. As far as 'Korea' is concerned, the father can be seen as the personification of the Irish government of the mid-twentieth century and, more generally, of all those countries whose domestic policies do nothing to keep young people at home, but seem on the contrary to encourage them to emigrate. These texts are in touch with realities that are still relevant today: aren't venal motivations at the root of many military engagements? How many young men are prepared to take part in a conflict and kill in order to improve their material situation and live better afterwards? 'Korea' also reflects the attitude of those fathers who knowingly sent their sons to war to make men of them. Is there a human motivation behind this behaviour? Is it due to the father's unspoken resentment towards the son who will outlive him, or the human need to kill what he loves?

The two stories raise fundamental questions. Through the conflicts and dramatic events they recount, they give the characters another dimension, reveal a different aspect of their humanity and of the humankind in general.[8] This is undoubtedly what makes them so contemporary. All these points in common, to which could be added the rigour and intensity of the narratives, devoid of useless gestures and superfluous words, justify the relation uniting the two texts. Grafted onto the biblical account of Isaac's sacrifice, 'Korea' can be seen as the hypertext of this extract from the Book of Genesis. It can be perceived as a response to this founding narrative, contextualized in a specific spatio-temporal universe, namely the Irish 1950s.

The intertextual relationship may not have been intended by the author, especially as 'Korea' never explicitly quotes the biblical episode. Readers who note this parallel can legitimately wonder if their own cultural background does not incite them to make spontaneous connections between the short story and the holy text. But does not the problem arise concerning any interpretative critical work inasmuch as any metatextual approach can give the text a meaning that the writer did not intend to give? What the text writes is more important than what the writer meant. By definition, the concept of intertextuality takes into account the links that literary works weave between themselves, without necessarily being concerned with the authors' awareness of the phenomenon. As a matter of fact, 'Korea' refers to texts of all kinds, not just literary myths such as the sacrifice of Isaac. Its intertextual practice may also draw on texts of lesser authority, so much so that not every reader will recognize the intertextual effect.

The question is which texts to turn to in order to illustrate this relation. It suffices to note the writers McGahern mentions in his interviews. Mention of their names suggests that our writer has read and appreciated their works. As a result, echoes between these texts and his own cannot be ruled out. As it happens, the names most frequently mentioned are those of

---

8   Eamon Maher examines this phenomenon of enlargement in his eloquent study *John McGahern: From the Local to the Universal* (Dublin: The Liffey Press, 2003).

Yeats, Beckett, Flaubert, Proust, but also Scott Fitzgerald and Hemingway. McGahern admires Hemingway for the simplicity, rigour and dramatic construction of his stories, and it is significant that 'Korea' implicitly refers to a short story by the American writer.

Hemingway's short story, entitled 'Indian Camp', is taken from the collection *The First Forty-Nine Stories*.[9] It takes place at night, and features a father and his son, Nick, in a boat. This initial scene, with its repetition of the verb 'to row' and mentions of darkness, fog and cold, gives the reader a sense of *déjà lu*. Along with the boy's uncle and two Indians, Nick and his father, a doctor, go to the bedside of an Indian woman who is having trouble delivering her baby. Like the protagonist of 'Korea', Nick finds himself in direct contact with nature, learning the simple gestures of life, in this case the possible complications of childbirth, hygiene conditions, and cutting the umbilical cord. His father justifies most of his actions by giving clear explanations to his son. After the birth, he is, like the father of 'Korea', excited and talkative, proud to have been able to perform a caesarean section with a pocket knife. But all hell breaks loose when the doctor discovers that the baby's father, seriously injured in an accident a few days earlier, has slit his own throat during his wife's delivery. As the young man in 'Korea' understands that his 'youth had ended',[10] Nick knows that his life will never be the same again. His father apologizes to him, and they both return home at daybreak: 'They were sitting in the boat, Nick in the stern, and his father rowing. The sun was rising over the hills. A sea bass jumped out, making a circle on the water.'[11] Like 'Korea', Hemingway's story ends as it begins, with father and son on a boat in the half-light. 'The Indian Village' is based on a cyclical structure mimicked by the circle in the water formed by the fish's leap. The cycle is also that of day and night, life and death: the newborn's entry into the world leads his father into death. In both texts, death has the last word: the American short story ends with the verb 'die', the Irish short story with the verb 'murder'.

---

9   Ernest Hemingway, *The Fifth Column and the First Forty-Nine Stories* (New York: Scribner, 1938).
10 McGahern, *The Collected Stories*, 57.
11 Hemingway, 'Indian Camp', *The First Forty-Nine Stories*, 95.

If this intertextual relationship is not fortuitous, Hemingway's writings can be said to have inspired, even influenced McGahern.[12] This notion of influence implies a chronological conception of history. For this reason, it is frequently reconsidered by intertextuality, which does not perceive textual connections in a chronological order. True, Hemingway's texts were written before McGahern's, but intertextuality works both ways as it suggests a conception of literary creation in which the writer, instead of being influenced, changes and reworks a previous text. A parallel observation of 'Indian Village' and 'Korea' highlights not only an impact of the first text on the second, but also a transformation of the first text by the second. The first text can thus be read with another eye. It is not so much the author who is influenced by the texts as the text itself that transforms others, even earlier ones. In this network, it may be interesting, after examining the intertextual relationship between 'Korea' and texts from the previous culture, to see the link the short story has with texts published later.

To this end, we need to look at authors who may have read McGahern's short stories. This is the case, for example, of Colum McCann, who was born in Ireland thirty years after McGahern, and thus belongs to the next generation of writers. As an Irish man of letters, McCann is necessarily familiar with the texts of his surrounding culture, of which McGahern's work is a part. And it is not impossible that 'Korea' left an indelible imprint on his mind. One of McCann's short stories, 'As Kingfishers Catch Fire', establishes an intertextual relationship with 'Korea'.

Published in 1997, 'As Kingfishers Catch Fire' tells the story of Rhianon, a young Irish woman who leaves her native Roscommon for New York in 1950. Generous by nature, she goes to Korea with the American troops, caring for the wounded. She regularly sends letters to her family, which are read to the entire village community in the cinema. She writes about the heat, the mosquitoes, the kingfishers, but also about the helicopters, the illnesses and the suffering of the soldiers. When Rhianon tells of her

---

12 This is the opinion of Michael C. Prusse in his article on this intertextual relationship: 'Brief Encounters between Fictional Universes: John McGahern and Ernest Hemingway' (conference 'Rewriting / Reprising in Literature Conference', Université de Lyon, 2, 13 & 14 October 2006), http://archives.univ-lyon2.fr/237/2/prusse_01.htm [accessed 23 November 2023].

encounter with one of them, whom she cares for and considers a saint because he radiates an unusual light, the village becomes enthusiastic about this love story between one of their own and a handsome soldier with the physique of a Hollywood star. But when Rhianon returns home at the end of the war, she is alone, neglected and gives birth to a stillborn child, the 'bastard' of a 'Korean soldier'. Slapped by her mother and ostracized from the community, she buys a farm and a refrigerator to keep her lover's three amputated fingers on ice. From then on, she leads a reclusive life of silence, isolation and disillusionment.[13] When Rhianon dies, the small village of Roscommon is stunned by a spectacular invasion of kingfishers. As her body is laid in the earth alongside her son, the birds take flight. No one notices that there are three fingers in the pocket of her dress.

Echoes of McGahern's short story can be found in McCann's. The spatio-temporal data are the same: the North-West of Ireland, the US, Korea, the early 1950s. Although the American flag is present in both stories, the US is merely a stopover between Ireland and Korea. Korea means death (Luke Moran and Rhianon's lover lose their lives there), while Ireland is characterized by pettiness and narrow-mindedness. The miserly greed of the father in McGahern's story is matched by the inhuman, inhospitable reaction of the disappointed villagers in McCann's. Only birds pay tribute to the departed woman: 'The kingfishers continued their onslaught, a salvo of them through the Roscommon sky, with a liquid movement of their wings.'[14] The mention of the military term 'salvo' echoes the discharge of firearms in honour of Luke Moran at his burial: 'Shots had been fired above the grave before they threw in the clay.'[15] Kingfishers reconcile the elements through their familiarity with air, water and earth. Moreover, the title of the story associates them with the fourth element – fire – which

---

13   Disillusionment is a common theme in the three short stories mentioned here. In McGahern, McCann and Hemingway, the protagonists lose their illusions as a result of their own experiences. In addition, the other characters – the father in 'Korea', the Indian woman in 'Indian Village' and the village community in 'As Kingfishers Catch Fire' – are equally disillusioned by the situations they witness.
14   Colum McCann, 'As Kingfishers Catch Fire', in *Phoenix Irish Short Stories*, edited by David Marcus (London: Phoenix House, 1997), 85.
15   McGahern, *The Collected Stories*, 57.

completes their communion with matter, whatever it may be. The surprising title of the story is a quotation from Gerard Manley Hopkins' 1877 poem 'As Kingfishers catch fire, dragonflies draw flame'.[16] Literature is indeed conceivable in terms of indefinite textual interactions. The image of the kingfishers which 'swooped down on rivers and fed on fish found in the icy water'[17] recalls 'Korea': 'The wings of ducks shirred as they curved down into the bay.'[18]

Similarly, bats are mentioned in both texts: 'The dark was closing from the shadow of Oakport to Nutley's boathouse, bats made ugly whirls overhead',[19] can be contrasted with 'At night bats flitted above the rice fields and somehow made her think of home, the movement of shadows'.[20] 'Night' echoes 'shadows', terms that are closely associated with the appearance of twilight animals such as bats. This theme of darkness, characteristic of McGahern's story, is also very present in McCann's, as evidenced by a whole semantic field, with the repetition of the term 'shadow', as well as its compounds: 'shade' or 'overshadow'. Similarly, the words 'evening', 'night' and 'black' are recurrent. As in 'Korea', the major scenes of the story take place in the evening, or more precisely at dusk, that is, at an intermediate period between light and shade. Significantly, Ireland is associated with this in-between time: described as 'dull, grey, monochromatic',[21] it lies at the junction between American brightness and Korean darkness. In the villagers' imagination, Rhianon's lover is a star, a blond, blue-eyed American soldier, whereas he is a small Korean man with hair as dark as his country's nights.

When he is close to death, this soldier's body is riddled with bullets and metal pieces. This detail recalls the prisoner's execution which haunts the father's memory at the beginning of McGahern's story: 'The officer then ordered them to fire, and as the volley rang, the boy tore at his tunic

---

16   With this reference, McCann's short story explicitly displays itself as an intertext, all the more so since the mention of its title is directly followed by an epigraph quoting the first line of the poem.
17   'As Kingfishers Catch Fire', 75.
18   McGahern, *The Collected Stories*, 57.
19   McGahern, *The Collected Stories*, 57.
20   'As Kingfishers Catch Fire', 78.
21   'As Kingfishers Catch Fire', 76–77.

over the heart, as if to pluck out the bullets, and the buttons of the tunic began to fly into the air before he pitched forward on his face.'[22]

The veteran's instinctive memory conjures up the buttons of the garment in the bursting furze pods on his honeymoon in Howth. This association of flowers with buttons, and implicitly with bullets, is a peculiar image. Yet it is not specific to McGahern's story, as it is also present in 'As Kingfishers Catch Fire':

> She was carrying the bastard child of a black-haired Korean soldier who, when he died, had set off a meteor shower over the landscape of his country, huge streams of light rivering upwards to the sky from some hillside where digit-shaped flowers burst out every spring in his memory.[23]

Set against the backdrop of a soldier's death and the memory of spring,[24] both texts link blossoming flowers to exploding war projectiles, associating natural, peaceful phenomena inherent to life with processes linked to a culture of violence, cruelty and death. The verb 'burst', applicable to both situations, has flowers as its subject in both stories.[25] It accentuates and justifies the analogy: bursts of death are answered by bursts of life.

These elements allow the reader to see in McCann's story a subtle composition with McGahern's. Unlike the relation the former establishes with Hopkins' poem, to which it explicitly refers, 'As Kingfishers Catch Fire' implicitly echoes 'Korea'. The convergence between the two texts can thus go completely unnoticed, especially as 'As Kingfishers Catch Fire' is not a well-known text. Identifying elements common to both stories highlights a relation of co-presence between them: McCann reconstructs fragments of 'Korea' with a different logic. This negotiation with another writer's text reflects the presence of dialogism, a notion at work in all intertextual relations, according to Julia Kristeva. As the Russian theorist Mikhail Bakhtin

---

22 McGahern, *The Collected Stories*, 54.
23 'As Kingfishers Catch Fire', 82.
24 The protagonist's parents' honeymoon takes place in May.
25 'The sea was below, and smell of the sea and furze bloom all about, and then I looked down and saw the furze pods bursting, and the way they burst in all directions seemed shocking like the buttons when he started to tear at his tunic. I couldn't get it out of my mind all day' ('Korea', 54–55).

shows, every literary statement is characterized by dialogism, because it is a response to other statements and bears the mark of a dialogue between two subjects.[26] Texts are elements of a vast network in which they interweave, understand one another and dialogue with one another. As a result, 'Korea' is enriched by a polyphonic composition in which voices other than McGahern's can be heard.[27]

26   Mikhail M. Bakhtin, *The Dialogic Imagination: Four Essays* (Austin: University of Texas Press, 1981).
27   Of course, other illustrations could have been given. For example, there are a number of echoes of James Joyce's work in McGahern's short story: the recurrence of the word 'clay' in 'Korea' is reminiscent of a short story from *Dubliners*, precisely titled 'Clay'. Similarly, typically Joycean notions such as paralysis, epiphany and the *non serviam* of the protagonist who escapes the nets in which he risks being trapped are also present in McGahern's story.

ANNE GOARZIN

4 Friendship and Literature

This *Festschrift* is a welcome opportunity to celebrate books and their readers and to explore what binds them together and what forms the basis of shared emotions in literature. For the contributors of this collection, Eamon Maher is unquestionably a central figure in the intellectual, academic, friendly and international connection between France and Ireland. However, my intention here is not to write an academic panegyric, but rather to reflect on what constitutes a 'lasting' or sustainable transmission – or a 'bountiful literary friendship' to echo the title of the book which has served as a reference for many scholars. In the opening chapter paying homage to the late Patrick Rafroidi, co-editors Haley and Murray state the solidity and durability of a bond which Eamon Maher has, in turn, developed over the course of his own academic career:

> The 'French connection' has never been severed by Irish people since the first Irish missionaries established cultural bases in France in the Middle Ages. Today it is instructive to drive through Normandy and Brittany and note how many towns are twinned with towns in Ireland. In that long reach of time, from the early Middle Ages to the present, the history of Irish-French relations and interconnections remains to be written. There is a history of affinity, mutual indebtedness, and diverse communication; a history that illuminates and modifies ideas, literature, and political developments; a history that interrogates the forces that shape identity. It is a history of friendship that has borne fruit in many ways.[1]

[1] Barbara Hayley and Christopher Murray (eds), *Ireland and France: A Bountiful Friendship* (London: Colin Smythe, 1991), x. See *Le Monde*, 24 November 1989, https://www.lemonde.fr/archives/article/1989/11/24/patrick-rafroidi-1930-1989_4162 082_1819218.html [accessed 24 April 2023, translation mine]: 'Born in Arpajon on 15 June 1930, a doctor in literature and the holder of agrégation in English, he spent his university career between Lille and Strasbourg, before being elected President of the University of Lille-III, then cultural attaché in London from 1981 to 1984. The founder and director of the Centre for Irish Studies and

This chapter offers to reflect on ways to establish common ground in literature, specifically between readers of the same author. To do so, it will rely on literary concepts such as the 'master form',[2] or the 'impersonal',[3] to explore McGahern's writings from the perspective of readers and reading.

Common literary ground

My conversation with Eamon Maher dates back to 2002, when he e-mailed me with a proposal to review the book I had just published with the Presses Universitaires de Rennes.[4] His reaching out surprised me at the time as I thought I had somewhat exhausted the discussion of McGahern's writings. Yet I could not but acknowledge the resonance of the text and our shared interest in McGahern's singular writing, or, as Marielle Macé puts it in *Façons de lire, manières d'être*, our wish to 'follow an author in his sentence':

> What does to follow a writer through a sentence mean? First of all, it means entering into the framing power of a style, identifying and actively appropriating what is obstinate in that style – the preference consists precisely in reviving that obstinacy […]

Research at Lille-III University, he also founded the twice-yearly journal *Etudes Irlandaises* […].' The book also pays tribute to Barbara Hayley, professor of literature and William Carleton specialist at St Patrick's College, Maynooth; who died prematurely in 1991. Likewise, this very collection offers me a chance to honour the memory of Cécile Maudet, an Irish literature scholar who passed away in 2023 at the age of 38, and who gifted me her friendship and the privilege of her bright conversation on McGahern, to whose work she was introduced during her Erasmus stay at Saint Patrick's College Drumcondra in 2005. She then wrote two master's theses on his novels before going on to complete her doctoral thesis on Colum McCann.

2   Marielle Macé, *Façons de lire, manières d'être* (Paris: Gallimard, 2011), 2022.
3   Jacques Rancière, *La Chair des mots. Politiques de l'écriture* (Paris: Galilée, 1998).
4   Anne Goarzin, *John McGahern: Reflets d'Irlande* (Rennes: Presses Universitaires de Rennes, 2000).

it means appropriating his mode of figuration, following in his footsteps and making his approach one's own, integrating this step in one's own tempo.⁵

In the course of this epistolary exchange, it became clear to us that we shared an attention to McGahern's own melody and to the world he makes available to his readers. With hindsight, this mutual impression appears best defined by Marielle Macé as the *'forme maîtresse'* of an oeuvre, which she theorizes by expanding on the significance of the 'standard sentence' (*phrase type*) in Proust or in Stendhal's works. These forms make their way into the readers' minds and stay with them; whether it is be 'elevation scenes' in the case of Stendhal or the verbal expression of a style of being or a presence in the world in the case of Proust. The 'standard sentence' can be recognized in all the works and they imply a degree of attention on the part of the reader to appreciate them. Their exemplarity accounts for

> the differentiating yet generic force of an author's style. These sentences are not only grammatical realities, but also decidedly situational: physical or experiential situations, sketches of gestures, perceptive windows; generic framings rather than images, movements rather than objects, they inscribe the question of style in the vast realm of attention and behaviour.⁶

What happens in the encounter with other readers is thus an opportunity to start a dialogue about what features of McGahern's style stick with us, and to step away from the comfort of what Macé calls '[o]ur cognitive style, the one that returns in a recognizable fold, in that repeated way we

---

5   Marielle Macé, 87–89, translation mine: 'Suivre un écrivain dans sa phrase qu'est-ce que cela veut dire? C'est, d'abord, entrer dans la puissance encadrante d'un style, parvenir à identifier et à s'approprier activement ce qu'il y a d'obstiné dans ce style – la préférence consistant justement à relancer cette obstination [....] c'est donc s'approprier son mode de figuration, lui emboîter le pas et faire sienne sa démarche, en modulant ce pas dans son propre tempo.'
6   Macé, 89, translation mine: '[...] la force à la fois différenciante et générique d'un style d'auteur. Ces phrases ne sont pas seulement des réalités grammaticales, mais engagent décidément des situations: situations physiques ou expérientielles, esquisses de gestes, fenêtres perceptives; cadrages génériques plutôt qu'images, mouvements plutôt qu'objets, elles inscrivent la question du style dans le vaste domaine de l'attention et du comportement.'

have of taking things and making use of them, [which is] undoubtedly the outline of our master form'.[7] The encounter of our distinct experiences of literature and of life also takes the literary text out of its context of academic study and inserts it into a living community of friendship, as Jacques Rancière puts it: 'The word has many other things to imitate than its meaning or referent: the power of the word that brings it into existence, the movement of life, the gesture of an address, the effect it anticipates, the recipient whose listening or reading it imitates in advance.'[8]

Readers in conversation

The collected essays in *Love of the World*[9] trace the influence of Proustian imagery[10] and of the French Realists on McGahern's writing. The literary company that McGahern keeps and that we, as readers, become acquainted with in the reading (e.g. McGahern appraisal of Joyce through the prism of Flaubert)[11] should not obscure the fact that the position that underpins McGahern's writing is primarily an experiential one. His *'phrase maîtresse'* is a subjective disposition to solitude, as he writes in 'The Solitary Reader'.[12] Yet far from hindering dialogue, this solitary way

---

7   Macé, 96, translation mine: 'Notre style cognitif, celui qui revient dans un pli reconnaissable, dans cette façon répétée que nous avons de prendre les choses et d'en faire usage, [qui est] sans doute le dessin de notre forme maîtresse.'
8   Rancière, 11, translation mine: 'Le mot a bien d'autres choses à imiter que son sens ou son référent: la puissance de la parole qui le porte à l'existence, le mouvement de la vie, le geste d'une adresse, l'effet qu'il anticipe, destinataire dont il mime par avance l'écoute ou la lecture [...].'
9   John McGahern, *Love of the World: Essays*, edited by Stanley Van de Ziel (London: Faber and Faber, 2009).
10 McGahern, 'Playing with Words', in *Love of the World*, 9–10.
11 See John McGahern, 'Dubliners', in *Love of the World*, 200–205, in which McGahern quotes extensively from the correspondence between George Sand and Flaubert.
12 McGahern, 'The Solitary Reader', in Love *of the World*, 87–88.

of being in the world gives rise to dialectical relationships. McGahern's literary form and style calls to our own: 'In reading, the draw of an object and the disposition of a subject are thus articulated and relaunched, [...] literary styles and cognitive styles interweave.'[13] His solitude as a reader and as a writer thus sets his reader's own solitude to work, opening up the text to new figurations.

In the account of McGahern's experience as a guardian of the Moroney's library, the time of reading unlocks the possibility of imagination and plenitude. As such, it stands in contrast to the busy and work-filled constraints of social and family life, or even politics. The experience of the completeness of solitary reading is made possible by the reconfiguration of the young boy's private space, with the library granting him independence from the Cootehall barracks, at a distance from the strained relationship with his father. Here, desire and pleasure take over from productivity ('those days not lived at all, the days lost in a favourite book').[14] It frees the reader from the guilt-fraught relationship to the idle time of Christian morality ('"The devil always finds work for idle hands" was one of the warning catchphrases'),[15] and gives free rein to the pleasure of the imagination and the lightness of conversation:

> During this time I was given the free run of the Moroney's library. [...] As a boy, I was sent to buy apples, somehow fell in conversation with Willie about books, and was given the run of the library [...] I didn't differentiate, I read for nothing but pleasure, the way a boy nowadays might watch endless television dramas [...] Nobody gave me direction or advice. There was a tall slender ladder for getting books on the high shelves. Often, in the incredibly cluttered kitchen, old Willie would ask me about the books over tea and bread. I think it was more out of the need for company than any real curiosity [...] Earlier that morning he must have gone through his hives [...] and while he was talking some jam fell into the beard and set off an immediate buzzing. Without interrupting the flow of his talk, he shambled to the door, extracted the two or three errant bees caught in the beard, and flung them into the air of the yard.[16]

13 Macé 94–99, translation mine: 'Dans la lecture s'articulent et se relancent ainsi l'allure d'un objet et les dispositions d'un sujet, [...] des styles littéraires et des styles cognitifs qui s'entre-façonnent.'
14 McGahern, 'The Solitary Reader', in *Love of The World*, 89–90.
15 McGahern, 'The Solitary Reader', in *Love of The World*, 87.
16 McGahern, 'The Solitary Reader', in *Love of The World*, 88.

The 'impersonal' nature of McGahern's text

'Everything interesting begins with one person in one place, though the places can become many, and many persons in the form of influences will have gone into the making of that single woman or man [....] Out of the particular we come on what is general, which is our great comfort, since we call it truth, and that truth has to be continually renewed. What is general and true has to be found again', McGahern writes.[17]

This renewed search fuels what Gilles Deleuze calls the *'fabulation function'* (*Fonction de fabulation*) of literary enunciation. It does not consist in imagining or projecting or a self;[18] rather it seeks to *restore* – a process, the possibility of life, becomings or powers.[19] McGahern himself calls it a literature 'without qualities' after Robert Musil – that is to say, a literature that is not pre-determined, without intentions, in the sense that it escapes social control or labels, and that it resists the dictates of conventions or literary fashions, as McGahern stresses: 'In a world governed by the desire for total control, the writer must be the caretaker of the possible.'[20] Beneath the story of the young reader therefore lies the potential story of all our encounters with literature.

In McGahern's writings, this tension between control and potential is internalized by characters who are overdetermined by their relationship to the political, the domestic and the territorial, while at the same time embodying a singularity that transcends their own selves. Thus Moran, the ageing farmer in *Amongst Women*, grapples with his own anger at a world that is slipping away from him and his bitter nostalgia for the dream of a Republic that would not have been sacrificed to the Treaty. In *The Barracks*, Reagan, a *Garda Siochána*, is trapped in a life marked by the absurdity of rules and repetition. In *The Dark*, the teenager caught between the domination of an abusive biological father and the injunctions of a priest tries

---

17   McGahern, 'The Local and the Universal', in *Love of The World*, 11.
18   Deleuze, *Critique et clinique* (Paris: Minuit, 1993), 14.
19   Deleuze, *Critique et clinique*, 13.
20   McGahern, 'A Literature without Qualities', in *Love of The World*, 181.

to open a passage to his own freedom. But it is with the female character in *The Barracks* that McGahern unleashes the full power of an impersonal vision, both literally and figuratively. Elizabeth Reagan is stripped of the power to say 'I' by what Deleuze terms a 'becoming too powerful [for her]':[21] she gains access to the vision of her own mortality, a condition that is both foreign and familiar, therefore articulating the neutrality of a 'we'.

Memoir (2005),[22] although it is based on McGahern's personal memories, also speaks on behalf of a people that is 'missing' in Deleuze's phrase.[23] The narrative contains the universality of a vanished community and traces the memory of the places associated with it – the sunken country lanes, the house at Aughawillan, the schools or the barracks. The conversations between the narrator's parents resonate through found letters. Beyond the recollection of personal heartbreak and of the boy's last goodbye to his mother and his subsequent grief, numerous voices reverberate is a text that conveys a collective experience of loss, real or metaphorical. But the realization of loss is counterbalanced by the potential of these experiences for literary creation, with many of them finding their way into novels or short stories:

> We grow into an understanding of the world gradually. Much of what we come to know is far from comforting, that each day brings us closer to the inevitable hour when all will be darkness again, but even that knowledge is power and all understanding is joy, even in the face of dread, and cannot be taken from us until everything is.[24]

---

21 Gilles Deleuze, 'La littérature et la vie', in *Critique et clinique*, 13. 'Ce ne sont pas les deux premières personnes qui servent de condition à l'énonciation littéraire; la littérature ne commence que lorsque naît en nous une troisième personne qui nous dessaisit du pouvoir de dire "Je" [...] certes les personnages littéraires sont parfaitement individués, et sont ni vagues ni généraux; mais tous leurs traits individuels les élèvent à une vision qui les emmènent dans un indéfini comme un devenir trop puissant pour eux.'
22 John McGahern *Memoir* (London: Faber, 2005).
23 Deleuze, 14, cf. 'La santé, comme littérature, comme écriture, consiste à inventer un peuple qui manque.'
24 McGahern, *Memoir*, 36.

In her chapter published in *Essays on John McGahern: Assessing a Literary Legacy*, Máire Doyle further examines the reasons for the relational failings of many of McGahern's characters:

> The lack of a fully developed society allowed the family to become the dominant unit, the kind of dominance he explores in particular in *Amongst Women* [....] The absence of manners, which for McGahern was a moral void, meant that people had no communal understanding of the ethically proper way to develop relationships with others.[25]

How, then, may collective enunciation be achieved when interactions are problematic or when friendship is acutely absent? Among other insights, Doyle identifies a resistance to friendship in the case of Moran in *Amongst Women*, or a rejection of female sociability in that of Elizabeth Reagan in *The Barracks*. She also notes that *That They May Face the Rising Sun*, McGahern's final novel, makes for an important exception to this enduring defiance, with its 'unequivocal celebration of community [...] friendships of varying hues emerge and disappear'.[26] These friendships are anchored in 'traditional neighbourliness – a reciprocity of time, labour and hospitality – a mutual generosity of spirit that each couple recognised in the other'.[27] This particular novel makes room for collective agency and worldliness where 'shared consciousness is strengthened with each return journey', according to Doyle's perceptive study.[28] Even though it anticipates the disappearance of a community and of a way of life for want of a younger generation to take its place, she emphasizes the openness and the exteriority of a narrative which lies in the affirmation of a friendly sociability, breaking the pattern of resistance to relationships, as exemplified by the incipit:

---

25 Máire Doyle, '"My Sweet Guide": Friends and Friendship in the Fiction of John McGahern', 146–161 in *Essays on John McGahern: Assessing a Literary Legacy*, edited by Derek Hand and Eamon Maher (Cork: Cork UP, 2019), 148.
26 Doyle, 'My Sweet Guide', 148.
27 Doyle, 'My Sweet Guide, 157.
28 Doyle, 'My Sweet Guide, 158.

> The doors of the house were open. Jamesie entered without knocking and came in noiselessly until he stood in the doorway of the large room where the Ruttledges were sitting. He stood as still as if waiting under trees for returning wildfowls. He expected his discovery to be quick. There would be a cry of surprise and reproach; he would counter by accusing them of not being watchful enough. There would be welcome and laughter [....]
>
> 'Hel-lo. Hel-lo. Hel-lo', he called out softly, in some exasperation.
>
> 'Jamesie!' They turned to the voice with great friendliness. As he often stole silently in, they showed no surprise. 'You are welcome.'[29]

In spite of the notable exception of this novel, the recurring difficulty of friendship or relationships across McGahern's writings still raises the question of what ultimately holds his *oeuvre* together. Here, I turn to Jacques Rancière's proposition that the five words uttered by Bartleby in Herman Melville's *Bartleby The Scrivener*, his negative preference and strange response ('I would prefer not to') undermines the normativity of literature. The clerk Bartleby 'gives up preferring', or 'prefers not to' copy, and in so doing he enacts a rupture with representation, and with the normativity of the *mimesis*. This is why Rancière asserts that Bartelby's refusal is performative: it is 'a material operation accomplished by the materiality of the text'[30] – that is, by the formula.

Likewise, if we are to trace a similar formula in the tendency of McGahern's characters to 'prefer not to' be with others or to avoid friendship, then what does this achieve? One could argue that the characters' solitariness and recurring 'preference not to' embrace relationships, to idealize them (*The Pornographer*) or their fear of depending on someone as far as romantic relations, or family or friends are concerned, only underlines the unbreachable distance between individuals. Perhaps the struggle to be in the world and to establish relationships is not just a matter of *mimesis*. It may also be a tell-tale sign of the characters' metaphysical resistance to the norm (church, family, nation).[31] Their individual difficulty in relating to

---

29   McGahern, *That They May Face the Rising Sun*, 1.
30   Rancière, *La chair des mots*, 179. Rancière refers to one of Deleuze's later essays entitled 'Bartelby et la formule', in *Critique et clinique* (Paris: Minuit, 1993), 89–114.
31   See Rancière, 181: 'La puissance propre de la littérature s'origine dans cette zone d'indétermination où les individuations anciennes se défont [....] La puissance

others materializes in a common aspiration (to prefer) not to be limited by a given model. What emerges from is a literary oeuvre that demonstrates an uncompromising vitality, unconstrainted by literary or social normativity while calling for a degree of humility:

> We have to discard all the tenets that we have been told until we have succeeded in thinking them out for ourselves. We find that we are no longer reading books for the story and all stories are more or less the same story; and we begin to come on certain books that act like mirrors. What they reflect is something dangerously close to our own life and the society which we live in.[32]

Conclusion: Recognition, not repetition

The scarcity of friendship that characterizes many of McGahern's works may be seen as a metaphor for McGahern's own solitary experience as a writer and, by extension, for his readers'. Indeed, how may we base a community of friendship on an experience constituted by the essential solitude of reading? For one, this can be achieved by recognizing the common ground of scholarly networks and the circulation of critical debate. The crisscrossing of networks such as AFIS or SOFEIR (of which Eamon Maher is an Honorary President) has fostered the development of academic critique, in France and Ireland. They also afford academics multiple opportunities to share experiences in ways that are considerate of other readers. In this context, many conversations have been initiated and sustained – one of which is still ongoing between an Irishman captivated by McGahern's French subtext and a Frenchwoman from Brittany who recognizes something intimately familiar in McGahern's Irish landscapes. Seamus Heaney's remarks in *The Government of the Tongue* seem particularly relevant here with regards to all 'imaginative arts':

---

nouvelle de la littérature se prend, à l'inverse, là où l'esprit se désorganise, où son monde craque, où la pensée éclate en atomes.'
32   McGahern, 'The Solitary Reader', 90.

> Poetry is more of a threshold than a path, one constantly approached and constantly departed from, at which reader and writer undergo in their different ways the experience of being at the same time summoned and released.[33]

Rather than an acknowledgement of the previously known, one can say that that there is something unexpected and joyful in being re-acquainted with texts and in agreeing to this inflexion of ourselves.

---

33   Seamus Heaney, *The Government of the Tongue: The 1986 T. S. Eliot Memorial Lectures and Other Critical Writings* (London: Faber, 1988), 108.

DEREK HAND

5 Elizabeth Bowen's 'The Good Earl': Escaping the Past

Elizabeth Bowen's short story 'The Good Earl' is something of a curio within her published oeuvre. Appearing in 1946 in *Diversion*,[1] it was not included in *The Collected Stories of Elizabeth Bowen*,[2] and it is not too difficult to understand the reason for its exclusion. In her writing Bowen hardly ever uses the first-person narrator, preferring the control and distance of the objective third person. In one collected story, 'Oh Madam', for example, she does make use of the first person which is, up to a point, successful.[3] The story of 'The Good Earl' is told from the point of view of a tenant on an Irish estate, not unlike the device employed by Maria Edgeworth in *Castle Rackrent* (1801). However, Edgeworth's Thady Quirk is a much more complete and nuanced creation than Bowen's unnamed narrator. Moreover, Edgeworth possesses the ability to capture Thady's Hiberno-English lilt, whereas Bowen's effort is simply embarrassing in comparison. Despite these obvious failings, however, 'The Good Earl' captures a moment in Elizabeth Bowen's developing engagement with Ireland in her fiction, and particularly her deployment of the Anglo-Irish

---

1   See Elizabeth Bowen, *The Bazaar and Other Stories* (Edinburgh: Edinburgh University Press, 2008). '"The Good Earl" appeared in *Diversion*, a book edited by Hester W. Chapman and Princess Romanovsky-Pavlovsky and published by Collins in 1946 (pages 133–146). Proceeds from the book were meant to benefit the Yugoslav Relief Society.'
2   Elizabeth Bowen, *The Collected Stories of Elizabeth Bowen*, with an introduction by Angus Wilson (London: Jonathan Cape, 1980).
3   See Patricia Craig, *Elizabeth Bowen* (Harmondsworth: Penguin Books, 1986), 115. Craig argues that Bowen is unable to handle colloquial speech except on very rare occasions.

Big House trope through which she interrogates her anxious link to a post-independence Ireland.

The story told is set back in time, the late nineteenth century, with reference made to Queen Victoria,[4] though the narrator is telling his listener about the past from the vantage point of the present. The tale concerns the Good Earl and his efforts to bring prosperity to his community by constructing a Hotel on the shores of a Lough.

On one level, the reader is presented with a cautionary tale – a fairy tale[5] – concerning the difficulty of making the transition from the past, through the present and on into the future. In an effort to right the wrongs of his forebears, the Good Earl 'became famous for being an improving landlord':

> [He] restored the Castle, which had been destroyed with neglect and riotous living in the preceding times; he renewed the roof and the lead piping and sealed up the cracks asunder in front and back; he stripped down the sullied brocades from the saloons and commanded copies from France and Italy; he brought a scholar from Dublin to list the books, and renewed the heads of the garden statues [....] He dispelled the dead from the nether part of the kitchen floor; and from the day the kitchen was repavemented no voice but that of the living was heard there.[6]

The Good Earl, in a very real way, looks toward the future: the past is overcome in the form of erasing the marks of 'preceding times' from the house itself and in the symbolic removal of the remains of his interred ancestors from beneath the kitchen floor. The emphasis is firmly placed on change, transformation and renewal – on the here and now of the 'living' world rather than on the 'dead' from the past. The scheme for the Hotel is part of this general overhaul, refocusing his and the community's attention on the future: 'The Earl conceived that the Hotel was to do great good to us country people by bringing foreign money into the land.'[7] The entire project puts the Good Earl's finances at serious risk.

---

4 Bowen, *The Bazaar and Other Stories*, 120.
5 Bowen, *The Bazaar and Other Stories*, 18.
6 Bowen, *The Bazaar and Other Stories*, 121.
7 Bowen, *The Bazaar and Other Stories*, 123.

However, his insistence that a steamboat is required for guests to get to the Hotel and for pleasure cruises completes the 'folly'. Phyllis Lassner sees this aspect of the story undermining creation myths that conveniently ignore the violence upon which 'civilization' is built.[8] The steamer as a hearse, Lassner argues, serves 'as a sign of the destructive solipsism of the Anglo-Irish Ascendancy'.[9] She believes that the Good Earl's plan is bought at the price of ignoring everybody, and everything, else – those who live on his estate and his family. Thus, the steamer is transformed into a hearse at the end of the story, bringing the body of the Good Earl home, having died abroad in his efforts to raise money for his scheme.

Reading the story as a form of fairy tale gestures toward a realm of simplicity and innocence, and certainly, the binary structure that underpins the narrative: past, present, improving landlord versus wastrels, would suggest that. At the level of fairy tale, then, the intended message is clear: single-minded ambition and wilful blindness to the needs of others is a dead-end. Ignoring people while focusing only on the 'bricks and mortar' of buildings is problematic.

As a fairy tale, too, the realities / facts of history do not need to be attended to, and in an Irish context, the nuances of history are ignored in order that broad gestures can be made. However, perhaps the story is best understood in the context of Bowen's writing of this period, particularly her history of her homeplace *Bowen's Court* (1942)[10] and an essay, 'The Bend Back' published in 1950. Doing so brings a certain complication to the narrative, expressing a certain anxiety for Bowen and her changing links to Ireland.

---

8   Phyllis Lassner, *Elizabeth Bowen: A Study of the Short Fiction*, Twayne's Studies in Short Fiction (Woodbridge, CT: Twayne Publishers, 1991), 17. Bowen herself does *not* ignore such violence and readily admits in *Bowen's Court* that the Big House and the land upon which it was built was gained and constructed because of an 'inherent wrong'.
9   Lassner, *Elizabeth Bowen: A Study of the Short Fiction*, 16.
10 Elizabeth Bowen, *Bowen's Court* with a new introduction by Thomas McCarthy (Cork: The Collins Press, 1998).

'The Bend Back'[11] deals with what Bowen feels is the phenomenon of 'Nostalgia' in the literary productions of her contemporary moment. She argues that nostalgia is not solely confined to art but it is a widespread hankering after, what she calls, 'the better days'.[12] The result, she declares, is that writers are 'retreating' from the present moment. While the sentiments are definitely coloured by her experiences of the Second World War, and the violence and destruction that war wrought, Bowen's Irish background and experience also inform her thought and argument. For example, she pinpoints the moment when these 'better days' ended in an Anglo-Irish context: the beginning of the First World War. She registers this turning point in her family history, *Bowen's Court*:

> It was an afternoon when the simplest person begins to anticipate memory – this Mitchelstown garden party, it was agreed, would remain in every one's memory as historic. It was, also, a more final scene than we knew. Ten years hence, it was to seem like a dream – and the Castle itself would be a few bleached stumps on the plateau.[13]

The old Anglo-Irish world was passing away and a New World coming into being. Bowen makes a clear distinction between that Old World and the present moment. In the pre-war world, she reminds us that:

> As a child of the period may remember – it was considered glory to be alive. 'The better days', if one needed them, were the future.[14]

At that time, the future was the focus: possibilities were, perhaps, infinite and the predicament of moving from the past through the present and on into the future was not such a problem because the world was an ordered and solid place:

> The past is only just over the frontier of living memory; it is the epoch of our immediate forebears. It is the youth of our parents, the prime of our grand-parents and great-grand-parents, which most subtly seem to have stolen our hearts away. A

---

11   Bowen, 'The Bend Back', in *The Mulberry Tree*, by Elizabeth Bowen (London: Vintage, 1979), 54–60.
12   Bowen, *The Mulberry Tree*, 54.
13   Bowen, *Bowen's Court*, 436.
14   Bowen, *The Mulberry Tree*, 54.

> particular spell is exercised by the nineteenth century; while we may think ourselves lucky in being clear of the taboos and restrictions of Victorianism, we hanker after its solidness, its faith, its energetic self-confidence, its domestic glow [....] The day-before yesterday represents at once the last and the best of the old order.[15]

Bowen emphasizes the connection with the past in terms of family, highlighting how 'continuity' between the past, the present and the future is, or can be, maintained. However, what is of significance is the overwhelming sense that what the past possessed and the present lacks is 'order' and, perhaps, 'purpose'. The present, then, is not orientated toward the future, is unable to deal with the future, instead the 'past' has now become the site of contemplation and, indeed, contention. This is the dilemma that Bowen perceives as pervasive in the modern world: such a focus on the past leads to a form of paralysis in the present.

Of note, too, is how memory itself, as an activity, is brought to the fore: it is memory which gives access to this nostalgic past and is a primal element in creating this past. After proclaiming the type of order, faith and solidity that the past offers those in the present, Bowen goes on to say:

> So it seems [...] (*sic*) We must not shy at the fact that we cull the past from fiction rather than history, and that art, out of the very necessity to compose a picture, cannot but eliminate, edit – and so, falsify.[16]

In other words, Bowen recognizes that what her characters celebrate in the past is a myth and not a reality. She realizes, too, that myths of history, rather than 'raw history' itself, cover over and sanitize the past, perhaps offering the consolation of 'continuity' where in fact there is none:

> As things are, the past is veiled from us by illusion – our own illusion. It is that which we seek. It is not the past but the idea of the past which draws us.[17]

No matter whether that as an illusion or indeed a delusion, the past exercises a powerful attraction on the collective contemporary imagination

---

15 Bowen, *The Mulberry Tree*, 57.
16 Bowen, *The Mulberry Tree*, 57.
17 Bowen, *The Mulberry Tree*, 58.

as Bowen sees it. At the close of her essay, she believes that there needs to be a readjustment of focus away from this 'past' toward the future in order that art, culture, and society can continue to 'forge something' that need to be taken in order to overcome the impasse she now feels the modern world faces.[18]

In light of 'The Bend Back', our understanding of 'The Good Earl' is complicated. The narrator, who speaks from the present, offers a nostalgic view of the past and the Good Earl as a much loved 'benefactor' among the locals.[19] The Earl himself is like the pre-World War I Anglo-Irish, as described in Bowen's essay when the hoped-for 'better days' were the future. Interestingly, then, the story contains a double relationship between the past and the future that might seem to work against each other. It is clear, as well, that Bowen's calling attention to the fictive and constructive nature of memory opens up the possibility of rereading the narrator's story for further revelations beyond the simple celebration of the Good Earl's actions.

As stated earlier, the structure of the story revolves around simple opposites: The Good Earl stands in contrast to his father, the Bad Earl, progress, science, and improvement, the future stands in opposition to the past of 'wicked doings' and 'injustices'.[20] Such a binary structure is to be discovered everywhere. The Good Earl travels the world with the implication it is there, in far-flung locations, that he learns of the future and its ways, which he can bring back to the local homeplace:

> He advocated to us many improved methods of doing all things, in the manner in which he had witnessed them done abroad; and he would dispute with the most stubborn farmer.[21]

Despite the narrator's positivity about the Good Earl, he goes on to say: 'We listened to him in patience, while we preferred it better to keep to our fathers' ways.' Thus, the irony is that the Earl's attempt to bring the

---

18   Bowen, *The Mulberry Tree*, 59.
19   Bowen, *The Bazaar and Other Stories*, 120.
20   Bowen, *The Bazaar and Other Stories*, 120–121.
21   Bowen, *The Bazaar and Other Stories*, 121.

'world' to his home is, in fact, an outward sign of Anglo-Irish blindness and inability to connect productively with the surrounding countryside.

There is a moment in the story when this solipsism noted by Lassner is complicated and deepened:

> The two looked below them upon the bends of the Lough and upon the Castle, and the demesne and upon the Protestant church with the graveyard and the Bible house, and upon the island having the ancient chapel, and upon the jetty expectant of the Steamer. Why, it is like a picture, says Lady Mary, when you can see the whole![22]

The fictive nature of the Big House is subtly referred to here: the House and the lands are the imposition of an imagination that has little to do with reality. Thus, being likened to a 'picture', Anglo-Irish life is seen to be radically cut off from lives going on outside this 'frame'.

Though there is a shift of emphasis away from the past in that the Good Earl resolutely sets his gaze on the future, there still remains an obsession with the bricks and mortar of buildings – in this instance, the projected Hotel. One result of this obsession is that real people are ignored, and in this story, it is the Good Earl's daughter, Lady Mary, whose feelings are not considered.

Due to the Good Earl's plans, an assistant to the agent of the estate is required and a Mr Harris is 'procured from Belfast city'.[23] He and Lady Mary fall in love, but as the Earl's plans deepen and his need for more money grows, Mr Harris, along with many other things, is sacrificed. Lady Mary's beseeching does no good; her father 'had no ear for her, being deep in plans'.[24] Mr Harris leaves for America, ignoring Lady Mary's wish to go with him, believing 'in his humbleness' that she is 'too lofty' for him.[25] The real tragedy of this story, then, is not to be found in the Earl's demise, as he vainly tries to make his dream a reality, but rather in the fate of Lady Mary.

Certainly, gender is an issue and her position is one of uncertainty. Opposites, we know, underpin the story told and how it operates. These

---

22   Bowen, *The Bazaar and Other Stories*, 129.
23   Bowen, *The Bazaar and Other Stories*, 124.
24   Bowen, *The Bazaar and Other Stories*, 131.
25   Bowen, *The Bazaar and Other Stories*, 131.

are mostly obvious and clear cut: the dead who are removed from beneath the kitchen in order that a new life might be imagined, the image of the modernity in the telescope versus the traditional world of folklore represented by the old 'mountainy woman'.[26] There are, though, other less obvious binaries at play within the narrative. For instance, Lady Mary is introduced in this way: '[T]he Lady Mary was the Earl and Her Ladyship's one child; God sent them no other, and no son.'[27]

More concerning than the easy male-female divide is the acknowledgement of an interaction between presence and absence and the powerful hold that absences can generate. Indeed, it might be argued that the simple order that opposites suggest, and the form of the fairy tale might aspire to, is undone or certainly challenged in this reading. What is clear is that what is not said may be as significant as what is. It is said that in the early drafts of this present story, quotation marks were used to indicate dialogue. The argument that their removal in the finished story 'enhances the mythic dimension of the fairy tale' might be so,[28] but it also has the effect of empowering the narrator who tells the entire story. In other words, we hear no other voice but his, the words of the characters are reported to us, like echoes on the wind. Their absence also suggests a kind of silence or act of silencing, and certainly, the predominance of moments of pictorial stillness within the story accentuates that pervasive silence.

More significant than the absence of speech, perhaps, is the presence of vision. Again and again, the reader is presented with characters 'looking' at the world around them. Earlier, it was remarked how notable is that moment when Lady Mary 'can see the whole' of the Big House demesne. Its entirety, encompassing the graveyard, the lough, the jetty, the castle, and the church, is a picture that contains everything: the past, the present and the future. They can see the 'whole' because the forest has been cleared. An act of violence on the landscape allows for a new picture of that world. It also, as we know, expresses its apartness from the landscape in which it

---

26 Bowen, *The Bazaar and Other Stories*, 132.
27 Bowen, *The Bazaar and Other Stories*, 122.
28 Bowen, *The Bazaar and Other Stories*, 357.

is situated. It is interesting that the word Protestant is used here, as it is elsewhere, while the word Catholic is absent.

The deployment of the 'Hotel' as the medium that will bring continuity and access to the future is of interest. Bowen's writing, so often concerned with the idea of home and anxiety about it, makes use of the hotel as an image of contrast, a place of transience, of people coming and going. Her novel *The Hotel* brilliantly exploits this. But her Anglo-Irish Big House, at times, also embraces something of the hotel in that idea of the transitory. *The Last September*, for instance, revolves around arrivals and departures. Interestingly too, the opening passages of her family history *Bowen's Court*, can be read as a brilliant positioning of the solidity of the house in the very centre of a natural landscape. The reader is presented with a unique Bowen's Court:

> [it] is not built on a river; it has no castle and belongs to no neighbourhood, being much lonelier in its situation than any other big house in the country round.[29]

In a sense, the reader is being offered a tour of the house – room to room, with areas of interest being pointed out and deliberated upon. It is as if she has foreknowledge of what would happen to many Big Houses that would eventually open their grounds and doors to tourists as hotels. She focuses only on the part of the house used for living and leisure, 'the working part of the house – the back stairs, pantry, bootroom, stairs down to the basement and north wing'[30] are passed over. The difference between these 'two' houses is reinforced when it is noticed that Bowen uses capitals when talking of the 'Library', the 'Dining Room' and the 'Hall', whereas the below stairs position is underlined with this obvious lack of capital letters. Again, the template for how a Hotel might operate is there, within the physical architecture of the Big House itself and its 'upstairs-downstairs' social division.

This is further developed in her history of the famous Dublin hotel, *The Shelbourne*, published in 1951.[31] As Robert Tracy notes, the unwieldy

---

29 Bowen, *Bowen's Court*, 20.
30 Bowen, *Bowen's Court*, 24.
31 Elizabeth Bowen, *The Shelbourne Hotel* (New York: Alfred A. Knopf, 1951).

subtitle of this history, 'A Centre in Dublin Life for more than a Century', sets it firmly in the category of Bowen's work which attempts to give Anglo-Irish institutions significance in modern Ireland.[32] Robert Tracy sees the Shelbourne Hotel in Bowen's history of it 'as a kind of ultimate and collective Big House'. As has been already said, the Hotel becomes another form of the Big House in that it will take on the role of the Big House in the future. The Good Earl in the story stresses that it will be the 'gentry' who will visit and patronize the place and spread their money around. It is a place and an image that is not intended to be for everyone.

In *The Last September*, reference is made to the economic ills of Ireland. Out walking the demesne of Danielstown, Lois and guests Marda and Hugo, who are visiting, come across a ruined mill. Hugo declares: 'another [...] of our national grievances. English law strangled the – '.[33] He is not allowed to finish his assessment of the economic relations between Britain and Ireland. Still, it indicates, as with the Good Earl's ambitions, a business venture that has, for whatever reason, failed. Of particular interest, though, is that image of the ruined mill. In *Bowen's Court*, it is said that Ireland is a 'country of ruins': 'Lordly or humble, military or domestic [...] ruins feature the landscape.'[34] All of these 'ruins stand for error or failure – but in Ireland we take these as part of life'.[35] The Big House's 'other' then is the ruin: the antithesis to the endurance and continuity the Big House aspires to. And yet, the conclusion of 'The Good Earl' undermines that notion of permanence.

At the end of the story, as the body of the Good Earl is brought up the channel on his prized steamer, we are presented with another picture of Anglo-Irish isolation:

> And it was the Castle now drew our eyes – for the shutters opened upon one terrace window, from which the Lady Mary stepped out alone. The height of the Castle and

---

32   Robert Tracy, 'Elizabeth Bowen: Rebuilding the Big House', in *The Unappeasable Host* (Dublin: University College Dublin Press, 1998), 232.
33   Elizabeth Bowen, *The Last September* (Harmondsworth: Penguin Books, [1929] 1987), 123.
34   Bowen, *Bowen's Court*, 15.
35   Bowen, *Bowen's Court*, 17.

the wide of the water made the Lady Mary appear to us very small. She advances to the balustrade of the terrace, to come as near the Steamer as she could come. She puts up her hand to shade her eyes from the almighty whiteness striking out from the its flank. We could not see her face to see did it change. She attentively, slowly turns her head, watching the Steamer proceed past her; she considers its wake and looks over the balustrade. Far below in the chopping and the heave of the wake's end the Castle's watery image is broken up.

There were few to perceive the Lady Mary turn around and go back and shut the window behind her, for the hundreds of us were now trampling down from the woods and speeding by on the tracks, and the shores and the stony places. We were gathered at the jetty to meet the Earl.[36]

There is a discernible movement in focus from the Good Earl toward Lady Mary and then back to the Good Earl at the close, emphasizing Lady Mary's isolation and detachment from the world about her. The tragedy, then, is hers alone in being alone and isolated. She is left to inherit the Castle, but little else is left to her in terms of a future. The man she loves has departed, never to return – and, if he did, he feels himself socially inferior to her. The awful consequence of this is not hard to ascertain. Like many of Bowen's characters, Lady Mary is a figure of impotence and sterility.

It has been argued that this story is a companion piece to an earlier story of Bowen's 'Her Table Spread'. Written in 1930 this story reflects Bowen's own concerns after inheriting Bowen's Court on the death of her father. In a sense, what Bowen portrays is a nightmarish – if somewhat comic – vision of herself if she had not been married when coming into her inheritance. Valeria Cuffe illustrates a kind of 'madness' that lack of opportunity induces in the Anglo-Irish post-1922. She has a hope that some men from the English Destroyer in the estuary will come up the hill to her castle and visit. It is a delusion and she, in turn, appears by the end of the story to have a very tenuous grip on reality. Owing to the time that this story is set, some readers might be forgiven in their belief that the Destroyer is a 'ghost ship' as this is post-independent Ireland. However, as is explained in the story itself: 'By a term of the Treaty, English ships

---

36   Bowen, *The Bazaar and Other Stories*, 133–134.

were permitted to anchor in these waters.'[37] Nonetheless, their presence is something of an anachronism, as is Valeria's interest in the ship and the men on board the ship. So, for all intents and purposes, the Destroyer *does* haunt the scene as described in this story, in that it represents the past and the burden of the past. It has been argued too that Valeria herself becomes something of a ghost figure haunting the castle as she rushes about on a hilltop waving her lantern in a demented fashion.[38] Not unlike Lady Mary, Valeria – and the Anglo-Irish that she symbolizes – is immature, and not fully grown: she, and they, are stunted in their growth. Though this story is, as Phyllis Lassner calls it, a 'romantic comedy',[39] there is still something rather disturbing in presenting a picture of such sterility and entrapment.

In both stories, the Big House's demise is guaranteed, as ultimately there will be no one in the future to hand it on to. The Good Earl failed to understand that survival cannot be found only through bricks and mortar. Perhaps this is an echo of the original Anglo-Irish desire to make roots through building homes. If this reading is accepted, then what ultimately undermines the Anglo-Irish in the New Ireland is their adherence to the founding myth. The image of the reflected castle being broken up in the water suggests as much.

'The Good Earl', as indicated, is perhaps rightly left out of Elizabeth Bowen's collected stories as its execution lacks the poise of her other writing, and most certainly, the deployment of the Irish narrator simply does not work. And yet, within the context of her writing of this period between the 1930s and 1950s, it does have its place. Like her other works of this moment, the autobiographical essays, the historical writing such as *The Shelbourne* and *Bowen's Court*, short stories and novels, it is obvious how it reflects her concerns with the position and fate of the Anglo-Irish Big House and its continuance in contemporary Ireland. She recognizes it needs to acquire a new role for it to survive both as an idea and as a physical reality. Bowen's 'rebuilding' of the Big House in her writing of this period is not simply an act of imaginative consolation for the very real loss of prestige and power

---

37 Bowen, *The Collected Stories*, 419.
38 Lassner, *Elizabeth Bowen: A Study of the Short Fiction*, 15–16.
39 Lassner, *Elizabeth Bowen: A Study of the Short Fiction*, 15.

experienced by the Anglo-Irish from the 1920s onwards; though, of course, there *is* an element of this in her writing. Accordingly, for all of her misgiving about the image of the Big House, and all that it represented, it is obvious that for her, it is still something to be actively engaged with, rather than passively sentimentalized. Though the shimmering of the water breaks up the reflected image of the castle at the close of 'The Good Earl', it does open up the possibility of the image eventually reassembling itself and being whole again. Her acts of writing then are, at some level, acts of survival.

PIERRE JOANNON

6 Reflections on the Relationship between Ireland and France

Friendly relations between countries are based on mutual understanding, common interest and / or shared experience. That we were both true Celts and faithful Catholics was once said to be the bedrock of the empathy between the French and the Irish. Dr Eamon Maher who has been ploughing the furrow of Franco-Irish relations for decades would probably agree that race and religion are not the lens through which one would nowadays attempt to examine our bilateral relationship, past or present.

Of much more weight in the building of this relationship is our respective involvement in the great historical struggle for the domination of Europe between Reformed England and Catholic France and later between the British Empire and revolutionary Napoleonic France. These wars connected France and Ireland more closely than anything previously on record.

However, the historical empathy between France and Ireland in the context of the ongoing Anglo-French rivalry goes beyond a purely tactical alliance based on the simplistic idea that 'the enemy of my enemy is my friend'. It goes far deeper than that, as the perception of France, either negative or positive, became an integral part of the intellectual construction of British and Irish national identities.

It was brilliantly established by historian Linda Colley in her 1992 compelling study entitled *Britons: Forging the Nation 1707–1837*: 'We can plausibly regard Great Britain', she wrote:

> as an invented nation superimposed, if only for a while, onto much older alignments and loyalties. It was an invention forged above all by war. Time and time again, war with France brought Britons, whether they hailed from Wales or Scotland or England into confrontation with an obviously hostile Other and encouraged them to define

themselves collectively against it. They defined themselves as Protestants struggling for survival against the world's foremost Catholic power. They defined themselves against the French as they imagined them to be, superstitious, militarist, decadent and unfree [...] Imagining the French as their vile opposite, as Hyde to their Jekyll, became a way for Britons – particularly the poorer and less privileged – to contrive for themselves a converse and flattering identity. The French wallowed in superstition: therefore, the British, by contrast, must enjoy true religion. The French were oppressed by a bloated army and by absolute monarchy: consequently, the British were manifestly free. The French tramped through life in wooden shoes, whereas the British – as Adam Smith pointed out – were shod in supple leather and, therefore, clearly more prosperous.[1]

It is worth noting that Professor Colley did not include the Irish in the list of people coming together under the name of Britons, for which francophobia was such a significant element in terms of national definition. This is because for many Irish, but not all it is fair to say, the French were more akin to the Self than the Other. No one has expressed it better than William Lecky, the famous nineteenth-century historian who, even though he was a staunch unionist, wrote at the outbreak of the Franco-Prussian war of 1870: 'In Ireland, we are passionately French, partly because we think ourselves rather like the French, partly because of the Irish Brigade which served under France, and partly because the English take the other side.'[2]

This affinity between Ireland and France led to many contacts and exchanges, so much so that for the Irish to ponder on France and the French was often to undertake a voyage of self-discovery. In *Doomsland*, a novel described in 1923 by the Evening Standard as 'the most complete emotional survey of the Ireland of our time', Shane Leslie portrays a man who discovers his Irish roots in the capital of France of all places:

> In these days, he wandered about Paris in the track of Irish exiles. Paris cemeteries were full of Irish graves, her archives were choked with Irish plots and documents. The Irish swarmed in French history. In old colleges and behind crumbling walls priests,

---

1 Linda Colley, *Britons: Forging the Nation 1707–1837* (New Haven: Yale University Press, 1992), 5 and 368.
2 *A memoir of the Rt Hon. W. E. H. Lecky*, by his wife, London, 1909, quoted in Alfred Duquet, *Ireland and France* (Dublin: Maunsel and Co., 1916), xxx.

soldiers, and secret agents had conspired. Through eighteenth century Paris passed the Wild Geese of the Irish Brigade. In Notre Dame knelt the victors of Fontenoy. From the Irish College priests passed to and fro between the two countries. It was an Irish abbé who remembered the right words to cry to Louis XVI at his execution, and an Irish physician accompanied Napoleon to St Helena. Here Wolfe Tone met the First Consul. Here Humbert and Hoche received orders for their invasion of Ireland. And the gorgeous sunset behind the mighty Arc de Triomphe goldenised the ashes of the anonymous myriads of Irish dead.[3]

Having fixed the boundaries of Irish francophilia and British francophobia within the parameters of identity building in both islands of the archipelago, let us consider the social, cultural and diplomatic dimension of the Franco-Irish connection. Throughout history, we can see it at work in religious matters, in politics and notably on the birth of Irish republicanism via the United Irishmen, in literature, and finally in our cooperation in the building of Europe during the last fifty years.

On the survival of the Catholic faith in Ireland, the influence of France cannot be underestimated. At the time of the Penal Laws, Irish would-be clerics, unable to gain religious education in Ireland, travelled to France to pursue their studies in French Catholic institutions and in a chain of Irish colleges protected and endowed by French kings and gentry. Irish seminaries were to be found in Paris, Toulouse, Bordeaux and Nantes as well as in Douai, Lille and Bourges. Founded in 1769, the Irish College which still stands in the rue des Irlandais, behind the Panthéon, in Paris, was one of the most important, if not the most important, sources of Irish ordinations in Europe. It sent no less than fifty bishops to the Irish Catholic Church. When the revolution broke out, there were 478 Irish ecclesiastical students on the continent of whom 348, nearly three-quarters, were receiving their education in France.

According to Lecky, no subsequent generation of Irish priests have left so good a reputation as this class of frenchified clerics:

> They grew up, he wrote, at a time when Catholicism throughout Europe was unusually temperate, and they brought with them a foreign culture and a foreign grace, which did much to embellish Irish life. Their earlier prejudices were corrected and

[3] Shane Leslie, *Doomsland* (London: Chatto and Windus, 1923), 246.

mitigated by foreign travel. They had sometimes mixed with a society far more cultivated than an Irish protestant country clergyman was likely to meet, and they came to their ministry at a mature age, and with a real and varied knowledge of the world. If they produced little or nothing of lasting value in theology or literature, they had at least the manners and feelings of cultivated gentlemen [...] and they were saved by their position from the chief vices and temptations of their class upon the continent. The leaders of a poor and unendowed church, which was appealing to the principles of religious liberty in order to obtain political enfranchisement, were not likely to profess the maxims of persecutors or to live the lives of epicureans.[4]

In order to undermine the French influence in religious affairs while, at the same time, exploiting the situation created by the closing of the Irish colleges and seminaries in France, the British government took the decision, in the Maynooth College Act, 1795, to establish and endow a college 'for the better education of persons professing the Popish or Roman Catholic religion'. Even though the new seminary in Maynooth counted among its professors several French refugees, the training at home of the Irish priesthood from 1795 onwards was the death knell of French influence on Irish church affairs. The persistent and often violent struggle between Church and State in nineteenth-century France alienated Catholic Ireland for good and made it impossible to renew the confessional tie ever since. Having for ever lost its influence over religion, France was quick to regain it in the field of politics and, to be more precise, in the realm of political philosophy.

The soft breeze of liberty coming from America turned into a tornado when the French Revolution erupted suddenly in 1789. That this seismic upheaval was to have immense repercussions in Ireland is hardly surprising. A substantial number of Irish people had always looked in the direction of France for inspiration, support or personal advancement. Before turning to the New World, it was in the Kingdom of France that the great bulk of Irish migrants settled throughout the seventeenth and eighteenth centuries. Furthermore, many of the causes which produced the French Revolution existed in Ireland: the landed interest separated from the commercial, the

---

4   W. E. H. Lecky, *History of Ireland in the Eighteenth Century* (London: Longman's Green and Co., 1913), vol III, 354–355.

gentry from the peasantry, the civil and ecclesiastical establishments from the people.

Ireland's response to the first episodes of the French Revolution was enthusiastic, bewildered and misconceived. The Anglo-Irish members of Grattan's Parliament rejoiced in the fact that the French had, at long last, acquired the freedom that the English had been enjoying since the Glorious Revolution of 1688, and the Irish since the achievement of the so-called parliamentary independence of 1782. For the radical enlightened dissenters of Ulster, mostly Presbyterians, the French Revolution marked the triumph of their egalitarian aspirations not only against the authoritarianism of Church and State and the social privileges of the aristocratic landed gentry but also against what they saw as the tyranny and obscurantism of the Catholic Church. For the Catholic weavers, labourers and tenant farmers who had taken the oath of the Defender secret societies, the French Revolution was reinstating France as the ally and avenger of the Catholics. Seeking French help right from the beginning, their objectives were simple: 'to knock the Protestants on the head and take their place'.[5]

The aristocratic worshippers of the French Revolution soon realized that Danton and Robespierre were not John Locke or William Molyneux in French garb; they quickly fell in line behind the great Edmund Burke, undoubtedly the most brilliant, articulate, and forceful opponent of the new order taking root on the continent.

As a result, the development of Irish republicanism produced an explosive blend of the cosmopolitan inclusive egalitarianism of the United Irishmen with the sectarian exclusive nationalism of the Defenders. It was the Right of Man against the Right of the People or, in other words, 'Liberté, Égalité, Fraternité' versus 'Ourselves Alone'. This dialectical tension between two opposite trends has been a characteristic of Irish republicanism down to the present day. 'On the one hand', says Richard Kearney, 'republicanism has promoted an enlightened universalism of world citizens. On the other,

---

5   Marianne Elliott, *Partners in Revolution: The United Irishman and France* (New Haven: Yale University Press, 1982), 42.

it has permitted a separatist nationalism which subordinates the universal rights of the citizen to the right of the nation-state.'[6]

As an antidote to such a drift, one should revisit Wolfe Tone's vision of a non-sectarian, democratic, inclusive Ireland. He stated his motives which are still as valid today as they were then: 'To unite the whole people of Ireland, to abolish the memory of all past dissensions, and to substitute the common name of Irishman in place of the denominations of Protestant, Catholic and Dissenter.'[7]

Following in his footsteps, the Young Irelanders made their pilgrimage to revolutionary Paris in the spring of 1848 from whence they apparently returned with the famous green, white and orange Irish flag modelled on the French tricolour.[8] It was displayed on 15 April 1848 in the Music Hall of Abbey Street in Dublin. John Mitchel's paper, *The United Irishman*, reported Thomas Francis Meagher's speech:

> From Paris, the gay and gallant city of the tricolour and the barricade, this flag has been proudly borne. I present it to my native land, and I trust that the old country will not refuse this symbol of a new life from one of her youngest children. I need not explain its meaning. The quick and passionate intellect of the generation now springing into arms will catch it at a glance. The White in the centre signifies a lasting truce between the 'Orange' and the 'Green', and I trust that beneath its folds the hands of the Irish Protestant and the Irish Catholic may be clasped in generous and heroic brotherhood.[9]

---

6   Richard Kearney, 'The Irish Heritage of the French Revolution: The Rights of the People and the Rights of Man', in *Ireland and France. A Bountiful Friendship*, edited by Barbara Hayley and Christopher Murray (Gerrards Cross: Colin Smythe, 1992), 40–41.
7   *Memoirs of Theobald Wolfe Tone Written by Himself*, edited by his son William Theobald Wolfe Tone (London: Henry Colburn, 1827), vol. 1, 64.
8   Pierre Joannon, 'Le drapeau tricolore irlandais et la France en 1848', in *Drapeaux et Pavillons*, Bulletin de la Société Française de Vexillologie, n°145, 3ème Trimestre 2020, 6–9.
9   Michael Cavanagh, *Memoirs of Gen. Thomas Francis Meagher* (Worcester, MA: The Messenger Press, 1892), 163–164.

Some twenty-two years later, France was still present in the hearts and minds of the Irish people, if we are to believe G. K. Chesterton who wrote in his *Irish Impressions*:

> Let's always keep in mind a historical fact I have mentioned already: the reality of the old Franco-Irish entente. It lingers alive in Ireland, and especially the most Irish parts of Ireland. In the fiercely Fenian city of Cork, walking round the Young Ireland monument that seems to give revolt the majesty of an institution, a man told me that German bands had been hooted and pelted in those streets out of an indignant memory of 1870. And an eminent scholar in the same town, referring to the events of the same 'terrible year', said to me: 'In 1870 Ireland sympathised with France and England with Germany, and, as usual, Ireland was right'.[10]

It should also be noted that, in the first Dáil, the Declaration of Independence was not only read in Irish and English but also, significantly, in French, as French was considered by many of the legislators to be the idiom of liberty. Several leaders of the Irish Free State believed that closer relations with France might have been one of the best ways to implement the Collins' policy of exercising freedom to achieve freedom for Ireland. In his splendid biography *Joseph Walshe and Irish Foreign Policy 1922–1946*, Aengus Nolan has revealed that 'at this time, some in Ireland hoped that Irish Foreign policy would turn from the Commonwealth and move more towards France. One suggestion was that a Franco-Irish *entente* be established by taking advantage of the growing disparity and disagreement between Britain and France at that time.'[11] However, if the old Franco-Irish entente was to be resuscitated, it was not in the realm of politics, but in the richer fields of literature.

The journey to Paris in search of models or inspiration was for many Irish writers a deliberate move to emancipate themselves from Albion while at the same time redefining their identity. Brian Fallon has put this cultural fascination in its proper historical context when he wrote:

---

10   G. K. Chesterton, *Irish Impressions* (London : Collins, 1920), 132–133; *Impressions Irlandaises*, Préface de Pierre Joannon (Versailles : Via Romana, 2016), 132.
11   Aengus Nolan, *Joseph Walsh, Irish Foreign Policy 1922–1946* (Cork: Mercier Press, 2008), 25–26 and 345 note 37.

It was not only admiration for French culture, French political structures and French thought which inclined the Irish intelligentsia towards Francophilia. France offered, in effect, an alternative to English domination or at least a corrective to it. France was republican while Great Britain was monarchist, and the fact that both had colonial empires was often conveniently overlooked in this Irish exaltation of France as the home of liberty, equality and fraternity. France was also seen as the land of artistic modernism and innovation, while English culture – as exemplified by a writer such as Galsworthy – was often considered stodgy, inward-looking and insular.[12]

Sydney Owenson, alias Lady Morgan, who was to Ireland what Madame de Staël was to France, visited Paris on several occasions after the fall of Napoleon. In June 1817 she published a two-volume vivid description of French society entitled *France*. The book was extremely successful but the Gallic influence over its author was considered very distasteful by the British Tory press in so far as she was making comparisons with her own country that were highly critical of the situation in Ireland. She was accused of irreligion, Jacobinism, indecency, vanity, and ignorance which demonstrate to which extent she had become more French than the French themselves. These perceived vices were then and still are very often used as terms of abuse that we, French, receive by the bucketful from the English gutter press. 'Like a cook with a heavy hand on the garlic', she was also criticized for using too many French expressions in her writing and in her conversation.[13]

George Moore, who came to live in Paris in 1873, wanted to be a painter. However, under the influence of Théophile Gautier and Baudelaire, he was to start the process by which he would instead become a man of letters. He met Mallarmé and Manet who painted his portrait, and Zola who impressed him greatly. Many years later, his friend John Eglinton would accurately write:

> His mind had taken its permanent shape in the French language; his standards were French standards; the liberators and instructors of his spirit were those who held

---

12   Brian Fallon, *An Age of Innocence: Irish Culture 1930–1960* (Dublin: Gill and Macmillan, 1998), 124.
13   Mary Campbell, *Lady Morgan: The Life and Times of Sidney Owenson* (London: Pandora, 1988), 134.

sway in Paris in the eighties. With a French subject he was serious and circumspect, but in most English authors everything seemed to him, just as to a Frenchman, a little odd and often a little ludicrous.[14]

Living the life of a typical French man of letters, Moore did not hesitate for a moment to claim that France was 'his own country', and French 'the language that should have been mine'.[15] On another occasion, he confessed: 'I am full of France.'[16]

Oscar Wilde also loved France dearly, so much so that he once described himself as 'Irlandais de race' but 'Français de sympathie'.[17] He spoke French fluently and was adamant that 'every artist should know French, and every gentleman'.[18] Like Moore he had rubbed shoulders with Mallarmé, Zola, Degas and Edmond de Goncourt. *The Picture of Dorian Gray* was clearly influenced by Joris Karl Huysmans, the author of *À Rebours*, masterpiece of the aesthetic and decadent movement. Wilde wrote his play *Salomé* directly in French and, when it was banned in London, he considered leaving England and becoming a French citizen.[19] The English, like Lady Bracknell, were not amused, and in order to poke fun at him, *Punch*, in its issue of 9 July 1892, published a caricature of Wilde in the uniform of a French trooper, which entitles him, in my opinion, to be called the last of the Wild Geese, with or without the final e.[20] France for him was the land of artistic and sexual freedom as opposed to the hypocrisy and philistinism of England. After his release from Reading jail, he crossed the channel never to return. He finally settled in Paris where on his death he was buried in the cemetery of the Père Lachaise. As one critic said aptly: 'France was the adoptive, encouraging and forgiving mother who welcomed him at the start of his literary career, embraced him during his years of success, and

---

14 John Eglinton, *Irish Literary Portraits* (London: Macmillan, 1935), 97.
15 George Moore, *Hail and Farewell* (Gerrards Cross: Colin Smythe, 1976), 257.
16 George-Paul Collet, *George Moore et la France* (Genève: Librairie Droz, 1957), 18.
17 Merlin Holland and Rupert Hart (eds), *The Complete Letters of Oscar Wilde* (London: Fourth Estate, 2000), 505.
18 Holland and Hart, *The Complete Letters of Oscar Wilde*, 1102.
19 Holland and Hart, *The Complete Letters of Oscar Wilde*, 531.
20 A reproduction of this caricature can be found in the *Album Oscar Wilde* (Paris: Gallimard, 1996), 151.

succoured him after his downfall.'[21] William Butler Yeats resided in Paris in the eighteen-nineties. He visited the downtrodden poet Paul Verlaine in his humble lodgings of the Rue Saint Jacques. In the autumn of 1896, whilst staying at the hotel Corneille, near the Odéon, he met John Millington Synge who was living on the attic floor of the hotel in the grip of a depression. Without guessing what a genius he would turn out to be, Yeats urged him to go to the Aran islands to 'find a life that had never been expressed in literature, instead of a life where all had been expressed'.[22] Yeats, himself, was greatly influenced by the French symbolist movement: he was indeed very fond of the poetry of Mallarmé and of the plays of Villiers de l'Isle Adam. In 1939, William Butler Yeats died at the Pension Idéal Séjour in Cap Martin on the French Riviera. According to Roy Foster, author of an outstanding biography of the poet, it was appropriate that he passed away on French soil as 'part of the pattern of his life is a linkage between Irish identity and an intellectual and aesthetic affinity with Europe, particularly France'.[23]

James Joyce, the other giant of Irish literature, owes Paris the recognition of his genius and the publication in English and in French of his magnum opus *Ulysses*. Burned in America, condemned in England, seized in Ireland, *Ulysses* was hailed as a masterpiece by influential French writers and critics like Valery Larbaud, Louis Gillet and Philippe Soupault. France was for a time the only Joycean stronghold against the philistinism of the outside word. We may say without exaggeration that, in that instance, Paris saved Dublin. And we may surmise that Joyce was thinking of France when he ascribes to himself the task to Europeanize Ireland and Hibernicise Europe, a mission that is well advanced but far from complete today! Many other Irish writers and poets came, or turned their attention, to France to find new ways of expressing their inner self.

---

[21] Anne Markey, 'French Culture and Oscar Wilde's Fairy Tales: An Unexplored Interlink with Neglected Works of Art', in *Reinventing Ireland through a French Prism*, edited by Eamon Maher, Eugene O'Brien and Grace Neville (Frankfurt: Peter Lang, 2007), 132.

[22] W. B. Yeats, *Autobiographies, Memories and Reflections* (London: Bracken Books, 1995), 343.

[23] Quoted in Lara Marlowe's Irishwoman's Diary, *The Irish Times*, 2 June 2009.

Reflections on the Relationship between Ireland and France

James Stephens lived in Paris before the First World War. He was a voracious reader of Honoré de Balzac and Anatole France. The last poem he set his eyes upon, on Christmas day 1950, on the eve of his death, was La Fontaine's fable 'La Mort et le Mourant', a perfect lesson of stoicism.

Brian Moore lived on the left bank of Paris in the fifties and sixties. France, he said, 'was a foreign country where I felt at home'.[24] And so did Brendan Behan. His play *The Hostage* represented Great Britain at the Théâtre des Nations in 1953:

> 'The fact of the matter', he wrote, 'is there is everything to fit an Irishman in France. He can find a good Irish excuse for getting into any political argument there. Paris, as the man said, est toujours Paris. Always her own sweet self. The talk about local politicians and other notabilities in a Paris bistro is like a breath of home to the Dubliner, far from the scurrilities of pub conversation in his native city, and just as intimately savage. And the Frenchman has good time for us.'[25]

The writer John Broderick, author of *The Pilgrimage* (1961) and *The Waking of Willie Ryan* (1965), was clearly influenced by François Mauriac. A critic has even suggested that, in these novels, 'he was attempting to re-invent himself as a French-style Catholic novelist'.[26]

Among poets, Brendan Kennelly has acknowledged four major influences on his large corpus of poetry, novels, plays and criticism: one is Irish, Kavanagh; one is American, Ginsberg; and two are French, Baudelaire and Rimbaud. John Montague who lived the last years of his life in Nice where he died in 2016 has claimed to have 'established a fertile dialogue between (my) old and new worlds, Ireland and France'.[27] The same can be said of Derek Mahon who has produced remarkable translations of Molière, Nerval, Valéry and Jaccottet. 'Mahon's francophilia', writes Terence Brown, one of the most perceptive contemporary critics and scholars, 'is more than

---

24 Brian Moore, 'Patrick Rafroidi: Before and After', in *Ireland and France. A Bountiful Friendship*, edited by Barbara Hayley and Christopher Murray (Gerrards Cross: Colin Smythe, 1992), 5–6.
25 Brendan Behan, *Confessions of an Irish Rebel* (London: Arrow Books, 1967), 205.
26 Madeline Kingston, *Something in the Head: The Life and Work of John Broderick* (Dublin: Lilliput Press, 2004), 122.
27 John Montague, *Company: A Chosen Life* (London: Duckworth, 2001), 121.

a simple regard for the qualities of French life and letters [...]. Rather it is an element in an imagination that has always been tantalized by the nature of alternative modes of consciousness and feeling'.[28] More precisely, Terence Brown adds that France has been for Mahon 'an imaginative escape route from the tedium of the provincial and the fixity of an inherited identity'.[29]

However, in terms of soul searching under French influence and reconstruction of oneself far away from Albion's grasp, I can find no better example than Samuel Beckett. To a Frenchman who once asked him if he was English, he is reputed to have answered 'Au contraire', on the contrary, a very explicit response albeit a minimalist one. The counterpoint of English being obviously French, Samuel Beckett not only decided to live in France, he also shared the fate of the French people during the war, played his part in the Résistance for which he was awarded the Croix de Guerre, and ended up writing his novels and plays directly in French. Whilst avidly interested in what was going on in Ireland, very much like James Joyce, he is the first example of a unique species: a Hiberno-French writer who can equally be claimed by the Irish and by the French as 'one of our own'.

The blossoming of the literary connection must not hide the fact that, since the beginning of the twentieth century until the early seventies, the relationship between our two countries had lost its impetus: 'Whether that ancient attachment between Ireland and France will revive', asked the ubiquitous Hilaire Belloc in 1932, 'the future only can show; it will depend in part upon the settlement of the French religious quarrel, in part upon the new orientation of international forces, more perhaps upon new factors in the culture of the West which we are only now beginning dimly to perceive'.[30] Belloc would be amazed to see that the French religious quarrel has been settled for good whereas the Irish are suddenly finding fault with their own religious institutions. But he was right in anticipating a new orientation of international forces. Europe has seen the binding together of

---

28 Terence Brown, 'Home and Away: Derek Mahon's France', in Hayley and Murray, *Ireland and France: A Bountiful Friendship*, 144.
29 Hayley and Murray, *Ireland and France: A Bountiful Friendship*, 147.
30 Richard Hayes, *Ireland and Irishmen in the French Revolution*, with a preface by Hilaire Belloc (London: Ernest Benn, 1932), xii.

twenty-seven countries of the old continent. And since the first of January 1973, Ireland is a member of that federation of nations.

It was to be expected that the old affinity between France and Ireland would re-emerge as soon as the imperatives of solidarity and mutual interest would take precedence over the untroubled solitude of isolationism. When Patrick Hillery was about to take up appointment as the first Irish Commissioner of the European Economic Community, he went to Áras an Uachtaráin where President Eamon de Valera said words to this effect:

> You don't mind, Paddy, if I give you a last bit of advice before you go. We have been cut off from Europe for a long time now and you are the first Irishman to have the honour of taking on this very important role as Commissioner in the European Community. I am sure it will be a new and sometimes strange experience for you. But remember this – stay close to the French – they were always our friends over the years and if you follow them you won't go too far wrong.[31]

France and Ireland are even closer since the British people voted to quit the European Union in 2016. After a lengthy and sometimes bitter negotiation during which France observed an unswerving solidarity with Ireland, the United Kingdom officially left the European Union on 31 January 2020.

As a direct consequence of Brexit, France is now Ireland's closest EU neighbour. Far from being a convenient and empty political slogan, this formula is the accurate description of the stimulating reality coming from the unprecedented proximity of our two countries. Lara Marlowe, the well-informed correspondent of *The Irish Times* in Paris, went so far as to write 'Brexit threw Ireland into the arms of France', a barely exaggerated statement.[32] This unexpected situation has created a window of opportunity for the strengthening of the Franco-Irish bilateral relationship in every dimension.

Irish Ministers made more than thirty official visits to France last year; their French counterparts a similar number to Ireland. Maritime crossings

---

31 Letter from former minister Michael O'Kennedy to the author, 15 January 1999.
32 Lara Marlowe, 'Ireland and France's ever-closer relationship is good news in a time of strife. Brexit threw Ireland into the arms of France, spawning a relationship that has never been better', *The Irish Times*, 25 November 2022.

between the French and the Irish coasts have quadrupled, from 12 to 45 weekly. French youths are the largest contingent of Erasmus students in Ireland, and France is the first destination abroad for Irish students. The French language is such an important medium on the world stage that Ireland has sought and obtained Observer Status at the Organisation Internationale de la Francophonie. Every year, 500,000 French tourists visit Ireland, and over 700,000 Irish tourists visit France.

Trade and investment between Ireland and France are flourishing.[33] France is Ireland's third biggest supplier, while Ireland is the seventh biggest supplier to France. In June 2023, the Irish Central Statistics Office (CSO) indicated that the value of goods and services imported and exported between Ireland and France totalled 30 billion euros in the previous year. Furthermore, France is the fourth largest investor in Ireland and employs around 12,000 people in the Emerald Isle; and Ireland is also a very important investor in France where Irish companies employ more than 30,000 people.

Both States are committed to promoting further opportunities to strengthen this vibrant relationship. Irish renewed ambitions for that relationship have been set out in *Ireland's Strategy for France 2019–2025: Together in Spirit and Action*, itself part of the Irish Government's *Global Ireland* strategy.[34] It aims to deepen the engagement of Ireland in France, at national and regional levels, politically, culturally, economically and diplomatically. The official visit of French President Emmanuel Macron to Ireland on 26 August 2021 was a significant reaffirmation of the solid partnership between Ireland and France. In Taoiseach Micheál Martin's words, 'the links between us are deep, and they have never been stronger'.[35] At policy-making level, the signing of the *Ireland-France Joint Plan of Action 2021–2025* by the then Irish and French Ministers for Foreign Affairs Simon Coveney and Jean-Yves Le Drian represented a major aspect of the visit of President Macron

---

33 Arlene Harris, 'Helping French and Irish Firms Say oui to Fruitful Collaboration', *The Sunday Business Post*, 28 November 2021.
34 Global Ireland: Ireland's Strategy for France 2019–2025, 'Together in Spirit and Action', Department of Foreign Affairs and Trade, 28 August 2019.
35 Lara Marlowe, 'Ireland and France's Ever Closer Relationship'.

to Ireland.[36] The plan outlines six priority projects to be implemented by 2025 whether that be supporting sustainability; increasing trade connectivity; fostering the digital economy; reinforcing education and research links; promoting the French language; fostering cultural cooperation; strengthening our people-to-people links; and deepening policy dialogue and cooperation in all areas.

In accordance with this joint road map, two ongoing major Franco-Irish infrastructure projects have been set in motion. The first one is the Celtic Interconnector, a planned 575 km undersea high-voltage underwater power cable that will link the southern coast of Ireland and the north-west coast of France.[37] Led by EirGrid and Réseau de Transport d'Électricité, it will be the first interconnector between Ireland and continental Europe. When completed in 2026 at a global cost of 1,623 billion euros, it will transport 700 megawatts of electricity, enough to power more than 450,000 homes.

> 'It is a major energy capital project', said the French Ambassador Vincent Guérend, 'and something which will be mutually beneficial. Whenever Ireland's renewable energy capacity will not suffice, France will be happy to provide backup with its nice clean nuclear energy. Whenever Ireland will have surpluses in due time with offshore wind, we will be glad to get it offloaded into the French or European grid.'[38]

At roughly the same time, in December 2021, the French multinational Alstom, global leader in innovation and provider of green mobility solutions, has won a ten-year contract with Irish Rail to deliver 750 electric and battery-electric rail cars for Ireland's DART+ system.[39] The new trains will deliver more capacity and decarbonization benefits to the local community of Greater Dublin.

36   https://www.dfa.ie/media/dfa/publications/JPOA--24-August-2021-Engish-Version.pdf [accessed 12 October 2023].
37   Florentin Collomp, 'Un câble électrique franco-irlandais', *Le Figaro*, 8 Septembre 2021 https://www.celticinterconnector.eu/ [accessed 12 October 2023].
38   https://www.franceireland.ie/news/n/news/ambassador-of-france-to-ireland-vincent-guerend-france-irelands-closest-eu-neighbour [accessed 12 October 2023].
39   https://www.alstom.com/press-releases-news/2023/3/alstom-and-irish-rail-reveal-full-size-model-dart-carriage-dublin [accessed 12 October 2023].

Political will, technology and cooperation on sustainable growth are thus contributing a new dimension of the enduring and deep friendship and historical, ideological and literary affinities going back centuries between France and Ireland. This major new trend fulfils the wish expressed by former French President Charles de Gaulle at Dublin Castle on 19 June 1969:

> There has been, it seems, for some generations past a kind of screen between Ireland and France, but it appears that that time has passed and that it is now possible for both of us to get through it, to find one another and to be together again in spirit and action. That is the impression I have gained in my brief stay amongst you and it is the wish I would like to express before I leave your country. That henceforth Ireland and France may get to know each other better every day, that they may meet and remain together in thought and action.[40]

---

40   Pierre Joannon, *L'Hiver du Connétable. Charles de Gaulle et l'Irlande*, Préface d'Arnaud Teyssier, Orléans, Éditions Regain de Lecture, 2023, 99.

ALEXANDRA MACLENNAN

7 The Importance of Being Eamon

Liber Amicorum is what some academic traditions might call this collective endeavour. This is a book of friends, of colleagues who have become friends with Eamon as a result of working with him, and who grew into themselves as academics because of working in Eamon's orbit. The English-speaking academic world uses the word *Festschrift*, which is noticeably more festive than the comparatively underwhelming French 'mélanges', and thus eminently more suited to convey the spirit of Eamon's career. It is in that spirit that I would like to use my space in the book of friends to show the importance of being Eamon, the singular intellectual and institutional fruitfulness of his academic way of being and its capacity to foster renewal for the future.

To do so, I have interviewed two of his Irish colleagues who have travelled the journey with him: Eugene O'Brien and Grace Neville. The picture that forms is that of a career journey driven by creativity, independence, collegiality, and an equally festive and hard work ethic. It is one that singularly shows how academic life is allowed to grow, thrive, and renew itself for the future.

The importance of creating a space

Eugene O'Brien recalls meeting Eamon for the first time at University College Cork conferences in the late 1990s on themes such as 'The Scattering – Ireland and the Irish Diaspora' (UCC, 1997), 'Space in Literature and Film Conference' (UCC, 1998), '1798, 1848, 1898: Revolution, Revival, Commemoration' (UCC, 1998). He remembers the new and stimulating transdisciplinary approach of those conferences asking speakers to respond to the themes from every discipline. Eugene had recently earned his PhD in English from the University of Limerick on 'Post-Structuralist Perspectives on Aesthetic Ideology in the Writings of Seamus Heaney', as had Eamon, in French literature, from NUI Galway.

Eugene asked Eamon a question about the paper he had given on Jean Sulivan, the French priest-writer to whom he had devoted his PhD. As virtually nobody in Ireland had heard the name before, attendees could be forgiven for wondering who was that Irish female writer they didn't know. They soon realized that he was talking not about a woman by the Scottish variant of Jane, but about a French man called *Jean*, and that the Irish-looking second name 'Sulivan' – bar one dropped letter – was made to rhyme with that French 'Jean'.[1] That Frenchified Irish name alone opens up a new province of the imagination. Over postprandial coffee during that conference, Eugene and Eamon had their first conversation about Irish Studies and French Studies and the connection between the two. A whole new area of endeavour was born out of that first symposiac moment: Franco-Irish Studies.

The first fruits of that foundational encounter were books. Eugene invited Eamon to publish a book on John McGahern[2] as part of the series he edited with Liffey Press on late twentieth-century authors such as Seamus Heaney, Conor McPherson, or John Banville.[3] The inaugural conversation

1   Eamon Maher, *Jean Sulivan (1913–1980): La marginalité dans la vie et l'œuvre* (Paris: L'Harmattan, 2008). Eamon has also translated Jean Sulivan. See *Anticipate Every Goodbye* (Dublin: Veritas, 2000). Eamon is preparing a new book which will include new archival material on Jean Sulivan discovered at the Institut Mémoire de l'Edition Contemporaine (IMEC) in Caen, Normandy.
2   Eamon Maher, *John McGahern: From the Local to the Universal* (Dublin: Liffey Press, 2003).
3   The series edited by Eugene O'Brien with Liffey Press on 'Contemporary Irish Writers and Filmmakers' ran between 2002 and 2006, and included nine titles devoted to Jim Sheridan (Ruth Barton), Neil Jordan (Emer Rockett and Kevin Rockett), Brian Friel (Tony Corbett), John Banville (Derek Hand), John McGahern (Eamon Maher), Brendan Kennelly (John McDonagh), Conor McPherson (Jerry Wood), Roddy Doyle (Dermot McCarthy), William Trevor (Mary Fitzgerald-Hoyt).

was pursued over book launches. For Eamon, writing a book is a party, which never fails to kindle a spark in his eyes, but *launching* a book is an even greater party still. Eamon *loves* a book launch, Eugene says, laughing, shaking his head with memories. 'He gets excited every time'. Just having a new book out is cause for great excitement. But then, 'he'll bask for maybe a week, and then it's what's next'.

And soon, more fruits appeared: conferences at IT Tallaght, Eamon's institution, in 2004 ('La France et la langue française face à la mondialisation') and 2005 ('Irish and Catholic? Towards an Understanding of Catholic and Irish Identities'). On the success of Tallaght's first Franco-Irish Studies conference which Eamon organized in 2003 ('Ireland and France: Cultural, Literary and Spiritual Bonds'), the institution endowed itself in 2004 with a perennial research structure, the National Centre for Franco-Irish Studies, of which Eamon became president. Significantly, it was in that new forum that Eugene was given the opportunity to deliver his first plenary lecture.

In a second foundational symposiac moment, Eamon, Eugene, and Grace Neville were having a drink after a conference dinner, and Eamon said that there was a need for an association in addition to the Centre. Grace remembers how Eamon has always looked for new, like-minded scholars with whom he could work towards a common goal, and she observes that over many decades, he has been fantastic at doing that. Back to that conference dinner drink: Eamon noted that there were a number of French organizations studying Irish history and literature, such as the French Society for Irish Studies (SOFEIR), founded in 1981, and Irish organizations studying French history and literature. Those in existence were either very French or very Irish, but there needed to be something in-between, an academic space for Irish and French scholars to look at the carry over between the two, to see what might be learnt from the cross-perspective. Irish Studies, as it developed abroad and especially in France, had indeed become shaped by literary and cultural theory, most of which originated in France. Eamon then thought of creating an Association for Franco-Irish Studies (AFIS) in 2005, an organization which has become extraordinarily vibrant and self-replenishing – Eamon's greatest accomplishment, as Eugene sees it.

The importance of publishing 'with Eamon Maher', or the 147-volume Schriftfest

The creation of AFIS initiated a long succession of books: a 147-volume writing festival. In 2007, Eugene, Eamon and Grace edited two comparative books with Peter Lang: *Reinventing Ireland through a French prism* and *La France et la mondialisation*. Those were volumes one and two of the Peter Lang 'Series in Franco-Irish Relations', and saw the first actual collaboration between the three friends looking together at their new Franco-Irish nexus. First, they had France and Ireland together in a book title, and now they had the adjective 'Franco-Irish' in a book edited with Peter Lang in 2008: *Modernity and Postmodernity in a Franco-Irish context*. In 2009, attention turned to *Issues of Globalization and Secularization in France and Ireland*, jointly edited by the Irish trio and Yann Bevant in Rennes.[4] The same year, the fifth AFIS conference was organized in Cork by Grace Neville and Eamon Maher on the topic 'France, Ireland and Rebellion', and the following year, in 2010, collaboration with the university of Rennes was pursued, giving birth to a volume entitled *War of the Words: Literary rebellion in France and Ireland*, co-edited by Eugene O'Brien with Eamon Maher.[5] Since then, a variety of editors have produced a total of 22 volumes to date.

And that is before even mentioning the 'Reimagining Ireland' series, which is the largest – both in output and in scope – Irish Studies collection in the world, with its 125 volumes to date. Luke Gibbons has said that as it interrogates and constantly reappraises notions of Irishness and the cultural and national specificities of Ireland by offering ever refined theoretical perspectives, it is a 'major intervention' which sees Irish studies 'come back to Ireland itself. The Reimagining Ireland series is at the cutting edge

---

4   Yann Bevant, Eamon Maher, Grace Neville, and Eugene O'Brien, *Issues of Globalisation and Secularisation in France and Ireland* (Frankfurt: Peter Lang, 2009).
5   Eamon Maher and Eugene O'Brien (eds), *War of the Words: Literary Rebellion in France and Ireland* (Rennes: TIR, 2010).

of what it means to be Ireland'.[6] In 2018, the *Reimagining Ireland Reader* was launched at IT Tallaght by President of Ireland Derek Hand, and the 100th volume was produced to great acclaim in 2021. Eamon's piece in the volume shows him looking forward and not looking back: the twentieth century is done, let's move on. That, Eugene says, is what sums up Eamon: it's always the next thing that is significant.

Moving on to the next book, that is.

The sheer energy Eamon commits to organizing, editing, communicating, keeping the series to the high standards in which he has conceived it, checking the quality of every contribution has earned Eamon international acclaim. Eugene's admiration is vibrant when he comments that 'it's a massive undertaking. It's just huge!' Colleagues realize at this point that although Eamon comes across as being easy going and relaxed, he is highly organized, and has very high standards as editor, which is something both Eugene and Grace have commented upon. Reading his uplifting emails to the community promoting other people's work and congratulating them on their publications, conferences or vivas, one might think that he praises everyone and everything. Those endorsements are made more meaningful when you have the chance to notice – preferably not at your own expense! – that he has a strong sense of personal ethics, and when something is right, it's right and when it's wrong, it's wrong. Eamon can also be quite critical, indeed quite robust. If he doesn't like something, he will call it like it is.

Colleagues have also commented on the importance of commitment for Eamon. When he commits to a book, you'd better have your chapter ready, because it is going to come out, and it is going to come out on time. Commitment trumps most personal setbacks that may come in the way of our good intentions. You won't get away with even breaking your right arm if he's waiting for you. He will phone you, comfort you, tell you to take it easy, offer practical advice, but when you think he is going to let you off the hook, that is when he is going to ask you when you are going to send your manuscript. Eamon comes from Tipperary, and so does Eugene, and they agree that Tipperary people are very stubborn, which may be why

---

6   See Luke Gibbons' endorsement on the series website https://www.peterlang.com/series/reir [accessed 29 October 2023].

Eamon takes 'no' as an opening for a negotiation and then moves on from there. But Eamon will always check in, and if there's a problem, he'll call. He'll call when we're discouraged, dispirited, but for him, the cure, the most comforting, uplifting thought is that new book that we're going to do. No time for self-pity: there is something new that needs to be done.

The titles of the books Eamon has edited show the scope of his interests and competence: Catholicism, literary rebellion, modernity, reinvention, globalization, the Celtic Tiger, and so many other areas. He looks at Irish society in general, and brings in new literary and wider cultural cross-perspectives on contemporary phenomena such as the crisis in Irish Catholic identity, and on the Celtic Tiger. The books he and Eugene co-edited more recently about the Celtic Tiger were his idea:[7] he thought someone needed to write about the Celtic Tiger from another perspective than an economic or accountancy perspective, even though an economist from the Central Bank of Ireland and Trinity College Dublin, Brian Lucey, was also invited to join in the editorial adventure. He has a massive enthusiasm for reading, for writing, for thinking, for doing collegial work.

His phenomenal record in collective research should not however overshadow his prolific and highly original record as an individual scholar. There is a singular broadness and scope in the way Eamon writes and thinks. He takes the time to read and write a great deal – books about established authors based on new archives and book reviews of emerging authors. Eamon likes phoning his colleagues to sound them out about those new authors. Eamon's interest in new ideas, new sources, new areas is key, says Eugene who admires 'his very fine mind in that sense', which has absorbed a great deal, from Sulivan to contemporary food and beverage studies. Creating an academic space for the contemporary is probably one of the most challenging forms of scholarship: without the safety net of the test of time, a substantial intellectual risk is involved. But that doesn't bother Eamon, because he trusts his own judgement and he senses what they are writing about. That, in Eugene's eyes, might be his defining academic factor: the

---

7   Eamon Maher and Eugene O'Brien (eds), *From Prosperity to Austerity: A Socio-Cultural Critique of the Celtic Tiger and Its Aftermath* (Manchester: Manchester University Press, 2014); Brian Lucey, Eamon Maher and Eugene O'Brien (eds), *Recalling the Celtic Tiger* (Oxford: Peter Lang, 2019).

new isn't something scary, or something we have to gatekeep. If something is new and it involves a Franco-Irish area, Eamon wants to do it.

The importance of leading from behind

'When you look at all the different strands together, it's a fine career, it really is', Eugene reflects. Quantitatively, his record speaks for itself. But more singularly, he has created his own ecosystem and developed his own academic style. His work on Franco-Irish academic relations has made him very popular in French diplomatic circles – and in France in general, where he has received the Palmes Académiques and was recently made honorary President of the SOFEIR. Eamon has also singularly attracted PhD students mostly from outside his institution, which is all the more remarkable given that he doesn't have a feeding system going through from his undergraduate teaching in his institution.

Sometimes, strong-willed and independent-minded academics can be tripped up along the way by some aspect of academic politics. Most of us will be dispirited; a lot of us will let that stop us. Eamon won't let those outside values get in his way: being Eamon, he will just keep going. If he is valued by the people he's working with, and by a community of scholars whom he respects, he'll keep doing what he's doing.

Eugene sees this as massively admirable, and we certainly all need to emulate that style of leadership, because it is easy to smile, praise and be generous and pro-active when the wind is blowing in our sails, but it's when the going is tough that you really see what somebody is made of. So Eamon finds ways around obstacles. 'Sure, we'll do it anyway': Eamon's way of doing things works nine times out of ten, but even for the one time it doesn't, he sees it as worth taking the knocks and standing up again to keep going. Eugene loves 'that stubbornness about him. He will just drive on to get what he needs to get'. That is powerful encouragement for us to persevere come what may in the pursuit of the common good, in an academic world which can all to easily become dominated by competitive, individualistic indifference. And he has done a huge amount of academic good.

If he most often succeeds in his goals, it is not only because of his innate stubbornness, his solid judgement and impressive intellectual calibre, but also thanks to his legendary sense of humour which is an essential component of his leadership style. He allows his humour to be irreverent and self-deprecating, and his colleagues recall laughing more on the phone with him than with anybody else, and certainly at his conferences more than at any other. AFIS reflects his personality, and the sense of ease and warmth which reinforce collegiality among participants turn conferences into academic celebrations.

For someone who is so driven by the work, Eamon is also extraordinarily driven by people as well, says Eugene. Most often indeed, it seems that it is one or the other. But Eamon loves people to be as good as they can be, and to get the chances they can get, and he's a great man for giving academic colleagues opportunities to do things, and to help them out if he can. He has succeeded admirably in encouraging young scholars and students to obtain doctoral and postdoctoral fellowships and break new ground in Irish Studies. Grace also says that that is one of the things she most admires him for: that he has fostered a young generation of academics. She adds that not that many academics spend as much time as Eamon does in order to ensure succession not of him individually, but to make sure that there is a new generation coming up. Joe Lee, chair of Modern History at UCC and then Professor of History at NYU, did that, and Patrick Rafroidi (1930–1989)[8] did that too. When Eamon retires, if

---

8   Patrick Rafroidi (1930–1989) was born of a French father and Irish mother, Constance O'Rahilly, from Listowel, Co. Kerry. Constance was one of fourteen siblings who included Alfred O'Rahilly, president of University College Cork, and uncle to Patrick Rafroidi. Another uncle and aunt were Celtic scholars. Following a *doctorat d'état* (*Irish Literature in English*: *The Romantic Period, 1789–1850*), he was a professor at the university of Lille between 1972 and 1980, serving as President of the university himself between 1976 and 1980. He then became a research fellow in Australia, served for three years as director of the Institut Français in London and cultural attaché between 1981 and 1984, going on to become chair of Anglo-Irish Studies at the Sorbonne between 1984 and 1987, spending one year as visiting professor at City University New York in 1985–1986, and then retiring in 1987. See his entry in the *Dictionary of Irish Biography* which describes him as an all-round scholar with a vast array of scholarly interests https://www.dib.ie/biography/rafroidi-patrick-a7569 [accessed 29 October 2023].

ever he does, the enterprise, Grace assesses, is in very good hands thanks to a fabric of different people from different disciplines and institutions he has managed to weave together. He has ensured that the next generation is solidly anchored and ready to take over.

Remarkably then, there is always a place for a doctoral or postdoctoral student in Eamon's conferences. He has seen to it that AFIS reinvents itself with new people coming in and studying new areas, such as food studies or tourism. There is the network of academics from France and other continental European countries that Eamon has introduced to Ireland. And also, because Eamon is open to all sorts of cultural studies, all sorts of thinking and writing, new ways of doing things, he has developed his way of mentoring students coming to him. With students who are in trouble, who are having issues, Eamon is solution-driven: 'You need to do this, and if it doesn't work you need to do this.' And he will tirelessly go over their work and keep going with them until a solution is found. That is why he is regarded as having done so well as a supervisor, and why so many students come to him as a supervisor.

Eamon has built collegiality to a rare level of intellectual quality and friendship. His loyalty is well known: as Eugene puts it, 'if you told Eamon you'd killed someone, he would say "ok, where do we bury the body?" He's that kind of guy. If he's in your corner, he's in your corner.' Transposed to work, that means that Eamon is not one to allow things to drift. He's on top of them all the time, and that's probably one of his most defining characteristics, and one of the strongest reasons why anyone would want to be associated with him.

He has developed a style of leadership 'from behind', as Grace analyses, adding that in that respect, he reminds her of Patrick Rafroidi whom she met in Lille when she came to teach as a lectrice aged 22. And indeed, Rafroidi was a man of vast intellectual culture and scope of endeavour, a gifted teacher, an ambassador of Irish culture in France, as Eamon is of French culture in Ireland. Rafroidi was a founder, having founded *Etudes Irlandaises* in 1972. Both of them were Officers in the Order of the Palmes Académiques. Both of them were broad, independent minds; both of them were gifted and inspiring educators and promoters of young people. Rafroidi had the same warmth, the same capacity 'to make people feel good about themselves, to make people feel important', says Grace, recalling how he was with the *lecteurs* and *lectrices* at the university of Lille at the time. Like Rafroidi, she goes on, 'Eamon gives people space, he gives them opportunities, in a very discreet way: he doesn't push them, but suddenly you realize you've published an article, given a paper, co-edited a book, and none of that would have happened without Eamon.'

Leadership is creating a working environment where people will feel understood, trusted, valued, and where they can grow to an ever-fuller version of themselves, and bring growth to the rest of the environment in the process. Like Rafroidi, Eamon has great confidence in the people around him, and he gives them space and as Grace beautifully and powerfully puts it, 'makes them rise to become the people that they could become with a little bit of encouragement and a little bit of positivity. He doesn't make them into the people they are, but he gives them the oxygen that enables them to operate at that level'. That is vitally important at a time when short-term contract positions have become commonplace in Irish universities, making the sense of belonging and the virtue of encouraging increasingly irrelevant to the present age.

The other colleague Grace mentioned with similar qualities to Eamon's is UCC's Joe Lee, who was not only a great academic but someone everybody wanted to work with. If he was on a committee, people wanted to be on the committee with him. Joe Lee, Patrick Rafroidi, Eamon Maher: three academic leaders with a 'pied piper quality to them', says Grace beautifully. She also thinks of her UCC colleague from the Department of Education Áine Hyland who was once thought of for the presidency of the country. Likewise, if she was on a committee, everybody was queuing to be on that committee, whereas normally, people run away from committees. In the same spirit, Grace comments on Eamon's ability to draw a crowd of people to events he organizes, such as his book launches in Dublin on a Thursday afternoon which can take a whole day out of people's calendars, when travel is involved. However difficult it might be for people, whatever else might be happening in the lives of the young crowd that attends those events without any obligation, they will do it for Eamon.

In his final assessment of Eamon's career, Eugene finds that nobody else 'in our game' has been so influential across individual research, group research, postgraduate supervision, and the collegiality of actually forming an association, and conference running and symposiums. In terms of being an academic, he says, he's the all-rounder, the 'full package'.

And Eamon has become that singularly powerful academic leader almost unwittingly, in a self-effacing, self-deprecating manner. That is because leads 'from behind', putting people on a path of growth, giving people their own space, giving them opportunities. In Grace's estimation, as an international consultant in higher education, it is very rare in academia which is increasingly about ferocious competition for promotions, grants, sabbatical leaves, beneath the rhetoric of collaboration. The temptation to become a self-centred academic is very strong. As a result, candidates for academic jobs sometimes show great potential, qualifications, energy and talent, and then they seem to collapse like a soufflé and you never hear about them again. They collapsed because they didn't have somebody like Eamon, who finds the best in people and helps them rise, to tell them: 'you're at that level, and now you can go further and further'. Encouragement in academia is very unusual. Eamon thus seems to go completely in the opposite direction. He has created a culture around him, an ecosystem where people can rise to the full realization of their individual personalities. He is a life-enhancing presence in Irish – and French – academic life, an agent of growth, the yeast in the academic dough, to paraphrase Luke 13:21.

I would like to end these reflections on being an academic with two concluding thoughts. First, when institutions have somebody like Eamon gracing them with his academic vitality and his capacity to become a national and international driving force, they have to cherish them. Eamon is an exceptional academic leader in the classical academic tradition evoked above vibrantly by Grace. And second, ultimately, growth is the only thing that matters, and not only Eamon's record but his own singular way of being an academic shows how it is done. Eamon is very unusual in the academic world, and he is precious. But for the future of the university as a place of intellectual vitality, we will need more first names to step into the Wildean title and perpetuate the importance of being Eamon.

CATHERINE MAIGNANT

8 French Theory and the Academic Study of Religion in Ireland

The academic study of religions has a short history in Ireland and its scholars are relatively few in number. Unsurprisingly they have from the start sought theoretical models abroad. Owing to historical links with France and the success of postmodern French theory in the English-speaking world, the United States in particular, at the time when the scientific study of religion started developing in Ireland, French models were a natural resource for Irish scholars.

Yet dialogue between French and Irish intellectuals on religious matters already had a long tradition when Tom Inglis wrote his seminal monograph on the Catholic Church in the 1980s. This tradition went back to the time when French professors at Maynooth contributed to shaping Irish Catholicism, from the creation of the seminary to the mid-nineteenth century.[1] It continued when Catholic sociology developed in both countries and exchanges between their experts were regular. French theory of the 1960s and 1970s then became influential from the 1980s and 1990s, when the academic study of religions started gaining ground in Ireland as the Catholic Church's influence progressively dwindled.

As had been the case outside Ireland for a number of years, it emerged as a fundamentally multidisciplinary research field, leading to methodological debates about the legitimacy of cross-fertilization between disciplinary theories. If history has remained largely immune from multidisciplinary theorization, other concerned disciplines, in particular the sociology of religions or Brian Bocking's study of religions have proved open to multiple theoretical influences, including French theory. Yet the younger generation

1   See Michael Turner, 'The French Connection with Maynooth College, 1795–1855', *Studies*, 70–277 (1981), 77–87.

of researchers seems to favour other sources, perhaps owing to the fact that French thinkers of the 1990s and 2000s are not as well-known abroad as their famous predecessors, Foucault, Derrida, Bourdieu, Lyotard or Baudrillard, among others. This article will argue that more recent French theory also has a lot to contribute to help make sense of recent religious developments in Ireland.

The late development of the academic study of religion and early influence of French theory

In his 2007 survey of the academic study of religion in Western Europe, Michael Stausberg (University of Bergen) noted that, together with Portugal, Ireland was 'a marginal blind spot on the map'.[2] If this comment certainly needs to be qualified, it is interesting in that it draws attention to the late development of this discipline in Irish universities. This specificity finds its origin in the privileged position of the Catholic Church in Ireland from the last decades of the nineteenth century, which explains why theologians initially controlled religious studies in Ireland. This was originally the result of papal strategy and of the contribution of Rome to the elaboration of Catholic sociology. Pope Leo XIII's 1879 encyclical, entitled *Aeterni Patris* began 'the radical restructuring of Catholic thought by the imposition of the philosophy and theology of St Thomas Aquinas as the sole system of ideas mandatory on all seminaries and colleges for the training of clergy'.[3]

This was the starting point of a political strategy aiming to restore a Catholic social order in an adverse European context. It was connected with the pope's programme of social reforms embodied in his 1891 encyclical, *Rerum Novarum*, one of the 185 encyclicals issued between 1878 and 1958 to

---

2   Michael Stausberg, 'The Study of Religion(s) in Western Europe (I): Prehistory and History until World War II', *Religion*, 37–34 (2007), 296.
3   Bill McSweeney, *Roman Catholicism: The Search for Relevance* (Oxford: Blackwell Publishers, 1980), 61.

the same effect. Peter Murray and Maria Feeney argue that, as a result, 'Irish Catholic writers constructed sociology as the social branch of ethics'[4] and the Thomistic concept of natural law provided an 'overarching framework'[5] of Irish Catholic sociology books. It was in this context that the Knights of St Columbanus endowed the Maynooth Chair of Catholic Sociology and Catholic Action in 1937. The first appointee, Fr Peter McKevitt was immediately sent to Louvain and then to Rome 'for further study'[6] and he only started teaching in Maynooth in 1939–1940. Only with the death of Pope Pius XII did 'the Catholic philosophical monopoly of Thomism'[7] based on 'the acceptance of a social code founded on the divine and natural law'[8] come to an end.

In the early stage, there seems to have been 'no dialogue with contemporary thinkers'.[9] Yet, quoting Newman and Mueller, Brian Conway suggests that 'Irish Catholic sociologists were well acquainted with the writings of Catholic sociology in France, Germany and the US', and that 'non-Irish Catholic sociologists knew of and responded to the writings of Irish Catholic sociologists',[10] but there was no central intellectual figure among Irish Catholic sociologists, who did not significantly contribute to contemporary methodological debates, contrary to some of their French colleagues.[11] French Catholic Sociologists included Canon Fernand Boulard, Henri de Tourville, Paul Descamps, M. Pinard, and mostly Frédéric Le Play

---

4   Peter Murray and Maria Feeney, *Church, State and Social Science in Ireland* (Manchester: Manchester University Press, 2018), 23.
5   Murray and Feeney, *Church, State and Social Science in Ireland*, 23.
6   Murray and Feeney, *Church, State and Social Science in Ireland*, 22.
7   Murray and Feeney, *Church, State and Social Science in Ireland*, 24.
8   Fr Crofts quoted in Murray and Feeney, *Church, State and Social Science in Ireland*, 24.
9   Murray and Feeney, *Church, State and Social Science in Ireland*, 23.
10 Brian Conway, 'Catholic Sociology in Ireland in Comparative Perspective', *The American Sociologist*, 42–41 (2011), 37. Quoting Newman's review of 'Vocation de la sociologie religieuse: Sociologie des Vocations', by Paroisses Urbaines: Paroisses Rurales, *The Furrow*, 10–16 (1959), 416–417; and Mueller, in Review of 'The Plan of Society' by Reverend Peter McKevitt, *American Catholic Sociological Review*, 7-2 (1946), 144–145.
11 Conway, 'Catholic Sociology in Ireland in Comparative Perspective', 37.

and Gabriel Lebras. Together they produced an impressive volume of publications. But they all opposed Emile Durkheim, their fellow-countryman and the founding father of the scientific study of religion,[12] on the grounds that he believed in the social origin of religion. There was obviously no question of any form of critical approach to the Church's analysis of social issues. Irish Catholic sociologists reviewed the works of their French counterparts and referred to them in their own writings, but they too made no reference to any secular sociology.

The 1950s witnessed two major evolutions in Irish Catholic sociology: first the introduction of empirical data to contribute to theological analyses of society and then the adoption of a scientific approach to social issues and religion itself, which 'shifted from being the repository of values guiding sociological investigation to becoming an object of sociological inquiry in itself'.[13] McKevitt's successor Fr Jeremiah Newman believed that sociology could thus contribute to helping the Church understand itself.[14] In the words of Brian Conway, 'sociology of religion superseded "religious sociology" and paved the way for the emergence of a sociology of Catholicism'.[15] It was Newman who gave Catholic sociology a new direction and eventually brought it 'into dialogue with the mainstream – and increasingly internationalized and professionalized – discipline elsewhere'.[16] A reader of European continental philosophy, he responded to Maurice Merleau-Ponty's and Henri Lefebvre's works by writing in defence of Christianity against communist and other left-wing philosophies. He and his fellow Irish Catholic sociologists increasingly took part in international networks and were confronted by the norms and methods that prevailed outside Ireland. Besides, most of the new generation of sociologists who trained in the 1960s and 1970s did so abroad and they brought back to Ireland the standard empirical secular scientific practices, which in the

---

12 Emile Durkheim, *Formes élémentaires de la vie religieuse*, 1912. For an analysis of this question, see William McCorkle Jr and Dimitris Xygalatas, 'Past, Present, and Future in the Scientific Study of Religion', *Thema*, XX-2 (2012), 150–151.
13 Conway, 'Catholic Sociology in Ireland in Comparative Perspective', 40.
14 Conway, 'Catholic Sociology in Ireland in Comparative Perspective', 47.
15 Conway, 'Catholic Sociology in Ireland in Comparative Perspective', 40.
16 Conway, 'Catholic Sociology in Ireland in Comparative Perspective', 47.

long run were to ensure that traditional Catholic sociology lost ground in university departments even though it did preserve an influence in terms of 'public engagement' and interest in 'rural life, family, education and religion'.[17] In fact, in Bryan Fanning and Andreas Hess's estimation, only the early 1970s heralded 'the beginning of the slow end of Catholic sociology's hegemony'.[18]

The specific context of Ireland was in the end to delay the development of the academic study of religion. The precursor and most prominent early researcher in that field was Tom Inglis, author of the first notable monograph corresponding to international standards of methodological rigour, *Moral Monopoly: The Catholic Church in Modern Irish Society*, published in 1987. Its revised 1998 edition, entitled *Moral Monopoly: The Rise and Fall of the Catholic Church in Modern Ireland* bore witness to the Church's loss of influence in the 1990s, which was a significant background to the development of the academic study of religion in Ireland. Yet it was not until 2002 that the first Irish non-clerical Professor of Sociology, Seán O'Riain, a specialist of institutional policy-making, was appointed at Maynooth. Prior to that date, many sociologists appointed to Irish universities were foreigners, as for instance Michel Peillon who was recruited to teach Marxist sociology in UCD in 1970. As concerns the study of religions specifically, the very first non-confessional department for the study of religions opened at UCC in 2008 only.

There, the study of religions was developed as a discipline in its own right by Brian Bocking and his team. Bocking defended the view that this discipline was polymethodic as it borrowed from other disciplines such as 'history, sociology, anthropology, philosophy, psychology, literary and cultural theory, languages and archaeology to understand religions'.[19] He also insisted that the discipline was concerned by all world religions examined in comparative or 'holistic' perspective.[20] His and his colleagues' approach

17 Conway, 'Catholic Sociology in Ireland in Comparative Perspective', 52.
18 Bryan Fanning and Andreas Hess, 'Sociology in Ireland: Legacies and Challenges', *Irish Journal of Sociology*, 23–1 (2015), 9.
19 Denise Cush and Catherine Robinson, 'Brian Bocking and the Defence of Study of Religions as an Academic Discipline in Universities and Schools', *Journal of the Irish Society for the Academic Study of Religions*, 3–1 (2016), 33.
20 Cush and Robinson, 'Brian Bocking and the Defence of Study of Religions', 33.

was from the start agnostic, and the questions connected to the 'ultimate truth of religious claims' were deliberately left out.[21] Apart from study of religions experts, there emerged a new generation of researchers based in different disciplines such as sociology of religions, history, anthropology, cognitive sciences and Irish studies understood as cultural sociology.[22] However significant their contributions, their number remains limited today, hence the 'neglect of important areas of concern', as Gladys Ganiel notes.[23] Besides, many studies lack an all-Ireland or a comparative international approach, if we except academic study of religions scholars[24] and a few sociologists of religion such as Brian Conway among others.

However, in keeping with international practices, theorization is seen as a priority today and contemporary scholars have developed innovating concepts, for instance, Ganiel's 'extra institutional religion'.[25] Yet for historical as well as methodological reasons,[26] interest in theorization is recent and Irish scholars have tended to borrow theories from abroad, in particular from France. This has also been justified by the topics of international concern which have been at the core of recent research: the secularization and modernization debate, globalization, de-institutionalization and pluralization to name but a few.

---

21 Cush and Catherine Robinson, 'Brian Bocking and the Defence of Study of Religions', 35.
22 Brian Fanning and Adreas Hess argue that the conceptual tools of cultural sociology offer 'an alternative to the primacy of literary theory within Irish Studies and have the potential to reinvigorate sociology in Ireland'. Fanning and Hess, 'Sociology in Ireland: Legacies and Challenges', *Irish Journal of Sociology*, 23–1 (2015), 17.
23 Gladys Ganiel, 'Understanding the Sociology of Religions in Contemporary Ireland', in *The Study of Religions in Ireland, Past, Present and Future*, edited by Brendan McNamara and Hazel O'Brien (London: Bloomsbury, 2022), 68.
24 Alexandra Grieser and Brian Bocking, 'The Study of Religions in Ireland: An Entangled History', in *The Study of Religions in Ireland*, 7–8.
25 'Extra institutional religion' refers to the way 'people describe their own faith practices as outside or in addition to the institutional church'. Gladys Ganiel, 'Understanding the Sociology of Religions in Contemporary Ireland', 66.
26 In particular the tensions between positivist quantitative sociology embodied in the ESRI and interpretative qualitative sociology based in Irish universities.

As elsewhere, French theory has contributed to shaping contemporary understandings of religious practices, institutions and even beliefs. Most influential among the quoted theories, Michel Foucault's approach of power relations, Jacques Derrida's deconstructive perspective, Jean Baudrillard's analysis of hyperreality and Gilles Deleuze's philosophy of immanence have been repeatedly applied to the Irish context. But a number of other philosophers and sociologists are also referenced, in particular Lyotard and his description of 'the postmodern condition', Bourdieu and his concept of habitus, but also Ricoeur, Braudel, Levinas, Barthes and Lacan. By far the author most obviously influenced by French theory, philosopher Richard Kearney studied in France and wrote a thesis under the supervision of Ricoeur, which explains this bias. In *Anatheism*, for instance, he refers to practically all the previously mentioned philosophers, but also to Julia Kristeva, René Girard, as well as Merleau-Ponty, Michel de Certeau, Bachelard and several French writers, including Camus and Proust. But *Anatheism* may hardly be considered relevant to the list of books pertaining to the academic study of religions. No more can Mark Patrick Hederman's numerous published works be considered as belonging to this category for he is an actor of religious change rather than an analyst. But the fact that prominent intellectuals such as Kearney and Hederman repeatedly refer to French theory is a sign of the influence wrought by these thinkers on innovative perspectives about religion in Ireland.

If we take into consideration the works published by sociologists of religion and other academic study of religion scholars, we note a similar tendency. Tom Inglis wrote an article entitled 'Foucault, Bourdieu and the Field of Irish Sexuality', in which he tested the validity of these two authors' theories in the Irish context.[27] He also refers to them (and more particularly Bourdieu) in *Moral Monopoly*, where he also quotes Lyotard, Durkheim, Braudel, among other French thinkers. The younger generation of scholars makes a more limited use of French theory, but Carmen Kuhling, for instance, does mention Baudrillard, Hervieu-Léger and Lacan, Gladys Ganiel refers to Danièle Hervieu-Léger and Eamon Maher quotes Bourdieu.

27   Tom Inglis, 'Foucault, Bourdieu and the Field of Irish Sexuality', *Irish Journal of Sociology*, 7 (1997), 5–28.

More French theory and possible avenues of investigation

Yet, if Irish experts of the academic study of religion have found French theory relevant for their analyses, they have so far drawn on the works of a limited number of internationally renowned philosophers or sociologists and in some cases a limited number of their works. A number of other perhaps less well-known theorists such as Michel Maffesoli, Luc Ferry, Gilles Lipovetsky or Marcel Gauchet, among others might also profitably be considered to enrich the reflection on religious matters. Indeed, they may be said to have contributed ground-breaking and sometimes illuminating analyses that may usefully be applied to Ireland. They provide an invaluable insight when it comes to examining such questions as man's relationships to the sacred and the divine in contemporary Ireland, new appreciations of the self and redefinitions of the relationship of the other to oneself, and new attitudes towards space and time in a religious context.

Frédéric Lenoir thus convincingly argues that the development of individualism and humanism have resulted in a dramatic evolution of people's attitudes towards structures of authority. Today, men can no longer be content with being passive witnesses. They question traditions and truths imposed from above. Ready-made answers have become unacceptable. Men are now at the centre of preoccupations, which explains why people are concerned with physical and psychological well-being in a worldview that values emotions and imagination more and more, at the expense of reason. Any analysis of contemporary religious phenomena in the Western world, he says, must take into account this all-pervading context.[28] In Luc Ferry's estimation, what is in fact at work today is a form of humanization of the divine and divinization of human beings, which leads to a representation of transcendence that is not only intelligible but entirely subsumed within the immanence of human subjectivity.[29]

---

28   Frédéric Lenoir, *Les métamorphoses de Dieu – la nouvelle spiritualité occidentale* (Paris: Plon, 2003), 55–56.
29   Luc Ferry, *L'homme Dieu ou le sens de la vie* (Paris: Grasset, 1990), 226.

In the words of U2, you can 'look for Baby Jesus in the trash',[30] and in those of the Cranberries, God is just 'the man above'.[31] Besides, all men may be presented as Christ-like figures. Describing his feelings as he sits in traffic jams every morning, Aidan Mathews significantly talks about other drivers as 'the Christ before me and the Christ behind me and the Christ to my left and the Christ to my right – in short, the persons who are the real presence of God in the world'.[32] As for Martin Drury, the director of The Ark, he claims that his 'preference is for [...] the celebration of humanity rather than some remote divinity'.[33] Analysing comparable phenomena in the Western world, Ferry notes that the man-God is also a humanist,[34] which allows him to criticize the Church on grounds of inhumanity or insensitivity. Whereas the Church laboured for rationalization, he privileges emotion over reason[35] and thus redefines transcendence as 'horizontal' (my neighbour is Christ to me) rather than 'vertical' (the creature below venerates God above).[36] This evolution might actually have been to a certain extent predictable. In his seminal work entitled *Le désenchantement du monde*, Marcel Gauchet suggests that Christianity is the religion that freed men from religions precisely because of its human dimension and its historical connection with the State, a theory that no doubt needs to be investigated in the Irish context.[37]

Talking from de-christianized France, Regis Debray, for his part, suggests that the desacralization of the world may be connected to the sacralization of images.[38] Whatever the situation in a secularized country, it is clear that the aestheticization of values that has been analysed by Gilles

---

30 U2, 'Mofo', in *Pop*, 1997.
31 The Cranberries, 'Just my Imagination', in *Bury the Hatchet*, 1999.
32 Aidan Mathews, 'The Annals of Hannah', in *The Splintered Heart, Conversations with a Church in Crisis*, Eamonn Conway and Colm Kilcoyne (Dublin: Veritas, 1998), 30.
33 The Ark is a cultural centre for children, *Sources, Letters from Irish People on Sustenance for the Soul*, edited by Marie Heaney (Dublin: Townhouse, 1999), 193.
34 Ferry *L'homme Dieu*, 226.
35 Ferry *L'homme Dieu*, 194 and ff.
36 Ferry *L'homme Dieu*, 124.
37 Marcel Gauchet, *Le désenchantement du monde* (Paris: Gallimard, 1985).
38 Régis Debray, *Vie et mort de l'image* (Paris: Gallimard, 1992), 415.

Lipovetsky and Jean Serroy as a central characteristic of the 'hypermodern' world does have a bearing on religious issues,[39] notably in Ireland. Mark Patrick Hederman, thus considers that art, beauty and artists can save man's relation to the Catholic God.[40] So does John O'Donohue, who invites his readers to contemplate God's creation in the hope that it will spark creative energy in them.[41] To the people who took part in the Celtic pilgrimages he used to organize in the West of Ireland, it is clear that 'aesthetic emotion could function as a social cement',[42] as Michel Maffesoli notes. It could also create the sense of a community in which shared sensory emotion could re-enchant the world and abolish time. Dany-Robert Dufour argues that our complex era, where disenchantment and re-enchantment coexist is best symbolized by the opposition between the binary scientific and the trinitarian archaic conceptions of the world. Each scientific step forward has always been counterbalanced by a regressive step backwards towards various forms of esotericism.[43] Lyotard wrote that if paganism existed, it was characterized by the refusal to acknowledge the legitimacy of any metadiscourse.[44] According to Dufour, if we free ourselves from God and all grand narratives, it means that we are looking for a new law, hence the emergence of postmodern neo-tribes, identified by Michel Maffesoli.[45] In the absence of legitimate grand narratives, men need to reinvent themselves and find like-minded others to find a new form of sociability.[46]

Frédéric Lenoir suggests that the fragmentation of religious thinking which the distrust for institutions and individualism have engendered is limited by the hunger to belong. As a result, the quest for meaning often

---

39 Gilles Lipovetsky and Jean Serroy, *L'esthétisation du monde* (Paris: Gallimard, 2013).
40 Mark Patrick Hederman, for instance *The Haunted Inkwell* (Dublin: Columba, 2001).
41 John O'Donohue, *Divine Beauty, The Invisible Embrace* (London: Bantam, 2004), 226.
42 Michel Maffesoli, *Au creux des apparences – Pour une éthique de l'esthétique* (Paris: Plon, 1990), 24.
43 Dany-Robert Dufour, *Les mystères de la trinité* (Paris: nrf Gallimard, 1990), 11.
44 Jean-François Lyotard, *Rudiments païens*, 1977, quoted by Dufour, *Les mystères de la trinité*, 265.
45 Michel Maffesoli, *Le temps des tribus – le déclin de l'individualisme dans les sociétés postmodernes* (Paris: La Table Ronde, 1988).
46 Dufour, *Les mystères de la Trinité*, 265–267.

involves a quest for social connectedness.⁴⁷ Michel Maffesoli argues that the stress on communion – if not fusion – with others may actually in part be seen as a direct effect of the 'orientalisation' of contemporary Western culture.⁴⁸ The identity formation process which is central to the contemporary reinvention of religion involves what Maffesoli calls 'ecstasy', literally coming out of oneself to fuse with the other. This implies that the individual both dissolves and finds himself in the group as a result of a process of identification with others.⁴⁹ If we take the Irish example of those who have vowed to devote themselves to the poor as part of their religious engagement, we may argue that both the marginalized and the people who care for them find their true identity as a result of mutual recognition. Identifying with the group gives a status to those who had none and allows people who place them at the centre of their lives to find themselves as they 'are challenged to look at the masks' they themselves 'are hiding behind'.⁵⁰

All find God as a result, and this induces a change of heart which leads to a spiritual rebirth. Sister Stanislaus Kennedy draws a parallel between '*gardening* the soul' and being alert to nature's cycles through the seasons.⁵¹ In his seminal analysis of what he calls contemporary tribalism, Michel Maffesoli notes that those who feel for nature suggest an alternative model that both signals the decline of a certain type of society and 'calls for an irresistible rebirth'.⁵² Commenting on the will to live and survive at any cost, he further highlights that popular forms of religious piety can be understood as an expression of the need to belong,⁵³ which aptly symbolizes the need for warmth and love that is the essence of life itself. As such they contribute to the restoration of a sense of community in the dehumanized late modern age. This alerts us to the link between the quest for

---

47   Lenoir, *Les métamorphoses de Dieu*, 104–105.
48   Michel Maffesoli, *L'instant éternel* (Paris: La Table Ronde, 2000), 203.
49   Maffesoli, *L'instant éternel*, 67.
50   Sr Stanislaus Kennedy, *Gardening the Soul: Soothing Seasonal Thoughts for Jaded Modern Souls* (Dublin: Townhouse, [2001] 2003), 319.
51   Kennedy, *Gardening the Soul*, 288.
52   Maffesoli, *Le temps des tribus*, 69.
53   Maffesoli, *Le temps des tribus*, 109–110.

rebirth and the care for the earth which has become a key preoccupation for Christians and non-Christians alike in a religious context.

As suggested previously, because the Christian Churches in general and the Catholic Church in particular have systematically tried to deny man's humanity, it has become common to seek religious models in oriental philosophies or in archaic societies. Examples in Ireland include contemporary Celtic Christianity, neo-paganism, Wicca and such an exotic cult as that promoted by the Fellowship of Isis. In this manner, French sociologist Michel Maffesoli argues, contemporary society seeks to redeem life and its diversity, even in its most sulphurous aspects:

> Contre le progressisme judéo-chrétien, s'employant à expliquer (ex-plicare, enlever les plis) toutes choses, s'affirme une pensée 'progressive', sagesse impliquant toutes les manières d'être et de penser, impliquant l'altérité, impliquant l'errance. Voilà bien la mutation post-moderne, celle qui accepte les 'plis' des archaïsmes prémodernes.[54]

The anthropocentrism of the postmodern age has indeed resulted in an overall celebration of life in all its aspects, especially in its emotional dimension. Maffesoli thus explains that the Judeo-Christian legacy became outmoded because it imposed constraints, modesty and asceticism, preached patience and resignation and therefore neglected and even despised the throbbing heart of life.[55] Vitalism stands at the heart of postmodern religious experiments as part of the wish to leave behind the 'totalitarian violence' of Christian universalism. In the eyes of Maffesoli, what has thus re-emerged is 'demonic wisdom', which encompasses all aspects of nature, thus blurring the distinction between good and evil.[56] As in Jung's tradition, Satan is the symbol of the imperfection of God's creation, the fallen angel who causes scandals and fans the flames of what René Girard calls mimetic crises.[57]

---

54 Michel Maffesoli, *La part du Diable* (*Précis de subversion postmoderne*) (Paris: Flammarion, 2002), 15.
55 Michel Maffesoli, *Le rythme de la vie – Variations sur les sensibilités postmodernes* (Paris: La Table Ronde, 2004), 45.
56 Maffesoli, *La part du diable*, 52.
57 René Girard, *Je vois Satan tomber comme l'éclair* (Paris: Grasset, 1999), 63.

Humanity must be reconciled with its imperfect human nature in all its aspects. Mark Patrick Hederman thus criticizes the Catholic Church's systematic denial of man's humanity and calls for the rehabilitation of what he calls 'the proper dark of the Roman Catholic tribe'.[58] Maffesoli sees the defence of multifaceted, sometimes contradictory identities as a central claim of our time, which means accepting evil as part of human nature.[59] As part of such a project, Donal Dorr suggests rethinking sexual morality[60] and claims that it is time for a change.[61] If we follow Jacques Ellul, sexuality has in the past decades acquired a new value in the Western world, connected as it is to what he considers to be the sacralization of the body:

> Le sexe n'est plus un domaine d'activité naturelle libre, il est un instrument de combat – combat pour la liberté. Liberté sexuelle? non point. La liberté tout court [....] Combat pour s'affirmer autonome et apte à vivre en soi, combat contre un ordre: il ne s'agit plus de désacraliser le domaine sexuel mais de désacraliser l'ordre par la transgression sexuelle [....] Mais comme toute force de transgression, elle devient aussitôt sacrée. Seul le sacré peut détruire le sacré.[62]

In a global context, not only are identities fully human but they may become multicultural as identity is chosen as much as inherited. Talking about postmodern religious trends in general, Maffesoli writes: 'I' is a perpetual nomad, who enjoys wearing different masks as he explores 'the plurality of worlds in the social space of polyculturalism' embodied in the polytheism of values. Absolute relativism is a must'.[63] When the priests and priestesses of the Fellowship of Isis dress up as Egyptian or medieval dignitaries, they perfectly exemplify this comment. The taste for exotic disguise also points at the desire to identify with several others "'I" is always somebody else. He is always elsewhere'.[64]

58   Mark Patrick Hederman, *Kissing the Dark* (Dublin: Veritas, 1999), 28.
59   Maffesoli, *La part du diable*, 16–17.
60   Donal Dorr, 'Rethinking Sexual Morality', *The Furrow*, 53–12 (2002), 651–657.
61   Donal Dorr, *Time for a Change: A Fresh Look at Spirituality, Sexuality Globalization and the Church* (Dublin: Columba Press, 2004).
62   Jacques Ellul, *Les nouveaux possédés* (Paris: Mille et une nuits, [1973] 2003), 122–123.
63   Maffesoli, *Le rythme de la vie*, 169–170.
64   Maffesoli, *Le rythme de la vie*, 169–170.

The individual can then invent a new identity or dream he is born to a new life. In extreme cases, such as that of Fellowship of Isis adepts, the devotee no longer has an individualized life. His very existence relies on his connection to others since the overall target is to merge into what may be considered a kind of generic self as defined by Maffesoli.[65] The other makes the individual accede to real life. It may be argued that pilgrim sociabilities have the same effect. Danièle Hervieu-Léger has indeed reached the conclusion that pilgrim religiosity, which has become so fashionable in the Western world under different guises, can be understood as a metaphor of 'an expanding form of religious sociability based on mobility and temporary associations'.[66]

In the model defined by Hervieu-Léger, self-validated beliefs become mutually validated beliefs through communion with others.[67] In the case of Celtic pilgrimages, this communion is based on personal testimonies and the exchange of personal experiences, which gives storytelling and the telling of one's own story a new meaning. Indeed, 'narrative self-construction' becomes the condition allowing the formation of the collective religious identity embodied in the group with which the individual identifies.[68] But it seems that such forms of spirituality largely rest on the fact that the group symbolically shares a territory for the duration of the mystical union. The site of worship is the only 'common denominator' between the worshippers, and this place becomes what Rilke called *Raum der Rühmung*,[69] the location where the glorification is held. In this understanding, the celebration place binds people together in an emotional communion. It actually creates the condition for a religious experience to be shared by creating the bonds that it was the original etymological function of religion to establish.

---

65 Maffesoli, *Le rythme de la vie*, 129.
66 Danièle Hervieu-Léger, *Le pèlerin et le converti* (Paris: Flammarion, 1999), 98.
67 Hervieu-Léger, *Le pèlerin et le converti*, 180–182.
68 Hervieu-Léger, *Le pèlerin et le converti*, 99.
69 Rainer Maria Rilke, 'Nur im Raum der Rühmung darf die Klage', in *Die Sonette an Orpheus*, I https://lyricstranslate.com/en/rainer-maria-rilke-nur-im-raum-der-ruhmung-darf-die-klage-lyrics.html [accessed 11 August 2023].

The concept of 'presenteism' has been used to refer to this aspect of the late modern ethos,[70] which implies the experience and sharing with others of a glimpse of an eternal present subsumed in a given place. Life has become a succession of brief moments of eternity that must be enjoyed as much as possible. This hedonistic ideal is sought within various groups with which the individual chooses to connect and identify for a short period during which he plays an appropriate role. Identities are then fragmented into a series of loose identifications. Nowhere is this phenomenon better exemplified than in Celtic pilgrimages. The only common denominator between the members of loosely connected 'post-modern tribes', as sociologist Michel Maffesoli calls them, may indeed very well be their perception of a 'sense of place', which makes them adopt a territory as part of their cultural and religious identity. The possibility of social connection relies on the existence of a common territory, he says. The territory thus binds together the members of a community.[71] For instance, virtual Ireland clearly plays that role for Celtic neo-pagans on the internet.

When Mark Patrick Hederman seeks to build an underground cathedral as part of his project to reinvent Catholicism,[72] he too contributes to reinventing a connection between religion – in his case the Catholic religion – and the Irish territory. He digs into the earth to root his cathedral deep into the matrix of Ireland, a good illustration of what Maffesoli calls 'the invagination of meaning',[73] which is identifiable in several other contexts. New religious communities, Wiccans, Shamans or other neo-pagans in particular, systematically seek roots in Mother Earth while at the same time inventing founding myths for themselves in which they see a contemporary version of ancient myths. For such people, *Muthos* has superseded *logos* and they connect to what Maffesoli calls 'the emotional memory' of tribal myths.[74] Connectedness and interconnectedness are key notions in this perspective. Sister Stanislaus Kennedy writes that 'we

---

70   Michel Maffesoli, *Notes sur la postmodernité – Le lieu fait lien* (Paris: Le Félin, 2003), 37.
71   Maffesoli, *Notes sur la postmodernité*, 70–76.
72   Mark Patrick Hederman, *Underground Cathedrals* (Dublin: Columba, 2010).
73   Maffesoli, *Le rythme de la vie*, 26.
74   Maffesoli, *L'instant éternel*, 125 and 129.

are interconnected not only here and now, in this time and in this space, but with everything in the past and in the future and into that unknown dimension we call eternity'.[75]

Gilles Lipovetsky argues that contemporary Western societies have in the recent past witnessed the emergence of a seeming need for privileged connections with the distant past, for continuity between past and present and for roots and shared memory.[76] This confirms that imagination and emotion lie at the heart of contemporary perceptions of human beings in their relation to religion or spirituality. Anthropologists and biologists have argued that imagination stands at the core of what it is to be human. In his seminal study of human nature, which he significantly entitled *Le paradigme perdu: la nature humaine*, Edgar Morin thus suggests that *homo sapiens* is also *homo demens*, and that it is precisely man's capacity to go beyond rationality which has allowed the extraordinary development of the human species. Imagination, Morin writes, plays a key role in defining human perceptions of reality. To him, the origin of religious feeling is to be found in the necessity for *sapiens* to be reconciled with death and must be understood as a response provided by imagination to unbearable grief and unacceptable loss. Reality and illusion, objective truth and myth thus go hand in hand, as do absence and presence, or life and death, which can coexist and be reconciled thanks to man's aptitude to be rational and irrational at the same time.[77] Favouring imagination at the expense of reason therefore effectively means going back to origins while denying the legitimacy of the Catholic construct based on reason.

This brief presentation is far from exhaustive but it gives an idea of the benefit to be derived both from the use of French theory and from the diversification of theoretical sources. It also means to attract attention to

75   Sr Stanislaus Kennedy, *Now Is the Time: Spiritual Reflections* (Dublin: Townhouse, 1998), 21.
76   Gilles Lipovetsky, 'Temps contre temps ou la société hypermoderne', in *Les temps hypermodernes*, edited by Gilles Lipovetsky and Sébastien Charles (Paris: Grasset, 2004), 89–90.
77   Edgar Morin, *Le paradigme perdu: la nature humaine* (Paris: Seuil – Points Essais, 1973), 107–126.

the possible diversification of themes or angles of approach to be taken into consideration as part of the academic study of religion in Ireland.

To conclude, we have seen that in spite of widely diverging contexts in France and Ireland, French theory of the 1960s and 1970s has been borrowed to compensate for the initial lack of secular theorization in the sociological field in Ireland. Yet it seems that authors of the following decades have not met with a similar success, which may be due to the increased contribution of Irish scholars to international debates, the loss of influence of French culture in Ireland and the pre-eminence of US or European theory in the field of social sciences.[78] Yet French theory of the late twentieth and early twenty-first century certainly deserves to be taken into consideration for the academic study of religion. It provides an original perspective on the contemporary Irish scene, more and more characterized by the concept of 'exculturation of Catholicism' coined by Danièle Hervieu-Léger to define the French situation and now applicable to Ireland in Hervieu-Léger's own estimation.[79] It remains to be seen if the latest developments in Ireland confirm what Gilles Lipovetsky suggested as early as 2004, that preoccupations with the future have become as important as the reference to the past in our 'hypermodern' society, which he opposes to its postmodern counterpart in that respect.[80] It might certainly be interesting, for instance, to investigate the spiritual dimension of Xtinction rebellion and eco-feminism to assess the relevance of this hypothesis and its expression in the contemporary religious psyche.

---

78   Mostly English-language sources. Among non-English speakers, we can mention the German philosopher Jürgen Habermas and the Swiss sociologist of religions Jörg Stolz.
79   Danièle Hervieu-Léger and Jean-Louis Schlegel, *Vers l'implosion. Entretiens sur le présent et l'avenir du Catholicisme* (Paris: Seuil, 2022), 150.
80   Lipovetsky, 'Temps contre temps ou la société hypermoderne', 71.

PATRICIA MEDCALF

9   1960–1989: The Making of a Guinness Drinker

The dawn of a new era

The first year of any new decade brings with it an air of excitement, hope and anticipation. Those who rang in 1960 could not have predicted that it would herald the start of one of the most eulogized decades in modern history, one that would unleash significant cultural, societal, political and economic change. In 1960, John Fitzgerald Kennedy narrowly defeated Richard Nixon in that year's Presidential Election in the United States, and despite its brevity, his presidency is associated with some of the most memorable events in modern history, most notably the Cuban Missile Crisis and the assassination of a serving US President. Meanwhile, in Ireland Seán Lemass was settling into a seven-year tenure as Taoiseach and Eamon De Valera was the country's only President in the 1960s.

1960 was the year that popular culture embraced Chubby Checker's *The Twist*, a catchy Rock 'n' Roll hit that invited teenagers to twist and contort their bodies in dance moves that caused concern among older generations. Harper Lee's classic, *To Kill a Mockingbird*, was published and movie goers were scared by Hitchcock's *Psycho*. Diego Maradona and Paul Hewson (Bono) were born in 1960, both men capable of eliciting global recognition with one-word names. Also born in 1960 was Eamon Maher, who like Maradona and Bono, is affectionately known by a single name moniker, Ned. A seismic year indeed, one that marked the start of unprecedented change in Ireland and the wider world.

Maher's arrival provided a welcome boost to Munster's declining population, which recorded a 3.2 per cent fall from 877,238 in 1956 to 849,203 in 1961's census. He was one of the 3,372 people residing in the busy market town of Roscrea, Co. Tipperary as recorded in that census.[1] This paper imagines the lessons that Maher might have learned in his formative years from the advertising output of Guinness at a time when there were few restrictions governing the promotion of alcoholic beverages and when the black stuff was still 'Good for you'. This might go some way towards explaining his preference for a pint of plain, his beverage of choice.

The formative years

It is quite possible that up until the age of 6, a visit to the local GP in Roscrea might have been rewarded with a story in the waiting room from Guinness's Doctor's Books series, the first of which were gifted to doctors between 1933 and 1939 and then again between 1950 and 1966. The elaborately illustrated books contained poems and recipes, which were inspired by testimonials from the medical profession backing up the 'Guinness is good for you' proposition. As described in a Guinness Archive fact sheet:

> The themed, lavishly illustrated books notable for their whimsical charm and overt literary parody, contained many lateral – and often ingenious – references to Guinness, both visual and verbal.

What better way to distract and console a young, ailing child in the unfamiliar environs of a waiting room than to read them poems that were brought to life with elaborate and imaginative pictures, while weaving Guinness into the fairy tales? Even if these books evaded him, a ready supply of less fantastical stories about Irish life was unleashed by Guinness in Maher's formative years. The reasons for this can be attributed to economic and social changes, which were triggered in the late 1950s after a prolonged period of stagnation and protectionism.

---

[1] Central Statistics Office, *Census of Population of Ireland 1961, Volume 1: Population, Area and Valuation of each District Electoral Division and of each larger Unit of Area* (CSO, 1963).

Just before Maher's birth, Seán Lemass, then Minister for Industry and Commerce, implemented the seminal 1958 economic programme entitled 'First Programme for Economic Expansion'. It is credited with being the catalyst for Ireland's transformation into an outward-looking, small but open economy. From then on, Ireland actively sought out opportunities with its European neighbours, including France, thus paving the way for Maher to enjoy a long love affair with all things French. Such a stance disrupted societal norms and marked the start of Ireland's transition into an economy fuelled by the industrial and services sectors. By the time Maher was 11 years old, employment in agriculture had fallen from 34.5 per cent of the Irish workforce to 25.9 per cent by 1971.[2]

Meanwhile, in tandem with the change in economic direction, Guinness marked its 200th anniversary in 1959 by creating advertisements aimed specifically at Irish consumers, a practice that gathered momentum throughout the 1960s. Back then, alcohol advertising regulation was light touch or even non-existent. Consequently, some of Maher's earliest memories might have involved the stories told by Guinness in its advertising. An early narrative that was dangled in front of him aligned the brand to Ireland's emerging economy with proud copy lines such as:

> Every day well over five million Guinnesses put new heart into who knows how many Guinness drinkers the world over;
>
> They (Guinness) are proud to be the largest private employer in the Republic, with almost 4,000 staff and employees. It is their policy to buy Irish materials and services where possible.

In 1966, the business journal, *Statist*, published an ad that featured a Guinness bottle with a tag labelled £7,000,000, and body copy recounting how:

> Guinness products account for 26% of all excise revenue. Guinness is Ireland's largest industrial export worth £7,000,000 a year. Guinness is good for Ireland.

---

2 Kieran A. Kennedy and Thomas Giblin, 'Employment', in *The Economy of Ireland: Policy and Performance*, edited by John W. O'Hagan, 5th edn (Dublin: Irish Management Institute, 1987).

To a young child whose uncle was employed by Guinness in St. James's Gate, such declarations made sense.

What made these ads somewhat outside the reach of a young child was that they were published in print format and despite Maher's subsequent mastery of the written word, they would have been beyond his young intellect. However, due to the democratization of the television, an invention that would shape popular culture in Ireland and the developed world in the 1960s and 1970s, this barrier was removed. With perfect timing and just a few months before Maher's second birthday, Ireland's first television broadcasting service was launched on 31st December 1961. Growing up in Roscrea, it was not possible for the Maher household to watch the British TV channels that would have been enjoyed by its Dublin counterparts from 1955 when 40 per cent of the Irish population was able to access British television broadcasts on the BBC and ITV.[3] The latter channel depended on advertising revenue and one of its earliest clients was Guinness, which was quick to embrace TV's potential as a way of bringing its messages to life in a more impactful manner. This might not have been the case if one of Arthur Guinness's descendants, Bryan Guinness's (Lord Moyne), vehement argument against the introduction of commercial television had succeeded. In his searing attack, he posited:

> I believe that the majority of manufacturers would prefer this expensive and extravagant race never to begin; they say very little about it, because if it does begin they realise that they may be forced by the snowball effect of competition to participate, and they do not want to have to eat their words. I, being Irish, have a logical mind, and I see no difficulty at all in saying that I do not want this expensive race to be run, but that if it is run we might be obliged to go in for it and would acquit ourselves creditably. I do urge on the Government the advisability of seeing whether industry as a whole wants this thing started. I am told that it is the most expensive form of advertising in existence in proportion to the results obtained.[4]

---

3   Diarmaid Ferriter, *The Transformation of Ireland 1900 to 2000* (London: Profile Books, 2005), 42.
4   HL Debate, 25 November 1953, Volume 184, column 632 https://api.parliament.uk/historic-hansard/lords/1953/nov/25/television-policy#S5LV0184P0_19531125_HOL_128 [accessed on 4 June 2019].

Rather fittingly from Maher's perspective, Guinness's first TV campaign in Ireland was known as the *Sporting Series*, which commenced in 1963 when he was just 3 years old. It is not difficult to imagine a young child in front of a black and white television set in a sitting room in Roscrea, transfixed, enthralled and influenced by this brand-new medium. The campaign featured hurling (essential for a Tipperary boy), Gaelic Football, cross-country running and cycling. Rugby was absent and its chapter in the Guinness story would have to wait. In all scenarios, the participants pushed themselves to their limits, spurred on by the rewards at the end – possible victory in their chosen pursuits and most definitely a Guinness. They established the link between exertion in sport and the reward of the *après* match conviviality in a pub. The final scenes played out through a fog of smoke and generous servings of Guinness. The ads concluded with varied declarations:

> 'And now, the best moment of all – a Guinness. That puts the strength back into a man. You've earned that Guinness' or 'When you've worked up a real thirst, you need a Guinness.'

While not yet old enough to sample this alluring combination, the seeds were most likely sown in Maher's young mind, ready to germinate when the time was right.

Lessons in love

By the time Maher was eleven, the numbers of married women at work had risen by around 60 per cent, despite a refusal by Jack Lynch's 1968 Government to adopt the 1952 UN convention on the political rights of women. They steadfastly refused to waive the law preventing married women from working in the civil service.[5] As a primary school teacher, Maher's mother was exempt from this law and continued to work,

---

5   Ferriter, *The Transformation of Ireland*, 569.

thus instilling in her family an appreciation of women in Irish society. Meanwhile, between 1965 and 1970, Guinness made women part of the narrative in some of its TV ads. Unusually for that time, women featured in bar scenes, an environ from which they were often discouraged and sometimes prohibited.

One such ad made a lasting impression on 5-year-old Maher. *Young Man – Dublin* featured a happy young couple in a bar. Standing at the bar, the woman followed the man's lead, and asked for a Guinness, but he was given a pint and she a glass. Based on his study of advertising in the US in the 1920s and 1930s, Marchand concluded that it was acceptable to portray women as 'modern' and enjoying 'male' activities, so long as their domestic responsibilities were not neglected.[6] Nonetheless, it was a significant moment because the presence of women drinking in bars in Ireland was a relatively new phenomenon and reflected a gradual change in Irish social mores. More importantly, *Young Man – Dublin* should be viewed as a significant piece of advertising because it heralded Maher's first crush, an unrequited love, which reignited in 2016 when he saw the ad again and was reminded of the object of his early affections. She remains forever young in his mind and signifies a lifelong appreciation of women. The young actress set the benchmark, which was reached, if not surpassed when he met and subsequently married Liz.

Another of Maher's passions, golf, featured in the 1966 ad, *Golfer*. Disappointingly, it did little to further the cause of women in Irish society. Instead, it re-enacted scenes from a typical golf club, most likely on a Saturday when women were not permitted to play golf at private clubs. Times have changed and, in most clubs, women enjoy equal status with men. While his love of golf continues to this day, he combines it with another, Liz, as the couple are known to team up for competitions and social outings.

---

[6] Roland Marchand, *Advertising the American Dream: Making Way for Modernity, 1920–1940* (Berkeley: University of California Press, 1985), 194.

A beginner's guide to the black stuff

While cause and effect are in no way implied, overall alcohol consumption per adult in Ireland increased very significantly in the decades following Maher's birth. Between 1960 and 1991, it rose by 83 per cent.[7] In 1959, alcohol consumption per head of population aged 15 and over, in litres of 100 per cent alcohol, was 4.67; by 1969 it had jumped to 6.80 litres; by 1974 it was 9.44 litres and in the year that Maher turned 18, it had risen again to 9.64 litres. By the time he had reached the legal age for purchasing alcohol in 1978, beer sales were not as dominant as they had been in the 1960s and the popularity of spirits and wine grew. While beer consumption grew to 5.79 litres, its share declined from 73.4 per cent in 1959 to 60 per cent in 1978. Over the same period, the share enjoyed by spirits and wine grew from 23 and 3.4 per cent to 34.75 and 5.8 per cent, respectively.[8]

In the 1970s, Guinness took on its competitors, which all vied for the attention of those who would celebrate their all-important eighteenth birthdays. Its canny marketing team, together with its advertising agency, Arks, acknowledged that Guinness was an acquired taste, one that took longer to acquire than most lagers. Guinness marked the start of the decade with a head-on tackle, which played on its longevity and self-confidence:

> If all these new ales and lagers confuse you – here's something that won't [....] In these changing times, at least one thing hasn't changed. Guinness.

While its taste and ritualistic attributes helped set it apart from its rivals, these did not resonate with many young consumers. The challenge for Arks was to write advertising copy that would transform these perceived

---

[7] Denis Conniffe and Daniel McCoy, *Alcohol Use in Ireland: Some Economic and Social Implications* (Dublin: Economic and Social Research Institute, 1993), General Research Series, paper number 160, xi.

[8] Brendan M. Walsh, *Drinking in Ireland: A Review of Trends in Alcohol Consumption, Alcohol Related Problems and Policies towards Alcohol* (Dublin: The Economic and Social Research Institute, 1980), 5.

negatives into positives. Therefore, the tone of many of Guinness's ads in the 1970s was educational and while he had not yet reached the legal drinking age, Maher might have noticed an ad in 1972, which broke the stout down into its constituent parts. It introduced the 'lesson' by advising the reader:

> But for those who would like to know a little more about Guinness – and cannot spare the time to visit our brewery at St James's Gate – we'd like to point out a few things about this pint. (The ad explained that the head) is cunningly designed to stay with the drink right down to the last drop. (An air of intrigue emerged): You must drink this mysterious darkness up through the head. This is part of the Guinness ritual. Because only by drinking it this way are you able to savour fully the unique Guinness taste – and isn't that why you bought your pint in the first place?

The Guinness foundations were firmly in place for the 17-year-old Maher, so that by 1977, he would probably have been reassured by a very timely ad, which was aimed at young, inexperienced drinkers. It admitted that drinking Guinness is challenging when compared to other drinks but belittled competing ales and lagers by presenting him and his peers with a challenge:

> Almost anybody can tame an ale or a lager. But a Guinness? That's different.

It foregrounded the pint's ingredients as a point of difference:

> Some people will tell you Guinness has a bit of a bite. That's the kiss of the hops. Refreshing. It brings out the true zest in the brewing barley. And it's one of the things that makes a Guinness a Guinness.

To allay any residual anxiety, the ad reassured Maher and other young readers that:

> Once you master that smooth sharp flavour, no ordinary beer will do. So tell your taste buds they're growing up. Who knows – they may even enjoy it.

In another ad, also on the eve of Maher's eighteenth birthday, Arks came up with a headline, which might have piqued his interest:

> The beginner's guide to goodness.

The ad copy within adopted an amicable, empathetic tone:

> Remember when 'a shandy' was as close as you'd come to ordering a drink? Then you moved on to lagers and ales. But sooner or later your taste buds blossom and grow up.

This may have encouraged Maher to ignore gateway lagers and go straight for the 'black stuff'. The tone was reassuring and predicted with great foresight that:

> It could be the beginning of a beautiful friendship.

Surviving recession in 1980s Ireland with a little help from Guinness

The teenage years are seminal in the formation and consolidation of tastes and preferences. So too are the twenties, which play out against the life changing backdrop of place, relationships and career. In 1982, Maher embarked on twelve years of teaching at the renowned secondary school, Clongowes Wood College in Co. Kildare. His time there coincided with one of the worst recessions in Ireland's short history, and he was lucky not to be among the 358,000 who were forced to emigrate between 1981 and 1990 (NESC 1991). This proved significant because while at Clongowes, he met Liz, his wife, and many people who went on to become lifelong friends.

Maher no longer required lessons in how to consume the black stuff, but Guinness could still reassure him in different ways. He needed to save money for marriage and a mortgage, but he knew from its ads in the early eighties, that Guinness was good value. It empathized with Irish adults by acknowledging, not ignoring, the dire economic circumstances that pervaded Irish consumers. In one such ad, a pint and a tankard glass of Guinness were set against a newspaper bearing the headline:

> Gloomy Forecast for '82 – Year of the drop.

While taxes rose and disposable income continued to drop, so too did the price of a pint of Guinness. Other headlines early in the 1980s included:

> A valuable pint (and) Take the smooth with the rough. Guinness. First and Lasts.

The entire series of ads signed off with the attention-grabbing tagline:

> You can't beat a Guinness for good value.

What better way for Maher to enjoy the company of new friends than with a Guinness, safe in the knowledge that it would not break the bank at a time of economic hardship.

Conclusion

This paper does not in any way suggest that Maher's life has been governed by his preference for Guinness over other alcoholic beverages. However, it does speak to his love of friendship and social interaction, much of which is enacted in a pub, the best place to enjoy a Guinness and conviviality. Why does he prefer a pint of the black stuff to other beers? Is it because he was born just eight months after Guinness first launched a series of ads aimed at the Irish market, an endeavour that continues to this day. Is it because of the lack of advertising regulation when he was a child? Is it because he might have watched the early adopters of television advertising in Ireland (with Guinness being amongst them) when Teilifís Éireann was launched on 31 December 1961, just short of his second birthday? Is it because Guinness produced such memorable ads that resonated with its audience? Or is it simply because of its flavour and innate ritualistic powers? Answers to these questions are beyond the remit of this author, but it does not really matter. Eamon Maher is loyal friend, colleague and mentor to those who know him and his contribution to

Irish academia is beyond dispute. What harm if some of his best ideas were hatched over a pint of Guinness?[9]

9   Unless otherwise stated, all copy from print and TV ads cited in this paper are reproduced with permission of the Guinness Archive, Diageo Ireland. Guinness adverts have changed over the years and they are continually evolving to take into account the changing society, advertising rules, as well as the internal standards, that make Diageo a responsible business. These adverts may contain historical product claims that are not now endorsed by Diageo. In making those adverts available, the intention is not to promote the benefits of drinking, but to show Guinness advertising over more than forty years.

SYLVIE MIKOWSKI

10 Children in Recent Irish Fiction

Many critics have noted as an obvious fact the centrality of the theme of children and childhood in contemporary Irish literature, whether it be through the publication of numerous memoirs and autobiographies, or of novels revolving around a child or adolescent character. According to those same critics, James Joyce's *A Portrait of the Artist as a Young Man* is the seminal,[1] foundational example of a childhood narrative in Irish fiction, which set the trend for a long time, an opinion expressed by Ciaran O'Neill and by Jane Elizabeth Dougherty in their respective chapters called 'The Irish Schoolboy Novel' and 'Mary Robinson and the Irish Literary Childhood', published in *Children, Childhood and Irish Society 1500 to the Present*,[2] a collection edited by Maria Luddy and James M. Smith. The volume is one of the few recent books actually devoted to the topic of childhood in Ireland, despite the claims to the importance of the topic as mentioned above, and despite especially the dramatic import of the revelations brought to light over the recent decades regarding the ill-treatment of children by the Irish state, with the tacit complicity of Irish ordinary people. Joseph Valente and Margot Gayle Backus, however, have made this the subject of their fascinating study *The Child Sex Scandal and Modern Irish Literature: Writing the Unspeakable*,[3] in which they apply psychoanalytical concepts to the reading of a few contemporary novels,

---

1 James Joyce, *A Portrait of the Artist as a Young Man* (1916) (New York: Viking Press, 1964).
2 Maria Luddy and James M. Smith (eds), *Children, Childhood and Irish Society, 1500 to the Present* (Dublin: Four Courts Press, 2014).
3 Joseph Valente and Margot Gayle Backus, *The Child Sex Scandal and Modern Irish Literature: Writing the Unspeakable* (Bloomington: Indiana University Press, 2020).

such as Edna O'Brien's *The Country Girls*,[4] Keith Ridgway's *The Long Falling*,[5] Tana French's *In the Woods*,[6] and Anne Enright's *The Gathering*.[7] Their thesis is that literature, and especially narrative fiction, can express the kind of trauma that society is either unable or unwilling to confront.

However, neither of these two very valuable volumes offers a survey of the diversity and plurality of the recent or not-so-recent production of childhood narratives in Ireland; indeed, their subject is either broader, as in the case of the first one, which embraces not only literary but also sociological and political aspects of childhood in Ireland through time; whereas Valente and Backus have adopted the single angle of child sexual abuse. There is no denial that what the authors call 'the child sex scandal' – meaning either child abuse at the hands of public institutions, such as the Catholic Church, or incest – looms large in recent Irish fiction, and other examples could be added to the list of works dissected in the volume (even if some are indeed alluded to) such as John McGahern's *The Dark*,[8] Edna O'Brien's *A Pagan Place*[9] and *Down by the River*,[10] Patrick McCabe's *The Butcher Boy*,[11] or Eimear McBride's *A Girl is a Half-Formed Thing*.[12] However, not all childhood narratives are about sexual abuse: first, other forms of child ill-treatment, such as neglect, lack of love, authoritarianism and brutality, are pictured in such stories or novels as John McGahern's *Amongst Women*,[13] 'Korea',[14] or in Claire Keegan's *Foster*.[15] The less harrowing genre of the novel of maturation, of the Bildungsroman, is also one of the

---

4 Edna O'Brien, *The Country Girls* (London: Hutchinson, 1960).
5 Keith Ridgway, *The Long Falling* (New York: Houghton Mifflin, 1999).
6 Tana French, *In the Woods* (New York: Penguin Viking, 2007).
7 Anne Enright, *The Gathering* (London: Jonathan Cape, 2005).
8 John McGahern, *The Dark* (London: Faber & Faber, 1965).
9 Edna O'Brien, *A Pagan Place* (London: Penguin Books, 1970).
10 Edna O'Brien, *Down by the River* (London: Farrar, Strauss & Giroux, 1992).
11 Patrick McCabe, *The Butcher Boy* (London: Picador, 1992).
12 Eimear McBride, *A Girl is a Half-Formed Thing* (London: Galley Beggar Press, 2013).
13 John McGahern, *Amongst Women* (London: Faber & Faber, 1990).
14 John McGahern, 'Korea', in *The Collected Stories* (New York: Vintage International, 1994).
15 Claire Keegan, *Foster* (London: Faber & Faber, 2010).

most frequent modes of narrating childhood in recent Irish fiction, about which a difference should be established between boys' childhoods, and the portrayal of Irish girlhood.

Again, it is often recognized that Joyce's *A Portrait* inaugurated the first category, in which we can place, among others, Frank O'Connor's collection of short stories *My Oedipus Complex*,[16] but also nearer to our times Seamus Deane's *Reading in the Dark*,[17] Glenn Patterson's *Burning Your Own*,[18] Roddy Doyle's *Paddy Clarke Ha Ha Ha*[19] or Hugo Hamilton's *The Speckled People*.[20] Each novel in its own different way exposes the sometimes difficult apprenticeship of masculinity in the context of either the Northern Ireland Troubles or of the Republic. The very word 'girl' on the other hand raises issues as to the expectations and pressures confronting young Irish women growing up. Here the template is perhaps Elizabeth Bowen's repeated portrayals of orphaned girls growing unwanted in a world full of constraints for women. But the genre of the Irish girlhood narrative was further defined by Edna O'Brien's *The Country Girls*, Nuala O'Faolain's *Are You Somebody?*,[21] or Éilís Ní Dhuibhne's *The Dancers Dancing*,[22] even though one can notice that examples of female *Bildungsroman* are fewer than male ones. These might also be overshadowed by the number of horrific female childhoods, punctuated by violence and abuse, such as recorded by Eimear McBride in *A Girl is a Half-Formed Thing*, Mia Gallagher in *Hellfire*,[23] or Anna Burns in *No Bones*.[24]

Here again, the context of either the Catholic, conservative Republic of Ireland, or that of the Northern Ireland Troubles, makes a difference and should condition our interpretation. Another distinction which should be

---

16 Frank O'Connor, *My Oedipus Complex and Other Stories* (London: Penguin Books, 1963).
17 Seamus Deane, *Reading in the Dark* (London: Jonathan Cape, 1996).
18 Glenn Patterson, *Burning Your Own* (London: Chatto and Windus, 1988).
19 Roddy Doyle, *Paddy Clarke Ha Ha Ha* (London: Minerva, 1994).
20 Hugo Hamilton, *The Speckled People* (London: HarperCollins, 2000).
21 Nuala O'Faolain, *Are You Somebody?* (New York: Henry Holt and Company, 1996).
22 Éilís Ní Dhuibhne, *The Dancers Dancing* (Belfast: Blackstaff Press, 2000).
23 Mia Gallagher, *Hellfire* (London: Penguin, 2006).
24 Anna Burns, *No Bones* (London: Flamingo, 2001).

made is perhaps between the character of a naive, innocent, lovable child, in keeping with the tradition inherited from the Victorian construction of childhood, and that of the deviant, 'queer', uncanny child, the template for which in late twentieth-century fiction would be Patrick McCabe's *The Butcher Boy*, another example being Emma Donoghue's *The Wonder*,[25] but also Jan Carson's *The Fire Starters*.[26]

The character of the innocent child raises the issue of ignorance and knowledge, in a society constrained by secrets, prohibitions, and repressions, many involving sexual conduct, but also more political matters, such as the involvement of one part of society in violent terrorist action in the past. The child is thus very often used as a kind of sleuth whose acute sense of observation allows him/her to decipher the signs leading to hidden truths. Seamus Deane's *Reading in the Dark* would be a perfect illustration of this trend, but Claire Keegan's *Foster*, recently adapted for the screen as *The Quiet Girl*, to a certain extent also meets the definition.[27]

The innocent child, according to Locke's view of the child as *tabula rasa*, a blank slate, must also be trained and educated in the principles underlying the state and its quasi-official religion, hence the number of Irish narratives focusing on the context of an educational institution, whether the convent school in Kate O'Brien's *Land of Spices*,[28] the Christian Brothers' school in John McGahern's story 'The Recruiting Officer',[29] or Doyle's *Paddy Clarke Ha Ha Ha*, the industrial school in *The Butcher Boy*, or the Irish summer camp in *The Dancers Dancing*. This last novel also highlights the role of the Irish language in the transmission of the national values the Irish child is meant to absorb, both inside the family circle and outside, so that nationalism, family conflicts and the Irish language all get combined in the child's predicament, as in Deane's *Reading in the Dark* or Hugo Hamilton's *The Speckled People*. What's more, in those two novels the emphasis on the Irish language lying at the core of the child's upbringing and awakening raises a more profound and universal question about the

---

25 Emma Donoghue, *The Wonder* (New York: Little Brown, 2016).
26 Jan Carson, *The Fire Starters* (Dublin: Doubleday, 2019).
27 *An Cailín Ciúin* (*The Quiet Girl*), directed by Colm Bairéad, 2022.
28 Kate O'Brien, *The Land of Spices* (1941) (London: Virago Press, 2006).
29 John McGahern, 'The Recruiting Officer', in *The Collected Stories*.

possibility for literature to recreate the voice and the consciousness of a child, who is first of all a being who cannot yet speak. The French word *enfant*, like the English one *infant*, both derive from the Latin *infans*, one who cannot speak, thus inviting a reflection upon the origins of language, as was undertaken by the Italian philosopher Georgio Agamben in his book *Infancy and History*: 'infancy', he argues, 'is the state of being human outside of language use.'[30] Much of the challenge for the writer of a childhood narrative is therefore to articulate an experience which by definition is, to use Valente's and Backus' word, 'unspeakable'.

First of all, I am using the phrase 'childhood narratives' to refer to either memoirs and autobiographies or fictional stories revolving around one or several child characters. As many commentators have noted, there was an outpouring of Irish memoirs and autobiographies published in the 1990s, at a time when Ireland reinvented itself as a liberal society, both in the sense that it embraced a hard-core version of economic neoliberalism, and started to adopt the societal standards of other advanced capitalist nations, allowing the citizens to indulge their individual desires without the control of state and church. Jane Elizabeth Dougherty links the renewed attraction for childhood narratives in the 1990s to the advent of Mary Robinson's presidency, noting that 'the maturation narratives that attended the Irish presidency of Robinson can be described as an "outpouring" not only in terms of the sheer number of books published but also in the enthusiastic reception that continues to greet this now-characteristic national genre'.[31] She proceeds to distinguish three different sub-genres of Irish childhoods, 'the sensational, the sentimental, and the lyric', including in this last category Frank McCourt's *Angela's Ashes*,[32] a much discussed and contested 'memoir'. Roy F. Foster for one has ironically expressed doubt about the authenticity of McCourt's narrative of a miserable childhood in 1950s

---

30 Giorgio Agamben, *Infancy and History, the Destruction of Experience*, translated by Liz Heron (London: Verso, 1993), 4.
31 Jane Elizabeth Dougherty, 'Coming of Age in the 1990s: Mary Robinson and the Irish Literary Childhood', in *Children, Childhood and Irish Society 1500 to the Present*, edited by Maria Luddy and James M. Smith (Dublin: Four Courts Press, 2014), 346.
32 Frank McCourt, *Angela's Ashes* (London: Flamingo, 1999).

Limerick, arguing that the book was designed for an American readership eager to be confirmed in their stereotyped imaginings of Ireland: 'the McCourt *œuvre*', he argues, 'apparently trading on misery, actually sells on synthetic moral uplift, contributing to the genre of idealized Irish personal history [...]. This partly relies on a determinedly unreal approach to present-day Ireland.'[33] Conversely, such fictional narratives as Edna O'Brien's *The Country Girls*, or entire passages from John McGahern's *The Leavetaking* were directly inspired by the writers' own memories of their childhood, as became obvious when these writers finally published their 'true' autobiography: Edna O'Brien entitled hers *Country Girl* in direct reference to the 1960s trilogy, and whole pages from McGahern's *Memoir*[34] correspond almost word for word with pages from *The Leavetaking*,[35] especially in the chapters recording the author's mother's death and the necessity for the young boy to leave her house in order to move in with his father in the police barracks.

The word 'childhood' might prove tricky as well, in so far as many of the narratives in question actually stage characters on the verge of adolescence, or situated at an age when the border between childhood and adolescence becomes blurred, in relation to puberty and the character's gradual awakening to sexuality. The protagonist's age can be problematic when he/she becomes the victim of a predator who violates a time of life defined by Freud as the latency period. Thus if 13-year-old Orla in *The Dancers Dancing* naturally opens up to the attractiveness of boys – one of the possible meanings of 'dancing' – the girl's psyche in Eimear McBride's novel is half-destroyed by the sexual assault by an older man she suffers at about the same age. We are not told the exact age of McGahern's narrator in *The Dark*, but we know that at the end of the book he enters university, which situates the prior events before the age of 18 and suggests that the narrative takes the protagonist from childhood to adolescence.

From another perspective, whether those stories can be described as narratives of childhood or of youth, seldom do they display any reference

33 Roy F. Foster, 'Selling Irish Childhoods', in *The Irish Story: Telling Tales and Making it up in Ireland* (Oxford: OUP, 2002), 174.
34 John McGahern, *Memoir* (London: Faber & Faber, 2005).
35 John McGahern, *The Leavetaking* (London: Faber & Faber, 1974).

to youth culture, even though the second half of the twentieth century saw the blooming of such a phenomenon, and as much as invented the character of the teenager: as Michael G. Cronin argues about O'Brien's *The Country Girls* and McGahern's *The Dark*, those Sixties novels contain no echo of the youth culture that became so vibrant at the time, as was reflected, he says, in the 'great crowds that thronged the Irish concerts of The Beatles in 1963 and The Rolling Stones in 1965'.[36] In *The Dancers Dancing* for instance, which is supposed to take place in 1972, the children are taught to dance traditional Irish dances at the daily *céilidh*; and even in such an up-to-date novel as Sally Rooney's *Normal People*,[37] Marianne and Connell's social life before they move to Dublin takes place in the very traditional local pub or dance-hall. Even though *Conversations with Friends*[38] could be said to reflect global youth culture more accurately, through its emphasis on social networks for instance, Frances and Bobbi's favourite activity seems to be performing in poetry-readings, again more in line with the Irish tradition of story-telling than with global youth cultures.

This seeming attachment to traditionally Irish forms of culture is revealing of the difficulties experienced by most children or adolescents in those contemporary narratives to emancipate themselves from their national and familial environment. This seems to contradict the set pattern of the Bildungsroman, an aesthetic model to which the Irish novel is often said to adhere: according to Fintan O'Toole for instance, 'the novel of growing up, from James Joyce's *A Portrait* to John McGahern's *The Dark* and Edna O'Brien's *The Country Girls*, is the quintessential Irish form'.[39] Joseph Campbell famously insisted that the narrative of education was based on what he called the 'monomyth' of the 'hero's journey', claiming that 'the standard path of the mythological adventure of the hero is a magnification of the formula represented in the rites of

---

36 Michael G. Cronin, 'Arrested Development: Sexuality, Trauma and History in Edna O'Brien and John McGahern', in *Impure Thoughts: Sexuality, Catholicism and Literature in Twentieth-Century Ireland* (Manchester: Manchester UP, 2012), 176.
37 Sally Rooney, *Normal People* (London: Hogarth, 2019).
38 Sally Rooney, *Conversation with Friends* (London: Hogarth, 2017).
39 Fintan O'Toole, 'Why Irish Writers Don't Grow Out of Adolescence', *The Irish Times*, November 6, 2010, 8.

passage: separation – initiation – return'.[40] But in many Irish youth narratives, the journey is either impossible or a circular one, the template being set again by Joyce in the story 'Eveline', in which the young woman, instead of fleeing the tyranny, exploitation and abuse ruining her life at home in Dublin, finds herself incapable of following her fiancé to Argentina. Even in such a hyped version of the Irish Bildungsroman as Rooney's *Normal People*, Marianne's trajectory, which initially takes her from a similarly oppressive home to emancipation through success at university in the big city, finally ends up nowhere but in Ireland, with an uncertain future ahead of her, whereas her boyfriend Connell sets off to the United States.

John McGahern also repeatedly illustrated the pattern of the failed *Bildungsroman*. Young Mahoney in *The Dark* manages to journey from his rural home to the capital city, but finally chooses a dull, inglorious job as a clerk, rather than indulging in dreams of escape and social elevation. The Moran daughters constantly return to the site of their less-than-happy childhood at Great Meadow in *Amongst Women*, from the places they have established themselves, whether it be Dublin or London.

Another aspect of the *Bildungsroman* is the capacity to assert one's own identity and to find one's place in society, a goal that the protagonists of recently published tales of child sexual abuse, either by McCabe, Anne Enright in *The Gathering*, Eimear McBride, or Mia Gallagher in *Hellfire*, etc., do not manage to achieve, revealing the persisting incapacity of Irish society to nurture its young and to favour their independence, as if Stephen Dedalus' view of his country as being defined by the 'three nets' of nationality, language and religion, was still relevant at the turn of the twenty-first century. However, as Shahriyar Mansouri in her PhD dissertation argues, the failed Bildungsroman has a powerful subversive function: by deviating from the standards of the genre, 'the modern Irish Bildungsroman is a radical literary vehicle that reveals a history that the conservative Irish society

---

40   Joseph Campbell, *The Hero with a Thousand Faces*, 2nd edn, Vol. 1 (Princeton: Princeton UP, 1968), 30.

decided not to acknowledge', and therefore can be defined as 'a resistant critical structure'.[41]

However, within the genre itself a distinction must be made between male and female novels of formation, since, as Jane Elizabeth Dougherty puts it, 'Few readers, whether casual or scholarly, can readily name an example of the Irish literary girlhood – unsurprisingly, as there are not many from which to choose.'[42] What's more, Dougherty discusses the peculiar use of the word 'girl' in an Irish context, a word which tellingly appears in the titles of O'Brien's trilogy as well as in Mc Bride's *A Girl is a Half-Formed Thing*, a phrase alluding to the idea of an incomplete, or impossible, formation for female children and adolescents. The phrase strangely echoes Cait's cry in O'Brien's *The Country* Girls, when she exclaims: 'But we're not females, we're girls', a phrase pointing at the in-betweenness of girlhood in Ireland.[43] 'Girls' have indeed not yet reached the age when their function as women is defined by society, as was done in the most official manner by the 1937 Constitution, which insisted on women's reproductive role, legally and politically confining women to what Simone de Beauvoir called their biological fate. The under-age female thus finds herself deprived of a proper identity and place until she can play her part. This situation is aptly illustrated by the film adaptation of Keegan's *Foster*, where the 'quiet girl's' presence in the family home goes literally unnoticed by her parents when she returns and they don't speak a word or spare a look at her, whereas the mother is overburdened by her numerous pregnancies.

The 'biological fate' embodied by the mother is a much dreaded or even rejected role-model in many narratives of Irish girlhood. This mother, often shown to be harassed by children and housework, proves unable to protect her children from the dangers of the outside world: in Paul Lynch's *Grace*,[44] the mother throws her daughter out of the house, arguably to save

---

41 Shahriyar Mansouri, 'The Modern Irish *Bildungsroman*: A Narrative of Resistance and Deformation' (PhD thesis, University of Glasgow, 2014), http://theses.gla.ac.uk/5495/ [accessed 24 October 2023].
42 Jane Elizabeth Dougherty, 'Nuala O'Faolain and the Unwritten Irish Girlhood', *New Hibernia Review / Iris Éireannach Nua*, 11/2 (Summer 2007), 50–65.
43 Edna O'Brien, *The Country Girls*, 72.
44 Paul Lynch, *Grace* (London: Little, Brown & Co, 2017).

her from the assaults of the landlord, but exposing her to even greater threats as famine is breaking out. In *The Gathering*, the mother is too distracted to notice what is happening to her son Liam; in *Foster*, the child narrator is sent away to distant cousins because her mother is expecting yet another baby and has little affection to bestow on the elder children. Mothers also seem obsessed by the family's reputation, forcing their daughters to conform to social norms, even in the middle of a civil strife, like the mother in Anna Burns' *Milkman*[45] who worries that 'middle-daughter' might be seen to be dating a married man, who is actually a dangerous stalker. In McBride's *A Girl is a Half-Formed Thing*, the mother is half-crazed by religious devotion, which blinds her to her daughter's predicament as she is raped by a male relative that the mother herself introduced into the home. Like so many other female characters in Irish fiction, Rooney's Marianne in *Normal People* is betrayed by a mother who is supposed to be a care-giver but proves either indifferent or neglectful, failing to protect her from her brother's violence, and driving her daughter to deep psychological instability.

This almost stereotyped depiction of the Irish mother has a counterpart in that of the brutal, impotent or absent father who looms large in boys' narratives. John McGahern set the trend for the depiction of the tyrannical, violent father who jeopardizes his son's future, as in 'Korea' where the father speculates on the financial compensation he would receive if his son died on the front line in Korea. In *The Butcher Boy* the father indulges in the ultimate form of abandonment by committing suicide. In Roddy Doyle's *The Woman who Walked into Doors*[46] and its sequence, *Paula Spencer*,[47] the father is the stereotype of the drunkard who gambles away the family's little money. As Michael G. Cronin puts it in conclusion to his study, recent Irish novels 'still attest to the enduring power of the narrative of family failure in Irish literature',[48] an opinion shared by Vivian Valvano Lynch discussing what she calls 'The Toxic Parents of Claire Keegan's Fiction':

---

45 Anna Burns, *Milkman* (London: Faber & Faber, 2018).
46 Roddy Doyle, *The Woman Who Walked into Doors* (London: Penguin Books, 1997).
47 Roddy Doyle, *Paula Spencer* (London: Viking, 2006).
48 Cronin, 'Arrested Development', 210.

'What should be going on in her settings', she writes, 'is the protection of and caring for the most innocent and vulnerable family members, that is, the children – however real the surrounding poverty and hardships may be. But many of Keegan's adults fail miserably at this basic human charge, some to the point of depravity.'[49]

In fiction from the North, however, domestic troubles combine with political ones to further deprive children of the protection and security they need. In *Burning your Own*, Glenn Patterson offered an example of a child confronted by the upsetting events taking place inside as well as outside his home, as strife and hostility tear his parents and the communities around him apart. In his efforts to make sense of these events, he is guided by Francie, a kind of wild child who instructs Mal in the intricacies of the history of the place and the distant causes of the conflict. Patterson's use of a child's point of view here serves the traditional purpose of naturalizing a realist depiction of the Troubles, meant to present the reader with facts and explanations. The child as bearer of the hermeneutic function of interpreting the apparently incoherent events happening around him is also central to Seamus Deane's *Reading in the Dark* where the young protagonist must literally translate from a forgotten, mysterious language – Irish – to accede the truth about his family history, revolving around the Northern Irish conflict.

On the other hand, the child's misapprehension of the events unfolding around him/her casts light upon the meaninglessness and intractability of the Troubles. Depicting the world through a candid-like consciousness that is still innocent, naive and unbiased allows the writer to expose and critique the absurdities of the conflict. In Anna Burns' *No Bones*, young Amelia remains in the dark as to exactly what is happening around her: 'Amelia stopped trying to explain. Some people just did things differently. The women in the household apparently had their own ideas about these house-burnings and about this war.'[50] In Kenneth Brannagh's recent film *Belfast*, the child's naive and ignorant point of view, when it comes to making out

---

[49] Vivian Valvano Lynch, "Families Can Be Awful Places': The Toxic Parents of Claire Keegan's Fiction', *New Hibernia Review / Iris Éireannach Nua*, Earrach, 19/1 (Spring 2015), 131–146.
[50] Anna Burns, *No Bones*, 4.

the difference between Catholics and Protestants for instance, highlights the absurdity of sectarian hatred, a point already made by Joyce at the beginning of *A Portrait* when Stephen wonders why Dante, the staunch Catholic woman, does not like him to play with Eileen, the Protestant girl he likes:

> And she did not like him to play with Eileen because Eileen was a protestant and when she was young she knew children that used to play with protestants and the protestants used to make fun of the litany of the Blessed Virgin. *Tower of Ivory*, they used to say, *House of Gold!* How could a woman be a tower of ivory or a house of gold? Who was right then?[51]

However, the traditional image of the naive or innocent child in Irish fiction is in several instances substituted by the more disturbing figure of the uncanny child. Jessica Balanzateguy has analysed the figure of the uncanny child in transnational cinema. She argues that

> the uncanny child becomes a potent embodiment of trauma [...] she becomes associated with repressed – or oppressed – historical traumas and derails politically sanctioned narratives of national progress and development [....] Within the narratives of all of the films I discuss, the children are usually victims of trauma, or at least have privileged insight into traumatic experience. More than this, they come to harness this trauma and propel it back into the realm of adult experience, subverting their victimized position to become threatening and powerful through their very trauma.[52]

The description matches the scenario of McCabe's *The Butcher Boy*. Francie Brady is a horror figure, a child turned monster, who was initially abandoned by parents who were themselves victims of the state's inability to provide for the citizens' welfare. Francie was then abused at the hands of the institutions in charge of him, especially the Catholic clergy, before he turned against society by savagely killing Mrs Nugent, who embodied the values upheld by a bourgeois, conservative state and was therefore complicit in the failure of Francie Brady's parents and the boy's subsequent imprisonment in an industrial school.

51 Joyce, *A Portrait of the Artist as a Young Man*, 42–43.
52 Jessica Balanzategui, 'The Child as Uncanny Other', in *The Uncanny Child in Transnational Cinema: Ghosts of Futurity at the Turn of the Twenty-First Century* (Amsterdam: Amsterdam University Press, 2018), 9–28.

Jan Carson recently provided a revised version of the uncanny child through what she herself defines as 'magical realism' in *The Fire Starters* and in *The Raptures*,[53] both featuring children endowed with supernatural features. *The Fire Starters* is set in Belfast in the context of the Post-Troubles era, and Carson imagines that the threat of a new outburst of violence in the Province, rekindled by Brexit, has become true, engineered by the city's children, who seem to make the fathers pay for their past sins. In keeping with Balazanteguy's definition of the uncanny child, the fire-starters thus become 'potent embodiments of trauma': Sammy, a former Loyalist paramilitary thug, discovers that his son is the one who encourages the young to destroy the city, as if in retribution for his father's criminal past. Jonathan, Carson's other protagonist, is also confronted by his daughter's monstrosity. The offspring of a human and a siren, the little girl threatens to grow up a siren herself and use her bewitching song to lead people to their destruction, an image Carson drew from mythology to suggest the nefarious effects of discourse and language in the context of the Troubles. In her next novel, *The Raptures*, Carson has imagined how the children of a community of evangelist Protestants are decimated by a strange disease, again seemingly in retribution for their parents' errors, and are resurrected in a parallel world. Carson thus resorts to the trope of the ghost-child, which Balazanteguy analyses as 'empower(ing) a previously repressed traumatic experience from the past to reemerge in, and disrupt, the present',[54] in keeping with Northern Ireland's present condition, where the hope of a better future seems constantly stalled by pathological returns to the conflictual past.

Ireland's traumatic past is also embodied by eerie children in Paul Lynch's *Grace* and Emma Donoghue's *The Wonder*, both evoking the Famine and its consequences. In *Grace*, the 14-year-old girl is not a threat herself but her fate does arouse the anxiety caused by the irruption of the unfamiliar in the guise of the familiar, according to Freud's definition of the uncanny. Her journey takes her from a most familiar place – her mother's house – to a most unfamiliar world – Ireland made strange and nightmarish

---

53   Jan Carson, *The Raptures* (London: Doubleday, 2022).
54   Balanzateguy, 'The Child as Uncanny Other', 19.

by starvation and death, as Grace encounters the most horrific signs of devastation on her way. In the process, the girl morphs into an uncanny version of herself: first, she dresses up as a boy, then she becomes capable of ventriloquism when her interior monologue becomes split between her own and that of her brother after he dies. Grace's connection with the uncanny is also enhanced by her superstitious beliefs in supernatural beings and apparitions, as well as the kind of trance she falls into after she is taken ill and is subject to delirium. The experience of the uncanny embodied by Grace is meant to stir in the readers' minds the anxiety accompanying the return of a repressed memory, in this case that of the Irish Famine.

Emma Donoghue also used the figure of an uncanny child in the context of the post-Famine era in *The Wonder*, set in rural Ireland but based on the real story of Sarah Jacob, a Welsh girl who in the nineteenth century claimed to have lived without food for several years. Here the homely and the unhomely also get mixed: 10-year-old Anna, whose condition people regard as a religious miracle, is in fact secretly fed by her mother every time she gives her a kiss, as the English nurse sent over to test her finally finds out. The nurse also discovers that Anna was in fact the victim of incest at the hands of her brother, a crime covered up by her parents. As a result, Lin Elinor Pettersson interprets Anna's 'fasting body as a site where the rhetoric of anorexia nervosa testifies to the traumatic consequences of incest',[55] thus exemplifying again the role of the uncanny child in re-enacting trauma. Interestingly, Pettersson also reads this historical drama as an indictment of the contemporary myth of the Irish family, which echoes Balazanteguy's claim that the uncanny child disrupts the narrative of linear progress in time: 'the horrifying qualities of the uncanny child figures', she argues, 'are located in their simultaneous resistance to national, cultural, and individual "growth"'.[56] In other words, Donoghue's nineteenth-century tale of the miracle child disrupts the contemporary national narrative of a mature society, who has supposedly grown out of a past fraught with poverty, famine, superstition and family abuse.

[55] Line Elinor Pettersson, 'Neo-Victorian Incest Trauma and the Fasting Body', *Nordic Irish Studies*, 16 (2017), 8.
[56] Pettersson, 'Neo-Victorian Incest Trauma and the Fasting Body', 22.

As Jane E. Dougherty puts it, Mary Robinson's tenure as president was indeed accompanied by 'metaphors of maturation, whether the image is of national rebirth, [...] or of national coming-of-age, with a young Ireland finally maturing'.[57] If we consider like Dougherty does, that the Irish child is used in literature and culture as a metaphor for the nation, then the number of recent childhood narratives seems to suggest that this maturing process is not yet quite achieved. However, this number may also signify that Irish people are now free to face the facts that were hushed and repressed for so long, a phenomenon also present in other Western countries following the #MeToo movement and the 'liberation of speech' which followed. The freedom to discuss the up-to-then repressed issue of the treatment of children in Ireland, but also the need to process the appalling revelations made in the early decades of the twenty-first century – such as the discovery of the mass graveyard containing the remains of unnamed small children at the Tuam Mother and Baby Home – drove artist and writers in particular to devise the proper aesthetic means to express and represent the extent of suffering, neglect, and cruelty, experienced by Irish children, and which became publicly exposed.

As a result, many contemporary narratives – even if some continue to resort to traditional realism, like Claire Keegan, or Emma Donoghue – employ innovative, if not experimental, stylistic devices to 'speak the unspeakable', to use Jane E. Dougherty's and Valente's and Backus' phrase. Joyce inaugurated the process in the first pages of *A Portrait* in which he imitated the way a child will wonder about the meaning of words:

> *Dieu* was the French for God and that was God's name too; and when anyone prayed to God and said Dieu then God knew at once that it was a French person that was praying. But though there were different names for God in all the different languages in the world and God understood what all the people who prayed said in their different languages still God remained always the same God and God's real name was God.[58]

---

57 Dougherty, 'Mary Robinson and the Irish Literary Childhood', 339.
58 Joyce, *A Portrait of the Artist as a Young Man*, 6.

John McGahern experimented with the use of the second-person pronoun 'you' throughout *The Dark*, as if to distance the homodiegetic narrator, whom we guess to be very close to himself as a child, from the terrible events he relates. Eimear McBride has often been compared to James Joyce in her use of the stream of consciousness, which disrupts ordinary language, thus reflecting a chaotic, disturbed mind. Paul Lynch has devised a lyric, unheard-of language – often resorting to neologisms – to mirror Grace's similarly disturbed flow of consciousness. As said before, Jan Carson mixes plain realism with surreal characters and events; Anna Burns in *Milkman*, like McBride, experiments with language, her style being based not on fragmentation but on systematic euphemisms and set formulae. In *Foster*, in which Keegan mixes plain English and Hiberno-English, as if in search of a new language, one obnoxious neighbour says to Kinsella: 'She's a quiet young one, this', to which Kinsella replies: 'She says what she has to say, and no more.'[59]

The exchange draws attention to the meaningful balance between language and silence in the context of not just child sexual abuse in Ireland, but more generally of the way that children, contrary to what the Church and the state claimed, were the first category of Irish citizens who failed to be well cared for and protected by its institutions. It was the writers' task to give a voice to those silent victims, to all those 'quiet' girls and boys, and to make that voice as clear and beautiful as possible.

---

59   Keegan, *Foster*, 59.

MARISOL MORALES-LADRÓN

11   Nuala O'Connor's *Nora* and the Challenges of Biographical Fiction[1]

In the introduction to *Nora: A Biography of Nora Joyce* (1988), Brenda Maddox describes the motivations of her ambitious project to unearth the life of Nora Barnacle in terms of doing justice to the decisive role she played in Joyce's literary achievements. To this end, Maddox approached Richard Ellmann, Joyce's most renowned biographer, who argued that Nora's life would not make a book, since her role had merely been Joyce's partner and the mother of his children, not a literary woman: 'There were few letters, he said, Joyce and Nora having so rarely been apart, and their friends were dead; there was not even material for a feminist treatise.' When years of research proved otherwise, Ellman changed his mind, acknowledging that a biography of Nora was 'waiting to be done' and, in fact, assisted Maddox in her endeavour with additional resources, contacts, and addresses.[2] Indeed, the almost 600 pages of a well-documented and very readable biography of Nora Barnacle demonstrated that there were gaps and empty spaces in her life, as well as overlooked letters and other sources of information that required to be studied in detail, which opened the path for further research on her and the Joyces as a family.

---

1   The research carried out for the writing of this article has been financed by the Spanish Ministry of Science and Innovation, through the projects: VOPAS: 'Voices of the Past: The Contextual Referent in Contemporary British and Irish Historical Fiction' PID 2022-140013NB-I00; and INTRUTHS 2: 'Articulations of Individual and Communal Vulnerabilities in Contemporary Irish Writing' PID2020-114776GB-I00.

2   Brenda Maddox, *Nora: A Biography of Nora Joyce* (London: Minerva, 1988), 2.

One of Maddox's major accomplishments was the portrayal of Nora as a full-sized woman, counteracting the common perception of her as a shadow of the iconic author. In her own words:

> I began this book liking Nora. I finished in awe of her [....] Nora was ordinary. Nobody who loves Joyce will underestimate what that conveys. She was amusing, courageous, spontaneous, and articulate; she talked and talked. Joyce listened and listened and put her voice into all his major female characters. I hope I have done her justice.[3]

Granting Nora agency and individuality enabled Maddox to bring her from the periphery to the centre of Joyce's universe. This symbolic movement was of a paramount importance in Joycean criticism, as it went hand in hand with a growing interest to probe into the role of women, female characters and feminism in his life and works.[4] Indeed, until the 1990s, scholarship had tended to minimize the leading role of Nora. Still today, when looking up the entry Nora Barnacle in the final index of most critical studies, one finds that she very rarely has a space of her own, being usually identified as Mrs Joyce – which is not completely accurate, as they married 27 years into their relationship – or included in Joyce's own entry. On those occasions in which her maiden name is used, the reference sends you to the '*See* Joyce, Mrs James' section.[5] Even Maddox's biography, though often addressing her as Nora Barnacle, bears the name Nora Joyce in the title of her book. Curiously, the first biography of Nora, which had been written some years before by the Galway parish priest

---

3   Maddox, *Nora: A Biography*, 4–5.
4   See, for instance, the early significant contributions by Suzette A. Henke and Elaine Unkeless, 'Feminist Perspectives on James Joyce', *The Canadian Journal of Irish Studies*, 6/1 (June 1980), 14–22; Henke's monograph *Women in Joyce* (U of Illinois P, 1982); or Bonnie Kime Scott, *Joyce and Feminism* (Bloomington: Indiana UP, 1984), among a much longer list that has kept growing throughout the years.
5   There are notable exceptions, like Declan Kiberd's *Ulysses and Us: The Art of the Everyday Living* (London: Faber and Faber, 2009), or – interestingly for the development of *Nora's* plot, which fictionalizes a possible reciprocated attraction between Stanislaus and Nora – George G. Healey's edition of *The Complete Dublin Diary of Stanislaus Joyce* (Ithaca: Cornell UP, 1971). Her maiden name has also been recalled in 'The Nora Barnacle House museum' of Galway, which recreates the turn-of-the-century home where she grew up.

Padraic Ó Laoi, had been published with the title *Nora Barnacle Joyce* (1982).

In addition to these biographies, fictional recreations of the Joyces have also nurtured the literary imagination since the 1980s. A play directed by Maureen Charlton, which premiered at the Dublin Theatre Festival in 1980, with the title *Nora Barnacle*, was soon followed by Edna O'Brien's account on the life of the couple, entitled *James and Nora*: *A Portrait of Joyce's Marriage* (1981). Some years later, O'Brien authorized a second fictional biography on the writer, with the title *James Joyce* (1999). Additionally, in recent times, more biographical novels have also appeared: Annabel Abbs' *The Joyce Girl* (2016), Joyce Garvey's *Lucia*: *The Girl Who Danced in the Shadows* (2017), and Alex Pheby's *Lucia* (2018), which focuses on Lucia Joyce and her distressing mental issues; and Frank McGuiness' *The Woodcutter and his Family* (2017), which devotes a chapter to each member of the family, even though Nora is portrayed as little more than a manipulative wife. Further attempts to reinscribe her life into history include Pat Murphy's film *Nora* (2000) – based precisely on Maddox's biography – and Nuala O'Connor's own novel *Nora*, which will be explored in the present discussion. Finally, it is worth noting the recent publication of Mary Morrissy's uchronian novel, *Penelope Unbound* (2023), which ingeniously devises what would have happened had Nora parted with Joyce after an unfortunate real incident experienced by the couple as soon as they arrived in Trieste.

The blossoming of historical and biographical fiction in the last decades has turned into a global phenomenon, possibly propelled by an increasing interest in revisiting the past to fill in gaps, unravel discontinuities and shed light on competing narratives. Though traditional historians have tended to disregard the historical novel on grounds of the nature of fiction and its freedom to manipulate reality and distort facts, thus rendering inaccurate descriptions of the past, historical fiction writers have defended the truthfulness of their accounts, less concerned with data and minute evidence and more with seizing the spirit, ethos and culture of the period. As I will argue throughout the present discussion, undervaluing historical novels – and biographical novels as subtypes – because they are not true to the past is equivalent to reckoning that history is faithful to the Truth – with capital letters – an assumption that would ignore biased, partial and informed interpretations that have served different purposes throughout the times. Neither documented historical accounts, which rely on a narration, nor historical novels, have the power to capitalize truth, which is a mere construction rendered through discourse. As Lackey explains: 'All writing is told from a particular perspective and is based on an arbitrary selection of facts, but there is one major difference between history and fiction. Fiction writers acknowledge that their work is fiction, while historians suggest that their work is not fiction by calling it history.'[6]

Although biographies and biographical novels belong to different categories, their boundaries are often blurred, since they both select, omit and shape a given reality that has been filtered by the author. As Shabert has explained, 'non-fiction and fictional biographies are conceived in a process of interpreting the evidence', something that can be illustrated by looking at Ellman's authorized biography of Joyce, which embellishes recorded material and facts with imagined accounts to make the text more readable and appealing. Not in vain, this biography has been described as 'a modern novel dovetailed into a biography' since he experimented 'with more subtle ways of combining factual information with speculation bordering on such fiction',[7] evidencing that 'authors of biofiction write neither history nor biography'.[8] Consequently, the biographical novel will be considered here as a type of historical fiction that gravitates around the life of a real figure, and that lies at the intersection of history, biography, memoir and fiction, partially sharing the features of these modes, but not fully fulfilling any. Besides, the boundaries that separate historical and biographical fictions from the tradition of life-writing (auto)biography, memoir or factional biography are indeterminate and further problematized by the author, who can be both subject and object of discourse, and by the intricate relationship between literature and history.

6 Michael Lackey, 'The Ethical Benefits and Challenges of Biofiction for Children', *a/b: Auto/Biography Studies*, 33/1 (2018), 7.
7 Ina Schabert, 'Fictional Biography, Factual Biography, and Their Contaminations', *Biography*, 5/1 (Winter 1982), 3, 2 and 12.
8 Michael Lackey, 'Ireland, the Irish, and Biofiction', *Éire-Ireland*, 53/1 & 2 (Spring/Summer 2018), 104.

In Ireland, the number of biographical novels that have engaged with the unearthing of the lives of forgotten and silenced figures from the past, including women, nobodies and marginal others, or that have offered alternative perspectives to official narratives, clearly abound. Writers such as Colm Tóibín, Emma Donoghue, Anne Enright, Joseph O'Connor, Colm McCann, Roddy Doyle, Mary Morrissy, Evelyn Conlon, Martina Devlin or Nuala O'Connor have challenged master narratives that approached history as a linear succession of events, leaving behind conspicuous silences that spoke volumes.[9] Aligned in this similar attempt at reshaping existing margins to accommodate new central spaces, O'Connor's *Nora* (2021) 'a work of biographical fiction based closely on the life of Nora Barnacle', stands out.[10] Hence, in what follows, I will argue that O'Connor's biographical work aptly contributes to dislodge the role occupied by the figure of Nora Joyce, in order to place Nora Barnacle centre stage, an early twentieth-century maverick woman who went against the grain, transgressed gender expectations and proved to be very advanced for her time. I will additionally contend that this genre grants O'Connor the possibility to give voice to the character, rendering a bold portrayal of a female self with an authenticity that had been absent in previous biographies, challenging, in turn, earlier 'truthful' biographical accounts.[11]

The writer of two previous biographical novels, *Miss Emily* (2015), which tells the story of poet Emily Dickinson from the eyes of a fictional Irish maid, and *Becoming Belle* (2018), about the life of feminist Isabel Bilton, a Victorian woman who was also ahead of her time, O'Connor's interest in the figure of Nora was long-standing. As she explained in an interview, she had read Maddox's biography in her teens, was later inspired

---

9   See Michael Lackey's *Ireland, the Irish, and the Rise of Biofiction* (London: Bloomsbury, 2021), the only study to-date that deals with the flourishing of this genre, though he does not include many of the authors that I have listed here.
10 Nuala O'Connor, 'On Writing Nora Joyce into Biographical Fiction', *Literary Hub*, 5 January 2021, https://lithub.com/on-writing-nora-joyce-into-biographical-fiction/ [accessed 12 September 2023].
11 For considerations of space, I am unable to provide a detailed analysis of the novel. Instead, I will focus on the potential of this genre to challenge received truths and unquestioned biased interpretations.

by the film and, eventually, after writing an essay for her Italian classes on Joyce and his friendship with Italo Svevo, she came to realize that Nora was far more interesting than the two men: 'Nora, I found, intrigued me more than either of the men. What was her life really *like*, I wondered?'[12] Feeling drawn to the character of Nora Barnacle, she embarked on the rewriting of the 'Penelope' chapter of *Ulysses* for a twenty-first-century reader, a work that had been commissioned by the Irish Writers Centre. Reshaped into a parodic version of Molly and Leopold Bloom's marriage, the story was initially included in her flash-fiction collection *Of Dublin and Other Fictions* (2013), and later in *Joyride to Jupiter* (2017), with the title 'Penny and Leo and Married Bliss'. The following incursion was her story 'Gooseen', published in *Granta*, awarded the UK's 2018 Short Fiction Prize and shortlisted for the Story of the Year at the Irish Book Awards.[13] Additionally, O'Connor had also won the 2018 *James Joyce Quarterly*'s fiction contest with her own version of Joyce's short story 'Ulysses', which the author had initially planned to include in *Dubliners*.[14] Still, sensing that Nora's life was not fully told yet, she began writing *Nora*, which would grant her enough space to breathe life into her and explore a different perspective from which to look at the rising of a young uneducated woman struggling to find her place in a convulsed Europe, amidst poverty and linguistic and social alienation. As O'Connor has explained:

> I wrote NORA not just out of curiosity, but also out of love. Biographical fiction, for me, is a way to honour women who've been smudged by history, downgraded as The Wife, as if as prop to some notorious man, a woman was not personally important and essential to her lover's success. I aim to resurrect these women – the Noras, Emily Dickinsons, Belle Biltons et al– and re-introduce them to the world as the rounded, wonderful, spiky people that they were. I don't want to make paragons of them, but I aim to get a feel for what their lived lives were like.[15]

---

12   Nuala O'Connor, 'On Writing'.
13   Nuala O'Connor, 'Gooseen', *Granta*, 16 June 2018, https://granta.com/gooseen/ [accessed 12 September 2023].
14   As Joyce had announced to his brother Stanislaus in 1906, though he changed his mind a year later. See O'Connor's prize-winning entry in the *James Joyce Quarterly*, 55/1–2 (2017–2018), as a part of the 'Clever, Very' series.
15   O'Connor, 'On Writing Nora'.

O'Connor's Nora *and the Challenges of Biographical Fiction*

Not surprisingly, *Nora* was soon critically acclaimed and was timely awarded with the 'One Dublin / One Book' 2022 prize, precisely the year of the celebration of *Ulysses*'s centenary, which has contributed to disseminate its wide reception. As it is customary with this award, the book was read and discussed in most libraries and literary clubs across Ireland, valuing 'the contemporary writers Joyce has inspired, as well as the woman who inspired him'.[16] Needless is to say that the reading of O'Connor's novel has not only reassessed the significance of Nora, but it has also contributed to redefine Joyce's image. As Anne Fogarty has explained in her own tribute to the centenary celebrations of *Ulysses*, 'Joyce has in recent decades transmogrified from a scandalous author, upstart outsider, and foreign import to a kindred spirit and congenial but always challenging artistic role model.'[17] In keeping with this, O'Connor forms part of a movement of women writing back, of which we find another suitable example in Mary Morrissy's *The Rising of Bella Casey* (2013), a novel that unearths the life of John O'Casey's sister, who had been written out of history, in spite of her pivotal role in his literary career.[18] Outside Ireland, a magnificent parallel would be the widely praised Maggie O'Farrell's *Hamnet* (2020), which gives voice to Shakespeare's ignored though remarkable wife Agnes Hathaway to tell her own story.

In O'Connor's embodiment of Nora, she breathes life into her in such a way that she surfaces as a real woman who happened to be attached to a literary genius and was doomed to be his satellite, fulfilling Joyce's own expectations. In a letter to his brother Stanislaus, he had boasted about his gifts affirming that: 'My mind is of a type superior to and more civilised than any I have met up to the present', and in a letter to Nora he had

---

16   Martin Doyle, 'Nora by Nuala O'Connor chosen for One Dublin One Book 2022', *The Irish Times*, 21 October 2021, https://www.irishtimes.com/culture/books/nora-by-nuala-o-connor-chosen-for-one-dublin-one-book-2022-1.4707200 [accessed 12 September 2023].

17   Anne Fogarty, '*Ulysses* 1922–2022: Creative Reinventions', *Estudios Irlandeses*, 18 (2023), 212.

18   See Marisol Morales-Ladrón's 'Mary Morrissy's *The Rising of Bella Casey*, or How Women Have Been Written Out of History', *Nordic Irish Studies Review*, 15/1 (2016), 29–42, for further insights into this issue.

prophesized: 'I hope that the day may come when I shall be able to give you the fame of being beside me when I have entered into my Kingdom.'[19] Being precisely 'beside' him marked Nora's destiny, often undermined and overlooked by seemingly androcentric Joycean scholars who saw an uneducated woman unappreciative of his geniality, until Kime Scott's seminal study on Joyce and feminism showcased her as an advanced woman for her time: 'Although she seems to have presented no intellectual or social challenge to him and to have offered a wealth of conventional allure, forbearance, and loyalty, Nora did not bow to male authority altogether. Her gifts of expression, her penchant for mockery, and her independent opinions seem to have been both a resource and a delight for Joyce.'[20]

Sidestepping Joyce to make space for the agentive female protagonist, Nora's apparent ordinariness makes her look extraordinary. The narrative thus unfolds more important matters in their daily concerns than writing, success or ambition. In fact, for most of her life, Nora had to manage an insecure, moody partner, who was full of contradictions, thought too highly of himself and distrusted people. Her struggles to keep him away from trouble, from alcohol and from other excesses are explored in detail. Not only was he irresponsible with money, mostly spent on drinks and good restaurants, while Nora had to take in washing to feed the children, he was also abusive and ungrateful to family and friends. It is notorious how, while Stanislaus supported them financially and in many other ways, he received little appreciation from his brother, who was in the habit of taking advantage of people, mistreating those who meant him well. Later in their lives, they also had to face health problems, including Nora's uterine cancer, Joyce's glaucoma and ulcer, and Lucia's schizophrenia. From this angle, the novel, then, unearths the real life of a figure who had challenged the limitations of women at the time. In her readiness to leave everything behind, including language, country and family, to start a new unmarried life with a young man she barely knew, *Nora* raises questions of what it meant to be a woman in a male-dominated society.

---

19 Quoted in Richard Ellman, *Four Dubliners: Wilde, Yeats, Joyce and Beckett* (London: George Braziller, 1988), 54 and 53.
20 Scott, *Joyce and Feminism*, 205.

This shift in perspective adds further value to an account that places the focus not on the writer or his literary achievements but on the ordinariness of their lives, blurring the boundaries between the public and the private. *Nora* is about the private lives of Joyce and Nora, their domestic struggles and concerns, and their lasting problems with money, alcohol, excessive outings, continuous exile, unsettlement and alienation. Both had escaped from provincial Dublin: Nora, from an abusive uncle and a misogynist society and Joyce from the narrow-mindedness and paralysis of his family and friends. In the novel, they are presented as a family struggling to survive in foreign countries, with foreign languages, very little means and health problems. As the author has explained, she was very interested in the family, in the four of them as a quartet, stressing that it is a compassionate book that aims at providing a truthful portrait of a couple who wrestled like everyone else in their daily lives.[21] In fact, the subtitle of the novel, *A Love Story of Nora and James Joyce*, underlines how despite the hardships endured, the couple remained together, and how it should be interpreted as:

> an homage to Nora as individual, woman, caretaker and mother, firstly, and secondly, to Joyce as life-partner, father, and genius writer. I try to look with empathy at two fresh young people leaving their island, not knowing what lies ahead. A couple who ages and grows together, while negotiating the travails of life.[22]

At the same time, one should note that the undermining of Joyce-the-writer in *Nora* is not only the result of the shift in focus, but a realist account of the initial little appreciation Joyce was receiving in the publishing world in which he was struggling to find his place. In a more than interesting article written by Anne Enright about her grandmother, who had worked in the 1930s with Joyce's sister, Eileen, she recounts how: 'Eileen did not admit to her literary connection, except privately. James Joyce was still a "dirty word", [...] a name mentioned only by my mother and grandfather', adding that his books were read 'hiding them away from her children under the quilt'. Enright herself explains that she 'was forbidden to read *Ulysses* in my teens and forced to read *Dubliners* instead', which she hated because: 'The

---

21 O'Connor, 'On Writing Nora'.
22 O'Connor, 'On Writing Nora'.

paralysis it describes among the Irish middle classes lived on, more or less exactly preserved, in the lives and conversational habits of my aunts.'[23]

In Nora's biography, Maddox affirms that 'James Joyce scarcely took a step without Nora'.[24] The extent to which he was dependent on her is highlighted in the initial pages of the novel, sprouting as Joyce's constant source of inspiration, a repository of oral stories, language and wisdom. It is well-known how, when they first met, Joyce was attracted to the Ibsenian resonances of her name, and to the way she spoke and told stories.[25] Not only the last chapter of *Ulysses* is believed to have been modelled on the writing style of her letters, free of punctuation and stylistic rules, she was also the model of many female characters. For Joyce, Nora epitomized Ireland, as the novel echoes in the initial pages:

> TO JIM I AM IRELAND.
>
> I'm island shaped, he says, large as the land itself, small as the Muglins, a woman on her back, splayed and hungry, waiting for her lover [....] Jim says I am harp and shamrock, tribe and queen. I am high cross and crowned heart, held between two hands. I'm turf, he says, and bog cotton [....] Jim styles me his sleepy-eyed Nora. His squirrel girl from the pages of Ibsen [....]
>
> 'Nora', Jim says, 'you are syllable, word, sentence, phrase, paragraph, and page. You're fat vowels and shushing sibilants.
>
> 'Nora', Jim says, you are a story.[26]

However, finding an authentic voice for Nora out of the insufficient remaining records was one of O'Connor's most enduring challenges, who felt that she had a duty with her real life. When Joyce's correspondence was published, Nora's replies were missing. Her letters were lost or had

---

23 Anne Enright. 'Priests in the Family', *London Review of Books*, 43/22 (12 November 2021), https://www.lrb.co.uk/the-paper/v43/n22/anne-enright/diary [accessed 12 September 2023].
24 Maddox, *Nora: A Biography*, 3.
25 As the author has explained, 'Nora was fully herself by the time she met Joyce and he loved the enigma of her as much as the charming stories of her girlhood that she fed him, and he used', O'Connor, 'On Writing Nora'.
26 Nuala O'Connor, *Nora: A Love Story of Nora and James Joyce* (New York: Harper Perennial, 2021), 5.

been destroyed and had never been reclaimed, somehow assuming that her voice was not relevant for Joyce's legacy. Nora was thus written out of scholarly research and of history. To write her biography, Maddox had access to some unpublished archives, preserved at Cornell University and the British Library, but still significant gaps of her life remained. For the creation of *Nora*, O'Connor has explained that she rewrote Joyce's letters that were under copyright and imagined her replies, trying to be as truthful and faithful as possible to the couple: 'I wrote Nora's part of the correspondence using Joyce's letters as a call-and-response guide. When he praised her for using certain stimulating phrases and words, I included them in her letters to him, in the voice I had invented for her.'[27] Although she admits that it was difficult to get things right, avoiding anachronisms and inconsistences, for which she had to conduct a lot of research, she has also admitted that when she revised her novel, she tended to forget what was real and what wasn't, which explains why Nora's voice in the book is so strong.[28]

Yet it is precisely out of those incomplete spaces and gaps of history where the writer of biographical novels invests meaning and raises questions that reveal other sides to the stories. Such is the case of the apparent attraction between Stanislaus and Nora, fictionalized in the novel as a result of their mutual admiration and love, as well as of Joyce's solipsistic nature, unbearable moods and unappreciative behaviour towards people. While this episode might strike the orthodox Joycean scholar, at the same time, it opens the path for alternative interpretations of their lives probing into another possible turn. Much in tone with this, O'Connor takes a further

---

[27] Nuala O'Connor, 'Imagining Nora Barnacle's Love Letters to James Joyce', *The Paris Review*, 31 March 2021, https://www.theparisreview.org/blog/2021/03/15/imagining-nora-barnacles-love-letters-to-james-joyce/?fbclid=IwAR3EEC8HcmuX8Re9dBcjdpqYvawN3fohnUNorY8UwRg_D233Brk5d-hFej4 [accessed 12 September 2023].

[28] Annalisa Mastronardi, '"Joyce and Nora's life had such detail, texture, triumph, sadness": An Interview with Nuala O'Connor', *Contemporary Irish Literature*, 26 August 2021, https://contemporaryirishlit.wordpress.com/2021/08/26/joyce-and-noras-life-had-such-detail-texture-triumph-sadness-an-interview-with-nuala-oconnor/ [accessed 12 September 2023].

step in her rendering of Nora's relationship with her daughter Lucia, questioning received assumptions that had demonized the mother-daughter bond. Though it was well documented that Joyce had initially refused to accept Lucia's possible mental disorder, and instead saw a superior intelligence and an artistic gift as symptoms of her geniality, scholarship has tended to blame Nora of providing insufficient care and attention to her daughter.

Like Nora, Lucia's life had also been written out of history. Although Carol Loeb Schloss engaged in the writing of a long biography of Lucia, she recognized gaps and inconsistencies due to missing letters that had been deliberately destroyed by Joyce's grandson, to medical records that had been burned and to the absence of C. G. Jung's own reports, who treated her as a patient for four months. In the novel, the more empathic view of Nora as a committed and concerned mother is apparent in the way she is given the chance to painfully voice how she feared that their unrooted lifestyle had affected the education of the children: 'Oh God, have we made her this way? Have we caused Lucy's riotous behaviour with our way of living, now here, now there? Jim always out by night, our rows by day?'[29] Additionally, her struggles to convince Joyce that Lucia had mental issues that had to be treated, the little advance in psychiatric therapy at the time and the unclear diagnosis of schizophrenia, while Lucia's dysfunctional and violent behaviour, setting her room on fire, appearing naked or disappearing for days on end, persisted. Hence, O'Connor's focus on the care and distress of the whole family, liberates Nora of her sole responsibility with this difficult struggle.

In Edna O'Brien's fictional biography of Joyce, she had declared that his complexity and multiple sides made it impossible to provide an accurate description of him: 'The truth is that the Joyce they saw was a fraction of the inner man. No one knew Joyce, only himself, no one could.'[30] As mentioned earlier, it was not until the 1980s that Joycean scholars began to recognize the leading role of women in the writer's life, without whom, he could not have achieved half of his fame. While his family assisted him in

---

29 O'Connor, *Nora: A Love Story*, 251.
30 Edna O'Brien, *James Joyce* (London: Penguin Lives Series, 1999), 165.

numerous ways, including Nora, his sister Eileen,[31] who moved to Trieste to help with the care of his children, or his aunt Josephine, who would keep him updated with news in Ireland and sent him newspapers and other sources of information, others also helped him. In the publishing world, some women were crucial: the couple Margaret Anderson and Jane Heap, who published the serialized version of *Ulysses* in the US facing prosecution and censorship; Sylvia Beach, who almost ruined herself to publish the complete version of *Ulysses* and endured Joyce's irrational demands and unremitting corrections to the text;[32] Harriet Shaw Weaver, another of his benefactors who supported him all the way through, while he spent her money on luxurious items, clothes, meals and alcohol. Joyce was truly dependent on all of them, and their shadows loom large in his life.

To conclude, I hope to have been able to demonstrate how, even if Nora did not understand a word of what Joyce wrote, she is an enduring voice in his life and work. Admitting that she saw Joyce as a 'sacred cow' and describing biofiction as 'a democratic and illuminating form', O'Connor has explained that she felt her novel was needed if only to counteract the misogyny of *Ulysses*.[33] Her attempt to fulfil this endeavour has involved sidestepping the icon to give Nora the chance to tell her own story and change the narrative. In this regard, she has followed Fogarty's affirmation that 'it is crucial to rethink Joyce's legacy and to make good the omissions in biographical accounts of him that create stock roles for the women in his life but rarely tarry long enough to dwell on their contribution and distinctive life experience'.[34] Placing her centre stage in O'Connor's novel

31 Eileen's husband committed suicide when she was on her way to Trieste to visit her brother and he had such a pain trying to break the news to her that he avoided the conversation as much as he could (Enright).
32 It is worth noting the recent publication by Kerri Maher of her novel *The Paris Bookseller* (2022), which recreates the life of Sylvia Beach and her partner Adrienne Monnier while she was running her bookshop in Paris 'Shakespeare and Co', funded to promote English and American writers and to disseminate their works.
33 Hilary A. White, 'Nuala O'Connor: 'I really don't believe in closing the bedroom door on my characters', *Independent.ie*, 10 April 2021, https://www.independent.ie/entertainment/books/nuala-oconnor-i-really-dont-believe-in-closing-the-bedroom-door-on-my-characters/40286300.html [accessed 12 September 2023].
34 Fogarty, *Ulysses 1922–2022*, 214.

not only highlights the extraordinariness of the ordinary life of a woman, a couple and a family, but it also serves to overturn assumptions about gender construction amidst the limitations women endured in a male-dominated world. To this end, it is worth quoting Annabel Abbs, the author of *The Joyce Girl*, who argues that biographical fiction allows readers to revisit history from an angle usually de-centred from the mainstream account:

> It can give a voice to the marginal, the disempowered and the suppressed [....] Novels like these dislodge the iconic male, giving centre stage to someone with a very different viewpoint. They also give us the opportunity to explore the experience of someone rarely included in historical accounts or biographies. Through them we experience historical change or personalities in a new way, perhaps in a more nuanced or complex way.[35]

---

35 Anabel Abbs, 'Why Should Be Trust Biographical Fiction?', *Irish Times*, 21 October 2016, https://www.irishtimes.com/culture/books/why-should-we-trust-biographical-fiction-1.2838176 [accessed 12 September 2023].

MARY S. PIERSE

12 Judging George Moore's 'Wild Goose': The Case of Ned Carmady

The short story entitled 'The Wild Goose' first appeared as one of the constituent chapters in *The Untilled Field* (1903) and it was also included in subsequent editions of that collection up to 1914.[1] When the third English (revised) edition of the volume was published in January 1926, George Moore inserted a prominent, preliminary note that is an important authorial statement.

Announcing changes to 'The Wild Goose', he alluded to influential artistic precedent for his actions and expressed the hope that 'the new edition of *The Untilled Field* will allow me to seek an outline that eluded me in the first version of 'The Wild Goose'; and should I find the needed outline, the story will become, perhaps, dearer to me than the twelve that precede it and that need no correction'. Although known for his frequent revisions, it is interesting to consider what might lie behind Moore's concentration on that particular story. Could the changes alter or undercut any previous, intended messages? Were they connected to reinterpretation of his own ambition to provide literary models for young writers in Ireland? Undoubtedly, several different hypotheses can be suggested regarding those questions, and others too, but the main focus here will be to look at aspects of Moore's artistic treatment of Ned Carmady, the 'wild goose'.[2]

---

[1] George Moore, *The Untilled Field* (London: T. Fisher Unwin, 1903); American and Continental editions also appeared in 1903. The second English edition was *The Untilled Field* (London: William Heinemann, 1914) and the revised, third English edition was published by Heinemann in 1926. The fourth edition (1931) had one important addition, the final chapter was 'Fugitives', loosely based on two previous stories from 1903. That edition was used by Heinemann for the Uniform edition in 1933 and the Ebury Edition in 1937.

[2] All page numbers in this chapter refer to the 1931 edition.

See Figure 1.

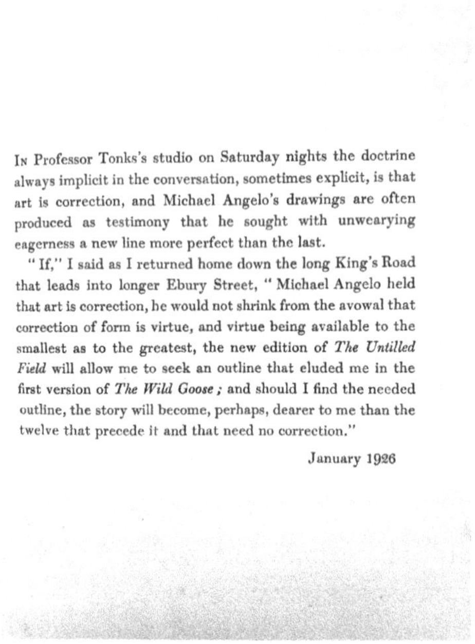

> IN Professor Tonks's studio on Saturday nights the doctrine always implicit in the conversation, sometimes explicit, is that art is correction, and Michael Angelo's drawings are often produced as testimony that he sought with unwearying eagerness a new line more perfect than the last.
> "If," I said as I returned home down the long King's Road that leads into longer Ebury Street, " Michael Angelo held that art is correction, he would not shrink from the avowal that correction of form is virtue, and virtue being available to the smallest as to the greatest, the new edition of *The Untilled Field* will allow me to seek an outline that eluded me in the first version of *The Wild Goose*; and should I find the needed outline, the story will become, perhaps, dearer to me than the twelve that precede it and that need no correction."
>
> January 1926

Figure 1

In its original form, this short story was an elaboration in English of Moore's story 'Tír-Grádh' that had featured in *An tÚr-Ghort* and whose title clearly conveyed its patriotic and nationalistic flavour, albeit permitting any differing interpretations conveyed by 'love of country' and 'patriotism'.[3] The note preceding the final iteration of 'The Wild Goose' reveals Moore's investment in, and attachment to, its composition, and underscores his engagement with the themes and characters in the story. Significantly, its rewriting occurs in a period when an artistic environment was once more an important part of the Moore social world. The convivial Saturday night gatherings of creative friends in the Chelsea studio of painter Henry Tonks reconfirms the centrality of visual art and

---

3   Moore chose to publish six stories, translated into Irish by Pádraig Ó Súilleabháin, in *An tÚr-Ghort* (Dublin: Sealy, Bryers & Walker, 1902), months ahead of their appearance with others in *The Untilled Field*.

architecture for Moore – and hence its recurrent interweaving into his prose – while that London location also firmly fixes the time in Moore's life when as 'the sage of Ebury Street', he looked back again at Ireland from his London home. Both artistic appreciation and some political revision might be seen as key elements in Moore's new approach, and interestingly so in the case of Ned Carmady.

All versions of the story relate the arrival in Ireland of Ned Carmady, described as an American journalist who had been born in Ireland, had spent most of his life in England, America and Cuba, and who harboured some stereotypical images of the Ireland and its people. He plans to write articles during his stay. His further education concerning Irish heritage and nationalist beliefs is undertaken by wealthy Ellen Cronin, whom he subsequently marries. She is portrayed as a determined and competent woman whose politics differ from those of her father, in that she aims for a new Irish Ireland. However, her Celtic renaissance views coexist with a hidebound subservience to reactionary codes promulgated by a recently vociferous and active Catholic clergy. As Ned, encouraged initially by Ellen, becomes immersed in efforts to promote Irish freedom, a chasm opens between their different life expectations and standards, and their paths diverge. Ned's total preoccupation with advancing that Irish cause leads him to perceive blockages on the route, and those obstacles are supported and underpinned by conservative Catholic clergy. His determination to confront and call out their opposition publicly in lecture and in print then clashes with Ellen's belief in submission to the dictates of those priests. The outcome leads to Ned's departure from a land where he sees no hope of victory.

There are contradictions, ambiguities and antithetical qualities in Ned which could render him a cardboard cut-out figure but yet many ingredients in the story are plausibly and fleetingly suggestive of a complex individual in the turbulent era of fin-de-siècle Ireland with its revolutionary ideas and Celtic Twilight infusions. Initially central to that representation are the notions he brings with him from America, and some are soon shattered. While he is personally impressed by the ancient stones of Newgrange, he assesses that his American readers would rather have descriptions of more modern life and so decides to engage in conversation with every local farmer and herdsman he meets. Convinced that it would be better to burn turf from the bog than to use coal, he then has to accept his landlady's use of seaborne, cheaper coal as there is no bog in the area. His expectations, in his own words, are 'based on the charm of tradition', and that comprehension envisages a wife wearing a frilly nightcap in bed, a practice not observed even in a previous generation.[4] Visiting a fair where he encounters a variety of local characters, he immediately decides that the genius of Ireland is in herding cattle, the Irish are 'The finest herdsmen and the finest horsemen'.[5] One cattle jobber points out a 'Mr Cronin, one of the biggest dairymen in the County of Dublin',[6] and Ned's encounter with the laconic Cronin leads to meeting Ellen. Ned settles into a routine of evening meals in Cronin's house, followed by billiards games with Mr Cronin, and some chat with Ellen. Gradually, his attraction to the beautiful woman brings him to the point where he weighs up 'if he would like to live in this queer, empty country' while he 'discovered himself to be without enough will to run away from Ellen's red hair and her turquoise eyes'. The indecision is clear: 'His mood veered like a gale all the next day.'[7]

Other glimpses of Ned show his impatience.[8] When they go fishing, Ned thinks they should give up after half an hour of catching nothing whereas Ellen 'was more persevering' and a big trout was eventually landed.[9] The slight descriptions of Ned's moods, attitudes and actions are sufficient to paint him as somewhat of a travelled but naive enthusiast, maybe even a rebellious butterfly, impulsive, impetuous, and ready to embrace the latest vogue. He is 'taken with the desire of political leadership',[10] and rapidly became 'convinced he was the very man Ireland needed'.[11] He travels Ireland to encourage involvement in the new political movement, and in pursuit

---

4   Moore, *The Untilled Field*, 170.
5   Moore, *The Untilled Field*, 150.
6   Moore, *The Untilled Field*, 154.
7   Moore, *The Untilled Field*, 163.
8   A remark by Mr Cronin could suggest a shrewd assessment: 'I'm afraid, Ned, you're a rolling stone' Moore, *The Untilled Field*, 162.
9   Moore, *The Untilled Field*, 165.
10   Moore, *The Untilled Field*, 169.
11   Moore, *The Untilled Field*, 170.

of that cause, goes back to America, presumably to rally support for Irish independence. While he is away, their baby is born, and Ned's immediate preoccupation is that a wet nurse should be obtained so that Ellen's figure would not alter: '[H]e had often thought of Ellen as a beautiful marble.'[12] Ironically, it is Ellen who evinces 'enticing, winning sensuality',[13] and who, remarkably for fiction of the period, tells him to 'kick off those pyjamas; I would be nearer to you.'[14] During conflict over Ned's anti-clerical stance, when Ellen asks if 'his resolution never to come into her room again was irrevocable, he answers: "I cannot tell you I am engaged upon my work and have no thought for anything but it".' His thoughts are that 'constancy is not everything; and it's a pity I cannot love her always'.[15] On the eve of his departure, her words are: 'Though it be for the last time, you need not be afraid to come into my room'; that offer is not accepted.[16] The frankness evident in Ellen's remark about pyjamas, and in the open invitation to her bed, is one of the notable changes from Moore's 1903 text when he wrote with a view to presenting short stories as models for young Irish writers while constantly and sharply aware of the censorious attitude of Fr Peter Finlay of the *New Irish Review*. Writing in 1914 from the fastnesses of Chelsea, he is minded to portray the multiple and oft-incongruous expressions of authentic life, particularly evidencing the paradoxical coexistence of uninhibited female desire with surrender to compliance with a clerical order that would limit or deny it.

As they drift apart, Ned seizes upon the vision and the associated folklore of wild geese departing south and he leaves, apparently to fight with the Boers in South Africa. He claims, 'There is nothing for me to do here.'[17] Ellen is forlornly accepting of an inevitability: '[W]hen one is so bent upon going as you are, it is better he should go at once. I give you your freedom.' She adds, 'I shall always welcome your return if you return.'

---

12   Moore, *The Untilled Field*, 176.
13   Moore, *The Untilled Field*, 178.
14   The word 'pyjamas' does not appear in earlier versions of the story, nor does Ellen invite Ned into her bed. Moore, *The Untilled Field*, 179.
15   Moore, *The Untilled Field*, 187.
16   Moore, *The Untilled Field*, 192.
17   Moore, *The Untilled Field*, 191.

Their closing exchanges acknowledge their bond and its rupture: 'Each follows his and her truth, Ellen;' is how Ned phrases it as he ponders on how he could leave his infant son forever while still saying that he will always love her and suggesting that distance would 'bring us into a closer and more intimate appreciation of each other'.[18] Perhaps grasping on to a faintly exculpatory idea, Ned determines that Ireland is epitomized by the shepherd's flute tune that he hears as he wanders through the mist of Howth and he labels it as 'the song of the exile, the cry of one driven out into a night of wind and rain, a prophetic echo. A mere folk-tune, mere nature, raw and unintellectual'.[19]

Neither Ned nor Ellen is allowed to emerge as totally admirable: Moore's less-positive depictions of Ned's activities, and his notions and actions, are counterbalanced by the portrayal of Ellen's unexpected subservience to clerical judgements on breastfeeding; his labours for a nationalist cause might merit commendation as could her resolute pursuit of Ned, her decisive views on moving house, and her assertiveness in plotting Ned's political career. This complexity is credibly human but, in Moore's revisions, it might also reflect some authorial indecision as to ingredients in its multiple constituent parts. A key to its interpretation may reside in 'Fugitives', the final story in the 1931 edition of *The Untilled Field*. This tale sees Ned Carmady in London and, rather than heading for the Boer war, he is now bound for America. In conversation with John Rodney (a sculptor) and the journalist Harding (so often a Moore *alter ego*),[20] Carmady says that ultimately, he 'may ramble back to Ireland'.[21] Harding's summation is: 'I am sorry for his wife, a pretty little red-haired woman, soused in Catholicism even as Martyin.' Significantly, Harding calls Carmady '[a] strange man, whom I never know whether I like or dislike'.[22] This may be the author's final verdict on his creation, and the misgivings of its uncertainty are expressive of a possibly personal and analogous conflict between artistic and

---

18   Moore, *The Untilled Field*, 192.
19   Moore, *The Untilled Field*, 191.
20   The journalist Harding had also made an appearance in *A Drama in Muslin* (1886).
21   Moore, *The Untilled Field*, 206.
22   Moore, *The Untilled Field*, 207.

personal choice, with perhaps an over-simplification of options, reducing them to a choice between creativity and domesticity.

While mulling on Carmady (or on Ellen), it would be important to consider some artistic elements inserted by Moore into 'The Wild Goose': one links to Tallaght, and the other has associations with Tipperary and ties two men named Ned. Tallaght (spelt as Tallagh in the story) is a central location in the story and both its architectural and natural beauty are foregrounded. When Carmady arrives in Ireland, he lodges in Fir House, an eighteenth-century manor house at the end of a long elm avenue, 'a stead built out of huge stones, only one degree removed from a Norman keep'.[23] A short walk away is the home of the Cronins at Brookfield, surrounded by 'wide pastures where cattle wandered or rested under trees'.[24] Brookfield also had a very long avenue, this time divided by three gates and lined by old yews. Ellen is proud that 'our yew avenue is often admired'.[25]

In addition to its pastures, Brookfield also had walled gardens, a tennis lawn, and a stream with a tributary that at one point, disappeared 'mysteriously underground'.[26] Carmady approves 'the pretty Georgian house, pillars and portico. "A manor-house in the eighteenth century"', he said, 'fallen into the hands of the middle classes in the nineteenth; and very happily fallen, too';[27] 'Walking back to Fir House, 'he could just distinguish the sluggish roll of the Dublin mountains, dim and grey'.[28] When Ellen wants to move from Brookfield to live 'on the other side of Dublin in a modern villa, he confessed his preference for Tallagh and the old seventeenth-century

---

23 Moore, *The Untilled Field*, 148.
24 Moore, *The Untilled Field*, 156.
25 Moore, *The Untilled Field*, 157. A picture 'Former Avenue to Tymon Lodge' (Kieran Swords, 26 October 1992) appears on the website of South Dublin Libraries https://hdl.handle.net/10599/4744 [accessed 20 October 2023]. It is from Séamus Ó Néill, *Firehouse History, Legends, People, Places* (South Dublin Council, 2010).
26 Moore, *The Untilled Field*, 164. Layout of the stream that 'runs through the old walled-in garden of Tymon Lodge' is confirmed in William Domville Handcock, *The History and Antiquities of Tallaght* (Dublin: Hodges Foster & Figgis, 1877), 124.
27 Moore, *The Untilled Field*, 160.
28 Moore, *The Untilled Field*, 163.

stead'.[29] It is on the toss of a coin that they move to Kingstown. Carmady's inclination is towards the ancient; Ellen's focus is on the optimal location for his new political career.

See Figure 2.

Figure 2

But it is Tallaght rather than Kingstown which is so recognizable in Moore's tale, and the depictions are linked to his own intimate knowledge of the area and its former comfortable estates, and to his personal life. Images of river, streams, and views of the area, and accounts of the layout within the demesne of Brookfield, all accord with historical records and

---

29 Moore, *The Untilled Field*, 170. Tallagh was the spelling on the Taylor and Skinner 1777 map of the route from Dublin to Tullow (Patrick Healy *All Roads Lead to Tallaght* (Dublin: South Dublin Libraries, 2004), 42. On William Duncan's 1821 map, the spelling is Tallaght (Healy, *All Roads Lead to Tallaght*, 10). Robert Newcomen's 1654 spelling is Tallaghe.

with what remains visible today.[30] The antiquity of Tallaght's history was very obviously attractive to Ned and reference to it would chime with the prominence of interest in antiquarian inheritance that was strong in the latter half of the nineteenth century.[31] In addition to the general antiquarian vogue, there had been an account in the 1890s – a mere ten years before Ned's arrival – of the remains of a funerary urn recently excavated in Tallaght, between Tallaght Castle and Greenhills, one described as being 'one of the most beautifully and richly decorated urns that has been found in Ireland'.[32] That of course was only one artefact from a district whose settlement history and treasures would fill innumerable volumes.

Tymon Lodge was the actual name of the house that is named Brookfield in 'The Wild Goose' and it was the place located by Moore for his lover, the English artist Clara Christian. She lived there for several years from 1901, and died there in 1906. Moore's description of the house that he then calls Moat House in *Hail and Farewell!*,[33] matches the portrayal in the short story, just as many of the incidents described therein correspond with his autobiographical account. The house is 'a moated

---

30   'The ground on both sides of the old Tymon Lane has been converted into a park, with plantations of trees, open grassy slopes and sports fields, with the Poddle River flowing through the middle of it' (Healy, *All Roads Lead to Tallaght*, 43).

31   Several finds in the Tymon area are reported by Patrick Healy *All Roads Lead to Tallaght* (Dublin: South Dublin Libraries, 2004), 43–44. In 1898, a cist was discovered which contained an encrusted urn, over cremated bone and a pigmy cup, along with a vase-shaped vessel, these Bronze Age (1500–1000 BC) prehistoric burials were in a flat cemetery. Healy also notes unearthing of nineteenth-century pipes (Healy, *All Roads Lead to Tallaght*, 47). Ellen's father smokes such a pipe (UF170).

32   Detailed information in Thomas Henry Longfield's entry in *Sketch Books of Irish Antiquities* (NLI: PD 1975 TX 34 (50a) 23 May 1892), 50–51. Longfield (a Fellow of the Society of Antiquaries) bought fragments of one urn that had been buried at a depth of 10 feet, from a Dublin antique dealer, Mr Halbert of High Street. Longfield reassembled much of the urn. A picture of a second urn and part of a food vessel was published by the RIA with an entry by R. E. Plunkett, 'On a Cist and Urns found at Greenhills Tallaght Co. Dublin' (Proceedings of the RIA 21 Section C, 1899).

33   George Moore, *Hail and Farewell!* (Gerrard's Cross, Bucks.: Colin Smythe, 1985), 432.

stead built in the time of Anne'; amongst the features recalled by Moore, in addition to 'some fine rooms', were 'a dining-room and a very handsome drawing-room'. Its moat is 'fed at the upper end by a stream, and it trickles away by the bridge into a brook'.[34] With a Carmady-like insensitivity to flora, Moore mentions a 'chestnut avenue',[35] whereas Ellen recognizes a yew avenue. Tymon Lodge was demolished in the 1970s but the avenue is still tree-lined and, according to South Dublin County Council, is a pathway between Carrigwood Estate and Firhouse Road.[36] The Poddle river, rising in Tallaght, was always called the Tymon River at its early point, and it flows to form a lake at Tymon Park. Moore, who walked many of the roads and streets of Dublin, was familiar with Clondalkin, Tallaght, Firhouse, Rathfarnham and their intersections, and chose to place cherished ingredients of his own story in the Tymon area of Tallaght. The meshing of his experiences with the fictionalized tale gives rise to innumerable hypotheses as regards where memoir starts and ends, and how true to Moore's life might be the actions and opinions ascribed to Ned Carmady. What is indisputable is the significance of Tallaght in both fact and this Moorian fiction.

Music in the tale provides a connection to Tipperary. The instances of George Moore's integration of music into his texts are several and, in each case, the underlying messages can be simple or multiple.[37] Music makes a very conspicuous appearance in 'The Wild Goose' where almost one entire page is given over to reproduction of the tune allegedly played by a shepherd in the mist and then written down by Ned Carmady. See Figure 3.

---

34 Moore, *Hail and Farewell!*, 270.
35 Moore, *Hail and Farewell!*, 432. Moore offers a self-deprecating apologia for his disinterest 'because I cannot remember the name of every trivial weed. I suppose it is that men don't care for flowers as women do; [...] We are interested in dogmas; they in flowers'.
36 Today, the Tymon Lodge site is occupied by the football pitch belonging to Scoil Treasa. See Mary S. Pierse 'Moore's Music: Reading the notes, Knowing the Score', in *George Moore: Influence and Collaboration*, edited by Ann Heilmann and Mark Llewellyn (Newark: University of Delaware Press, 2014), 53–67.
37 See Mary S. Pierse 'Moore's Music: Reading the notes, Knowing the Score', in *George Moore: Influence and Collaboration* (Newark: University of Delaware Press, 2014), 53–67.

Judging Moore's 'Wild Goose': The Case of Ned Carmady 169

Figure 3

This is the air that Ned disparages as 'a mere folk tune', as 'raw and unintellectual'.[38] Unbeknownst to him, his transcription gives the lie to his interpretation, and hence very subtly further undermines Ned's own authority. He copies the tune in the key of E-flat major, a key most usually employed to convey love, devotion, courage, determination, and sometimes the heroic – as in Beethoven's Eroica symphony and Emperor concerto, and Mozart's Die Zauberflöte – and thus very far from 'melancholy'. Since Ned is presented as a competent violinist who had ambitions to join the orchestra of the New York opera house, and subsequently played what Ellen called 'Bach's interminable twiddles' on the piano in the Kingstown villa,[39] both key choice and his misunderstanding of the

38 Moore, *The Untilled Field*, 191.
39 Moore, *The Untilled Field*, 180.

air show him as functionally deaf when it came to Irish music. Failing to interpret the import of the key signature, and hence its distance from 'a mere folk tune', appears to be downgrading by Moore of Ned's suitability to lead the proposed new Irish political movement since Ned denigrates what is culturally espoused by its programme and misconstrues its wider significance. In failing to recognize the air, he misses the further import of its history and referential tentacles.

Ned was not alone in his ignorance. The somewhat surprising placement of music on the page seems not to have invited critical interpretation, and the melody has been generally unheeded in literary commentary. Recent enquiries to musicologists and specialists in traditional music failed to find one who could recognize the air. However, the tune can be definitely identified as 'Éamonn an Chnoic' (Ned of the Hill), a song that tells of the rapparee Edmund O'Ryan from Tipperary.[40] His story had very widespread recognition in the nineteenth century and was told in multiple prose and poetry versions in two languages. While some feats were embellished to a degree that qualifies them as legends, much of the core account has been verified by historians. Moreover, the importance attached to popular interpretation of Éamonn an Chnoic's life and deeds is reflected by the choices of Padraig Pearse and Thomas McDonagh to make poetic translation of the verses.[41] It was probably Mrs Frances Peck who gave an initial nineteenth-century fillip to the story when she published a romance entitled *The life and acts of the renowned, chivalrous Edmund of Erin, commonly called Emun ac Knuck, or Ned of the Hills*.[42] Her book was commended by Daniel O'Connell (then Lord Mayor of Dublin) to whom she gave a copy in 1842. In her preface, she admits that there was an

---

40 It was a serendipitous coincidence that, when it was played by violinist Karla Kennedy at a George Moore event in the Museum of Literature Ireland in November 2022, I recognized the tune.

41 The translation by Thomas Mac Donagh is in NLI MS 10,999/6/5. According to Róis Ní Ógáin, the Pearse translation appeared in *The Irish Review* in 1911 (*An Duanaire Gaedhilge* (Baile Átha Cliath: Comhlucht Oideachais na h-Éireann, 1921–1930), 106).

42 Frances Peck, The life and acts of the renowned, chivalrous Edmund of Erin, commonly called Emun ac Knuck, or Ned of the Hills (Dublin: S. J. Macken, 1842).

Edmund O'Ryan who was active after the battle of the Boyne, but she situates her 'Emun' eight hundred years earlier and he is renowned for strength, sporting prowess, harp playing, and knowing all the songs of the country.

Despite the era in which she places him, she notes a nineteenth-century reality in one interesting footnote: 'Ned of the Hills or Emun ac Knuck is one of the popular songs of Ireland this day. This tune is played by every itinerant musician; and its fame has been perpetuated by Mr Moore and Sir John Stevenson.'[43] The combined attentions of Edward Bunting and Charlotte Brookes, and later of Peck, O'Connell, Lady Morgan, and Thomas Moore, and followed by the interest of Pearse and Mac Donagh, are surely sufficient to establish that both song and tale were widely known and understood when Moore incorporated his reference.[44] It was Ned Carmady who was out of tune. In this instance, the contrast intimated between Ned Carmady and Ned of the Hills allows at least a critique of Carmady's superficial understanding of Ireland and its history. Does his affinity with classical music block appreciation or construal of native culture? Has his objectification of Ellen blinded him to their differences? Certainly, any juxtaposition of Carmady's vacillations against the image of an heroic, creative Eamonn / Ned must, at a minimum, dilute approval of Carmady even if there is agreement with the latter's diagnosis of Irish societal ills.

43   Peck, The life and acts of the renowned, chivalrous Edmund of Erin, 54.
44   By 1900, scholars had established that the 'real' Eamonn or Ned was born into very comfortable circumstances in Co Tipperary. Intending to be a priest, he was educated on the continent and while visiting Ireland, shot a tax collector and so was outlawed. He subsequently fought on the side of King James at the Boyne, and after Aughrim and Ballyneety, he and others were known as rapparees. Tales of his generosity and bravery abounded and there is documentary evidence extant for some elements. With a price on his head, he was killed in his sleep by a presumed friend who then failed to collect the money because Ned had been pardoned just hours earlier. For the airs and words, see Edward Bunting *General Collection of the Ancient Irish Music* (Dublin: Hime, 1798); much additional history is given in *The Journal of Irish Folk Song Society*, xxiv (1927), 36–49, 52. For more recent assessments see Séamus Ó Catháin, *Irish Life & Lore* (Dublin: Mercier Press, 1982), 18–21; Stephen Dunford, *The Irish Highwaymen* (Dublin: Wolfhound Press, 2005); Dáithí Ó hÓgáin, *The Hero in Irish Folk History* (Dublin: Gill & Macmillan, 1985), 186–187. There are numerous other sources.

Hypotheses may abound, and there are several potential clues, but no certain authorial position on characters can be decoded in 'The Wild Goose'.[45] What is palpable is George Moore's determination to provide a rich text that conveys atmospheres of fin-de-siècle Ireland and its many shades of societal and political complexities. In realizing this creative task, Moore enhances his literary text with visual imagery, musical and cultural resonances, and most striking amongst them are the echoes of Tallaght and the insertion of a musical key to Tipperary's Eamonn / Ned.

An afterword

There is a shining light in the Franco-Irish academic world who has ties to Tallaght and to Tipperary, a wonderful man whose multiple achievements in several areas are matched by a generosity of spirit and a firm commitment to everything he undertakes. Eamon Maher merits the level of acclaim given to Éamonn an Chnoic – and, most emphatically has no affinity with a character named Carmady.

---

45 This accords with a Moorian assertion (in a letter to Nancy Cunard) that 'the artist must be eccentric, stand aloof and disdainfully'. *GM: Memories of George Moore* (London: Rupert Hart-Davis, 1956), 137.

MARÍA ELENA JAIME DE PABLOS

13 Trauma and Artistic Creation in *Another Alice* by Lia Mills

Introduction

Lia Mills, born in Dublin in 1957, is a notable Irish academic and writer of novels, short stories, autobiographical literature, essays and reviews. In 1996, she published her debut novel, *Another Alice*, and it was nominated for *The Irish Times* Irish Fiction Prize. In this work, the author narrates the story of Alice Morrissey, a young woman who desperately struggles to overcome the trauma of having been psychologically, physically and sexually assaulted by a violent, alcoholic and schizophrenic father with the complicity of a mother, who 'seem[s] to be deaf and blind in relation to the incestuous abuses taking place at home'.[1] This chapter examines how the protagonist, with the help of a psychotherapist, learns how to overcome trauma and become a triumphant survivor, 'another Alice', through artistic creation.

In her introduction to 'Lia Mills Interviewed by Caitriona Moloney', Moloney makes emphasis on the psychological nature of *Another Alice*: 'Mills brings considerable expertise to bear on the psychology of the abused child and woman.'[2] Later on, Lia Mills confesses herself that

---

1   María Elena Jaime de Pablos, 'Incest, Gender and Abjection in *In Night's City* and *Another Alice*', in *Las inéditas: voces femeninas más allá del silencio*, edited by Yolanda Romano Martín and Sara Velázquez García (Salamanca: Ediciones Universidad de Salamanca, 2018), 446.
2   Caitriona Moloney, 'Lia Mills Interviewed by Caitriona Moloney', in *Irish Women Writers Speak Out: Voices from the Field*, edited by Caitriona Moloney and Helen Thompson (New York: Syracuse University Press, 2003), 181.

she has done 'a lot of reading in psychology'.[3] This is why I choose to the psychoanalytic approach – following Julia Kristeva's and Boris Cyrulnik's theories – to carry out the analysis of the protagonist of the novel, from victim to survivor of sexual assault, giving focal attention to art as the engine of her identity transformation.

The impact of incest on Alice's mind: A traumatic childhood

Father-daughter incest, a taboo topic rarely discussed in Ireland before the 1990s as it had been contained 'within the private sphere, the space of male privilege',[4] became the 'focus of an increasingly body of sociological, psychoanalytic, [...and] clinical discourse; [and] the subject of modern novels'.[5] Notable amongst the most accomplished novels are: Dorothy Nelson's In *Night's City* (1982), Jennifer Johnston's *The Invisible Worm* (1991), Lia Mill's *Another Alice* (1995) and Edna O'Brien's *Down by the River* (1997).[6] Through their fiction, Dorothy Nelson, Jennifer Johnston, Lia Mills and Edna O'Brien make 'visible the situation of thousands of girls who are sexually abused by men close to them and then forced to remain silent regarding the source of their traumatic grief'.[7] They take part

---

3   Moloney, 'Lia Mills Interviewed by Caitriona Moloney', 182.
4   Kathryn A. Conrad, *Locked in the Family Cell: Gender, Sexuality, and Political Agency in Irish National Discourse* (Madison: The University of Wisconsin Press, 2004), 82.
5   Jane M. Ford, *Patriarchy and Incest from Shakespeare to Joyce* (Gainesville: University Press of Florida, 1998), 1.
6   Adding to the number of incest narratives produced in the late 20th century, are two relevant short stories: Leland Bardwell's 'The Dove of Peace' in the collection *Different Kinds of Love* (Dublin: Dedalus Press, 1987), and Mary Dorcey's 'A Noise from the Woodshed', in the collection *A Noise from the Woodshed: Short Stories* (London: Onlywomen Press, 1989).
7   María Elena Jaime de Pablos, 'Child Sexual Abuse and Traumatic Identity in *Down by the River* by Edna O'Brien', in *Identities on the Move. Contemporary Representations of New Sexualities and Gender Identities*, edited by Silvia Pilar

in the public debate on father-daughter incest thereby indicating that this practice 'can be named, explored, criminalized, and so, perhaps controlled'.[8] Indeed, by 'contributing to the acknowledgment of this hidden reality of Irish family life, by uncovering its patriarchal roots, by exposing its dreadful consequences for girls and women both physically and psychically, they are also collaborating with its eradication'.[9]

Even in late twentieth-century Ireland, social, religious and political forces join to perpetuate patriarchy. The 'Patriarchal law, the law of the father' not only 'decrees that the father is the absolute ruler of the household, but also that the "product" of sexual union, the child, shall belong exclusively to the father, be marked by his name.'[10] In *Another Alice*, the protagonist literally confesses that, in childhood, her father, Michael Morrissey, made her feel that she was one of his properties: 'He was my father, [therefore] he owned me.'[11] Far from displaying parental protection and affection, Michael, 'the beast',[12] 'the slavemaster',[13] 'the sworn enemy',[14] 'the monster',[15] sexually abuses his little daughter. Unable to feel any sense of compassion for her, this despotic character is ready to manipulate and torture her vulnerable body nearly to death as if it were inert, insensitive and worthless matter. The following lines from *Another Alice* illustrate this assertion. In them, Alice remembers the excruciating physical and

---

    Castro Borrego and María Isabel Romero Ruiz (New York: Lexington Books, 2015), 53.
[8]   Christine St. Peter, 'Petrifying Time: Incest Narratives from Contemporary Ireland', in *Contemporary Irish Fiction. Themes, Tropes, Theories*, edited by Liam Harte and Michael Parker (New York: Palgrave MacMillan, 2000), 131.
[9]   Jaime de Pablos, 'Incest, Gender and Abjection in *In Night's City* and *Another Alice*', 452–453.
[10] Jane Gallop, 'The Father's Seduction', in *Feminisms REDUX*, edited by Robyn Warhol-Down and Diane Price Herndl (New Brunswick, NJ: Rutgers University Press, 2009), 156.
[11] Lia Mills, *Another Alice* (Dublin: Poolbeg, 1996), 78.
[12] Mills, *Another Alice*, 345.
[13] Mills, *Another Alice*, 345.
[14] Mills, *Another Alice*, 39.
[15] Mills, *Another Alice*, 39.

psychological pain that she experienced every single time that she was sexually assaulted by her father:

> Then he starts. He takes my right hand and begins to squeeze it, crushing it. The pain is excruciating and, as I try to pull away, it rises up my arm. When I stop fighting, he stops moving and, if the pain doesn't go away, at least it doesn't grow [...] but it's still there, and it's bad, and after a while I can't stand the tension any more, knowing what comes next. I deliberately move my legs away from him so he will come to it straight away. If it has to happen, just do it, I want it to be over. So I move my legs and he pushes his way inside me and oh, Jesus, the pain is searing and splitting me, it's going to split me in two, my whole body is going to split up the middle like a wishbone when you pull it apart, how can anything be so big and be inside me? [...] I'm bleeding, but I don't have to do anything about it, because if I don't my whole body will bleed away to nothing and then it will be over, I'll belong to him.[16]

Michael regards Alice's body as a 'puppet', as a 'rag doll with floppy limbs and empty head'.[17] In his eyes, she is, resorting to Foucault's expression, a 'docile body', which is understood as 'the body as object and target of power [...] the body that is manipulated, shaped, trained, which obeys, responds, becomes skilful'.[18] According to Susie Orbach, Michael's brutal depravity is intended 'to show that the master of the body is not its inhabitant but its torturer'.[19] The perpetrator colonizes Alice's body, which he marks – as his own – with his sweat, blood and sperm: 'I am marked with his scum. I am his, I belong to him.'[20] Michael also tries to colonize her mind by convincing his daughter that she has an abject body and a pernicious soul: 'He tells me what I am, *dirty, filthy, slut, evil*.'[21] As 'discourse constructs the subject', [22] Alice's father uses its effective power to

---

16   Mills, *Another Alice*, 316.
17   Mills, *Another Alice*, 220.
18   Michel Foucault, *Discipline and Punish: The Birth of the Prison* (New York: Vintage Books, 1977), 136.
19   Susie Orbach, *Bodies* (London: Profile Books, 2009), 108.
20   Mills, *Another Alice*, 346.
21   Mills, *Another Alice*, 347.
22   Judith Butler, *Bodies that Matter: On the Discursive Limits of 'Sex'* (New York: Routledge, 1993), 8.

materialize her identity in derogatory terms. Judith Butler calls this 'identity through injury'.[23]

The protagonist is induced to perceive herself as bearer of a stigma: 'a mark of disgrace or infamy [...] impressed on a person', which has 'debilitating psychological effects', since the shame it generates 'corrodes wellbeing and damages your sense of self'.[24] The experience of sexual abuse is so unbearable for her, that she needs – as a defence mechanism – to detach herself from her body, where the horrendous sexual assaults take place. She becomes a split subject, her mind, the part of her that she still controls, escapes from her body, the perpetrator's property – 'an empty shell'. Through this act of resistance, she tries to preserve her real self from defilement:

> Don't touch me with your dirty eyes I hate you. I can't stop you looking, touching, but that's not me you see, not me you feel. That's a shell and I'm not in it. I've left you far behind. I can escape, I will escape, I have escaped and you're so stupid, carrying on as if I was there when I'm not. That's not me. An empty shell pretending to be a person – no, a thing – for you to paw and prod and suck on. It's not a person, body, you've made it something else, your slave. Your thing. Don't touch me. Don't.[25]

Since Alice's body belongs to her father, it turns out to be, in the phraseology of Hélène Cixous, 'the uncanny stranger [...] the nasty companion', and as such, it is attacked by the protagonist even after her father's death.[26] Her self-destructive behaviour ranges from anorexia and addictions to drugs and alcohol to self-inflicted pain and suicidal attempts. Using Orbach's terms, Alice expresses with her self-damaged body what she is unable to confess with words; she wants 'to bring attentiveness to a body that has been neglected, disregarded or mistreated' and amplify her pain as 'a mechanism of self-communication and self-expression'.[27]

---

23   Judith Butler, *The Psychic Life of Power: Theories in Subjection* (Stanford: Stanford University Press, 1997), 105.
24   Imogen Tyler, *Stigma: The Machinery of Inequality* (London: Zed Books, 2021), 9.
25   Mills, *Another Alice*, 344.
26   Hélène Cixous, 'The Laugh of the Medusa', in *Feminisms REDUX*, edited by Robyn Warhol-Down and Diane Price Herndl (New Brunswick, NJ: Rutgers University Press, 2009), 419.
27   Orbach, *Bodies*, 108.

Eventually, as another psychological mechanism of defence, records of horrible sexual abuse in childhood are erased from her conscious memory – by ignoring a cruel reality at a conscious level, the pain it entails becomes lighter; however, the ghosts of the past, hidden at the subconscious level, continue to haunt her through recurrent flashes and nightmares.

Resilience through artistic creation

Deeply wounded, Alice does not 'know how to live in the world'.[28] Even in adulthood, she 'finds herself trapped in an outside-of-meaning, repetitive, marginal and invisible existence'.[29] This mood prevents her from enjoying a satisfactory emotional life, which provokes in her a sense of anger that negatively affects her relationship with Holly, her daughter. As she does not want to become an abusive parent like her own ones, she looks for professional assistance in order to solve her psychological problems.

A psychotherapist, Ruth, helps Alice to achieve a state of resilience, one defined by the psychologist Boris Cyrulnik as 'the ability to succeed, to live and to develop in a positive and socially acceptable way, despite stress or adversity that would normally involve the real possibility of a negative outcome'.[30] This is the revealing way in which she introduces herself to her psychotherapist: 'I'm like a cylinder. The surface is smooth and hard, it reflects back to people whatever they want to see. But inside […] it's completely hollow. A vacuum. […] there's no one there.'[31]

---

28 Mills, *Another Alice*, 369.
29 María Elena Jaime de Pablos, 'Expropriated Bodies: Victims of Father-Daughter Incest in Three Contemporary Irish Novels', *Revista Canaria de Estudios Ingleses*, 73 (2016), 40.
30 Boris Cyrulnik, *Resilience. How Your Inner Strength Can Set You Free from the Past* (London: Penguin Books, 2009), 5.
31 Mills, *Another Alice*, 246.

Alice presents herself as a commodified being that adapts to people's expectations because she feels an existential void, lacks a sense of identity and is prey to a frustrating melancholic mood. As she has forgotten the source of her grief, Ruth urges Alice to make an effort to confront her buried memories and they come back to her mind 'like falling snow, silent and heavy'.[32] However, as María Armental Romero comments, 'Alice's efforts to work through her memories, to liberate herself from the bad dreams, madness and fantasies which she has secretly kept, passes inevitably for the articulation of the narrative of her abused body.'[33] This narrative is not a written, but a visual one. She chooses the art of photography to offer portraits of damaged objects, harmed animals or disempowered people of a transgressive nature to represent an abject reality that is usually hidden to preserve the existing morality and culture and give focal attention to those who have been seriously abused like herself, but have survived. She is very fond of portraying broken dolls – in reference to her broken childhood – and injured birds – in allusion to the suffering that powerful beings inflict on those whom they regard inferior to themselves in order to take control of them.

Through her camera, Alice transforms images of vulnerability and suffering into unquestionable works of art.[34] According to Julia Kristeva, 'the artistic experience, which is rooted in the abject it utters' purifies it; for Alice, art is a means to achieve catharsis par excellence.[35] Following Boris Cyrulnik's ideas, her artistic work, highly iconic and extremely original, would have both an aesthetic effect and a therapeutic effect. From the aesthetic point of view, her photographs 'warm [... her] up by inducing a sense of beauty, and even happiness.'[36] Although Alice's photographs represent

32   Mills, *Another Alice*, 350.
33   María Armental Romero, '*Daddy says I mustn't tell because it is a secret*. The Subversion of the Irish Father-Daughter Creed in Lia Mills's *Another Alice*', in '*To Banish Ghost and Goblin*' *New Essays on Irish Culture*, edited by David Clark and Rubén Jarazo Álvarez (A Coruña: NETBIBLO, 2010), 55.
34   Art is a relevant phenomenon in Lia Mill's life, she has worked on different public art commissions and as arts consultant.
35   Julia Kristeva, *Powers of Horror: An Essay on Abjection* (New York: Columbia University Press, [1980] 1982), 17.
36   Cyrulnik, *Resilience: How Your Inner Strength Can Set You Free from the Past*, 277.

life exposed to abuse and degradation by tyrannical power, her technical skills elevate these pictures of the abject – generally understood as repugnant – to the category of sublime; by doing this, her 'abject' art becomes attractive to others, whose gaze is not only centred on its aesthetic features but also on its subversive content, since the abject 'disturbs identity, system, order. [It …] does not respect borders, positions, rules. [And it represents …] the in-between, the ambiguous, the composite'.[37]

From the therapeutic point of view, through the art of photography, she is able to transform her suffering 'into a story without words that is similar to an advertisement'.[38] According to Boris Cyrulnik, wounded people create a representation of the traumatic event that they can understand, it can be 'the turning point of [… their] personal history, a kind of dark guiding star showing [them] the way' to bounce back.[39] A camera helps Alice to put a distance between her and her trauma, so she can contemplate it, understand it and come to terms with it. She transforms her psychological wounds into artistic photographs that invite her, and others, to produce meaningful interpretations of the painful realities that they represent, thus showing the link between creativity and suffering, but also between creativity and healing. Examining the relation between the abject, art and catharsis, Arthur Danto states that the 'redemptive task of art is not to make [...] surplus beauty, but to beautify what is initially as remote from beauty as [... the abject]'.[40] Alice's pictures represent an oxymoron, in Cyrulnik's words 'a wonderful horror'.[41]

Alice's camera provides her the means to acquire a voice – due to the sensory immediacy of pictures – with which to narrate her past and make visible her existence in the present. 'When words are silenced [in Alice's case by a protecting memory], objects [pictures] become a language'.[42] Thanks to her photographs, which tell stories similar to her own, she talks

---

37 Kristeva, *Powers of Horror: An Essay on Abjection*, 75.
38 Cyrulnik, *Resilience: How Your Inner Strength Can Set You Free from the Past*, 196.
39 Boris Cyrulnik, *The Whispering of Ghosts: Trauma and Resilience* (New York: Other Press, 2005), 12.
40 Arthur Danto, *Mapplethorpe* (London: Jonathan Cape, 1992), 330.
41 Cyrulnik, *Resilience: How Your Inner Strength Can Set You Free from the Past*, 160.
42 Cyrulnik, *Resilience: How Your Inner Strength Can Set You Free from the Past*, 234.

fully and freely about herself – although not explicitly – through a socially acceptable practice. The beauty in Alice's pictures lets her see herself as a damaged person through a different lens, the art in them purifies that part of her that she has always linked to defilement, abjection, chaos and death.[43] Art allows her to overcome trauma by reconstructing herself as a proper and clean body and to recover her original psychosomatic unity. Art is, in this way, an effective healing tool to such an extent that her photos, although portraying abuse, do not re-enforce notions of victimhood, but of resilience.

As she becomes an accomplished and admired photographer, her art not only contributes to improvement in her self-esteem, self-respect and self-confidence – all of this gives her a sense of power that helps her to fill the existential void that marks her experience with a terrible sense of anguish, but also connects her to society and culture, since the audience engages with Alice's emotion-evoking images. Exposing to others the damaged side of nature, and receiving a positive feedback for it, makes her burden lighter.

At the end of the novel, Alice's attitude is that of the triumphant survivor: 'This is who I am. I survived all that',[44] who has learnt to 'denaturalize' sexual abuse, to cope with its effects and to reappropriate her own body in order to experience a pleasing sense of wholeness:

> She was white hot, luminous. She could feel herself glow with energy. Her blood sang, it was better that any high she'd ever known. Liquid, molten, silver and shining, she was coming together again, like mercury, all the dispersed parts of herself flowing into each other. She held herself ready and let them fill her. When it was over she felt clear and new.[45]

Alice is so willing to leave trauma behind and enjoy life that her new goal is 'to live well'. 'No longer hollow, fragmented, silent, depressed or isolated, Alice is now ready to make deep and lasting changes in her life, to explore new places, and enjoy fresh experiences in the company of the

---

43 For a more detailed analysis of abjection in *Another Alice*, see 'Incest, Gender and Abjection in *In Night's City* and *Another Alice*' by María Elena Jaime de Pablos.
44 Mills, *Another Alice*, 350.
45 Mills, *Another Alice*, 353.

person she most loves, Holly.'⁴⁶ At this stage, she perceives herself as a part of living nature, as a worthy human being entitled to love and happiness:

> An ache of love caught in her chest. The whole country seemed to stretch out in front of them. Limitless' [...] She and Holly sang along together, loud. 'Take these sunken eyes and learn to see' [....] They smiled widely at each other in the mirror, still singing. Alice looked at the road ahead. She felt the pressure of happiness build in her until she was sure she would burst, lift from the ground and soar. Nothing, not even the gravity, was strong enough to hold her down. The sky bent over her in a wide blue curve and she flew to meet it. Strong. Forgiven.⁴⁷

Both Alice and Holly show their state of joy and hope in the future by singing 'Blackbird', a song that The Beatles included in their *White Album*, released in 1968. This song also tells the story of a damaged being, a blackbird that has to learn to fly with broken wings to survive and is ready to do it, which implies to begin life anew: 'Blackbird singing in the dead of night / Take these broken wings and learn to fly / All your life / You were only waiting for this moment to arise.' The fragment that Lia Mills chooses to include in her novel belongs to the second stanza of the song: 'Blackbird singing in the dead of night / Take these sunken eyes and learn to see / All your life / You were only waiting for this moment to be free.' Flying and seeing life from a different perspective let the bird enjoy happiness and freedom.

By singing, which involves the art of music, the bird makes itself visible and heard; with its trill, it narrates its plight, presenting itself as a vulnerable, but resistant creature. Only inner strength and positive attitude can save it from a sure death. The role of the poetic voice, which – out of love and care – drives the bird into motion, is also very relevant. Alice's journey towards her psychological salvation resembles that of the blackbird, whereas psychotherapist Ruth's impulse for vital change resembles that of the song poetic voice.

The new Alice articulates the unspeakable about incest through the art of photography,⁴⁸ that helps her to understand that the abuse that she had

---

46 Jaime de Pablos, 'Incest, Gender and Abjection in *In Night's City* and *Another Alice*', 451.
47 Mills, *Another Alice*, 392.
48 Jaime de Pablos, 'Incest, Gender and Abjection in *In Night's City* and *Another Alice*', 450.

suffered was not her fault and that she was not dirty, but 'hurt'.[49] She learns to accept and respect her body – which once represented 'otherness' – to knit herself together, forging the bond between body and mind anew in order to experience a gratifying sense of selfhood. She feels love for herself because she has worked hard to overcome adversity and has achieved victory over suffering: 'Something warm stirred inside her. She was shocked to realise that what she felt was love. As she recognised it, it grew. Love for herself, both then and now. Love and a fierce kind of pride.'[50]

By charting 'the passage of Alice from wounded denial and inner loathing to self-knowledge and acceptance',[51] Mills implies that people who have suffered brutal abuse may develop the ability to adapt and bounce back from adversity in order to reach and enjoy well-being – provided that they are determined to do it and receive the support necessary to achieve it – and that they may turn to artistic creation as an effective healing tool.

Alice's pictures provoke a third effect, a social effect. By presenting damaged objects, animals and people in an artistic way, thus making them more socially acceptable, she aims to generate a feeling of sympathy for them in those who pay attention to their situation of vulnerability. These illustrations of life are meant to activate people's social conscience and ethical responsibility in relation to the suffering of those who need to overcome a state of anguish, sadness and / or fragility. In this way, Alice's photographs, like Lia Mill's novel, can be called 'disturbatory art' since it is intended 'to modify, through experiencing it, the mentality of those who do experience it'.[52] Thus, it contributes to the transformation of the community in which it is consumed by making it more ethically self-conscious, more sensitive and more engaged with damaged people.

---

49   Mills, *Another Alice*, 350–351.
50   Mills, *Another Alice*, 350.
51   Anne Fogarty, '"The Horror of the Unlived Life": Mother-Daughter Relationships in Contemporary Irish Women's Fiction', in *Writing Mothers and Daughters*, edited by Adalgisa Giorgio (New York: Berghahn Books, 2002), 112.
52   Arthur Danto, *Encounters and Reflections: Art in the Historical Present* (Berkeley: University of California Press, 1990), 299.

EAMONN WALL

14 He Lived among These Lanes: Bioregional John McGahern

In this exploration of John McGahern's fiction and non-fiction, I will reach out to see how easily his work can find shelter under the umbrellas of ecocriticism and bioregionalism, and take a route that brings his life and work into dialogue with Wendell Berry's and Gary Snyder's, two American father figures of environmental writing. First, two definitions to serve as guides. Cheryl Glotfelty defines 'ecocriticism as the study of the relationship between literature and the physical environment' before proceeding to elaborate that 'all ecological criticism shares the fundamental premise that human culture is connected to the physical world, affecting it and affected by it'[1] Lynch, Glotfelty, and Armbruster have defined bioregionalism as being motivated by the desire 'to address matters of pressing environmental concern through a politics derived from a local sense of place'.[2] Robert L. Thayer, Jr. believes that a bioregion is 'literally and etymologically a "life place" – a unique region definable by natural (rather than political) boundaries [....] The bioregion is emerging as the most logical locus and scale for a sustainable, regenerative community to take root and *take place*'.[3] In addition to its focus on place in the widest sense, culture, also in its largest sense, plays a central role in the bioregionalist vision and less so in ecocriticism. A key term in bioregionalism is

1 Cheryll Glotfelty, 'Introduction: Literary Studies in the Age of Environmental Crisis', in *The Ecocriticism Reader*, edited by Cheryll Glotfelty and Harold Fromm (Athens, GA: University of Georgia Press, 1991), xviii–xix.
2 Tom Lynch, Cheryll Glotfelty, and Karla Armbruster (eds), *The Bioregional Imagination: Literature, Ecology, and Place* (Athens, GA: University of Georgia Press, 2012), 2.
3 Robert L. Thayer, Jr., *LifePlace: Bioregional Thought and Practice* (Berkeley, CA: University of California Press, 2003), 3.

reinhabitation 'that is, not only learning to live-in-place, but doing so in an area that has been disrupted and injured through past exploitation', as Berg and Dasmann point out.[4] My argument is that the latter terms – bioregionalism and reinhabitation – provide us with new avenues to explore McGahern's work. It turns out that ecocritical readings of McGahern's are less persuasive than bioregional ones.

In 'Literature without Qualities', John McGahern details his own position regarding the connection between ideology and writing:

> The work of a writer does not define itself in advance, even in the case of a writer who appears to identify and conform perfectly with his own time or when his hope is to be exemplary and right-thinking. If he is a great writer, his work is shaped in the writing itself first of all, and then in successive re-reading and the intervention of specific poetic elements, which bypass ideological notions [....] A writer's work does not define itself by intentions but by results.[5]

McGahern is firmly focused on vision and aesthetic. Should ideology occupy the writer's field of vision before he begins composing, his creative powers will be hamstrung, and his sight blurred. Elsewhere, he declares: 'I write because I need to write. I write to see. Through words I see.'[6] The author must avoid ideologies and instead work with the fundamental building blocks of writing: words. Writing of McGahern, Declan Kiberd makes note of two salient aspects of his art. The first is that his fiction is 'anthropological rather than political', an indication that his vision is not ecological.[7] McGahern's work appears to be so profoundly and deeply focused on people that larger spaces play no visible roles. In fact, interaction between humans and non-humans in McGahern's fiction appears negligible, particularly in his early work. His fiction is deeply anthropological: it has been created to dramatize and describe the lives led by men, women, and children from the War of Independence to close to the present.

---

4   Peter Berg and Raymond Dasmann, 'Reinhabiting California', *The Ecologist*, 7/10 (1977), 35–38.
5   John McGahern, *Love of the World: Essays* (London: Faber & Faber, 2009), 181.
6   John McGahern, *Love of the World: Essays*, 9.
7   Declan Kiberd, 'Introduction', *Love of the World: Essays*, xiii.

Often, both the outdoor and indoor settings are so narrowly drawn that we must imagine what a field or kitchen looks like. McGahern's powerful characters and the highly charged crises they provoke so overwhelm the spaces where actions occur that setting lapses from our field of vision. Always, McGahern draws us towards people. Landscape can seem empty. As the eco-critic Harold Fromm has depressingly noted, 'all life continues in existence by feeding on other life, favouring itself at the expense of everything else'.[8] In McGahern's fiction, male authority figures are often exemplars of this dictum, and this is an aspect of the type of behaviour and outlook that McGahern obsessively traces in his work, particularly in the novels *The Barracks*, *The Dark*, *Amongst Women*, and in the short story 'Gold Watch'. Larger-than-life characters overwhelm the living world. Kiberd provides an extract from *That They May Face the Rising Son*, McGahern's final novel, that emphasizes another aspect of the author's aesthetic – the need to be separate rather than connected, to be of oneself and not of everything else, and of the essential independence of art and the artist from whatever structures are outside of him:

> Often he sat in silence. His silences were never oppressive and he never spoke unless to respond to something that had been said or to say something that he wanted to say. Throughout, he was intensely aware of every other presence, exercising his imagination on their behalf as well as on his own, seeing himself as he might be seen and as he saw others.[9]

Kiberd adds that 'if McGahern's tastes were fastidious, his instincts were democratic, but rooted in the conviction that there is something inherently beautiful about a silent experience of pure imagination'.[10] Whatever McGahern might have felt as a citizen of the world, he sought to carefully separate the dross that came his way from his artistic vision. The environmental ideologies would have found no leverage at his desk. What is described in this brief scene from the novel is a trigger moment when the

---

8 Harold Fromm, 'Aldo Leopold: Aesthetic Anthropocentrist', *Interdisciplinary Studies in Literature and Environment*, 1/1 (Spring 1993), 43.
9 John McGahern, *That They May Face the Rising Sun* (London: Faber & Faber, 2002), 36.
10 Declan Kiberd, 'Introduction', *Love of the World: Essays*, xxi.

imagination is freed from its restraints to become itself, to take off on the wings of language into conjecture and drama. Whereas the scholar requires dogma to underpin his / her work, the writer sees it as something to avoid. At the same time, the publication of three volumes of McGahern's non-fiction – *Memoir* (2005), *Love of the World: Essays* (2009), and *The Letters of John McGahern* (2021) – forces us to view McGahern in another light as a man very much in tune with his environment. The late McGahern is green and bioregional. As we look backwards from his later to his early work, we can, with the aid of eco and biological critical values, discover that for all his protests to the contrary, McGahern always brought ideology to his work.

Writing of McGahern in mid-career, Eamon Maher notes:

> But throughout his literary career, McGahern has been attempting to find the right way of conveying the image that is at the heart of his creativity. This task brings him on a circular path back to his rural roots in the north-west midlands of Ireland. He returned there at the end of *The Pornographer* and has not left it since. His attitude to this setting has changed considerably.[11]

The earliest letter written from Foxfield is dated 10 May 1974.[12] Maher identifies two important aspects of McGahern's career: first, the image, like the word, is central to his aesthetic and an abiding driver of his imagination, and, second, his return to live in the north-west midlands of Ireland that provides his work with a bioregional consciousness and which is, in fact, a reinhabitation of a damaged environment. After McGahern and his wife settle in Co. Leitrim his work begins to change in subtle ways with the keys to this change more evident in his essays than in his fiction. While McGahern sought to partition his fiction from the extraneous world outside, he allowed himself free reign in his non-fiction, a genre he did not consider his essential art. But in his later fiction, from *Amongst Women* on, he is less guarded in this respect. *That They May Face the Rising Son* is a novel with a wider focus and a more open style

---

11 Eamon Maher, *John McGahern: From the Local to the Universal* (Dublin: Liffey Press, 2003), 98.
12 Frank Shovlin (ed.), *The Letters of John McGahern* (London: Faber & Faber, 2021), 366–367.

than anything McGahern had attempted previously. Its guiding voice is brought magnificently into focus on the opening page by the tolling bell which unites its disparate parts:

> The morning was clear. There was no wind on the lake. There was also a great stillness. When the bells rang out for Mass, the strokes trembling on the water, they had the entire world to themselves.[13]

In *Amongst Women*, Moran, the old patriarch, understands toward the end of his life that 'to die was never to look on all this again. It would live in others' eyes but not in his. He had never realized when he was in the midst of confident life what an amazing glory he was part of.'[14] Here, Moran embraces the non-human that he bypassed when he was so busy working his land for profit and survival. Now aware of his own frailty, he begins to absorb the fields' permanence. Both *Amongst Women* and *That They May Face the Rising Son* are elegies, though not always fond ones, for vanishing times and people. While he is contemplating the death of one civilization, McGahern is simultaneously imagining that which will replace it. The crude and violent characters that populate and terrorize in such late stories as 'Creatures of the Earth' and 'Love of the World' seem all the darker for their modernity.[15] Though the titles of these stories suggest an environmental consciousness, they might also be viewed as being highly ironic.

While his work might sound a death knell for his home region, McGahern contributed to its economy and essential character by farming. He downplayed this role, 'The myth of Farmer John is not my doing. Over the years many TV crews have been here who wanted me to play the farmer. This I always refused. I was a writer who happened to live on a farm.'[16] But McGahern improved his farm. He was an active farmer albeit on a small scale. Writing to Niall Walsh on 10 July 1977, McGahern notes, 'We bought

---

13 McGahern, *That They May Face the Rising Sun*, 1.
14 John McGahern, *Amongst Women* (London: Faber & Faber, 1990), 179.
15 John McGahern, *Creatures of the Earth: New and Selected Stories* (London: Faber & Faber, 1992).
16 Shovlin, *The Letters of John McGahern*, 798.

4 in-calf cows, and they've had four calves, all heifers. One of them got joint ill, but was treated, and seems all right, if a little shaky. We've started to put up a shed, and seem owned as well by the acres.'[17] By settling at Foxfield and making improvements, John and Madeline McGahern not only learned 'to live-in-place, but [were] doing so in an area that has been disrupted and injured through past exploitation'.[18] For a long time, Leitrim was Ireland's poorest and most underpopulated county, in a part of Ireland that had been ravaged by colonization, dispossession, famine, depopulation and poverty. In short, in bioregional parlance, the McGaherns had reinhabited a distressed region at a time when the bureaucrats in Brussels saw such outposts of the Common Market / EU as being fit for nothing but tourism. Like Wendell Berry in Kentucky and Gary Snyder in California, McGahern was part of a resistance movement. All three fought with both fists: the pen and the plough.

It is useful to place McGahern's life in Leitrim alongside Wendell Berry's in Port Royal, Kentucky. Writing of his life on his farm, Berry refers to himself as an agrarian, 'We agrarians are involved in a hard, long, momentous contest, in which we are so far, and by a considerable margin, the losers. What we have undertaken to defend is the complex accomplishment of knowledge, cultural memory, skill, self-mastery, good sense, and fundamental decency – the high and indispensable art – for which we can probably find no better name than "good farming".'[19] McGahern is a more circumspect farmer-thinker who does not view his decision to be a writer who happens to live on a farm as an overt political act. I can't imagine McGahern calling himself an agrarian. But, like Berry, through his writings and activities, he is engaged in efforts to preserve the soul and land of a community. Berry's describes his return to Kentucky in messianic terms:

> I could never bring myself to want to live in any other place. And so we returned to live in Kentucky in the summer of 1964, and that autumn bought the house whose roof my friend and I had looked down on eight years before [....] Thus I began a

---

17 Shovlin, *The Letters of John McGahern*, 444.
18 Lynch, Glotfelty and Armbruster, *The Bioregional Imagination*, 3.
19 Wendell Berry, 'The Agrarian Standard', in *The World-Ending Fire: The Essential Wendell Berry* (Berkeley: Counterpoint, 2017), 133.

profound change in my life. Before, I had lived according to expectation rooted in ambition. Now I began to live according to a kind of destiny rooted in my origins and in my life [....] In buying the little place known as Lanes Landing, it seems to me, I began to obey the deeper causes.[20]

Not only was Berry making a journey back to a resonant place, but he was also assuming the responsibility of taking on a deeper role both as a custodian of the land and as an author whose work would be focused on that place. In *Memoir*, McGahern describes his journey home in 1974:

I came back to live among these lanes thirty years ago. My wife and I were beginning our life together, and we thought we could make a bare living on these small fields and I would write. It was a time when we could have settled almost anywhere, and if she had not liked the place and the people we would have moved elsewhere. I, too, liked the place, but I was from these fields and my preference was less important.[21]

It suited McGahern to return to the north-west midlands of Ireland and settling there, as I have argued, did influence how he thought and how he wrote. It was familiar place, the territory of his early life where the memories of his mother abounded; however, as he admits, it was on account of his wife feeling comfortable in the area that the decision was made to settle at Foxfield. During the same decade when McGahern settled in Leitrim, Gary Snyder made his home in northern California, 'moving into the Sierra foothills of northern California in the 1970s, into an area that had been devastated by hydraulic gold mining, he built a house, planted trees, raised children, and explored the terrain. His departure from industrial society and turning back to the land was "a moral and spiritual choice", a seeking for a life committed to a place'.[22] McGahern might not have seen his return as being guided by 'a moral and spiritual choice', for I see no evidence of this, but it was as firm a commitment to a place as Snyder's.

20 Wendell Berry, 'The Making of a Marginal Farm', in *The World-Ending Fire: The Essential Wendell Berry* (Berkeley: Counterpoint, 2017), 39.
21 John McGahern, *Memoir* (London: Faber & Faber, 2005), 2.
22 Katsunori Yamazato, 'Kitkitdizze, Zendo, and Place: Gary Snyder as a Reinhabitory Poet', *ISLE*, 1/1 (Spring 1993), 1.

Bioregionalism is perfectly suited to understanding Irish writing. As McGahern believed, for Irish people loyalty is primarily local rather than national and place is a core value in Irish writing, 'everything interesting begins with one person, in one place. The universal is the local without walls. The place itself has walls'.[23] If we extract the activist / ideological element, we can argue for McGahern – living and working as he did in Co. Leitrim – as a bioregional writer. On a practical level, he participated in the local woodland project by planting trees on his land. Everything that McGahern achieved in Foxfield mirrors what Snyder, a father figure of environmentalism and bioregionalism, achieved in northern California. As Denis Sampson has pointed out, McGahern is a 'regional writer'.[24] Often, this can be a dangerous label to apply to a writer; however, in McGahern's case it is quite correct. Snyder and Berry are also regional writers; however, like McGahern, neither their range nor audience has been limited by this definition because these writers appeal to broad swathes of readers. Environmentalists and bioregionalists favour regions over states and nations: if more attention is paid to smaller and more natural units, then the damage caused by big thinking (colonialism, industrialization, and development) can be corrected. A further environmental aspect present in McGahern's work is eco-feminism. The prevalence of so many remarkable women in his work opens the door for eco-feminist explorations of his work.

A change of emphasis is obvious in McGahern's later work. For one, animals play important roles in the short story 'Creatures of the Earth' – a cat and basking sharks – while both the violence with which they are treated and the empathy for their fate that McGahern draws from his reader attests to his movement away from a strictly anthropological view of the world to one that embraces the non-human. Animals are also fondly written about in both *Memoir* and in his essays. In a letter to Niall Walsh of 20 April 1992, McGahern writes with grief at the death of the family's cat, 'The old black cat Fats with the four white paws that we had for 13 years

---

23   Maher, *John McGahern: From the Local to the Universal*, 10.
24   Denis Sampson, *Outstaring Nature's Eye: The Fiction of John McGahern* (Washington, DC: Catholic University of America Press, 1993), xii.

died in January. It was kind of silly but it was like watching a whole happy part of our life go.'[25] In an accompanying note to this letter, Frank Shovlin notes that McGahern 'loved animals and had a particular liking for cats'.[26]

An attentiveness to the natural world and the non-human is a recurring feature of his non-fiction. Examples abound:

> There is nothing dramatic about the landscape, but it is never dull. On the low drumlins around the countless lakes the soil is hardly an inch deep. Beneath it is either channel-compacted gravel or daub (a sticky blue clay), and neither can soak up the heavy rainfall. Irregular hedgerows of whitethorn, ash, green oak, holly, wild cherry, sloe and sycamore divide the drumlins into rushy fields. The hedges are the glory of these small fields, especially in late May and early June when the whitethorn foams out into streams of pink and white blossom. The soil's very poorness is what saved these hedges from the bulldozer, when great trees and old shrubs were being levelled and 'rationalized' for machinery through Europe in the 1960s and 1970s.[27]

Not only does McGahern patiently observe but he also highlights how vulnerable these trees, shrubs, and bushes are. Interviewed by Dennis O'Driscoll, Seamus Heaney was asked if 'a poem can stop an SUV? "I think"', Heaney replied, "that one answers itself. What has happened, however, is that environmental issues have to a large extent changed the mind of poetry"'.[28] Of course, neither the lyric nor the essay can compete with the JCB; however, what both can do is raise consciousness in the hope that the bureaucrat will pause before ordering the great machines into the verdant field. Like Berry and Snyder, McGahern understands the primacy of the local, those places that undercut such received boundaries as state, county, and national demarcations. Snyder's *Turtle Island* is quite large while McGahern's is miniscule by comparison:

> Though I have written only about a small area, less than thirty miles, it would nevertheless be considered enormous by the local people. Except for football and politics, the county divisions mean little to them. For those who live around Mohill,

---

25   Shovlin, *The Letters of John McGahern*, 654.
26   Shovlin, *The Letters of John McGahern*, 653.
27   McGahern, *Love of the World: Essays*, 19–20.
28   Dennis O'Driscoll, *Stepping Stones: Interviews with Seamus Heaney* (London: Faber & Faber, 2009), 444.

Rockingham, eighteen miles away, might as well be Syracuse (New York or Sicily). It is each single, enclosed locality that matters, and everything that happens within it is of passionate interest to those who live there [....] But once the news crosses a certain boundary, eyes that a moment before were wild with curiosity will suddenly glaze: news no longer local is of no interest.[29]

One task that environmental writers and scholars set us is to remap where we live. If we can do this, we will make an important first step towards understanding and guarding the area where we reside. Like what Snyder achieved in *Turtle Island*, though on smaller scales, both Berry and McGahern remapped their home places.[30] McGahern helped preserve the culture of where he lived by making it central to his work. In various essays, he remapped his bioregion and the watersheds that form its veins and arteries, 'The whole region is dominated by water. As the Erne is in the North, the Shannon is the great river of the South, and it rises in the low chain of mountains that crosses the border.'[31] Environmentalists ask us to be loyal to watersheds rather than counties – watersheds that erase county, state, and national boundaries. To follow this path is the route to new ways of thinking that will allow us to better care for our planet. In another essay, 'Life as It Is and Life as It Ought to Be', McGahern recounts a role he played in the preservation of documents recording details of the lives of members of the local Protestant community. Willie Booth, the man who owned the documents, called on McGahern for help in saving them now that he had grown old and had no family. McGahern and Booth 'discussed the possibility of restoring the small Protestant church in Fenagh as a library or museum to house these records.'[32] Eventually, with community and government help, the church was restored, and the archive was preserved. If attention to culture is central to bioregionalism, McGahern is certainly involved in the preservation of the culture of his bioregion.

---

29   McGahern, *Love of the World: Essays*, 24.
30   Gary Snyder, *Turtle Island* (New York: New Directions, 1974).
31   McGahern, *Love of the World: Essays*, 23.
32   McGahern, *Love of the World: Essays*, 160.

Eamon Maher has explored the structure of *That They May Face the Rising Son* and observed, 'Let us now consider the novel with these few ideas at the back of our minds. There is no real plot, no strong central consciousness to hold our attention. What we have is a community, made up of middle-aged to old inhabitants, whose lives have not changed significantly for several decades.'[33] Though bioregionalists reinhabit blighted places in hopes of revitalizing them, these depopulated areas have never been empty. People have remained clustered in small but rich communities; they carry unrecorded cultures forward. As Maher points out, McGahern served the particular community of his narrow hinterland by imagining it, by affording it a central place in writing, by making its culture a part of our own, by revealing to us both our closeness to it and our distance from it. If the community provided McGahern with material, he, in return, afforded it a place on the maps he had drawn. Artist and community were working in tandem and were co-dependent. This is exactly the form of cultural engagement that Paula Gunn Allen, the Laguna Pueblo / Sioux writer, advocated when she wrote: 'Literature must, of necessity, express and articulate the deepest perceptions, relationships, and attitudes of a culture, whether it does so deliberately or accidentally.'[34]

Just as ecocriticism and bioregionalism and the other scholarly practices that connect ecologies with writing have evolved and continue to do so, so too did McGahern's own attitudes to and representations of his rural environment change over time from the cold, stark lucidity of *The Barracks* to the more nuanced and weathered surfaces of *That They May Face the Rising Son*. Maher directs us to the absence of 'plot [and a] strong central consciousness' in the final novel and I would argue that these are absent because McGahern sought a more natural form to frame this novel, one that would allow a community to breathe rather than be curtailed by the artificiality of plot, and suffocated by a guiding consciousness.[35] As a result, *That They Face the Rising Sun* is the most natural and organic of McGahern's

---

33 Maher, *John McGahern: From the Local to the Universal*, 123.
34 Paula Gunn Allen, 'The Sacred Hoop: A Contemporary Perspective', in *The Ecocriticism Reader*, edited by Cheryll Glotfelty and Harold Fromm (Athens, GA: University of Georgia Press, 1991), 260.
35 Maher, *John McGahern: From the Local to the Universal*, 123.

novels. It is both a bioregionalist text and a novel that retains what Kiberd refers to as its 'experience of pure imagination'.[36] Though McGahern would probably disagree with Paula Gunn Allen's belief that 'the significance of a literature can be best understood in terms of the culture from which it springs' because such ideas give too much agency to matters that are beyond the writer's field, I would make the point that McGahern's work and the times they evoked and the characters he invented are inseparable from the times and places of his own life and the communities he was part of.[37]

36   Kiberd, 'Introduction', *Love of the World: Essays*, xxi.
37   Allen, 'The Sacred Hoop: A Contemporary Perspective', 241.

HARRY WHITE

15 *Fifth Business*: George Moore and the Cultural History of Music in Ireland

My intention in this short essay is to make admittedly very modest amends for having hitherto overlooked George Moore completely in my work on the relationship between music and the Irish literary imagination.[1] *Mea maxima culpa*. And yet it would appear that I am anything but alone in this kind of dereliction. Notwithstanding the formidable heft of recent Moore scholarship, 'GM' (to use that well-beloved abbreviation) continues to lie offshore, like a vast Cunard liner waiting to dock in port.[2] In the words of one recent commentator, Moore (to alter the likening) 'tends on the whole to be denied a place at the top table'.[3] For many people, indeed, Moore remains 'yesterday's man' (another commonplace description) and a forgotten hero of the *fin-de-siècle*.[4] He is the neglected precursor of James Joyce; he is the *bête noir* of the Irish Literary Revival in general and of Yeats

---

1   I would like to thank the distinguished Moore scholar, Mary Pierse, who invited me to take part in a symposium on George Moore that took place at the Museum of Irish Literature, Dublin, in November 2022. The original version of this essay was delivered on that occasion, at which Eamon Maher was present. His generous comments afterwards prompted me to revise this essay in his honour.

2   This simile occurred to me because Maud Cunard (1892–1948), husband of Sir Bache Cunard (owner of the famous shipping line) was Moore's lover and mistress.

3   See Gerry Smyth, *Music and Sound in the Life and Literature of James Joyce* (Cham: Palgrave Macmillan, 2020), chapter four ('Joyce, George Moore and the Irish Wagnerian Novel)', 123–144, here at 126. I am indebted to this essay for its close reading of Moore's fiction in relation to music.

4   The phrase is used to characterize Moore in Gerry Smyth, '*Evelyn Innes* and the Irish Wagnerian Novel', in *Music Preferred*: *Essays in Musicology, Cultural History and Analysis in Honour of Harry White*, edited by Lorraine Byrne Bodley (Vienna: Hollitzer Verlag, 2018), 335–349; here at 336.

in particular; he is the English Zola, and so on: something, to paraphrase Philip Larkin, is always pushing Moore to the side of his own life. The prolific nature of Moore's vast literary estate is surely complicit in this enterprise, to say little of the writer's exceptionally extensive network of friends and enemies in Paris, Dublin and London. Above all, perhaps, as Adrian Frazier makes clear in his magisterial biography of Moore, GM's resistance to school or party, or to any prevailing category of reception history, impeded his afterlife as a self-standing artist. Frazier adds that 'he died as neither an Irish patriot nor a Roman Catholic', but that was perhaps the least of it: he belonged, it seems, everywhere and therefore nowhere.[5]

It is true that GM reminds me of another Irish Catholic who worked in the world at large and who spent the latter part of his life in Britain, namely his namesake, Thomas Moore, who died in 1852, the year of GM's birth. Tom Moore has also endured something of a half-life in literary reception history, even if this shadowy state of affairs has improved considerably over the past twenty years. I once asked Declan Kiberd about Tom Moore's absence from *Inventing Ireland* (which first appeared in 1995) and he told me that he had simply forgotten about him, which is a sure enough indication of how far Moore had fallen out of sight by then. One of Tom Moore's biographers, Helen Hoover Jordan, remarked in 1975 that 'critics observed that the author of *Lalla Rookh* and the *Irish Melodies* would not produce a School of Moore, as the School of Wordsworth or Byron had arisen, because no other poet could work in the two media of music and poetry'.[6] The critics were right: the lustre of Moore's reputation in the years following the publication of *Lalla Rookh* (in 1817) no more secured his position as an English romantic than it redeemed his ambiguous standing as an Irish proto-nationalist. To 'work in the two media of music and poetry' was to fall between two stools. I'm tempted to suggest that something

---

5   See Adrian Frazier, *George Moore, 1852–1933* (New Haven: Yale University Press, 2000), xii. At the very close of his biography, Frazier quotes Moore as having said: 'Myself was my nation' (468).

6   See Helen Hoover Jordan, *Bolt Upright: The Life of Thomas Moore* (Salzburg: Institut für englische Sprache und Literatur, 1975), vol. 1, 273.

similar may have happened to George Moore, and that he, likewise, fell between the two stools of French symbolism and Irish modernism, even if many scholars recognize Moore's fiction (and in particular his novel *The Lake*, from 1905) as a fundamental source for Joyce's stream of consciousness in general and the achievement of *Ulysses* in particular. And this is to say nothing of a host of other premonitory achievements on Moore's part, not least in relation to Joyce's *Dubliners* and its debt to *The Untilled Field*. But in summoning TM in relation to GM (so to speak) I am in danger of merely adding to that conjunctive reception history which has so strikingly determined George Moore's significance in the present day. Even the website of the George Moore Association, in its persuasive reading of Moore as a fundamentally transitional figure, locates Moore's life and work under the governance of a recurring preposition: *from* the nineteenth to the twentieth century, *from* naturalism to modernism, *from* fiction to autobiography, *from* Ireland to France and Britain, and so on.[7] In a similar way, the meaning we attach to Moore is perpetually defined, at least in part, by reading him in relation to his forbears and contemporaries: Moore and Edward Martyn, Moore and Wagner, Moore and Yeats, Moore and Shaw, Moore and Eduard Du Jardin, and of course Moore and Joyce. In each case, Moore's dependence is mandatory. Given these habits of reception history, the conjunction 'Moore and Music' also seems to arise as a natural consideration, not only in relation to Moore's musical dependencies as a writer of fiction but also in relation to the cultural history of music in Ireland. It is the latter that will preoccupy me in this essay, even if I have occasional recourse to Moore's novels in the tentative enterprise of restoring GM's role in that (musical) history.

---

[7] See the home page of the George Moore Association https://www.georgemoore association.org [accessed 24 August 2023], which identifies Moore as 'a transitional, boundary-crossing figure' whose achievement is defined in such terms.

I

I once remarked that 'music is the sovereign ghost of the Irish literary imagination'.[8] Thus identified as a formative presence in the work of Tom Moore, John Millington Synge, Bernard Shaw, W. B. Yeats, James Joyce and indeed Samuel Beckett, it is difficult to overlook that recurring pattern of musical beginnings and verbal endings which, with the notable exception of Yeats himself, underpins the emergence of an Irish literary modernism haunted by the absence of actual music (which is to say its sounding forms) and yet preoccupied by its condition of meaning. Even in Yeats's case, the rival claims of music and poetry remained of acute account from his own immersions in literary Wagnerism right through to the broadcasts he made for the BBC on the subject of speech as music in the closing years of his life. Yeats, the implacable enemy of music *per se*, nevertheless conceded its dangerous and ineffable sway over the certain good of words alone.[9] And this antagonism was fortified by another rival claim which initially dogged Yeats's emergence as poet and indeed as a man of the theatre: that claim, of course, was the short-lived but immensely influential ascendancy of the Irish language as an indispensable agent of cultural revival. It is a commonplace, but nevertheless a controversial one, to argue that Yeats's vision of Irish cultural autonomy overcame the Gaelic League and won the day. Even Synge, after all, wrote his plays in English. Irish itself, like music, was remaindered or marginalized in this grand enterprise. The Abbey Theatre was preponderantly an English-language institution (it still is), and although traditional music would become, partly on this very account, a vigorous emblem of the Free State, a kind of Irish-language *manqué* (and now the definitive global signature of Irishness itself), Irish music in the European tradition all but lapsed into silence.

8 See Harry White, *Music and the Irish Literary Imagination* (New York: Oxford University Press, 2008), 3.
9 See Colton Johnston (ed.), *W. B. Yeats, Later Articles and Reviews, Uncollected Articles, Reviews and Radio Broadcasts Written after 1900* (New York: Scribner's and Sons, 2000), 265–277.

Even today, the history of art music in Ireland between the turn of the century and the founding of the Irish Free State in 1922 remains fugitive and insecure. It is a safe bet, for example, that the operas of Robert O'Dwyer, Michele Esposito, Geoffrey Molyneux Palmer and Thomas O'Brien Butler, all of whom set Irish-language libretti and / or operas on Irish subjects between 1901 and 1910, are (with one or two fleeting exceptions) unknown to Irish cultural history, despite the vigorous remembrances of the Decade of Centenaries that has just come to a close.[10] One might even say that the prospect of imagining Ireland operatically was a fitful but unmistakable episode doomed to silence after the revolution of 1916, when in the words of one contemporary musician (Joseph O'Neill), 'Dublin was principally interested in war and politics', adding that the city 'sank into its humdrum musical life' following the Tailteann Games opera festival of 1924.[11]

Beyond the purview of specialized scholarship, George Moore's part in this hidden history remains little-known. I draw attention to it here not to exaggerate Moore's influence on Irish opera (which as far as I can see was vestigial), but rather to indicate the extent to which Moore's own profound immersion in Wagner's operas and music dramas (which, among much else, had explicitly shaped both the plot and characterization of his 1898 novel *Evelyn Innes*, in which the composer Ulick Dean is based on Yeats himself) underwrote his ambitions for *Diarmuid and Grania*.[12] *Diarmuid and Grania* was the play which he co-wrote with Yeats for the Irish Literary Theatre in 1901. Moore's ambitions, in fact, transcended the actual production of the play (at the Gaiety Theatre, Dublin in October of that year, in a double bill with Douglas Hyde's Irish-language play, *Casadh*

---

10 For an appraisal of these operas see Axel Klein, 'Stage Irish, or The National in Irish Opera 1780–1925', *Opera Quarterly*, 21/1 (2005), 27–67. Recent research by Maria McHale (as yet unpublished) shows that the vigorous operatic culture which prevailed in Dublin between 1900 and 1916 (McHale documents over 1,000 performances of opera during this period) died away in the early years of the Free State.

11 See Joseph O'Neill, 'Music in Dublin', in *Music in Ireland Symposium*, edited by Aloys Fleischmann (Cork: Basil Blackwell and Cork University Press), 251–262, here at 254.

12 I should add in passing that to imagine Yeats as a composer surely gives the game away as far as Moore's musical ambitions were concerned: a more unlikely model for a fictional composer could otherwise scarcely be envisaged.

an tSugáin [*The Twisting of the Rope*]), but they also conflicted with Yeats's dramaturgy and poetic-dramatic diction. Anyone who has read J. C. C. Mays' excellent introduction to his edition of the manuscript materials of *Diarmuid and Grania* (published by Cornell University Press in 2005) must know that GM ultimately was intent on *Diarmuid and Grania* not as a play but as an opera.[13] His correspondence with Edward Elgar leaves us in no doubt in that regard. Moore would continue in his attempts to persuade Elgar to cut the text, reshape it as a libretto and set it as an opera for years afterwards (right up to 1914 he was expressing to Elgar his disappointment that this did not transpire). Of course, it was Elgar who had written the brief incidental music for the original production (at GM's request) but it is perhaps no less significant that Moore told Yeats during rehearsals for the first (and only) production of *Diarmuid* that their play didn't matter: '[W]hat matters is *The Twisting of the Rope*; we either want to make Irish the language of Ireland or we don't; and if we do, nothing else matters.'[14] Moore's reference here to the English title of Douglas Hyde's play, *Casadh an tSugáin*, which Moore rehearsed in his own home in Ely Place is nevertheless disingenuous, given that as early as August 1901, Moore had written to Elgar offering to re-set *Diarmuid* (or even to abandon the topic altogether) in favour of a full-scale opera libretto.[15] Everyone was lying to everyone else it seems, or at least being evasive about their intentions: for one thing, Yeats had no intention whatever of making Irish 'the language of Ireland', at least not in artistic terms, and for another, both he and Moore had engaged English actors to play in *Diarmuid*, an ultimately

---

13   See J. C. C. Mays (ed.), *Diarmuid and Grania Manuscript Materials, by W. B. Yeats and George Moore* (Ithaca, NY: Cornell University Press, 2005). Mays' introduction to these materials (xix-li) meticulously details the genesis of the play, the circumstances of its writing and rehearsal, the working relationship between Yeats and Moore, the efforts which Moore subsequently made to persuade Edward Elgar to write an opera on the same subject (including his offer to recast the play as a libretto) and the play's initial reception history.
14   Cited in Mays, *Diarmuid and Grania* (from Moore's *Hail and Farewell*), 'Introduction', xxxix.
15   For the details of this correspondence, see Mays, *Diarmuid and Grania*, xli-xliii. Moore had first approached the French composer (of Irish descent) Augusta Holmès in Paris to write the music for the play, but she declined.

poor decision summed up by Gerard Fay (as Mays reports) as follows: the production had 'this place in Irish theatre history: that it was the last time Dubliners had to call in English actors before they could see a production of an Irish play'.[16]

Despite its poor reception, *Diarmuid and Grania* was initially well-received by the Irish press, and a now famous review of the first performance by Synge (published in France) partly explains why:

> It happened that during an interval of Diarmuid and Grania, as was the custom in this theatre, the people in the gallery began to sing some of the old popular songs. Until that moment these songs had never been so heard, sung by so many people together to the old, lingering Irish words. The whole auditorium shook. It was as if one could hear in these long-drawn-out notes, with their inexpressible melancholy, the death-rattle of a nation. First one head, then another, was seen to bend over the programme notes. People were crying. Then the curtain went up. The play re-started in a deeply emotional atmosphere. For an instant we had glimpsed, hovering in that hall, the soul of a nation.[17]

For Seamus Deane, who cited this passage in an essay on Synge published almost forty years ago, its significance relates directly to the disappearance of Irish as an artistic medium (redeemed, perhaps by the Hiberno-English of Synge's own plays).[18] But I cite it for another reason. If Synge glimpsed 'the soul of a nation' in these Irish-language songs, neither he nor anyone else on that night could have anticipated the cultural eclipse that this visionary moment would entail. And even if George Moore himself persisted for a while longer with the Gaelic League (and with Douglas Hyde in particular), this was, according to Hyde himself, a disaster waiting to happen.[19] Less than a year after *Diarmuid*, however, Moore's famous 'Gaelic Lawn Party' took place on 19 May 1902, at which he hosted and directed a production of Hyde's play, *The Tinker and the*

---

16 See Mays, *Diarmuid and Grania*, xxxix.
17 Synge's review is published in his *Collected Works, II: Prose*, edited by Alan Price (London: Oxford University Press, 1966), 381–382.
18 See Seamus Deane, 'Synge and Heroism', in *Celtic Revivals* (London: Faber and Faber, 1985), 51–62, here at 61–62.
19 From an unpublished letter by Hyde referenced in Mays, *Diarmuid and Grania*, xxxviii–xxxix.

Fairy, with incidental music by Michele Esposito (an Italian composer resident in Dublin since 1886 and the 'uncrowned king' of the Royal Irish Academy of Music).[20] Adrian Frazier remarks that 'this was Moore's idea of a delightful Irish theatre, and indeed it was, but it lasted for only one performance'.[21] Yeats and the Fay brothers, meanwhile, were headed in a different direction. And so, ultimately, was Moore. But one could argue that without the incidental music which Esposito wrote at Moore's behest for this occasion, Esposito would never have written his second and last opera, which sets a libretto by Belinda Butler based on Hyde's play and performed by the Dublin Amateur Operatic Society at the Gaiety Theatre in March 1910. It was never heard of again (Esposito did not take a curtain call at the final performance of the short season in which it was given, but left the theatre in deep despair).[22] By then, the brief flowering of original Irish opera in Dublin was at an end. It carried forward into something other than itself, as in Synge's *Playboy of the Western World* and Joyce's *The Dead*, to say little of the literary Wagnerism of Moore's *The Lake*. And therein lies the point: like Synge's 'soul of a nation', Irish-language opera, or Irish opera of any kind, fluttered briefly in the cultural consciousness of the emerging nation, and then disappeared. George Moore's part in this fleeting appearance was perhaps more avocational than effectual, but it was nevertheless highly significant, even if his dreams of opera came to nothing.

---

20 See Jeremy Dibble, 'Esposito, Michele', in *The Encyclopaedia of Music in Ireland*, edited by Harry White and Barra Boydell (Dublin: University College Dublin Press, 2013), vol. 1, 358–361; and Declan Kiberd, 'George Moore's Gaelic Lawn Party', in *The Irish Writer and the World* (Cambridge: Cambridge University Press, 2005), 91–104.
21 See Frazier, *George Moore*, 311.
22 See Jeremy Dibble, *Michele Esposito* (Dublin: Field Day Publications, 2010), 131–135. The full score of the opera was nevertheless published by Breitkopf und Härtel (Leipzig) in 1910. It seems characteristic of the fate of opera in Dublin that the company which gave Hyde's opera folded in 1911.

II

There is a second musical consideration which attaches to Moore and which I would like to inspect briefly before bringing this paper to a close. To that end, I enlist his exact contemporary, the Irish composer Charles Villiers Stanford (1852–1924) in relation to Moore himself and also in relation to Bernard Shaw (1856–1950) and Edward Elgar (1857–1934). Although I have been unable to ascertain any link whatever between Moore and Stanford (even if it seems inconceivable that they did not know each other), there are instructive parallels to be drawn between the reception histories of both artists. If ever the phrase 'yesterday's man' (or 'forgotten hero') has afflicted a composer, it is Stanford. Born in Dublin, but resident in London and Cambridge for most of his life (he left Ireland aged 18), Stanford was to prove decisive in the reanimation (one might say rehabilitation) of British musical life between c. 1880 and his death. As a prodigiously gifted composer, conductor and professor of composition, Stanford's musical achievement was immense. Twelve operas, seven symphonies, three piano concertos, a host of oratorios and choral music and without question one of the greatest musical settings of the Requiem mass are among his many accomplishments, forgotten though many of these now largely are.[23] It is impossible nevertheless to give the merest account of music in Victorian and Edwardian Britain without privileging his works. And yet, despite a compelling revival of interest in Stanford's oeuvre during the past thirty years, it remains the case that the greater number of his compositions has never been performed in Ireland. Moreover, he has not been reclaimed as an Irish composer (a designation, incidentally, which extends beyond national ascription, given Stanford's immersion in the music of the country of his birth). Unlike Oscar Wilde (another contemporary, born in 1854), Stanford, like Moore, if to a greater

---

23 For an outstanding biography of Stanford, see Jeremy Dibble, *Charles Villiers Stanford: Man and Musician* (Oxford: Oxford University Press, 2002). A revised and expanded version of this study will appear in the series *Irish Musical Studies* (published by Boydell & Brewer) in 2024 to mark the centenary of Stanford's death.

degree, remains in the waiting room of Irish cultural history. And also like Moore, he has long since been overtaken in the annals of reception history by a kindred soul. In fact, I would argue that Moore's eclipse by Joyce compares closely to the diminishment of Stanford's reputation in favour of Elgar. If we ask, as Moore scholars do, why *The Untilled Field* and *The Lake* axiomatically defer to *Dubliners* and *Ulysses* (to say little of the similarly deferential ranking of *Hail and Farewell* in relation to *A Portrait of the Artist as a Young Man*), we might well ask in turn a similar question of Stanford's *Requiem* in relation to Elgar's *The Dream of Gerontius* or, indeed of Stanford's symphonies and Irish rhapsodies in relation to Elgar's orchestral music.[24]

As for answers to such questions, the prevailing response in the case of Moore and Stanford would appear to have been: 'Thank you very much, gentlemen, but *we'll* take it from here.' In Stanford's case, this sense of cultural eclipse, moreover, was hastened by the antics of Bernard Shaw. Shaw's mockery of Moore and Stanford alike can partly be explained by his determination to position himself as the natural heir to Richard Wagner, a preposterous ambition, but one which gained traction because of Shaw's controversial but widely-disseminated readings of Wagner, and also because of his influence as the most popular music critic in England during the 1880s and 1890s.[25] It is true that after he established himself as a dramatist, Shaw's jeering savagery in relation to German and English music alike abated, but by then the damage was done. Without a moment's further scruple, moreover, he took up the case of Edward Elgar, whose allegiance to the oratorio and the symphony did not trouble Shaw one whit, despite the fact that he had attacked the English cultivation of both genres as being a 'stone dead' enterprise in his galley years as a critic.[26] But Shaw's animadversions would

---

24 Both vocal works were first performed at the Birmingham Triennial Festival: the *Requiem* in 1897 and *The Dream of Gerontius* in 1900.
25 On Shaw's influence as a music critic see Harry White, '"Making Symphony Articulate": Bernard Shaw's sense of music history', in *British Musical Criticism and Intellectual Thought, 1850–1950*, edited by Jeremy Dibble and Julian Horton (Woodbridge: The Boydell Press, 2018), 102–117.
26 Shaw used this phrase in a review of Stanford's Irish Symphony published in the Pall Mall Gazette, dated 18 May 1888.

not have been enough to remainder Stanford to the past tense of British and Irish cultural history. The same might be said for Yeats's later repudiation of Moore (to say little of Joyce's callow attack on Moore in 'The Day of the Rabblement'). A force greater than personal animosity or ambition was responsible in either case for the recessionary progress of Moore and Stanford into the half-light of cultural remembrance.

We might identify this force as *the desire for a masterwork*, by which I intend the purposed unfolding of Joyce's art in particular through the agency of a singular renunciation of the writer's busy catalogue in favour of a very small number of works that would exhaust the genres to which these belonged.[27] Elgar, albeit less extremely, moved in the same direction: two symphonies, one set of orchestral variations and one oratorio comprise the masterworks by which he claims our permanent attention. By comparison, the restless extravagance and prolificity of Moore's catalogue, and the industrious pursuit by Stanford of virtually every generic model available to him came to appear supererogatory to this desire.

Declan Kiberd's supremely persuasive identification of 'the national longing for form' in postcolonial literature (following Homi K. Bhabha) articulates a related concept which we might engage in seeking to explain this preference.[28] In this respect, *Ulysses* is more than a novel, and Elgar's First Symphony is more than an orchestral masterpiece. However, differently, both works respectively answered and indeed satisfied this longing for form in Irish writing and English music to a definitive degree. In Elgar's case, the First Symphony was also the first *English* symphony to achieve a truly international reception history, precisely on account of its transcendent Englishness and its post-imperial romanticism. Joyce's *Ulysses*,

27   Although this is my own argument, I am clearly indebted to David Lloyd, *Anomalous States* (Durham, NC: Duke University Press, 1993) and to Lloyd's discussion therein of this desire.
28   See Declan Kiberd, 'The National Longing for Form', in *Inventing Ireland* (London: Jonathan Cape, 1995), 115–132. It is perhaps germane to this identification that in *Ulysses*, George Moore is nominated (with some irony) as a person capable of satisfying this longing: 'Our national epic is yet to be written, Dr Sigerson says, Moore is the man for it.' See James Joyce, *Ulysses* [1922] (Harmondsworth: Penguin Classics, 2000), 246.

likewise, would become definitive of Irishness in the very avant-garde of European fiction. We may argue that Joyce's Wagnerian impulses and musical dependencies summon the vital precedent of Moore, just as we might legitimately insist that without Stanford, Elgar would never have made his way to the top table. We may even seek to find a place there for Stanford, and indeed for Moore, through the agency of increasing their listenership and readership. But however we proceed, whether or not as advocates of Moore (or Stanford, for that matter), our fundamental obligation is not perhaps advocacy, but a better understanding of the labyrinths of cultural and political history from which such figures emerge.

When I sat down to write the first version of this paper, the epigraph to Robertson Davies' novel, *Fifth Business* (published in 1970) floated up to my mind.[29] Here, I offer it as an envoi:

> Those roles which, being neither those of hero nor Heroine, Confidante nor Villain, but which were none the less essential to bring about the Recognition or the denouement were called the Fifth Business in drama and Opera companies organized according to the old style; the player who acted these parts was often referred to as Fifth Business.

That is how I now think of Moore, in terms of the cultural history of music in Ireland, most especially at the turn of the twentieth century. He is indeed essential to its meaning and circumstance, not only because his own musical reliances so closely adumbrate those which shaped Joyce's fiction, but more narrowly still on account of his avocational interest in imagining Irish experience through the agency of opera. The denouement of Ireland's literary renaissance would entail a decisive repudiation of this agency, but a wider scholarly reception for George Moore would, I think, deepen our understanding as to how and why this happened. It might also promote the circulation of Moore's own fiction, in which the animating presence of music is exemplary. I am unlikely to forget as much in the future.

---

29   Robertson Davies (1913–1992) was a Canadian novelist, playwright and academic whose success as a writer was suddenly internationalized by the publication of *Fifth Business* in 1970. *Fifth Business* (Montreal: Macmillan, 1970).

PILAR VILLAR-ARGÁIZ

16 Transparency and Secrecy in the Poetry of Colette Bryce

This chapter explores the concept of secrecy in relation to ideas of transparency, dissidence and resistance as represented in a sample of poems by Northern Irish writer Colette Bryce. Secrecy and silence have been part of the Irish experience in Northern Ireland, especially during the period of the Troubles. As Bryce claims in a 2014 interview with respect to the title of her poem 'Don't speak to the Brits, just pretend they don't exist':[1]

> That was a piece of advice you'd hear on the streets when I was growing up because the soldiers were physically very present in our area, on foot patrols and so on. The 'Don't speak' part of that title seems significant to me, and I think that comes into other poems as well. The idea of suppression not only of speech but, by extension, thought. Difficult truths.[2]

In another interview years later, Bryce further comments: 'I had grown up in a culture of secrecy, so in some ways writing always felt like a rebellion against this, and it took time, distance and courage to begin to write. Writing can seem incredibly exposing, whereas I'm a naturally private person.'[3] So, secrecy becomes a potent motif in Colette Bryce's poetry,

---

1 The title of this poem by Colette Bryce alludes to Seamus Heaney's well-known poem 'Whatever You Say Say Nothing'. See David Wheatley, for an enlightening analysis of the use of strategies of evasion, secrecy and silence in the work of Northern Irish poets such as Seamus Heaney, Paul Muldoon and Ciaran Carson. David Wheatley, '"That Black Mouth": Secrecy, Shibboleths, and Silence in Northern Irish Poetry', *Journal of Modern Literature*, 25/1 (2001), 1–16.
2 Alex Pryce, 'Little Windows, Difficult Truths – Colette Bryce talks to Alex Pryce', *Poetry London*, 1 October 2014, http://poetrylondon.co.uk/little-windows-difficult-truths-colette-bryce-talks-to-alex-pryce/ [accessed 21 February 2019].
3 Adam Wyeth, 'Dam Wyeth Interview with Colette Bryce', *Non-Fiction*, 23 (July 2020), https://www.themanchesterreview.co.uk/?p=11583 [accessed March 27 2023].

which she explores in various ways, and not necessarily concentrating on its negative connotations.

This chapter examines the poetry of Colette Bryce in order to propose an analysis of the productive nature of secrecy in the aesthetic terrain and challenge the ideal of transparency that has been blindly accepted by so many Western commentators. The poems chosen for analysis place secrecy, rather than transparency, in the foreground. They do not demand us to consider the secret as a problem to be solved or eventually disclosed; they require us to respect this secret as secret. As I intend to show, Bryce interrogates in various ways the thought structures which have conditioned the public sphere. She raises awareness about the discursive mechanisms on transparency / secrecy used by institutions. Secrecy in her work might therefore be understood as a form of resistance to hegemonic ways of thinking. Bryce advocates a new form of knowledge that is not available through acts of disclosure, but by non-transparency and secrecy. Influenced by Derrida and other prominent scholars on Secrecy Studies (such as Birchall, Han, etc.) who maintain that secrecy is an essential element of all democracies (because absolute transparency is an expression of totalitarianism),[4] I argue that Bryce advocates the need to preserve privacy and secrecy as vital for transformative interpersonal relations. Bearing this in mind, I propose a different conceptualization of secrecy as productive rather than regressive, by offering an alternative way of viewing the secrecy-transparency nexus.

I will first analyse a few poems from her collection *Self-Portrait in the Dark* (2008), where Bryce explores the thought structures which have conditioned the public sphere, raising awareness about the discursive mechanisms on transparency / secrecy used by institutions. In poems

4   For Derrida, privacy and secrecy need to be preserved in all democracies, as absolute transparency is an expression of totalitarianism. In *A Taste for the Secret*, Derrida equates transparency with the imposition of hegemonic discourses: '[T]he demand that everything be paraded in the public square and that there be no internal forum is a glaring sign of the totalitarianization of democracy [...] if a right to the secret is not maintained, we are in a totalitarian space.' Jacques Derrida, 'I Have a Taste for the Secret', in *A Taste for the Secret*, by Jacques Derrida and Maurizio Ferraris, translated by Giacomo Donis, edited by Giacomo Donis and David Webb (Cambridge: Polity, [1997] 2001), 1–92, 59.

such as 'A Spider' and 'Vertical Blinds', Bryce offers a powerful critique of the ideal of transparency in today's world, by denouncing the seemingly 'transparent' boundaries which limit individuals socially, politically and sexually speaking. Her work denounces the digital panopticon that Byun-Chul Han explores in his work, a concept that will be developed in depth.[5] Secondly, I will draw on a few poems from various collections (*The Heel of Bernadette* (2000), *The Full Indian Rope Trick* (2005), *Self-Portrait in the Dark* (2008) and *Ballasting the Ark* (2012)), where Bryce proposes a radical form of secrecy, an intransparency and ambiguity which is highly subversive.[6] Challenging sharply the perceived advantages of the transparent digital world, Bryce advocates a space of secrecy and privacy which needs to be preserved, by means of mysterious self-portraits, which prevent any form of absolute self-exposure, and tropes of concealment which favour genuine interpersonal relationships.

Bryce has fought incessantly against the many ideological boundaries separating people. These are the boundaries she has felt in terms of religion, nationality, and sexuality: her Ulster childhood as a Catholic, and later as a lesbian, and as a Northern Irish woman living in England. The omnipresence and oppression that these transparent boundaries exert on her life is observed, for instance, in one of her most powerful poems, 'A Spider', where Bryce engages in a powerful exploration of how the self is placed in the world by means of a personal anecdote of trapping a spider in a glass:

> I trapped a spider in a glass,
>
> a fine-blown wineglass.
>
> It shut around him, silently.
>
> He stood still, a small wheel

---

[5] Byun-Chul Han, *The Transparency Society* (Stanford: Stanford University Press, 2015).
[6] Colette Bryce, *The Heel of Bernadette* (London: Picador, 2000); *The Full Indian Rope Trick* (London: Picador, 2005); *The Observations of Aleksandr Svetlov* (London: Donur Press, 2007); *Self-Portrait in the Dark* (London: Picador, 2008); *The Whole and Rain-domed Universe* (London: Picador, 2014); *Selected Poems* (London: Picador, 2017).

of intricate suspension, cap

at the hug of his eight spokes,

inked eyes on stalks; alert,

sensing a difference.[7]

The wineglass in the poem becomes a microcosm of the social control to which Bryce, like other individuals, is exposed in today's world. This universe of surveillance, characterized by permanent visibility and transparency, was well explained by Foucault in *Discipline and Punish: The Birth of the Prison*, by the image of the Panopticon: 'The Panopticon is a machine for dissociating the see / being seen dyad.'[8] Foucault borrows this idea from Jeremy Bentham's panopticon writings; the 'celebrated, transparent, circular cage with its high tower, powerful and knowing' becomes a metaphor of modern power and the modus operandi of disciplinary power in nineteenth-century French society.[9] He continues: 'Disciplinary power [...] is exercised through its invisibility [....] In discipline, it is the subjects who have to be seen. Their visibility assures the hold of the power that is exercised over them.'[10] Disorder, difference and heterogeneity are in this instance regulated by a power dynamic of constant surveillance which eradicates any privacy. The subjects are exposed to a gaze without even knowing whether there is somebody watching them or not.

In a similar way, Bryce draws our attention – by means of the transparent glass which entraps the arachnid – to the usually unseen modes of social control, which Michel Foucault identifies as 'discipline', an invisible but all-seeing form of surveillance. She describes a normative surveillance society whose spying methods have become invisible to individuals. The spider inside the wineglass senses this entrapment but is not able to visualize

---

7   Bryce, *Self-Portrait in the Dark*, 3; *The Whole and Rain-Domed Universe* (London: Picador, 2014); *Selected Poems* (London: Picador, 2017).

8   Michel Foucault, *Discipline and Punish: The Birth of the Prison*, translated by Alan Sheridan (New York: Random House, [1975] 1977), 201–202.

9   Foucault, *Discipline and Punish*, 208.

10   Foucault, *Discipline and Punish*, 187.

the walls separating it from the outside, or the gazer controlling it.[11] In addition, this physical space recorded by Bryce becomes a metaphor for what Han identifies as the 'digital panopticon' of contemporary life, in reference to how social media and internet create the illusion of intimacy, of proximity, fostering 'a space of absolute closeness' where there is no inside and outside.[12] As Han exposes in *The Transparency Society*, this universe of total monitoring exposed by Foucault is replicated in our contemporary digital, virtual age.[13] The transparency society, according to Han, creates an illusion of sameness where there are no boundaries: 'The compulsion for transparency dismantles all borders and thresholds. Space becomes transparent when it is smoothed, leveled, and emptied out.'[14] As he continues,

> Today the entire globe is developing into a panopticon. There is no outside space. The panopticon is becoming total. No wall separates inside from outside. Google and social networks, which present themselves as spaces of freedom, are assuming panoptic forms [....] people are voluntarily surrendering to the panoptic gaze. They deliberately collaborate in the digital panopticon by denuding and exhibiting themselves.[15]

In the second part of the poem, the speaker identifies with the experience suffered by the spider inside the glass, as her life is also enclosed within invisible boundaries:

> I meant to let him go
>
> but still he taps against the glass

---

11   As O'Reilly (2008) notes, the spider can also be understood as a metaphor of the 'double-edged power' of the woman artist, contained within the glass wall of the male tradition, precisely because of her dangerous effect. This link between female art and the spider may also be explained by the influence the French artist and sculpture Louise Bourgeois exerts on her work (see, for instance, poems such as 'Seven in Bed' or 'A little girl I knew when she was my mother'; and also 'The Poetry Bug', 2018: 41, where she defines her art as having 'eight root-like/ tentacles or feelers, rough/ like knuckly tusks of ginger/ clustered at the front').
12   Han, *The Transparency Society*, 35.
13   Han, *The Transparency Society*, 46.
14   Han, *The Transparency Society*, 31.
15   Han, *The Transparency Society*, 49.

all Marcel Marceau

in the wall that is there but not there,

a circumstance I know. [*italics original*][16]

Bryce destabilizes the dominant position of the subject in relation to the insect, as she sympathizes with the spider's entrapped condition. Although the speaker apparently occupies the world outside the wineglass, she is also exposed by similar boundaries, although not so visible at first sight. This is the danger of boundaries, that they can hide themselves at first, not visibly apparent, but still there. These are the boundaries she felt in terms of religion, sexual orientation and nationality. As Lucy Collins claims, 'Growing up in Derry during the Troubles, Bryce's understanding of the relationship between personal and political has been shaped by the claustrophobic nature of domestic and civic life in the province and by the impact that sectarian violence has on the lives of individuals.'[17] Such claustrophobia is indeed reflected in the image of the enclosed spider, with whom Bryce identifies. This enclosure is reflected in the carefully balanced form of the poem itself, with thirteen verse lines which are largely rhythmically regular, with the exception of the penultimate line ('*in the wall that is there but not there*'), which is longer, disrupting the metrical pattern.

The poem thus begins with a simple domestic anecdote which acquires a wider significance for the speaker in the end. In this way, the poem records the 'happy procedure' of the 'well-made poem', or 'conventional' poem that David Lloyd detects, which is repeatedly adopted as a convention in much contemporary poetry:

> the happy procedure of the poem that commences with a 'vividly realized experience, draws from it some metaphoric thread, and winds up with a moral payload, validated by a nice turn of phrase, that brings metaphor and experience into graceful concord

---

16 Bryce, *Self-Portrait in the Dark*, 3.
17 Lucy Collins, *Contemporary Irish Women Poets* (Liverpool: Liverpool University Press, 2015), 79. See also Gerarld Dawe's chapter on Colette Bryce, which revisits the impact of the Troubles in her poetry. Gerald Dawe, *Dreaming of Home: Seven Irish Writers* (Oxford: Peter Lang, 2022), 55–62.

again. The procedure of the 'well-made poem' is handily available for recycling and the world yields ample material for exploitation in this mode.[18]

Indeed, together with writers including Leontia Flynn, Sinéad Morrisey and Caitríona O'Reilly, Colette Bryce has been identified as belonging to the 'formal turn' in the Irish poetry of the 1990s and early 2000s, in reaction against the influence of the more experimental poetics of Medbh McGuckian, Ciaran Carson and Paul Muldoon.[19] Nevertheless, Bryce's poetry moves beyond this simplistic identification of 'conventional', formal poetry, in its varying use of strategies and techniques. However, it is true that the spider serves as a metaphorical vehicle for the expression of the subject's situation in the poem. As is typical in her work, a domestic scene offers a profound political reflection. The poem examines how difficult is to escape this form of entrapment, mostly when these boundaries remain largely transparent, invisible and they cannot be perceived easily from the outside. By means of the comparison of the world-famous mimer, Marcel Marceau, the poem largely allows us to consider the dynamics of exclusion and surveillance which limit individuals in real life and how unconscious we may be of these traps.

This theme is also reflected, visually and structurally, in one of her most attractive and enigmatic poems in the collection, 'Vertical Blinds', a playful poem constructed on two vertical columns separated by a midline long caesura. The repeated phrase in the poem, 'Vertical blinds / stand sentry at her life', suggests the numerous boundaries outside / inside, home / public sphere that circumscribe the speaker's life. The blinds the speaker describes in her living room are 'sentries' which protect her from some sort of external menace, but also some soldier-like figures which prevent her from stepping outside other zones. They are both symbols of immunitarian protection and simultaneously of enclosure. The vertical blinds thus symbolize those boundaries the female character has to cope with:

---

18 David Lloyd, 'Introduction: On Irish Experimental Poetry', *Irish University Review*, 46/1 (2016), 10–19, 11–12.

19 Tara McEvoy, 'Formalism and Contemporary Irish Women's Poetry', *A History of Irish Women's Poetry*, edited by Ailbhe Darcy and David Wheatley (Cambridge: Cambridge University Press, 2021), 390–408, 390–391.

> Vertical   blinds
> stand sentry at her life
> switch   on a whim
> to admit   or refuse light.[20]

Drawing inspiration from two different domestic settings (a spider within a glass and the ordinary house blinds in the living room), Bryce seems to suggest that all individuals are circumscribed by boundaries, however invisible they might be at first sight. In this setting, her life becomes a sort of social performance; the woman is perceived as 'Puppet – compliant / at the tugging of a string'. The internal world projected from the outside becomes 'a cinema screen's / oriental projection'.[21] Nevertheless, these borders are also necessary, Bryce seems to suggest, as this allows her not to be exposed totally to the outside, thus preserving her Otherness and singularity from being fully revealed. In the poem, the total essence of this woman cannot be fully grasped or disclosed as light can only be revealed at intervals, 'on a whim / to admit or refuse light'. In a world of apparently no boundaries, as Han explains, 'Meanings arise only at thresholds and in transitions, indeed through obstacles.'[22] This is so because these thresholds and boundaries 'are zones of mystery, uncertainty, transformation, death, and feat, but also of yearning, hope and expectation.'[23] Indeed, the thresholds of the vertical blinds allow the speaker to inhabit an in-between zone which favours both enclosure and liberation at the same time. On the one hand, the taut strips of the blinds are limiting her life in this 'masked gloom / of a living-room', enclosing her like the 'bars of a cage / gripped with a clip'.[24] Nevertheless, these blinds also enigmatically exemplify forms of liberation, because they allow her to escape confinement by sailing ships that lift her far:

20 Bryce, *Self-Portrait in the Dark*, 29.
21 Bryce, *Self-Portrait in the Dark*, 28.
22 Han, *The Transparency Society*, 31.
23 Han, *The Transparency Society*, 32.
24 Bryce, *Self-Portrait in the Dark*, 29.

>   at top
>   they are sails
>   a fleet
>   carry her
>   from all
>
>   and tail
>   of ships
>   that will lift
>   far
>   of this.[25]

In this refusal and admission of light, the image of the woman becomes ambiguous, both graspable and ungraspable at the same time; although as a 'puppet' behind blinds, she also manages at times to escape far away.

Indeed, Bryce explores in her poems a form of subjectivity in challenging ways, and one of her most common traits in this act of self-exploration is to avoid any act of easy, appropriative self-disclosure. As someone raised in Northern Ireland but who has also been used to living elsewhere (Barcelona, London, Dundee and now in the North of England), the movement between spaces is commonplace in her poems, thus reflecting a fluid identity and nomadic sensibility which is not attached to a particular place. As Collins puts it, Bryce's 'ambiguous relationship to place [...] troubles the sense of a unitary self, so that the speaker is simultaneously visible and concealed from the reader'.[26]

One of the most challenging poems in her collection where Bryce engages in experimental forms of subjective self-introspection is 'Self Portrait in a Broken Wing Mirror'.[27] Defying the easy enclosure of the spider in the previous poem, Bryce describes a self who is not confined by invisible, transparent walls; her projection in the broken wing-mirror of her car

---

25 Bryce, *Self-Portrait in the Dark*, 29.
26 In her chapter on Colette Bryce, Paula Meehan and Mary O'Malley, Collins maintains that 'All three poets meet the aesthetic and ethical challenges that attend the representation of private matter in poetic form, either by addressing the practice of representation directly or by creating an imaginative world with which subjectivity itself acquires new perspectives', Collins, *Contemporary Irish Women Poets*, 82. McEvoy also notes that Bryce's work is informed by an international perspective which defies the traditional opposition Irishness vs. Englishness, displaying her affinity with places, traditions and cultures different from her place of birth, McEvoy, 'Formalism and Contemporary Irish Women's Poetry', 392.
27 Bryce, *Self-Portrait in the Dark*, 12–13.

defies any form of easy containment as its many parts seem to exceed (even explode) any mode of artistic representation:

> [...] that's me, a cubist depiction: my ear,
> its swirly and ridge of pearly cartilage,
> peachy lobe and indent of a piercing
> not jewelled for years [....]
>
> The ear is parted neatly from the head
> by breaks in the glass, a weird mosaic
> or logic puzzle for the brain to fix.
> The eyebrow, stepped in sections, stops
> then starts again, recognisibly mine.
> The nose, at an intersection of cracks,
>
> is all but lost except for the small sculpted
> cave of a shadowy nostril. The eye
> is locked on itself, the never-easy gaze
> of the portraitist, the hood half open,
> the hub of the pupil encircled with green
> and a ring of flame.[28]

Bryce mediates through the poetic text a very challenging form of subjective self-introspection. The speaker's image is perceived from the outside as 'a weird mosaic / or logic puzzle for the brain to fix'. The self seems to be exploded in different parts (the ear separated from the head, the eyebrow 'stepped in sections', the nose 'at an intersection of cracks'), like a Picasso Cubist image, altering the self / other binary, which seems to be constituting the individual's identity.[29] Poems like this challenge the

28   Bryce, *Self-Portrait in the Dark*, 12.
29   This stated awareness of 'the problematic nature of self-representation', *Contemporary Irish Women Poets*, 81, is not only a distinctive feature of Bryce's work, as it is also

ideal of the transparent self (and by extension the ideal of a transparent society). Her self-portrait exhibits a mysterious lack of definition, 'an impenetrability and hiddenness' (in words of Han) which 'defies representation'.[30] This form of occlusion and otherness in turn challenges the so-called 'transparency' of contemporary times and the portrayal of the human being as 'glassy'.[31] Against the digital panopticon of today's world, where everyone yields to a 'voluntary self-illumination and self-exposure', Bryce offers a broken image of herself.[32] The digital new age depends on a prominent hypervisibility and exhibitionism of the self. By contrast, as Bryce reveals in an interview, her poems eschew all notions of transparency, 'They reveal vivid things, little windows, but you never really get to see a whole picture.'[33] The fissured images of the speaker in 'Self Portrait in a Broken Wing Mirror' are never smooth and transparent but full of mystery and hiddenness. This in turn challenges the hypervisibility and exhibitionism of the digital new age, where individuals of the 'digital panopticon' abandon their private sphere in their urgent need to put themselves 'on display without shame'.[34]

As Han explains, the society of transparency depends on exhibition versus the cult value: 'things become commodities; they must be displayed in order to be'.[35] This society of exhibition is 'a society of pornography. Everything has been turned outward, stripped, exposed, undressed, and put on show. The excess of display turns everything into a commodity: possessing 'no secret', it stands 'doomed [...] to immediate devouring'.[36] Bryce challenges this pornographication, overexposure of the self, such 'an absolutization of the Visible and the External'.[37] As Han claims, 'Transparency

---

        present in the poetry of other contemporary voices such as Paula Meehan and Eavan Boland. But what makes Bryce's poetic exploration of the self different, however, is its departure from realism.
30   Han, *The Transparency Society*, 17.
31   Han, *The Transparency Society*, viii.
32   Han, *The Transparency Society*, viii.
33   Bryce, 'Little Windows, Difficult Truths'.
34   Han, *The Transparency Society*, 46.
35   Han, *The Transparency Society*, 9.
36   Han, *The Transparency Society*, 11.
37   Han, *The Transparency Society*, 12.

makes the human being glassy', and this open exhibition of the self 'possesses no deep hermeneutic structure'.[38] By contrast, there is no hypervisibility in Bryce's poem, no transformation of herself into a commodity. The image reflected on the broken mirror of her car is fragmented, obscure, displaying all the 'negativity of Otherness'.[39] Her face is a countenance that is not transparent. As Han suggests, images which display their 'brokenness' can trigger mental reflection and aesthetic contemplation.[40] As he claims, borrowing from Kant, 'an object is sublime when it exceeds representation, any effort to picture it'.[41] It is then that beauty emerges. Bryce engages in such an act of contemplative lingering by gaining aesthetic distance to her self-reflection.

This poem could be set beside the title poem of the collection: 'Self-Portrait in the Dark (with Cigarette)'.[42] In both cases, there is a necessity for secrecy in her work: Bryce not only addresses her inability to describe herself in full but also the fact that she does not wish to disclose herself openly either. Whereas in the previous poem, the speaker's self-portrait can only be done through a broken wing-mirror, here the speaker reflects on her position in the dark, as she is observed from the outside, thus inhabiting the estranged position as the Other. The speaker occupies, once again, the position of witness rather than agent. These two poems, in the words of McEvoy, 'testify to the distorting effects of mediating subjectivity through poetic text',[43] and in some way, deconstruct, in the assessment of Williams, 'the so-called 'transparency' of the lyric utterance'.[44] In both

---

38   Han, *The Transparency Society*, viii, 12.
39   Han, *The Transparency Society*, 12.
40   Han, *The Transparency Society*, 13.
41   Han, *The Transparency Society*, 22.
42   Bryce, *Self-Portrait in the Dark*, 4–5.
43   McEvoy, 'Formalism and Contemporary Irish Women's Poetry', 404.
44   Nerys Williams, '"A Song Said Otherwise": Susan Howe, Maggie O'Sullivan, Catherine Walsh', *A History of Irish Women's Poetry*, edited by Ailbhe Darcy and David Wheatley (Cambridge: Cambridge University Press, 2021), 409–430, 411. Collins also remarks that 'the lyrical impulse commonly evokes a coherent self' (Collins, *Contemporary Irish Women Poets*, 93).

poems, self-representation becomes not only the subject of the poetic process but also the object of it.[45]

Indeed, the preservation of singularity and secrecy is at the core of Bryce's portfolio of poetic identities. Bryce addresses, in line with other contemporary poets such as Paula Meehan (see 'Note from the Puzzle Factory' and 'Zealot') and Doireann Ní Ghríofa ('Facetime'), the possibilities and challenges opened up by the new world of the technological advances, especially in digital media. In her poem 'Phone', from her collection *The Heel of Bernadette*,[46] the speaker finds that the new technological advances ease human (and in this case, personal) relationships. 'Though we've come to hate this line', the speaker abruptly begins, they keep on calling, as this enables them to surpass the pain of physical distance, fulfilling their 'desire / at least to hear and to be heard'. The phone line acts as a bond that strengthens and sustains their emotional attachment:

> For this becomes a web,
>
> becomes a hair, a strength, a thread,
>
> a harness between us, in all fairness,
>
> you in my hereness, me in your thereness.[47]

The digital benefits of phone conversations are, nonetheless, counteracted in other poems such as 'Where are You?', in which Bryce addresses the limits of modern technology and the impossibility of connecting properly. The speaker comments on how mobile conversations are truncated with her lover as Wi-Fi connections are lost:

> The denizens of outer space
>
> float about their business
>
> or slowly drift away.
>
> Earthbound,

45   Collins, *Contemporary Irish Women Poets*, 94–95.
46   Bryce, *The Heel of Bernadette*, 20.
47   Bryce, *The Heel of Bernadette*, 20.

> I'm losing you.
>
> There's not the reach on the line.
>
> Somewhere in the universe
>
> your voice is breaking up again.[48]

'Sin Música', from the same collection, also deals with the failings of modern-day technology; in particular, it draws on the limits of electronic mails to encapsulate feelings and emotions:

> *The words cover more than they reveal.*
>
> *I lift these lines from your virtual letter.*
>
> *How short they fall*
>
> *of real meaning. Your actual*
>
> *touch was so much better*
>
> *than words.* [italics original][49]

This sentiment, in a way, is also recorded in poems such as 'Once', also from the same collection, where Bryce – inspired by a poem from Denise Riley – claims that there are some words such as 'sweetheart' or 'darling', 'the known / words, the beautiful outworn / words', that can only be used once their accuracy, or communicative function is gone.[50] In today's digital panopticon, as Han explains, 'the practice of 'postprivacy' [...] demands an unrestricted mutual uncovering' between the self and the other.[51] Challenging the current transparency world, Bryce suggests that this uncovering is never total, as it can never replace the humanness involved in physical contact between human beings. At the same time, she suggests that the boundaries between the you and the I need to be maintained at all times. The digital panopticon runs the risk of falling into a

---

48 Bryce, *Self-Portrait in the Dark*, 25–26.
49 Bryce, *Self-Portrait in the Dark*, 35.
50 Bryce, *Self-Portrait in the Dark*, 42.
51 Han, *The Transparency Society*, 16.

symmetry of the 'sameness' which inhibits all forms of otherness and mystery, and such conditions are necessary for the preservation of singularity.

Indeed, Colette Bryce's poetry seems to defend the need for privacy in socio-political life: this privacy involves the condition of secrecy which guarantees the preservation of singularity. In her 2012 collection, *Ballasting the Ark*, Bryce focuses on animals who depend on secrecy and privacy for their survival, like lobsters or hermit crabs. The later, for instance, needs to overcome daily the 'perils of the shoreline', retreating quickly in the presence of danger:

> Hiddenness
>
> is the default policy.
>
> A low profile, a bent
>
> for privacy. Only
>
> the lucky and
>
> the fighters survive.[52]

As Collins claims, a concern in Bryce's work is the exploration of 'the philosophical and cultural implications of the concept of privacy and its role in larger constructions of identity'.[53] In particular, she focuses on one of her poems, 'Re-entering the Egg', where Bryce describes home in terms of the metaphor of a doll's house, 'the front of which can be opened to reveal all the rooms at once', and where each family member occupies a room separated from the other ones.[54] The poet brings to the forefront the issue of 'The ethics of breaching family privacy', as she reaffirms the distance between observer and observed: 'Out of time they go about their lives / unaware of our scrutiny. / Close it up. That is enough for now.'[55]

Indeed, the construction of genuine relationships based on values such as privacy, confidence and trust is a constant in her work. While in

---

52 Bryce, *Selected Poems*, 76.
53 Collins, *Contemporary Irish Women Poets*, 81.
54 Collins, *Contemporary Irish Women Poets*, 86.
55 Bryce, *The Whole and Rain-Domed Universe*, 7; Collins, 86.

'Where Are You?' lovers speak 'in a confidential tone', in other poems such as 'Riddle', Bryce advocates the value of secrecy between the self and the other.[56] Although the speaker wishes to break up with her partner, she will maintain the secrets her lover confided in her. The speaker's coat and its pockets serve as metaphors for those experiences (some of them painful), that she will not disclose in the future:

> As much as you confide in me,
>
> if you think that I'll be coming back
>
> you're on the wrong track.
>
> Our tryst will be intense but short.
>
> I mean to travel, go abroad, so ask just this:
>
> a single kiss, then one caress; no more, no less.
>
> I wear my intentions clear as a coat, but a coat
>
> of secrets to be kept – small betrayals, pleas
>
> of the heart – all stuffed into its pocket's depth,
>
> or stitched into its silk and hem.
>
> My new love may just cut my throat,
>
> Or tear me apart, to discover them.[57]

What Bryce suggests in the lines above is that secrecy / privacy in human relationships is necessary. Drawing on the work of sociologists such as Simmel,[58] Han opines that some degree of opacity is needed between the self and the other if the attraction and the 'eros' is to be maintained.[59] He also refers to Baudrillard, for whom eros depends on the 'intuition of something in the other that remains forever secret for him, something

---

56   Bryce, *Self-Portrait in the Dark*, 25; *The Full Indian Rope Trick*, 43.
57   Bryce, *The Full Indian Rope Trick*, 43.
58   Georg Simmel, 'The Sociology of Secrecy and of Secret Societies', *American Journal of Sociology*, 11 (1906), 441–498.
59   Han, *The Transparency Society*, 16.

that I can never know directly about him but which nevertheless exercises a fascination upon me from behind its veil of secrecy.'[60] Similarly, Bryce suggests that mystery and concealment are necessary conditions for sustained pleasurable, in-depth human relations. In the words of Han: 'The negativity of concealment transforms hermeneutics into erotics. Discovering and deciphering occur as pleasurable laying-bare.'[61]

Another poem in which Bryce advocates the need for privacy in human relationships is 'Car Wash'.[62] This poem portrays a lesbian couple who use the concealment of the interiority of a car wash to give free reign to their love. Although they cannot exercise their love openly in public, their concealment from the outside is also a guarantee of the consolidation and strength of their love. Bryce deconstructs patriarchy from within by using a traditionally male experience for her own benefit: 'The business of driving / reminds us of our fathers'.[63] Inside a car wash in Belfast, two women 'in a kiss / in a world where to do so / can still stop the traffic.'[64] Concealment for them is essential for giving free reign to their love and passion. Both find themselves 'delighted by a wholly / unexpected privacy / of soap suds pouring, no, / *cascading* in velvety waves'. Once again, in the words of Han, 'the negativity of the secret, the veil, and concealment incite desire and make pleasure more intense.'[65]

All these poems attest to the value that secrecy, mystery and concealment acquires in Colette Bryce's poetry. Against the logic of transparency that determines the present-day world, Bryce's poetry favours the importance of magic and mystery. In poems such as 'Itch', from her first collection, Bryce describes with humour the power that Catholicism still exerts in twenty-first-century Ireland: Jesus 'lives / deep in the ditch of my mother's ears', and thus the latter cannot hear what her daughter tells her, because of the religious 'interference' of Jesus' whispering: 'the whispering like wishes

---

60 Jean Baudrillard, *The Transparency of Evil: Essays on Extreme Phenomena*, translated by James Benedict (London: Verso, 1993), 166. Quoted in Han, 25.
61 Han, *The Transparency Society*, 19.
62 Bryce, *Self-Portrait in the Dark*, 6–7.
63 Bryce, *Self-Portrait in the Dark*, 6.
64 Bryce, *Self-Portrait in the Dark*, 7.
65 Han, *The Transparency Society*, 15.

of Jesus softly breathing there'.[66] The presence of Jesus in her mother's ear is 'unreachable' to her, and it is this sense of mystery, not only of religion but also of other practices in life, that her poetry constantly celebrates. Her second collection, *The Full Indian Rope Trick* (2005), is drawn to the power of magic, delusion and appearance, the interplay between illusion and reality, artifice and truth. This is observed, for instance, in two of her most celebrated poems, 'The Full Indian Rope Trick' and 'Fabio's Miracle'. The first begins with a line that is sharply challenged as the poem enfolds: 'There was no secret.'[67] The speaker performs a magic trick (which is described as 'unique, unequalled since') in Guildhall Square, Londonderry, 'in front of everyone', as she miraculously climbs through a rope that has risen up from the ground. At the end of the poem, she is both 'long gone' and 'still here'. As Bainbridge puts it, 'the poem is as elusive and slippery as the trick itself. It is a childhood fantasy, a painful rite of passage, an artistic statement, a comic wind-up, a self-consciously self-contradictory flight of bravado.'[68]

Another poem belonging to this collection, 'Fabio's Miracle' also draws on the power of mystery and enigma. As Rhoanne Pryce explains, this poem is based on the story of the apparently weeping Virgin Mary statue in the garden of Fabio Gregori in Civitavecchia, Italy, an event in 1995 which aroused 'much Catholic devotion, speculation, investigation'.[69] The scientific tests on the Madonna statue demonstrated that the tears were blood, but male blood, revealing that there was more trickery than mystery in this miracle. In Bryce's poetic retelling of this event, mystery is maintained, as the speaker concludes by saying: 'I knelt and raised / my eyes to meet her raw, clawed face / her livid gaze. One of us smiled.'[70] At the end,

---

66   Bryce, *The Heel of Bernadette*, 13.
67   Bryce, *The Full Indian Rope Trick*, 17.
68   Charles Brainbridge, 'Review: *The Full Indian Rope Trick* by Colette Bryce Review – a Great Escape', *The Guardian*, 29 January 2005, https://www.theguardian.com/books/2005/jan/29/featuresreviews.guardianreview12 [accessed July 22 2020].
69   Alexandra Rhoanne Pryce, *Selective Traditions: Feminism and the Poetry of Colette Bryce, Leontia Flynn and Sinéad Morrissey* (Oxford: Washam College). Thesis submitted for the degree of Doctor of Philosophy to the Faculty of English Language and Literature University of Oxford, 2013), 86–87.
70   Bryce, *The Full Indian Rope Trick*, 30–32.

we do not know whose smile the poem is recording (that of the miraculous statue or of the unscrupulous deceiver), and thus the mystery remains unresolved. Here, the poetic voice is playing with us in poems where we do not know if the miracle truly happens or if it is simply a delusion. As in the previous poem, the ending of this poem allows several meanings to emerge at once, creating an ambiguity. By maintaining the enigma in her poems, Bryce challenges the transparent language of today's world, which 'harbors no ambivalence'.

All in all, Colette Bryce constantly plays with the tropes of appearances, masks, and illusion. While in some of her poems, she inserts readers in a panopticon mode of vision, in others she offers enigmatic self-portraits, playing with dynamics of hiding and unfolding, absence and presence. The abundance of mysterious, magic motifs can be understood as a direct challenge of the transparency of today's world and the need for privacy and secrecy if one's singularity is to be preserved. My analysis of Bryce's work from the perspective of Secrecy Studies is particularly relevant if we consider that poetry is a literary genre more intimately connected with secrecy than others. Jacques Derrida claims that absolute, unconditional secrecy is related to poetry.[71] Clare Birchall also claims that secrecy is constitutive of poetry itself: '[I]t's a poem's resistance to being illuminated that shows how truly poetic it is [....] the native mode of the poem might be secrecy [....] For a poem to cleave to what makes it unique, it must tend toward the elliptical.'[72] As Birchall later claims, the 'experience of the poem is dependent on non-transparency: arguably, we cannot read or experience a poem as poetic without secrecy'.[73] Non-transparency and secrecy are indeed vital in Bryce's representation of interpersonal relations, the constitution of poetic identities and literary acts of self-exploration. The author offers an alternative way of viewing the secrecy-transparency dyad as generally

---

71   Jacques Derrida, *Points [...] Interviews, 1974–1994*, translated by P. Kamuf (Stanford: Stanford University Press, 1992), 201.
72   Clare Birchall, 'Transparency, Interrupted: Secrets of the Left', *Theory, Culture & Society*, 28/7–8 (2011), 60–84, 69.
73   Birchall, 70. For an enlightening exploration of secrecy in its relation to poetry, see Jo Walton and Ed Luker, 'Poetry and Secrecy', *Journal of British and Irish Innovative Poetry*, 10/1 (2018), 1–36.

perceived in institutionalized discourses in the West, by connecting transparency with surveillance and control, while conceptualizing opacity and secrecy as proper starting points for the representation of alternative singularities which escape the confinement of those invisible boundaries (or 'vertical blinds') which limit individuals, 'a circumstance', as Bryce says in 'A Spider', she well knows.[74]

---

74   Bryce, *Self-Portrait in the Dark*, 3, 29.

BRIAN J. MURPHY AND MÁIRTÍN MAC CON IOMAIRE

17 Generous Curiosity: Connections, Community and Commensality in Research

Due to the competitive nature of the Academy, some commentators have questioned whether it was possible to form true friendships in academia.[1] Thankfully, there are glimmers of light and hope among a number of research communities which manage to do just that. This chapter will discuss two such communities, one focused on Franco-Irish Studies and the other focusing on Food Studies.[2] They negotiate conferences, peer-reviewed journals and monographs without it becoming a 'blood sport' and to the best of their ability avoid the inducement of shame and humiliation often associated with the comments of Reviewer 2.[3] The theme of this chapter is born out of a lifetime's engagement with generous curiosity, which stems from a number of serendipitous life moments and meetings. It focuses on the important role that unique research communities can play in both our professional and personal lives. It builds on sociologist Ray Oldenburg's explanation of the need for third places in our lives beyond our first place (the home) and our second place (work). It suggests that certain unique research communities might in themselves be a version of an enhanced definition of third place. Many personal research journeys

---

1   Kate Eichhorn, Lincoln Allison, Alice Kelly, Helen Lees, Michael Marinetto and Scott Rich, 'Are True Friendships Possible in Academia?' *Times Higher Education*, 15 March 2022, https://www.timeshighereducation.com/depth/are-true-friendships-possible-academia [accessed 20 November 2023].
2   The National Centre for Franco-Irish Studies (NCFIS), the Association of Franco-Irish Studies (AFIS), and The Dublin Gastronomy Symposium (DGS) are all further explained within this chapter.
3   Michael Marinetto, 'There Is No Escape from Reviewer 2', *Times Higher Education*, 15 March 2022, https://www.timeshighereducation.com/opinion/there-no-escape-reviewer-2 [accessed 20 November 2023].

have been positively affected by such third places and the supports and opportunities they provide. This chapter argues for their continued success in an often challenging and sometimes hostile environment.

Drawing on Oldenburg's book *The Great Good Place*,[4] where the importance of place in our lives is foregrounded, the chapter uses a widened third-place lens to consider how it might apply to contemporary research communities in Ireland. In the book, Oldenburg proffers individual chapters that deal with a variety of physical places including the French café, the English pub, and the classic coffeehouse. He recognizes their importance and examines how such places can provide refuge in an often-hostile environment. He introduces us to the concept of third place and stresses its importance in contemporary society. Beyond our home and our work, these third places perform very important functions in our lives. They provide places of community, support, engagement and commensality. In his volume, Oldenburg laments the loss of third places, particularly in modern America. He looks to Europe to find good evidence of thriving third places. However, some would argue that recent world events such as the COVID-19 pandemic, global unrest and economic recessions have further weakened the ability of even these European third places to survive.

One of the later parts of his book details the threats to third places and is entitled 'A Hostile Habitat', and this chapter concludes with the recognition that all third places can be placed under threat from the very environment that they once thrived in. Oldenburg suggests that the third places he describes have a number of features in common:

> The third place has to be on neutral ground.
>
> The third place is a leveller.
>
> Conversation is the main activity.
>
> Regular customers are key.
>
> As a physical structure it often has a low profile.
>
> The mood is playful.
>
> It acts as a home away from home.[5]

---

4   Ray Oldenburg, *The Great Good Place* (Philadelphia: Da Capo Press, 1998).
5   Oldenburg, *The Great Good Place*, 20–42.

For the purposes of this work it can be argued that the attributes of third places as described by Oldenburg can be extended and mapped onto entities other than the defined physical places explored in his book. To do this we need to broaden our thinking around the idea of third-place attributes and take the idea beyond the confines of physical place into a world where other further qualities like commensality, professional courtesy, friendship, supportive environments and collegiality may play a role.

Oldenburg wrote *The Great Good Place* in 1998. Given the period, his work could not fully consider how issues like social media and other developing technologies might ultimately influence our interpretations of place. Ideas around the important places in our lives have now moved beyond the physical locations described by Oldenburg. In recent years we have learned how to share and meet in virtual spaces, often physically alone but somehow together.[6] The concept of Zuckerberg's Metaverse has started to leak into the lived reality of our everyday lives. Our gaze now often looks inward rather than outward through the medium of phone screens. Never have our third places been so important and yet never have they been under so much threat. One way to protect ourselves in this changing environment is through the promotion of spaces and communities that provide an opportunity for analysis and discussion of all aspects of our cultural lives in a curious, supportive, and interdisciplinary manner.

Third place, *terroir*, and opportunities for soul

Our society today has become disjointed and that has consequences. We no longer live in or near the places where we grew up and we are

---

[6] The 2020 Dublin Gastronomy Symposium was one of the first events to pivot to online and managed to use a number of techniques to provide a personal convivial experience in the online space. See Anke Klitzing and Brian J. Murphy 'Visionary, Convivial and Resilient: A History of the Dublin Gastronomy Symposium and Review of the DGS 2020 Online', *European Journal of Food, Drink, and Society*, 1/1 (2021), https://arrow.tudublin.ie/ejfds/vol1/iss1/9/ [accessed 20 November 2023].

frequently devolved from the first communities who raised us. We travel long distances for education, for pleasure, and for work. The world has become smaller and more accessible for many, through enhanced incomes and budget air travel. Communities like the European Union allow freedom of movement across twenty-seven countries for work and education. Due to rising property prices and difficulties in accessing the housing ladder in Ireland, many of us may never own a property in the place we might choose to settle down into. All of this inevitably leads to a separation of community. While some may argue that the aforementioned enhancements in technology help facilitate deeper communication, many feel we are getting farther away from each other. Ireland is now the loneliest country in Europe.[7] Many have proposed that places such as cafés, pubs, and even the church can provide an antidote to this. And yet such third places are proving increasingly difficult to access. Restaurants are struggling, pubs are closing, and faith communities are declining. Furthermore, the recent pandemic has added to a new sense of separation through a blurring of the lines between our traditional first and second places, as many of us work from home for at least part of the week.

In a radio interview in January 2023, Irish comedian Tommy Tiernan, when trying to analyse the success of his TV chat show, embarked on a discussion around what he describes as his general interest in 'opportunities for soul'. He suggests that part of the success he has observed in both his own shows and in many other cultural arenas is attributed to the opportunities such spaces provide for soul. In the piece he offers no definition for that soul, but rather a suggestion that 'there are lots of opportunities

---

[7] Saoirse Mulgrew, 'Ireland Has the Highest Levels of Loneliness in Europe, New Study Finds', *Irish Independent* [online], 7 June 2023, https://www.independent.ie/irish-news/ireland-has-the-highest-levels-of-loneliness-in-europe-new-study-finds/a1717927937.html [accessed 5 August 2023]. The survey was carried out as part of a European Parliament pilot project by the European Commission's Joint Research Centre (JRC) in collaboration with the Directorate General for Employment, Social Affairs & Inclusion (DG EMPL). For a UK comparison see also Thomas Thurnell-Read's 2021 report https://repository.lboro.ac.uk/articles/report/Open_arms_the_role_of_pubs_in_tackling_loneliness/13663715/1 [accessed 20 November 2023].

for soul but there are places, certain shows, certain arenas where they don't want that, they want it business and they want it fast and they don't want any actual human honesty or vulnerability'.[8] In some ways his description could be likened to Amy Trubek's definition of *terroir* in that it is hard to define human contribution and intervention that makes the difference in an otherwise physical exchange.[9]

The word *terroir* crops up regularly in the field of food studies and according to many foodies this is what gives a food or drink its sense of place. But it has been suggested that the word can evoke something much more fundamental. Trubek, who wrote *The Taste of Place: A Cultural Journey into Terroir*, insists that 'culture, in the form of a group's identity, traditions and heritage in relation to place, must also be part of the equation'.[10] There are strong similarities between Oldenburg's third-place requirements, Tiernan's opportunities for soul and Trubek's broader definition of *terroir* in that they all seek to describe a sometimes illusive quality that allows a sense of community to shine through. Interestingly, Tiernan's comment that some places can be 'hostile to soul' mirrors Oldenburg's chapter entitled 'A Hostile Habitat',[11] a subject we shall return to later. However, given the suggestion of a certain similarity between the three concepts mentioned above, it seems reasonable to investigate whether the communities that we choose to engage with, both professionally and personally, can fulfil the demands for Tiernan's soul provision, Oldenburg's third place or even Trubek's sense of *terroir*.

---

8   Tommy Tiernan interviewed by Ray Darcy on The Ray Darcy Show, RTE radio, 6 January 2023 https://www.rte.ie/radio/radio1/clips/22192782/ [accessed 4 November 2023].
9   Amy Trubek, *The Taste of Place: A Cultural Journey into Terroir* (London: University of California Press, 2009), 91.
10 Trubek, *The Taste of Place*, 91.
11 Oldenburg, *The Great Good Place*, 203–229.

The GAA community as a third place

There are examples of communities close to home that might be described as third places that have come close to demonstrating the aforementioned opportunities for soul and a sense of *terroir*. The most prominent of these is perhaps the local Gaelic Athletic Association (GAA) club. Many GAA club strongholds owe their success to the hard work of a small cohort of dedicated men and women. *Terroir* people might be an apt moniker for such a group.[12] The sense of 'club pride' that such people convey to others, stems from their personal relationship with both the club as a place and with members of that community. *Terroir* people in the GAA are special people who give a club its identity, its sense of place, by giving a lifetime of commitment and dedication. They work hard for the club, they run teams, organize events, chair meetings, and fundraise. Above all, they encourage players to be proud of the club. The GAA has faced many serious challenges in recent years, from emigration during lean years, to competition from other pursuits during boom times and recently one of the biggest challenges of all, COVID-19.

Thankfully, though, the community has remained strong throughout, and most GAA clubs have maintained a wide group of dedicated parents, who still give of their time freely every week to help out in the interests of their children and the local community. But sometimes if you look closely enough, some lucky clubs also have a small cohort of those *terroir* people who are the incarnation of the spirit of the place. In a sense they allow the club to become a true third place. Their commitment provides opportunities for soul. Long after their own children have grown up and moved away, these *terroir* people continue to maintain the beating heart of their local GAA club. Like the turf beneath their feet, they remain a club constant. They quietly go about their work organizing, chairing and fundraising. Most importantly, they nurture a club tradition rooted in a

---

12 See Brian J. Murphy, '"Pride of Place": GAA Clubs and the Community around Them', *RTE Brainstorm*, 26 April 2022, https://www.rte.ie/brainstorm/2022/0426/1294332-gaa-clubs-community-society-culture/ [accessed 20 November 2023].

pride of place that allows the community to feel a true sense of belonging, a true sense of *terroir*.

Third-place research communities

The case of the local GAA club is useful in that it provides an important example of an entity that moves beyond the physical places described by Oldenburg into the broader concept of a 'third place' community. We can suggest that similar qualities are evident in two distinct but related research communities that emerged in Ireland since the turn of the millennium. These are a Franco-Irish Research Community that originated in the early 2000s in what was then the Institute of Technology, Tallaght (IT Tallaght) and a Food Studies Research Community that emerged around the same time in what was then the Dublin Institute of Technology (DIT), Cathal Brugha Street. Like the GAA, both research groups are based on a sense of community in the truest sense, both provide opportunities for soul and both thrive due to the sustained efforts of the *terroir* people that maintain their contribution as third places.

Franco-Irish research community

The Franco-Irish research community began as a collaboration between two academic communities in France and Ireland. Starting in the early 2000s, initial professional friendships led to the emergences of two main research arms: The Association of Franco-Irish Studies (AFIS) and The National Centre for Franco-Irish Studies (NCFIS). AFIS is an international collaborative network of institutions and scholars based in TU Dublin. It hosts international conferences and events on the links between Irish Studies in France and Ireland. The association is chaired by the current president Dr Sarah Nolan from the Institute of Art, Design and Technology, Dun Laoghaire, who succeeded its instigator and founding president, Dr Eamon Maher. AFIS has published a wide range of conference proceedings both in Ireland and in France over its twenty-year history. The NCFIS, under the direction of Dr Eamon Maher, is a research centre based in TU Dublin and provides another important Irish research hub. Though historically focused on more traditional humanities research areas such as literature and history, over the last decade it has encouraged and supported several other research areas including food, tourism and sport.

The food studies research community

During the same period, a separate research community emerged in DIT / TU Dublin in the area of Food Studies led by Dr Máirtín Mac Con Iomaire. The origins of this community coincided with the development of a new liberal / vocational paradigm of culinary education in DIT in the 1990s, and with the attendance of Irish scholars at the annual Oxford Symposium of Food and Cookery (1979–present).[13] Gastronomy and food studies provided core liberal arts modules throughout the four years of the BA (Hons) Culinary Arts. Lecturers and students on the programme were energized by the latest developments in the world of gastronomy, as can be seen from attendees at the Oxford Symposium.[14] The

---

13 For a history of culinary education in Ireland, see Máirtín Mac Con Iomaire, 'From the Dark Margins to the Spotlight: The Evolution of Gastronomy and Food Studies in Ireland', in *Margins and Marginalities in Ireland and France: A Sociocultural Perspective*, edited by Catherine Maignant, Sylvain Tondeur, and Déborah Vandewoude (Oxford: Peter Lang, 2021), 129–153.

14 Early Irish attendees at the Oxford Symposium were Myrtle Allen, Darina Allen, Regina Sexton, Elizabeth Erraught, John Mulcahy, Dorothy Cashman, Tara McConnell and Máirtín Mac Con Iomaire. This provided a network of global food writers and scholars and an outlet for disseminating research on Irish food culture. Pádraic Óg Gallagher funded a student scholarship to the Symposium each year for the most promising student in Gastronomy on the BA (Hons) Culinary Arts.

first graduates of the BA (Hons) Culinary Arts were showcased in *The Irish Times* in 2004[15] and over the years many of the course's graduates have built careers both in Ireland and internationally as culinary educators, entrepreneurs, award-winning chefs and restaurateurs,[16] product development chefs, and as thought leaders within the broader food media. Gastronomy modules featured on postgraduate programmes from 2007. Postgraduate and doctoral research into food history soon followed, research which is continuously expanding and developing.[17] From this point on, it is evident that Irish food history was on a secure footing within academia and the wider community.

The role of serendipity

A key serendipitous moment in the nexus of Irish Studies with Food Studies was when Brian Murphy organized a Gastronomy Day in Tallaght in 2011. This was the first time Eamon Maher, Brian Murphy and Máirtín Mac Con Iomaire would meet, along with Dorothy Cashman and Tara McConnell. They instantly gelled, recognizing in each other like-minded souls who cherish the concepts of generous curiosity, conviviality, fun, and friendships. By the following year, they had collectively organized the first biennial Dublin Gastronomy Symposium, held at the School of Culinary Arts and Food Technology, Cathal Brugha Street in 2012, now relocated to the TU Dublin campus at Grangegorman.[18] The Symposium

---

15   Deirdre McQuillan, 'School for Foodies', *Irish Times Magazine*, 28 February 2004.
16   Many of these graduates have provided wonderful commensal memories for members of both AFIS, NCFIS, and DGS over the last decade.
17   For a general overview of the expansion of culinary arts, food studies and gastronomy education in Ireland with a list of food-related doctoral research, see Máirtín Mac Con Iomaire, 'Applying the Food Lens to Irish Studies', *Reimagining Irish Studies for the Twenty-First Century*, edited by Eamon Maher and Eugene O'Brien (Oxford: Peter Lang, 2021), 19–38.
18   Dublin Gastronomy Symposium https://arrow.tudublin.ie/dgs/ [accessed 20 November 2023].

was directly influenced by the Oxford example, but augmented with genuine Irish hospitality, that first gathering leading to the publication of *'Tickling the Palate': Gastronomy in Irish Literature and Culture* as part of the Peter Lang Reimagining Ireland series.[19] Often misunderstood as accidental, serendipity requires sufficient background knowledge, an inquisitive mind, creative thinking and good timing, involves both chance and sagacity, leading it to be paraphrased as 'accidental wisdom'.[20]

The meeting in Tallaght in 2011 brought like-minded people together who could sense a shared vision and an openness to work collectively to become more than the sum of their individual parts. This led to a gastronomy / food studies stream at the subsequent AFIS conferences, and to numerous publications. Both communities absorbed best practice from each other, with the high tide lifting all boats. The DGS partnered with the French Embassy and with Fáilte Ireland to enable international keynote speakers. The AFIS gathering soon became a biennial event running at the alternate years with the DGS. Food and commensality became a marker of AFIS, while publishing proceedings and book launches became a regular feature of the DGS. Both communities attracted new members, many of which would become active across both AFIS and the DGS, influenced by the conviviality and openness of both organizations. Peer-reviewed journals emerged from each community,[21] with some of the combined members becoming involved in both. A special issue of the *Canadian Journal of Irish Studies* in 2018 focused on Food Studies, and had contributors from both research communities.[22] It is safe to say that over a decade on from

---

19 Máirtín Mac Con Iomaire and Eamon Maher (eds), *'Tickling the Palate': Gastronomy in Irish Literature and Culture* (Oxford: Peter Lang, 2014).

20 Ohid Yaqub, 'Serendipity: Towards a Taxonomy and a Theory', *Research Policy*, 47 (2018), 169–179; Isabelle Rivoal and Noel Salazar, 'Contemporary Ethnographic Practice and the Value of Serendipity', *Social Anthropology* 21/2 (2013), 178–185.

21 The *European Journal of Food, Drink, and Society* was conceived by Michelle Share, Dorothy Cashman and Yvonne Desmond at the gala dinner of the Dublin Gastronomy Symposium https://arrow.tudublin.ie/ejfds/; The *Journal of Franco-Irish Studies* (JOFIS) became a vehicle for postgraduate students to publish and gain experience of editing and organize a journal https://arrow.tudublin.ie/jofis/.

22 This special Food Issue of the CJIS included articles from both the AFIS and DGS communities, for example, Eamon Maher, Dorothy Cashman, Eugene O'Brien,

the first gastronomy parallel session at the AFIS conference in Limerick, that food and beverage studies are now firmly on the radar of Irish studies researchers. Indeed, researchers from across both communities have contributed chapters to the latest interdisciplinary volume *Irish Food History: A Companion*.²³

The importance of Conviviality and Commensality

Anthropologists have long known the power of sharing food and drink together, and how it cements bonds of friendship and respect. Immanuel Kant (1724–1804) was renowned for his dinner parties, which had rules (between three and nine people), and trifold stages to the conversation during the dinner: (a) Narration, that is, exchange of news (b) Ratiocination, that is, lively discussion of the diversity in judgement at the table (c) Jest, that is, play of wit.²⁴ Many of these traits are found in Oldenburg's theory. Toussaint-Samat terms 'sacramental drunkenness – a communal experience which seals alliances [...] an experience of shared intoxication which [...] takes a group out of their normal state of mind, out of time, freeing them from the conditioning of the outside world'.²⁵ There is much evidence of successful academic research clusters bonding and exchanging ideas and projects over regular

---

Marjorie Deleuze, Máirtín Mac Con Iomaire, Elaine Mahon, and Tricia Cusack, with reviews of book or plays written by Brian J. Murphy, Grace Neville, Éamon Ó Ciosáin, and Séamus O'Kane. The cover featured the award-winning dish by Mark Moriarty, a graduate of BA (Hons) Culinary Arts who had won the San Pellegrino World Young Chef of the Year in 2015. See *Canadian Journal of Irish Studies*, 41 (2018), https://www.jstor.org/stable/26435222 [accessed 12 October 2023].

23   Máirtín Mac Con Iomaire and Dorothy Cashman, *Irish Food History: A Companion* (Dublin: EUT+ Academic Press, 2023).
24   https://www.anthologialitt.com/post/the-dinner-parties-of-immanuel-kant; https://branemrys.blogspot.com/2010/07/immanuel-kants-guide-to-good-dinner.html [accessed 20 November 2023].
25   Maguelonne Toussant-Samat, *A History of Food*, translated by Anthea Bell (Oxford: Blackwell, 2009), 35.

meals or libations. Take, for example, C. S. Lewis and J. R. R. Tolkien's informal discussion group, The Inklings, who met each Tuesday at The Eagle and Child pub in Oxford.[26] In Cambridge, Charles Babbage, John Herschel, William Whewell, and Richard Jones met every Sunday morning to discuss science in what became known as The Philosophical Breakfast Club.[27] The dining table or the pub becomes a third place, not work and not home, a neutral ground where conversation is intellectually stimulating and challenging, and sometimes irreverent, with a playful mood. It is in these informal settings that new ideas are exchanged and that future collaborations are often discussed and agreed. These settings provide a space for Tiernan's 'soul' and Trubek's intangible '*terroir*', the hard-to-define human contribution and intervention that makes the difference, but these occasions of 'soul' require '*terroir* people' to make them happen. Eamon Maher is undoubtably a '*terroir* person'.

Unbeknownst to each other at the time, both the Franco-Irish Research Community and the Food Studies Research Community had a number of important founding principles in common, primarily having generous curiosity at their core. Most if not all academics are curious, but not all are generous in their curiosity, willing to share their learning and knowledge and also admit to the gaps in their knowledge. With the philosophy that every day is a school day, and that the more we learn, the more we realize how much there is still to learn, the spirit of generous curiosity lifts all boats and ensures fun along the journey rather than focusing solely on the destination. They certainly fulfilled many of Oldenburg's previously mentioned third place requirements, but also provided a focus on attributes that moved beyond research community norms at the time. One of the most important of these was the sense of genuine support that they offered within the research arena. Both were initiated separately by Maher and Mac Con Iomaire at a time when research agendas were often fraught with conflict as more traditional academics fought for recognition of

---

26 See Lincoln Allison's 'The Lunch Clubbables' in Eichhorn et al. 'Are True Friend Possible in Academia?'; see also https://en.wikipedia.org/wiki/The_Inklings [accessed 20 November 2023].
27 Laura J. Snyder, *The Philosophical Breakfast Club: Four Remarkable Friends Who Transformed Science and Changed the World* (Oregon: Broadway Books, 2011).

their place within the broader academic community. Both communities offered something different, particularly to new younger researchers.

Conclusion

It is clear that both the Franco-Irish and the Food Studies research communities discussed in this chapter can, and do, function as third places. They offer something unique to members that goes beyond the confines of standard academic output. Like the aforementioned local GAA club, these communities are guided by *terroir* people who promote a research agenda that is both rigorous and prolific. But what makes them unique is their willingness to be driven by a spirit of generous curiosity that can sometimes be rare in academia. They know the importance of ensuring an inclusive, supportive and commensal environment that recognizes both the professional and personal needs of the contemporary researcher. They offer a rare mix of academic rigour coupled with the desire to derive enjoyment from the dissemination of research work. The nature of that dissemination, be it through conference or publication is always supported by an opportunity to engage with one another as friends thus providing 'opportunities for soul' as mentioned earlier. Both communities recognize the importance of sitting at the table together to break bread or share a glass. The word commensal itself means, quite literally, eating at the same table and is a founding principle of both groups. There is an importance to nurture this form of thinking and also to ensure succession plans for these organizations.

However, if one can successfully argue that research communities such as these are in fact a version of Oldenburg's third place, one must also take on board the words of warning expressed in his chapter: 'A Hostile Habitat.' When referring to the third places in his book he suggests: 'Like all living things, the third place is vulnerable to its environment. Far more important than the architecture and appointment of these establishments is the habitat in which they may or may not be able to blossom or thrive.'[28] This phrase reminds us of

---

28   Oldenburg, *The Great Good Place*, 203.

Tiernan's earlier reference that 'there are lots of opportunities for soul but there are places, certain shows, certain arenas where they don't want that, they want it business and they want it fast and they don't want any actual human honesty or vulnerability'.[29] The research communities mentioned in this chapter, and others like them, depend on opportunities to meet in person, to share commensal experiences so that the generous curiosity that is so core to their existence can be maintained. They frequently find themselves living in a hostile environment in academia.

While Oldenburg's third places are under attack from planners, increasing costs and competing places in the private sphere, research community third places are under threat from a bureaucratic system that is attempting the 'businessification' of higher education.[30] Research output seems increasingly restricted by regulations, cost-benefit analysis and bureaucratic decisions that stifle creativity. There is little space for true communities to develop. These new structures do not always recognize the benefit of supporting a conference with opportunities for engagement beyond the lectern. They often seek the financial advantage of moving things online rather than allowing face-to-face academic engagement, the very essence of what the two communities mentioned in this chapter are all about. And so, it behoves all members of these communities to persistently argue for, defend and protect the precious spaces these unique research-focused third places hold in academia. By doing this we can support the true *terroir* people in our research communities and ensure that future generations of researchers can benefit from the same spirit of generous curiosity that has proved so important to us all over the past twenty years.

---

29   Tiernan, *Interview*, 2023.
30   Peter McLaren, 'Critical Pedagogy and Class Struggle in the Age of Neoliberal Globalization: Notes from History's Underside', in *Neoliberalism and Education Reform*, edited by E. Wayne Ross and Rich Gibbons (Cresskill, NJ: Hampton Press, 2006), 257–288, 278, 285.

EUGENE O'BRIEN

18 'To write poetry after Auschwitz is barbaric [...]': Micheal O'Siadhail's *The Gossamer Wall*

The Holocaust is a defining event of the Western world that seems to resist definition. Jean-François Lyotard speaks of how the 'impossibility of quantitatively measuring it does not prohibit, but rather inspires in the mind of the survivors the idea of a great seismic force'.[1] The reason for the almost unrepresentable nature of the event has been summarized by Raul Hilberg:

> I believe that the Holocaust was a watershed event in human history – the most extreme case of genocide that has yet occurred. What distinguishes it from other genocides are two factors: first the totality and scope of intent – that is, the goal of killing every last Jew, man, woman and child, throughout the reach of the Nazi empire; and second, the means employed – namely, the harnessing of the administrative / bureaucratic and technological capacities of a modern nation state and western scientific culture.[2]

It is the sheer efficiency and commodification of a slaughter of a people for no other reason than that they are of one particular race that seems to be almost beyond our ability to represent. That so much of Western technology and scientific knowledge was used to enable the mass-genocide of 6,000,000 Jews seems impossible to contemplate, especially as most of us writing about this are doing so using the very products of that post-Enlightenment technology ourselves to write about it and locate the information. To write about this is to write about western Europeans like

---

1 Jean-François Lyotard, *The Differend: Phrases in Dispute* (Minneapolis: University of Minnesota Press, 1988), 56.
2 Raul Hilberg, *The Destruction of the European Jews* (London: Holmes & Meier, 1985), 251.

ourselves who became part of a murder machine, thousands of people involved to greater or lesser degrees in the vast machinery of extermination: a watershed indeed, and one that many of us find hard to put into words.

The whole issue of whether it can be remembered or recalled and whether our language and structures of signification are able to comprehend the Holocaust or Shoah is a fraught one. In early 1973, the year she died, the celebrated Austrian poet and novelist Ingeborg Bachmann visited Auschwitz and Birkenau during a reading tour of Poland. She remarked: 'I don't understand how one can live with them nearby [....] There is nothing to say. They are simply there, and it leaves you speechless.'[3] Writing in *Prisms*, Theodor Adorno made one of the most emphatic and oft-quoted comments about the intersection between the poetic, the political and the ethical, when he said that to write poetry after Auschwitz would be barbaric. The remark is quoted, and indeed mis-quoted, a lot in academic and theoretical discourse, but very often in a manner that does not take account of its full context. Adorno is speaking, not about the value of art as a redressal or a voicing or come form of cathartic or empathic response to barbarity and horror but rather about culture and about its contemporary state:

> The more total society becomes, the greater the reification of the mind and the more paradoxical its effort to escape reification on its own. Even the most extreme consciousness of doom threatens to degenerate into idle chatter. Cultural criticism finds itself faced with the final stage of the dialectic of culture and barbarism. To write poetry after Auschwitz is barbaric. And this corrodes even the knowledge of why it has become impossible to write poetry today. Absolute reification, which presupposed intellectual progress as one of its elements, is now preparing to absorb the mind entirely. Critical intelligence cannot be equal to this challenge as long as it confines itself to self-satisfied contemplation.[4]

If poetry after Auschwitz was barbaric for Adorno, one wonders what his views would be on poetry about Auschwitz? This chapter will examine

---

3   Emma Garman, 'Feminize Your Canon: Ingeborg Bachmann', *Paris Review*, 9 July 2019, https://www.theparisreview.org/blog/2019/07/09/feminize-your-canon-ingeborg-bachmann/#more-137776 [accessed 6 December 2023].
4   Theodor W. Adorno, *Prisms* (London: Spearman, 1967), 34.

just such a book, *The Gossamer Wall: Poems in Witness to the Holocaust*, by Micheal O'Siadhail, and will look at the value of poetry as a form of remembrance and witness, as well as looking at O'Siadhail's own sense of why such a book is relevant, and in his view, necessary. In a conversation with me, O'Siadhail, who is a fluent German speaker, discussed the centrality of this quote to his own thinking about the book:

> Of course, we are confronted with the famous statement of Theodor Adorno: '*nach Auschwitz ein Gedicht zu schreiben ist, barbarisch*': to write a poem after Auschwitz is barbaric. I think he later withdrew this sentiment but I know what he meant. At first it's not easy to square such evil with such beauty.[5]

As an exemplar of this, he quotes the first three lines of 'Glimpses':

> After a tough day selecting who'd live or die,
>
> For light relief Mengele had the camp cellist
>
> Anita Lasker play him Schumann's *Träumerei*.[6]

The notion that the aesthetic should in some way civilize those of us who enjoy and appreciate it died in examples like this one, in the sense that Mengele could butcher others in an almost Fordist industrialized process, and then come home and listen to Schumann. The most frightening thing is that normal people, people of culture and civilization, could become a willing part of this process:

> Friends, colleagues, clients that shied away.
>
> Slow isolation. Unprimrosed slide to a hell.
>
> Blind-eyed Northeim doesn't want to know.[7]

---

5   Conversation with the author, 12 January 2022.
6   Micheal O'Siadhail, *The Gossamer Wall: Poems in Witness to the Holocaust* (Tarset, Northumberland: Bloodaxe Books, 2002), cited in this chapter from Micheal O'Siadhail, *Collected Poems* (Tarset, Northumberland: Bloodaxe Books, 2002), 394–471, 465.
7   O'Siadhail, *Collected Poems*, 420.

At the end of 'Education After Auschwitz', Adorno recounts the time that Walter Benjamin asked him if there were really enough torturers in Germany to carry out the orders of the Nazis.[8] As it turned out, there were more than enough, as barbarity was normalized.

Interestingly, one of the poems in the book, 'Never', begins with the question that arises from consideration of Adorno's quotation:

> That any poem after Auschwitz is obscene?
>
> Covenants of silence so broken between us
>
> Can we still promise or trust what we mean?[9]

It might indeed, seem problematic to address the role of art and Auschwitz, standing in synecdoche for the 6,000,000 deaths of the final solution, in a work of art itself, but as is often the case, when Adorno's comment is placed in the broader context of Adorno's philosophy, the seeming declarative statement becomes more complex and O'Siadhail offers an interesting supplement to Adorno's perspective.

Of course, this perspective is far broader than the oft-quoted comment, as this comment, a text in itself, needs to be set within its context in order to more fully comprehend its full meaning. In Adorno's later thinking, Auschwitz is a very resonant metaphor, and the quote needs to be located in this developing context. Jacques Derrida's broader work has made this very point in the seemingly contradictory declarations *'il n'y a pas de hors-texte'* ('there is nothing outside the text'),[10] and *'il n'y a pas de hors contexte'* ('there is nothing outside of context').[11] For Derrida, any text, any sentence or statement, needs to be set within its framing context, and these two need to be seen as interacting if any sense of a full meaning is to be recuperated. This sense of the complexity and the difficulty of fully understanding any

---

8   Theodor W. Adorno, *Critical Models: Interventions and Catchwords*, translated Henry W. Pickford (New York: Columbia University Press, 1998), 191.
9   O'Siadhail, *Collected Poems*, 467.
10 Jacques Derrida, *Of Grammatology*, corrected edition, translated by Gayatri Chakravorty Spivak (Baltimore: Johns Hopkins University Press, 1997), 158.
11 Jacques Derrida, *Limited Inc*, translated by Alan Bass and Samuel Weber (Evanston, IL: Northwestern University Press, 1988), 136.

text without noting its shifting relationship with its context needs to be addressed, hence, as well as the context of the quote, it is also valuable to look at Adorno's own reassessment of his comment on Auschwitz.

Writing in *Negative Dialectics*, Adorno noted that 'perennial suffering has as much right to expression as a tortured man has to scream; hence it may have been wrong to say that after Auschwitz you could no longer write poems'.[12] For Adorno, this was an experience which fundamentally changed our perspective on society; he seemed to be suggesting that to write poetry in, and about, a culture which could produce such industrialized extermination of human beings, was in some way to avoid facing the inherent horror at the heart of that culture. It was a way of participating in reification (*Verdinglichung*), a process wherein human interactions, relationships and connections are seen increasingly as things or products, and where concepts become fixed, or thing-like, so they appear fixed and unchanging despite changing contexts. This allows people to avoid responsibility as they seem to be accepting what is natural or unchangeable:

> Victims, perpetrators, bystanders who'd known
>
> Still cast questioning shadows across our own.
>
> Some barbarous. Mostly inaction or indifference.[13]

While writing in 1965, collected in *Metaphysics: Concepts and Problems*, Adorno made the point that he did not anticipate his comment being taken literally as 'it is in the nature of philosophy – and everything I write is, unavoidably, philosophy, even if it is not concerned with so-called philosophical themes – that nothing is meant quite literally. Philosophy always relates to tendencies and does not consist of statements of fact'.[14] This is an important *caveat*, and it is also interesting in terms of how

12 Theodor W. Adorno, *Negative Dialectics*, translated by E. B. Ashton (London: Routledge, 1973), 362.
13 O'Siadhail, *Collected Poems*, 469.
14 Theodor W. Adorno, *Metaphysics Concepts and Problems*, translated by Rodney Livingstone, Edmund Jephcott, Howard Eiland and others, edited by Rolf Tiedemann (Stanford: Stanford University Press, 2001), 110.

O'Siadhail views Adorno's notions of poetry after Auschwitz. Adorno sees his comments as being interpreted within an over-simplistic, almost instrumental, binary opposition; he argues that people think he is saying either that 'after Auschwitz one cannot write any more poems; so either one really cannot write them, and would be a rogue or a cold-hearted person if one did write them', or that he is wrong, and 'has said something which should not be said'.[15]

For Adorno, the framing contextual discourse of philosophy means that this very simplistic explanation is only partial, a point he goes on to extrapolate at length in the same essay, where he stresses that any sense of full meaning is to be found in a negotiation, or a Kantian vibration, between the very different perspectives:

> Well, I would say that philosophical reflection really consists precisely in the gap, or, in Kantian terms, in the vibration, between these two otherwise so flatly opposed possibilities. I would readily concede that, just as I said that after Auschwitz one could not write poems – by which I meant to point to the hollowness of the resurrected culture of that time – it could equally well be said, on the other hand, that one must write poems, in keeping with Hegel's statement in his Aesthetics that as long as there is an awareness of suffering among human beings there must also be art as the objective form of that awareness.[16]

Here I am using the term 'negotiation' in quite a specific sense. Derrida traces the etymology of 'negotiation' to the Latin *negotium*: 'not-ease, not-quiet […] no leisure'.[17] He sees this 'no-leisure' as the 'impossibility of stopping or settling in a position […] of establishing oneself anywhere'. This process is typified by the image of a shuttle, what he terms '*la navette*, and what the word conveys of to-and-fro between two positions, two places, two choices' in a process of 'going back and forth between different positions'.[18] The vibration of which Adorno speaks has similarities to this Derridean shuttling between texts and contexts. A different

---

15   Adorno, *Metaphysics Concepts and Problems*, 110.
16   Adorno, *Metaphysics Concepts and Problems*, 110.
17   Jacques Derrida, *Negotiations: Interventions and Interviews, 1971–2001*, edited by Elizabeth Rottenberg (Stanford: Stanford University Press, 2002), 11.
18   Derrida, *Negotiations: Interventions and Interviews, 1971–2001*, 12.

context can easily elide a sense of horror, and replace it with a reified form of memory that something horrible has indeed happened, but it was in the past and does not affect us in the present:

> A world that lusts for life soon loses interest.
>
> For years tattoos of memory travel incognito.
>
> They didn't understand, they didn't want to know.[19]

Adorno puzzled over this sense of meaning pulled between opposite polls throughout his work, and his notion of dialectical criticism developed from this seeming aporia.

This contradictory position, of being part of a culture while at the same time attempting to offer a critique of the ideology of that culture, is discussed in his essay 'Cultural Criticism and Society'.[20] For Adorno, cultural criticism was by definition a problematic enterprise: the cultural critic 'is not happy with civilization, to which alone he owes his discontent'.[21] The two subject positions from which criticism may be offered are seen as those of immanence and transcendence, and both positions are fraught with difficulty. The immanent critic participates in the culture: he or she is shot-through with the ideologies and attitudes of that culture, and hence has little chance of making any real objective statements about this position of 'total immanence', and therefore is doomed to repeat the errors of the culture.[22] The transcendent critic, on the other hand, 'aims at a totality', and assumes an 'Archimedean position above culture and the blindness of society'. However, such a position, 'outside the sway of existing society', is 'fictitious',[23] and ultimately as monological as that of a position within ideology. Adorno's answer to this dilemma is the notion of 'dialectical criticism', which takes up a position in culture and not in culture at the same time. It is a position which takes full account of the resistances and difficulties that theory, politics, literature, and other constituents of society cause

---

19 O'Siadhail, *Collected Poems*, 459.
20 Adorno, *Prisms*, 17–34.
21 Adorno, *Prisms*, 19.
22 Adorno, *Prisms*, 26.
23 Adorno, *Prisms*, 31.

in seemingly monadic systems and structurations. As Adorno puts it: the dialectical method must relate the knowledge of society as a totality and 'the mind's involvement in it to the claim inherent in the specific content of the object that it be apprehended as such'.[24] In this sense, the position of transcendence is achieved dialectically by looking at a microcosmic part of a totality, and by then relating that to the macrocosm.

So to return to the statement that writing poetry after Auschwitz is barbaric, I think it is clear that there is a lot to be unpacked; for Adorno, so much of his post-war work and writing was driven by the need to ensure that 'never again' ('*nie wieder*') would such a holocaust happen. He opens his essay 'Education after Auschwitz', by stating that 'the premier demand upon all education is that Auschwitz not happen again [....] Every debate about the ideals of education is trivial and inconsequential compared to this single ideal: never again Auschwitz'.[25] He reiterates this in *Negative Dialectics*, when he says, again channelling Kant, that 'a new categorical imperative has been imposed by Hitler upon unfree mankind: to arrange their thoughts and actions so that Auschwitz will not repeat itself, so that nothing similar will happen'.[26] I would argue that O'Siadhail's book is very much in the service of this aim, as by delineating the horrors of Auschwitz through poetry, memories and witnesses are created that will resonate and vibrate in the minds of readers. In Hegelian terms, this art will be the objective form of that awareness of the suffering in Auschwitz. The associative language of poetry, which has the ability to embody and enunciate aspects of experience that are not really captured by more normative discourses, allows for a different mode of memory and witness. Poetry allows us to feel the affects of the despair, hopelessness and sheer instrumental cruelty of the *Shoah*; poetry enables emotion, feeling and affect to be studied with some precision because 'affect resides in the language of literature not in speaking *about* feelings but in the very speaking and way of speaking'.[27]

---

24 Adorno, *Prisms*, 33.
25 Adorno, *Critical Models: Interventions and Catchwords*, 191.
26 Adorno, *Negative Dialectics*, 365.
27 John Brenkman, *Mood and Trope: The Rhetoric and Poetics of Affect* (Chicago: University of Chicago Press, 2020), 9.

This book makes it clear that O'Siadhail grasps Adorno's sense that something very central in the intra-human experience has been shattered by the Auschwitz experienced. It also embodies Derrida's notion that philosophy, '*finds itself again* in the vicinity of poetics, indeed, of literature' [*italics original*]:[28]

> As though things can be too big for us close-up
>
> and need the slow-down of both time and distance;
>
> a wider angle, the gradual adagio of truth.
>
> So complex, so tangled as if we have to wait
>
> on some riff of imagination to refract detail,
>
> some fiction to shape elusive meanings of fact.[29]

O'Siadhail, like Derrida, is all too aware that a change of perspective and of genre can change the nature of what is being examined and, crucially, the meaning that results from this trans-generic examination. In this sense, to achieve Adorno's injunction of 'never again', poetry with its fictional but real truth, is necessary if another Auschwitz is to be avoided. A respectful, ruminative, thoughtful account of how we, who were not there, can witness and remember what happened, and crucially, allow ourselves to hear and read the attitudes and mindsets that enabled, and resisted, this horror, means that we will be far less-inclined to repeat these horrors.

O'Siadhail's awareness of Adorno's perspective on poetry is clear from a short sequence in the 'Prisoners of Hope' section of *The Gossamer Wall*, near the end of the book, where the phrase 'never again' is repeated across four poems:

---

28 Jacques Derrida, *Sovereignties in Question: The Poetics of Paul Celan*, edited by Thomas Dutoit and Outi Pasanen (New York: Fordham University Press, 2005), 44.

29 O'Siadhail, *Collected Poems*, 397.

'Glimpses'

Imagined surprises, surprises beyond our ken.

Dream and reality feeding circuitries of hope;

A promise to remember, a promise of never again […][30]

'Imagine'

The benign are keeping a watch over us.

Imagine another black sun,

An all-knowing stony insomniac Argus?

As never before we promise never again […][31]

'Repair'

The sudden riffs of surprise beyond our ken;

Out of control, a music's brimming let-go.

We feast to keep our promise of never again.[32]

'Never'

Never, never again. Pleading remembrance

Whispers through the gossamer wall:

Promise us at least this.[33]

The first two examples repeat the phrase at the end of a stanza, using the rhetorical device of epistrophe, and the effect is to foreground the Adornoesque invocation. The second two examples involve the rhetorical device of symploce, as the end of one poem is repeated directly, and with added emphasis, at the start of the next one. These examples of symploce and epistrophe foreground the sense of singularity that attaches

---

30   O'Siadhail, *Collected Poems*, 465.
31   O'Siadhail, *Collected Poems*, 466.
32   O'Siadhail, *Collected Poems*, 467.
33   O'Siadhail, *Collected Poems*, 467.

to the holocaust; they also underline that the poems are looking at both the present and the future, so as well as remembering and witnessing, there is also a didactic and optative sense in which we remember so that we may not repeat. It is an attempt to avoid a societal Freudian repetition compulsion. For Freud, compulsive action is 'a repetition of what is forbidden',[34] and he sums it up in the terms 'fixation to the trauma' and 'repetition compulsion'. He gives the examples of a man who has had a long-forgotten mother-fixation in his childhood but who will later 'seek for a woman on whom he can be dependent, who will feed and keep him', and of a girl who 'was seduced in early childhood', and who may in later life 'orient her later sexual life towards provoking such assaults over and over again'.[35] It is only by working through these experiences that this compulsion can be stopped, and these poems attempt just such a process as we are placed in a number of different positions and feel their intensity, danger and hopelessness.

A lot of these poems are written in the present tense, which allows for the immediacy of what is happening to affect the reader: as well as remembering the past, poetry allows us to witness it in a messianic poetic time wherein the affect is more immediate. The poems elicit emotion, and they make us feel the blackness and the pain through symbol and metaphor. One thinks of Paul Celan's 'Fugue of Death' (*'Todesfuge'*), where he speaks of the 'Black milk of daybreak we drink you at night / we drink you at noon death comes as a master from Germany',[36] which shows that the camps brought about an inverted life, a death-in-life as even what was supposed to be nourishing was black and death-infected. It is an image that conveys the hopelessness of a life in a camp, where one was living but had no future or hope. We feel this in Celan's work, and in that of O'Siadhail, as opposed to just cognitively knowing it. For Celan, every item of food, every meal, everything put in the mouth, just prolongs the death in life

---

34 Sigmund Freud, *Totem and Taboo: Resemblances between the Psychic lives of Savages and Neurotics*, translated by Abraham Arden Brill (New York: Moffat, 1918), 86.
35 Sigmund Freud, *Moses and Monotheism*, translated by Katherine Jones (London: The Hogarth Press and the Institute of Psycho-Analysis, 1939), 122.
36 Paul Celan, *Selected Poems*, translated by Michael Hamburger and Christopher Middleton, edited by Al Alvarez (Harmondsworth: Penguin, 1972), 33.

of the camps. This ability to affect us emotionally is a very strong quality of poetic discourse. As Brian Massumi has argued, emotion or affect, is a subjective content, 'the sociolinguistic fixing of the quality of an experience which is from that moment onward defined as personal', it is 'intensity owned and recognized'.[37] For him, affect is that which escapes what we can rationally express and is something that images and symbols and sounds can embody: 'intensity is the unassimilable'.[38]

This intensity is far from barbaric, to revert to Adorno's *dictum*: instead it forms a bulwark against forgetting that barbarity, as it keeps the victims of that barbarity before us and with us, not as dead memories or statistics, but rather as haunting presences which can be felt in the lines of the poems. O'Siadhail looks at all of the broad overviews and the numerical horror of the camps: 'Paths of Auschwitz paved with ash and bone',[39] and 'the crying silence of six million faces'.[40] However, he also focuses on individuals, stemming from his reading of a number of books on the Holocaust. In his acknowledgements, he lists some of the books he has read, broad history, overviews but also testimonies of those who were there: Primo Levi's *If This Is A Man*,[41] *The Truce*,[42] *The Drowned and The Saved*[43] and *Moments Of Reprieve*;[44] Charlotte Delbo's *Auschwitz and After*,[45] Elie Wiesel's *All Rivers Run to the Sea*,[46] Etty Hillesum's *An Interrupted Life*,[47] Anne Frank's *The Diary of a Young Girl*,[48] Jacques Lusseyran's *And there was*

---

37   Brian Massumi, *Parables for the Virtual: Movement, Affect, Sensation* (Durham, NC: Duke University Press, 2002), 28.
38   Massumi, *Parables for the Virtual*, 27.
39   O'Siadhail, *Collected Poems*, 464.
40   O'Siadhail, *Collected Poems*, 464.
41   Primo Levi, *If This Is a Man* (New York: Orion Press, 1959).
42   Primo Levi, *The Truce: A Survivor's Journey Home from Auschwitz* (London: Bodley Head, 1965).
43   Primo Levi, *The Drowned and the Saved* (New York: Summit Books, 1988).
44   Primo Levi, *Moments of Reprieve* (New York: Summit Books, 1986).
45   Charlotte Delbo, *Auschwitz and After* (New Haven: Yale University Press, 1995).
46   Elie Wiesel, *All Rivers Run to the Sea: Memoirs* (New York: Knopf, 1995).
47   Etty Hillesum, *An Interrupted Life: The Diaries, 1941–1943; and Letters from Westerbork*, translated by Arnold J. Pomerans, foreword by Eva Hoffman, introduction and notes by Jan G. Gaarlandt (New York: Henry Holt, 1996).
48   Anne Frank, *The Diary of a Young Girl* (London: Constellation Books, 1952).

light[49] and Anita Lasker-Wallfisch's *Inherit the Truth*.[50] This allows him to focus in individuals which makes the affect all the more intense and personal:

> Birkenau's chronicler Lewental
>
> Buries his thermos in the ash
>
> Of Crematorium III, journal
>
> For a final revolt, a cache
>
> Of testimony, resistance of word,
>
> Troves of memory interred.
>
> Four hundred pages of diary
>
> In the minuscule hand of Etty
>
> Hillesum [....]
>
> [....] As smoke from burning wood the will
>
> To survive leaves a ghosted heart;
>
> Parents and sons of Olga Lengyel
>
> Chambered, her husband once sighted.[51]

It is easier to empathize with individuals, and the present tense makes us imaginatively share their ordeal, and their desire that this ordeal be both recorded and witnessed. The rhyming of 'ash' and 'cache', and of 'word' and 'interred', is deliberate as an associative chain of connection between language and death is foregrounded across the book in this type of chiasmus. There is also a chiasmatic structure in the way in which the book as a whole is constructed, a point made by O'Siadhail himself:

---

49   Jacques Lusseryan, *And Then There Was Light: The Autobiography of a Blind Hero of the French Resistance*, translated by Elizabeth R. Cameron (Edinburgh: Floris Books, 1985).
50   Anita Lasker-Wallfisch, *Inherit the Truth: A Memoir of Survival and the Holocaust* (London: Thomas Dunne Books, 2000).
51   O'Siadhail, *Collected Poems*, 443.

I don't think I originally saw the structure of The Gossamer Wall; it seemed to evolve. I'm not sure at what point it became clear that it would be a chiasmus; Figures (describing the camps) are at the core and each side, before and after, the sections mirror each other in reverse order. Directly before the camps is Descent with first Northeim (how a town in the middle of Germany succumbed to the Nazis) and then Battalion 101 (how individuals became inured to evil). After the camps come Refusals, firstly Spoors (showing the bravery of individuals who resisted the Nazis) and the Le Chambon (relating how a Huguenot village in South East France stood up to the Nazis). In a word, the individuals who went along with the Nazis are set off against those who resisted them and the town, Northeim, that yielded to the Nazis is contrasted with the village Le Chambon which outwitted them. Finally, the build-up in the first section Landscapes is mirrored by the final section Prisoners of Hope. The purpose of the chiasmus is clearly to suggest contrasts.[52]

Hence the book is shaped in something of triptych, with Northeim, Auschwitz and La Chambon as the three panels, with the third panel offering the sense of hope that keeps a light burning in the awfulness of the Nazification of Germany and the annihilation of the Jews: 'In Jeremiah's darkest scroll a jazz of hope.'[53] David Ford, a really fine commentator on O'Siadhail's work, makes the point that he 'evokes this biblical tradition that can show hope stirring "even in the deepest cries of silence"'.[54] The structure of the book allows for that earlier mentioned interaction and shuttling between text and context, as the core of the book are the concentration camps, which are contextualized as the end-point of two thousand years of persecution and anti-Semitism. *The Gossamer Wall* takes the two villages as synecdoches of attitudes to the Jews. It shows the descent of Northeim, a 'city of ten thousand / nooked where the Leine and Ruhme meet'; a 'snug county seat plump in the heartland',[55] to Nazism and the war in which ordinary men can become hardened killers in Battalion 101. He also shows the resistance of the village of Le Chambon on the 'granite Plateau du Velay',[56] to Nazism by protecting groups of fleeing Jews.

52 Conversation with the author, 12 January 2022.
53 O'Siadhail, *Collected Poems*, 464.
54 David F. Ford, *Christian Wisdom: Desiring God and Learning in Love* (Cambridge: Cambridge University Press, 2007), 139.
55 O'Siadhail, *Collected Poems*, 412.
56 O'Siadhail, *Collected Poems*, 447.

O'Siadhail's The Gossamer Wall 257

It is an epic poem, composed of a series of lyrics, which together blend narrative and imagistic and symbolic modes to proffer a reading and enunciation of the Holocaust in a way that is unique in that there is a shuttling between horror and pity; between past and future; between poetry and philosophy; between hope and despair and between good and evil which offers an affective truth of the Holocaust in ways that cannot be caught by any other discourse. The implications of the Holocaust or the future are strong and are not avoided:

> Still the stamped forearms of first witnesses.
>
> Indelible warnings: this might happen again.
>
> Still a moment when testimony and story meet
>
> Before the last attesting faces will retreat
>
> To echo chambers of second-hand remembrance.[57]
>
> An intersection, at once cadence and overture,
>
> Hinge and turning point, the moment when
>
> The pasts we shape begin to shape our future.[58]

There is a depth of analysis here, as he realizes that the past does not come to us, readily packaged; instead it is we who give shape to the pasts and the plural is noteworthy as the book offers a broad range of pasts as it comes to terms with the enormity of what transpired. O'Siadhail also includes images of hope noting that '[a]t least a marriage each day at Bergen-Belsen. / Obstinacy of survival, slowly reassembled life'.[59]

We hear about the Jews who die; we also hear about those who die trying to save them. As well as couplets, sonnets and various poetic devices, he also uses zig-zag rhyme, a form adopted from Irish-language poetry, to further bind together different ideas, stories and memories. It is very

---

57 O'Siadhail, *Collected Poems*, 396.
58 O'Siadhail, *Collected Poems*, 396.
59 O'Siadhail, *Collected Poems*, 396.

deliberate and part of O'Siadhail's poetic technique of using the sound of words to reinforce the patterns of meaning. As he explains himself:

> It binds the whole narrative in an understated way, which manages the flat tone which I deliberately adopted in order to let the true horror of what happened take its own effect. Another favourite is the zigzag rhyme, where a word in each line rhymes (or occasionally half-rhymes) with one word anywhere in the following line. I use this frequently in *The Gossamer Wall* to chain together a deliberately sober account:
>
> Company platoons *surround* the village.
>
> *Fugitives* are shot. The others *round*
>
> them up in the market. *Anyone gives*
>
> trouble, *gun* them with infants or *feeble*
>
> or any who *hide*. *Able*-bodied men
>
> set *aside* for camps as 'work Jews'. [*my italics*].[60]

These echoes of language, hauntings of rhyme, half-rhyme and assonance, allow for the subtleties of the connections set up in the book between the present and past, as lines become 'echo chambers of second-hand remembrance'.[61] David Mahon makes the point that this type of poetry with its tangled rhyme-scheme suggests a reading of history 'as a complex process of untangling the "*tangled*" events in order to "*shape elusive meanings of fact*".'[62]

So we hear about 'Leopold the thief', who 'feeds his protégés [...] in his *pied-à-terre*, / a Lvov sewer': only ten of these survive. We hear about 'Albert the local masseur', taking food to his 'fosterlings underground'; we hear 'Priest Lichtenberg', who protested after *Kristallnacht*, and who 'dies *em route* to Dachau'; we hear of 'Austrian Anton Schmidt', who tried to 'flit' Jews by truck to Bialystok: 'he too forfeits the light', and in the present

---

60 O'Siadhail, Ford and Tolstoy, *Say But the Word*, 9.
61 O'Siadhail, *Collected Poems*, 396.
62 David C. Mahan, *An Unexpected Light: Theology and Witness in the Poetry and Though of Charles Williams, Micheal O'Siadhail and Geoffrey Hill* (Eugene, OR: Pickwick Publications, 2009), 121.

tense, we are with him imaginatively as this happens. A villager from Poland also tries to save some Jews, but with tragic consequences:

> A Roszak Zaporska unnamed tended
>
> Six in his cowshed. Raided he's gunned
>
> As he fled for his life. Gendarmes return
>
> To wipe out wife, daughter and son.[63]

These names, bound tightly to their narrative by all sorts of rhymes (note the harsh, thematic rhyming of 'tended' and 'gunned'), show the echoes and spectral presences that are betokened by the gossamer wall of the book's title. Indeed, that sense that there is only a thin veil between us and those who were killed, and that they are in some way with us in the present, is taken from *Fugitive Pieces* by Anne Michaels. The protagonist of her novel was continually aware of the proximity of a sister Bella who had died in the Holocaust: 'I felt her presence everywhere, in daylight, in rooms I knew weren't empty [....] Watching with curiosity and sympathy from her side of the gossamer wall.'[64] This sense that we are haunted by the memories and presences of those who have died is strong in O'Siadhail's writing; the present tense, and the echoes and ghosts all suggest that the memory is a living one:

> Behind a flimsy partition ghost parents call,
>
> Siblings eavesdrop behind a gossamer wall.
>
> A doubleness only revenants understand.
>
> Wounded alone know the wounded land.[65]

The sense of wounding and near-death echoes the writing of Paul Celan, as does the idea of ash as a signifier for the memory of the Shoah, and of the Holocaust:

---

63 O'Siadhail, *Collected Poems*, 444.
64 Anne Michaels, *Fugitive Pieces* (New York: Vintage Books, 1996), 31.
65 O'Siadhail, *Collected Poems*, 445.

> That half-death,
>
> suckled big with our life,
>
> lay around us, true as an ashen image.[66]

Ash is almost the product of the Holocaust, a word whose meaning, as noted by Derrida in *Glas*, refers to fire and burning: 'all (*holos*) is burned (*caustos*)'.[67] Derrida, writing about the Holocaust in *Cinders*, makes the point that ashes are 'the better paradigm for what I call the trace – something that erases itself totally, radically, while still presenting itself',[68] and O'Siadhail also uses the evocative term 'trace' to describe the four hundred pages of Etty Hillesum's 'crammed story' which will resurface forty years later as a remembrance of the camps: 'Spoor of life. A trace.'[69]

Art, language and memory are all, epistemologically, traces of something written in a present which is over as soon as the full stop is put at the end of the sentence. Remembrance is many-faceted, flawed, fallible but in this case, it needs to be repeated over and over so that what happened here cannot be forgotten. This book, with its pervasive use of the present tense, and the extended metaphor of ghostly memories hovering beside us behind a gossamer wall, brings the memories to life in our minds and in our imaginations, and this is important because it is the western, post-Enlightenment European culture that brought this about: as Derrida aptly put it, 'Nazism was not born in the desert', and he goes on to extend the metaphor, adding that even if it grew in a European forest, 'it would have done so in the shadow of big trees, in the shelter of their silence or their indifference but in the same soil'.[70] His point is that this is part of the civilization of which we are a part, of its culture, its technology and its very essence:

---

66   Celan, *Selected Poems*, 87.
67   Jacques Derrida, *Glas*, translated by Richard Rand and John P. Leavey (Lincoln: University of Nebraska Press, 1986), 241.
68   Derrida, *Cinders*, 43.
69   O'Siadhail, *Collected Poems*, 443.
70   Derrida, *Of Spirit*, 109.

> We all know this, but it has to be constantly recalled. And even if, far from any desert, it had grown like a mushroom in the silence of a European forest, I will not list these trees which in Europe people an immense black forest, I will not count the species. For essential reasons, the presentation of them defies tabular layout. In their bushy taxonomy, they would bear the names of religions, philosophies, political regimes, economic structures, religious or academic institutions. In short, what is just as confusedly called culture, or the world of the spirit.[71]

The traces need to be kept alive, the ashes need to be poked. 'Celan's burden of so much ash to bless',[72] is always countered by the opposing view of irrepresentability: 'How can one bless ashes in German?'[73] Poetry is probably the best way to encompass this aporetic imperative of the need to remember and represent that which is too huge to remember and represent, as if 'the all-burning [Holocaust] destroys up to its letter and its body, how can it leave or keep the trace of itself and breach / broach a history where it preserves itself [precisely] in losing itself?[74]

Giorgio Agamben sees poetry as a central point of differentiation between biological life 'which lives only to maintain itself, and human poetic life, which lives in order to create forms'.[75] In other words, Agamben sees poetry as a central defining human characteristic, speaking about 'the poetic status of man [sic] on earth'.[76] In a philosophical swerve, which echoes the thinking of Heidegger, he says that man has a poetic status because 'it is *poiesis* that founds for him [sic] the original space of his world'.[77] Poetry, for Agamben, is deeply imbricated with thinking, making, and form, all of which are central attributes to being human. The memories and diaries and witness gathered together so ethically and aesthetically in *The Gossamer Wall* is both a witness and a testimony to this.

---

71 Derrida, *Of Spirit*, 109–110.
72 O'Siadhail, *Collected Poems*, 446.
73 Derrida, *Sovereignties in Question: The Poetics of Paul Celan*, 63.
74 Derrida, *Cinders*, 44.
75 Claire Colebrook, 'Agamben: Aesthetics, Potentiality, and Life', *The South Atlantic Quarterly: The Agamben Effect*, 107/1 (2008), 107–120, 109.
76 Giorgio Agamben, *The Man without Content*, translated by Georgia Albert (Stanford: Stanford University Press, 1999), 42.
77 Agamben, *The Man without Content*, 63.

MICHAEL CRONIN

19 Is There a Translator in the Text? Language, Identity and Haunting

Gearailt lives and works in Brussels. He is contacted by an Estonian colleague who has difficulty identifying words in the recorded speech of a dying woman whose family want to know what she is saying. He recognizes the Irish term for a ringed plover, *feadóg chladaigh*. So begins the unravelling of the false identity of Hanna, who claims to a Jewish survivor of the wartime destruction of the Jewish population in Estonia but is, in fact, Muraed, a native Irish speaker from Inis Mór, fleeing her own troubled history. Gearailt's own identity issues are less ethnic than professional:

> Feadóg chladaigh. An dá fhocal Gaeilge ba spéisiúla a dtáinig Gearailt trasna orthu ó thug sé an Bhruiséil air féin is ó tharraing sé chuige ceird mhíthrócaireach an aistriúcháin.[1]

For the Irish-language translator, real life is elsewhere. The unmerciful task of translation a poor substitute for the blandishments of the oral tradition:

> Ní aistritheoir a bhí ann de réir nádúir, ach fear béaloideasa. B'fhearr leis go mór fada a bheith ag plé le hamhráin agus scéalta agus gnásanna traidisiúnta ná a bheith ag iarraidh Gaeilge na leabhar a chur ar imeachtaí Choimisiúin na hEorpa.[2]

---

1 Tadhg Mac Dhonnagáin, *Madame Lazare* (An Spidéal: Barzaz, 2021), 55. *Feadóg chladaigh* [ringed plover]. The two most interesting words in Irish that Gearailt had come across since coming to Brussels and since he had started on the unmerciful job of the translator.
2 Mac Dhonnagáin, *Madame Lazare*, 56. In essence, he was not a translator but a folklorist. He much preferred dealing with songs, stories and traditional customs that trying to put the proceedings of the European Commission into formal Irish.

The disdain for translation, the perception of it as an unwarranted intrusion, an unwelcome burden, is not new in Irish. The most notorious example of this sustained hostility to the translation in the first half of the twentieth century was the ritual disparagement of the translation initiatives of the state publishing house, An Gúm.[3]

In a review of *Fíon Gearmánach*, a collection of Irish-language translations of German poems by the Cork scholar, Tadhg Ó Donnchadha (Torna), the reviewer in the journal *An Stoc* noted peevishly:

> D'fhéadfamis a rádh, maidir leis an leabhar seo go bhfuil sé go réidh ar cheann den chuid is fearr a tháinig amach fá'n nGúm, ach tá faitchíos orainn nach mbeadh a sháithe de mholadh annsin aige.[4]

The discomfort or denial has played out even more strikingly in the systemic failure to treat translation as a language policy issue. From John Walsh's excellent and comprehensive *One Hundred Years of Irish Language Policy 1922–2022*, it is apparent that at no stage in the last one hundred years of policy formation has any serious consideration been given to the nature, practice and impact of translation despite the fact that translation is an inescapable fact of the daily experience of an Irish-language speaker in everything from tax returns to weather reports.[5] Any demand for the increased provision of services in Irish leads inevitably to the increased presence of translated language but where are the public debates on the form, utility and deployment of translation? An illustration of how this problem is likely to become more acute was unwittingly provided by events preceding the centenary celebration of the Easter Rising in 2016. On 6 November 2014, in a note to government officials, the senior media adviser to Heather Humphreys, the then Minister responsible

---

3   Gearóidín Uí Laighléis, *Galláin an Ghúim* (Baile Átha Cliath: Coiscéim, 2017).
4   Cited in Ailbhe Ní Ghearbhuigh, *Fíon Gearmánach: Torna agus Filíocht na Gearmáinise*, 196–217, in *Tintúd-Aistriú: Papers on Translation in Irish Tradition*, edited by Ken Ó Donnchú (Cork: Cló Torna, 2022), 211. One could say, with respect to this book that it is one of the best things that an Gúm has published, but I am afraid that would be poor praise indeed.
5   John Walsh, *One Hundred Years of Irish Language Policy 1922–2022* (Berlin: Peter Lang, 2022).

for, *inter alia*, Irish-language affairs, recommended that among the eight headings on the draft 1916 commemoration programme (Remembering the Past, Relatives, Commemorative Stamps, Culture Programmes, Irish Language, Our Young People, Community and Diaspora), the Irish language should be placed near the bottom of the list just ahead of postage stamps.[6] The Irish-language version of the programme which appeared on the official commemorative website was unintelligible. It had been, along with sections of the 1916 Proclamation itself, translated by that mischievous Lord of Language, Google Translate.

What is telling in this sorry debacle is not so much the cultural obtuseness or the linguistic ignorance of the media adviser than the ready recourse to automation. The translation was unmasked in 2014 because of the less advanced state of translation technology. However, the advent of neural MT and Deep-L, and the greater availability of Irish-language training data for MT systems, means that it is far less likely that unintelligibility would now be the predicted outcome of the of the use of MT. The greater embedding of automated translated language into the everyday language lifeworlds of Irish-language speakers has two legible consequences. On the one hand, there is the question of the range and nature of the translation outputs and their impact on the use and development of the language. On the other, there is the epistemic consequence of translation perceived as an instantaneous, ubiquitous activity which renders invisible the layers of mediation (linguistic, temporal, spatial) that make it possible. In other words, the cultural and institutional marginalization of translational reflexivity risks being further compounded by technical advances. It is for this reason, among many others, that the establishment of centres of reflection on translation in the Gaelic world, is of such primary importance to the speakers of both Irish and Scots Gaelic. Treating translation as a factor of primary importance in both the historical experiences and future developmental possibilities of speakers of different varieties of Gaelic is long overdue and will contribute to the urgent need for critical reflexivity in what we do with and how we think about translation. In this context, translation needs to

---

6   Harry McGee, 'Gaeltacht Department Sought Relegation of Irish in 1916 Event', *The Irish Times*, 9 February 2015.

be thought of less as a necessary evil and more as a redemptive partner in creating viable language worlds for different members of the Gaelic family.

So what does thinking about translation mean for the languages we speak and where we are situated? I want to suggest that for our purposes, there are consequences at three levels: the level of perception, the level of inclusivity, and the level of relationality.

Level of perception

In 858 Johannes Scotus Eriugena at the request of the Emperor Charles the Bald, grandson of Charlemagne, produced a new translation of the writings of Dionysius the Areopagite. Dionysius's work was especially prized because it was an attempt to bridge the world of classical learning with the doctrine of Christian revelation. Translation in such a tentative interface demanded vigilance. Pope Nicholas I in a letter to Charles the Bald requested that the translation be sent to Rome as there were doubts about its orthodoxy. The papal librarian, Anastasius, was given the task of examining and correcting the translation. Returning the edited text to the Carolingian monarch in March 860, Anastasius expresses surprise at the linguistic competence of the Irish translator:

> It is a wonderful thing how that barbarian, living at the ends of the earth, who might be supposed to be as far removed from the knowledge of this other language [Greek] as he is from familiar use of it has been able to comprehend such ideas and translate them into another tongue: I refer to John Scotigena, whom I have learned by report to be in all things a holy man.[7]

The trilingual Eriugena (Gaelic, Latin and Greek) is a source of wonder for the Vatican scholar but note how his puzzlement is expressed spatially – Eriugena is living at the ends of the earth, *finis terrae*. This is the quintessential Graeco-Roman terrestrial paradigm. Set out on foot or on

---

7   James Kenney, *The Sources for the Early History of Ireland* (New York: Columbia University Press, 1929), vol. 1, 582.

horseback from Athens or Rome and after weeks and weeks of travelling and the occasional boat journey, you will arrive at the edge of the world. It is a trope that has endured from the geography of Ptolemy to *The Banshees of Inisheerin*, the Gaelic world as remote, far removed, edgy, and peripheral. Let us consider this paradigm in the light of another set of translations, this time from Latin into Gaelic. Between the eleventh and thirteenth century, Gaelic scholars produced a series of translations of texts relating to the heroic wars of Graeco-Roman antiquity: accounts of the Trojan war in *Togail Troí*, the story of Alexander the Great in *Scéala Alaxandair*, Aeneas's arrival in Italy in *Imtheachta Aeniasa*, the campaign of the Seven against Thebes in *Togail na Tebe* and the Roman civil war between Caesar and Pompey in *In Cath Catharda*.[8] Michael Clarke points out, for example, that the dating of the Book of Leinster, with its copy of *Togail Troí* 'establishes beyond doubt that the beginning of the Irish antiquity sagas predates that of the principal equivalent Continental tradition, the Old French *romans d'antiquité*, and this is a further reminder that Middle Irish literary creativity was far from backward-looking or isolated in the Europe of its time'.[9] Clarke, in his analysis of the most extensive and ambitious of these translations, the 61,000 word *In Cath Catharda*, shows how the translator deftly weaves together a detailed knowledge of indigenous, heroic literature with a rich awareness of contemporary European warfare so that 'we are kept guessing as to whether to picture Caesar as a figure more resembling Conchobhar Mac Nessa or an aristocratic knight of the thirteenth century'.[10]

Indeed, this confident handling of material can be traced to a more general preoccupation with the possibilities of translation in the Gaelic tradition. Caitríona Ní Dochartaigh has written of the intense interest of monk scholars not only in the translations of Jerome but in his theoretical reflections on translation. This interest is apparent in the Old Irish glosses

---

8   Michael Cronin, *Translating Ireland: Translation, Languages* (Cultures, Cork: Cork University Press, 1996), 8–46.
9   Michael Clarke, 'Translation and Creativity in the Antiquity Sagas: The Arming of Julius Caesar in *In Cath Catharda*', 23–49 in *Tintúd-Aistriú: Papers on Translation in Irish Tradition*, edited by Ken Ó Donnchú (Cork: Cló Torna, 2022), 24.
10 Clarke, 'Translation and Creativity', 43.

explaining Jerome's prefaces to his translations of the Psalms in the Vulgate in a manuscript now housed in Milan.[11] The monk translators, strongly influenced by the Ciceronian substrate to Jerome's practice that eschewed literalism for a communicative engagement with the target language and culture, worked towards an increasing vernacularization of Latin ecclesiastical literature in the late eighth century. As Ó Dochartaigh observes, 'The Old Irish Treatise and Penitential as well as the Milan glosses and commentary are witnesses to this enterprise of vernacularisation and profound engagement with Latin source-texts.'[12] What emerges in the Gaelic tradition is not belatedness but contemporaneity, not residual copying but creative making.

The evidence of translation activity through the centuries indeed leads one to posit a wholly different paradigm for the Gaelic world, what I want to call the *quadrivial* as opposed to the *peripheral* paradigm. Quadrivial is derived from the Latin word for crossroads *quadrivium* and describes the Gaelic world as lying at a crossroads of influence running North-South from the Scandinavian world to the Iberian peninsula and beyond and East-West from continental Europe to the Americas. Underpinning this quadrivial paradigm is a shift from terrestrial to maritime readings of culture, prefigured in the Irish case by Bob Quinn's *The Atlantean Irish*[13] and articulated more recently in the scholarly works of David Brett, *A Book around The Irish Sea: History without Nations*,[14] and Nicholas Allen, *Ireland, Literature and the Coast: Seatangled*.[15] No longer hostage to the Graeco-Roman forms of definitional peripherality, prioritizing maritime channels of influence allows for the emergence of the Gaelic world as a quadrivial

---

11 Caitríona Ó Dochartaigh, 'Conceptualising "Translation" in the Early Medieval Latin/Irish Linguacultural Context', 1–22 in *Tintúd-Aistriú: Papers on Translation in Irish Tradition*, edited by Ken Ó Donnchú (Cork: Cló Torna, 2022), 2.
12 Dochartaigh, 'Conceptualising "Translation"', 7.
13 Bob Quinn, *The Atlantean Irish: Ireland's Oriental and Maritime Heritage* (Dublin: Lilliput Press, 2005).
14 David Brett, *A Book around the Irish Sea: History without Nations* (Dublin: Wordwell Books, 2009).
15 Nicholas Allen, *Ireland, Literature and the Coast: Seatangled* (Oxford: Oxford University Press, 2021).

space with translation in the spatial and symbolic sense at its heart. Whether speaking about the incorporation of Norse loan words into Gaelic, the translation activities of sixteenth-century Gaelic scholars in southern and northern Europe or the fortunes of Irish-Gaelic and Scots-Gaelic speakers on the Atlantic seaboard of North America, there is a distinct sense of the Gaelic world being at the crossroads of continuous transformation (not all of which, of course, were positive) rather than being stranded on an autarkic, self-regarding ledge, revelling in photogenic isolation. Shifting to the quadrivial paradigm demands a different level of perception of the role and value of translation in the Gaelic world as the activity itself is seen as core rather than peripheral.

Level of inclusivity

If one of the tasks of any reflection on Gaelic translation is to chart out the history of translation practice in the languages contained with the Gaelic tradition, it is important that we consider who it was did these translations and how they were done. This means challenging certain perceptions of cultural activity that remain embedded in sets of ideological assumptions that can distort our readings of the historical record or actual practice. Anthony Cordingley and Céline Frigau Manning in their introduction to a collection of essays on collaborative translation note that the 'popular image of the lonely translator is strikingly at odds with the reality of his or her work within the profession'.[16] They claim:

> Even if one defines translation narrowly, limiting it to decoding a source text and writing it in another language, throughout history the practice has not always been assumed to be a solitary affair. From Antiquity to the Renaissance, translation was frequently practised by groups comprised of specialists of different languages with varied skills.[17]

16 Anthony Cordingley and Céline Frigau Manning, *Collaborative Translation: From the Renaissance to the Digital Age* (London: Bloomsbury, 2016), 1.
17 Cordingley and Frigau Manning, *Collaborative Translation*, 1.

The rise of philosophical individualism throughout the sixteenth and seventeenth century with the advent in politics of the citizen and in economics of the consumer challenges the hegemony of the collective. The Romantic preoccupation with the force and sanctity of original expressiveness privatizes the demiurge, the sole genius brooding over their emerging, singular creations. The temptation in the post-Romantic Age can be to construe translation history as a Gallery of Greats, a pantheon of heroic individuals who single-handedly inflect the direction of the culture or the language. To show the limits of this approach I want to refer briefly to the practice of a translator in Irish, Pádraig de Brún, who as translator in the twentieth century of Homer, Dante, and Racine would seem to answer to the description of the sublimely individual talent. At the end of a day working on one of his translations, he would ask one of his neighbours in the West Kerry Gaeltacht to come to his house and go over the translations with him, checking the translations for accuracy and idiomaticity. In a lament he penned for one of his collaborators, Peats Mhicil O'Connor, he acknowledges his debt:

> Léinn duit ó am go ham na haistrithe a rinneas
>
> Ó dhrámaí stáitse an chlú ón bhFrainc is ón tSeana-Ghréig
>
> Thaitníodh a gcúrsaí leat, is chuirfeá feabhas is cruinneas
>
> Ar mo lag-iarrachtaí le briathra an bhreithimh réidh.[18]

The novelist and critic, Alan Titley, is intrigued by the collision of cultures in de Brún's kitchen, 'Nach aoibhinn an smaoineamh é go raibh Racine agus Hóiméar agus Dante ag scoilteadh focal leis an gCeithearnach Caolriabhach agus leis an nGobán Saor agus le Fianna Éireann ar leac

18   Brian Ó Cuív, 'Metrical Features in de Brún's Coiméide Dhiaga Dante', 139–147, in *Miscellanea Wagner: Miscellanea Celtica in memoriam Heinrich Wagner*, edited by Séamus Mac Mathúna and Ailbhe Ó Corráin (Uppsala: Studia Celtica Upsaliensia, 1997), 153–154.
From time to time I would read my translations to you
Of famous plays from France and Ancient Greece
You liked the way of them, and you improved, made sharper,
My poor efforts with the words of the wise judge.

Language, Identity and Haunting 271

na cistine sin.'[19] The contact was, of course, not as surprising as it may have sounded. We know that seven centuries earlier there were already stylistic convergences between the *Táin Bó Cuailgne* and *Togail Troí* and 'resonances between the depiction of Cú Chulainn in the *Táin* and that of Achilles in Latin poetry and mythography derived ultimately from the Homeric tradition'.[20]

However, at the level of inclusivity, it is noteworthy that there is a democratic or horizontal dimension to the translational practice as local farmers with rudimentary formal education cooperate with a renowned academic scholar and onetime president of University College Galway. Titley notes this tendency more generally in surveying a number of the leading translations produced by the state publishing house in the interwar period, 'fág gur daoine ardoilte ba ea formhór na ndaoine a bhí ag dul do haistriúcháin, ní raibh léann an scoláire ach ar fhíorbheagán díobh'.[21] This raises the question of whether translation practices in minority or minoritized cultures are more socially inclusive by virtue of the fact that it is often more politically or economically marginalized sections of the community that will have levels of competence in the language not readily available elsewhere. They possess a linguistic or cultural capital which is not the sole monopoly of elite groups in the society. In analyses of translation practice, it is instructive to remain attentive to the collaborative dimension and how the social distribution of native speakers and new learners plays out in the realization of translation projects.

19 Alan Titley, *An Scéim: An Gúm 1926–2016* (Baile Átha Cliath: An Gúm, 2020), 38. Isn't it wonderful to think of Racine and Homer and Dante splitting hairs with the Ceithearnach Caolriabhach, the Gobán Saor, and Fianna Éireann on that kitchen floor.
20 Clarke, 'Translation and Creativity', 24.
21 Titley, *An Scéim*, 41. Although many of those involved in the translations were highly skilled, very few of them had advanced formal education.

Level of relationality

The French philosopher Bruno Latour, who passed away recently, notes that the designation of a new geological epoch, the Anthropocene, serves to mark climate change not just as a transitory event, a 'passing crisis' but rather as 'a profound mutation in our relation to the world'.[22] In other words, what place do humans now occupy in the world and, in turn, how they relate to the other organisms and entities with which they share the planet? The climate crisis has fundamentally challenged the doctrine of human exceptionalism, whereby humans are masters and possessors of the natural world and thus uniquely equipped to subordinate it to their own needs. Rather than asserting human autonomy and supremacy, the crisis has revealed human dependency and vulnerability. What the profound mutation in our relation to the world demands is a new way of thinking that allows us to explore *how* humans might now relate to the world they inhabit. That relation is, of course, powerfully mediated through language, and places are rarely understood separately from the words used to describe and interpret them. A telling indicator of the ecological pressure on the language force field is the publication of a succession of works in English in Ireland interrogating the Gaelic underpinning of native understandings of place. Sharon Arbuthnot, Máire Ní Mhaonaigh and Gregory Toner, *A History of Ireland in a 100 Words*;[23] Manchán Magan, *Thirty-Two Words for Field: Lost Words of the Irish Landscape*;[24] Doireann Ní Ghríofa, *A Ghost in the Throat*;[25] Kerri ní Dochartaigh, *Thin Places*[26] and Manchán Magan, *Listen to the Land Speak*,[27] are all works that in

---

[22] Bruno Latour, *Facing Gaïa: Eight Lectures on Climate Change* (Oxford: Polity, 2017), 8, 9.
[23] Sharon Arbuthnot, Máire Ní Mhaonaigh, and Gregory Toner, *A History of Ireland in 100 Words* (Dublin: Royal Irish Academy, 2019).
[24] Manchán Magan, *Thirty-Two Words for Field: Lost Words of the Irish Landscape* (Dublin: Gill, 2020).
[25] Doireann Ní Ghríofa, *A Ghost in the Throat* (Dublin: Tramp Press, 2020).
[26] Kerri Ní Dochartaigh, *Thin Places* (Edinburgh: Canongate, 2021).
[27] Manchán Magan, *Listen to the Land Speak* (Dublin: Gill, 2022).

their different registers grapple with a fundamental translation problem. Kerri ní Dochartaigh, working through the traumatic legacy of paramilitary and state violence in her native Derry, situates her own personal losses in a wider framework of dispossession:

> The loss of the ability to name both the landscape and the creatures we share it with in Irish began to sink in. An incomparable loss has been touching the wider world, growing with each newspaper report we hear, during my lifetime. Somehow I had always viewed that loss of wild things as being unrelated to the loss in my homeland, as though they could not be spoken of in the same breath. But I started to feel an ache, a deep sorrow, when I began to see it all in the clear light of day. How interconnected, how finely woven every single part of it all was.[28]

The more-than-human world she gestures to is opaque. For it to be made meaningful, it requires a particularizing translation into Irish which restores an animate, ecological presence to lands voided by the colonial erasures of a *terra nullius*. It is the translational shortfall, 'the loss of the ability to name both the landscape and the creatures we share it with', which reveals the extent of alienation. Restorative ecology – the recovery of a resilient and sustainable relationship to the more-than-human world – lends a particular urgency to the project of studying and promoting translation across the Gaelic world. Translation both nourishes and is nourished by language. Translation contributes to the broadening of horizons in a language but there are no translators without competent speakers of the language.

Translation in its toxic form is substitutive – the substitution of the weaker language by the more powerful language. The assumption here is that everything can be successfully captured (the verb is not innocent) by the dominant tongue, Caliban's postcolonial illusion that acquiring the language of the master is sufficient to the creation of a viable identity. It is the awareness of the limits to this book that inform the work published over the last four years, a reappraisal of Calibanism as an ideology of redemption. Translation in its positive sense is additive. The argument here is for more translation into Gaelic not less. The building of a sustainable

---

28 Ní Dochartaigh, *Thin Places*, 20.

lifeworld is paralleled by the construction of a resilient language world. Translation, in this respect, can become an integral part of the project of biocultural diversity, adding to what speakers can know, do and think in a language that for more than two millennia has meticulously mapped the Gaelic archipelago.

I began with a fictional Irish-language translator in the European Commission, and I want to end with a real one, Diarmuid Johnson. He is the author of *Seacht dTír Seacht dTeanga*,[29] an account of his linguistic and translational wanderings through Welsh, Polish, Breton, German, Romanian, Irish, and English. Speaking of the particular challenges of learning the *Gwened* dialect of Breton, Johnston confesses, 'Má bhí dúshlán san éagsúlacht seo dom, bhí lón léinn agus léirmhachnaimh ann chomh maith.'[30] Language variety and linguistic difference are, of course, the core challenges for the translator. They also provide, as Johnston rightly signals, ample opportunity for study and deep reflection. We no longer need to be uniquely haunted by the ghosts of our historical inadequacy but can be guided by the different levels of perception, inclusivity and relationality to embrace a progressive translation manifesto for our Gaelic worlds.

---

29 Diarmuid Johnson, *Seacht dTír Seacht dTeanga* (Indreabhán: Lebhar Breac, 2021).
30 Johnson, *Seacht dTír Seacht dTeanga*, 107. If this variety was a challenge for me, it was also an opportunity for learning and deep reflection.

VIC MERRIMAN

20 At Someone's Expense: Nation, Fulfilment, and Betrayal in Irish Theatre

Throughout the twentieth century, Ireland's theatre artists were ostentatiously in dialogue with moments of historical significance and the forces that shaped them. While this may have been expected in the work of the Abbey and Peacock theatres, which aspired to, and regularly achieved, an avowedly public role, it is also true of plays produced on other stages. Ireland's public plays interrogate social, political and historical questions, and works by Bernard Shaw, JM Synge, Sean O'Casey, Tom Murphy, and others have both testimonial and prophetic capacities. For most of the period since independence, Irish electoral politics, and the business of government, has been widely understood as the concern of the population in general rather than the preserve of elite groups. The use of the single transferrable vote in multi-seat constituencies, and the enduring ferocity of rivalries rooted in civil war politics, ensures a vigorous campaigning culture and relatively high voter participation. A turnout of 70 per cent of the electorate at the general election of 2011, called after the acceptance of terms for an EU / IMF 'bailout' following the Global Financial Crisis (GFC), produced an unprecedented rejection of the hitherto hegemonic Fianna Fáil party, in what was called 'a riot at the ballot-box'.

As it had done a century before, early twenty-first-century theatre provided a platform on which to interrogate the concerns of the day. A series of plays dramatizing the perceived – and later verified – venality of the political classes, included *Ariel*, by Marina Carr[1] and *Hinterland*, by Sebastian

1 https://irishplayography.com/play.aspx?playid=30682 [accessed 12 December 2023].

Barry[2] (both Abbey Theatre, 2002), *Sky Road*, by Jim Nolan (Theatre Royal, Waterford)[3] and *Boss*, by Thomas Hall (Granary Theatre, Cork, 2008). Nor were the entrepreneurial or 'business-leader' classes spared, in works including, David McWilliams's *Outsiders* (Peacock Theatre, 2010) and Julian Gough's *The Great Goat Bubble* (Mick Lally Theatre, Galway, 2013).[4]

This striking interplay between critical artefacts and historical events has been evident since the foundation of the national theatre, even in the period of Eamon De Valera's political dominance, widely regarded as culturally unremarkable (1932–1959). *Bunreacht na h-Éireann*, a new constitution for the Irish Free State, was ratified by referendum on 1 July 1937, and came into force on 29 December that year. This was a document in which the state asserted its exceptional ethno-national quality as a confessional entity, which had been achieved, and would be sustained, at the expense of certain groups – women, as a sex, people of no property, 'non-Catholics' and apostates, and intellectuals. In this context, Paul Vincent Carroll's excoriation of the human costs of the social and cultural hegemony of an authoritarian Catholic Church, *Shadow and Substance*, is an extraordinary intervention. More remarkably, it was staged at the National Theatre two months before the Church's 'special position' in the life of the nation was institutionalized in Article 44 of *Bunreacht na h-Éireann*. *Shadow and Substance* included strong autobiographical material, and Carroll followed John Millington Synge and Bernard Shaw[5] in articulating the human consequences of the contradictions and cruelties of the Church-State compact.[6]

2   https://irishplayography.com/play.aspx?playid=30690 [accessed 12 December 2023].
3   https://irishplayography.com/play.aspx?playid=32419 [accessed 12 December 2023].
4   https://irishplayography.com/play.aspx?playid=33563 [accessed 12 December 2023].
5   Ben Levitas, 'These Islands' Others: *John Bull*, the Abbey, and the Royal Court', in *Irish Theatre in England: Irish Theatrical Diaspora*, edited by Richard Cave and Ben Levitas (Dublin: Careysfort Press, 2007), 15–33.
6   See, Victor Merriman, '"To Sleep Is Safe, To Dream Is Dangerous": Catholicism on Stage in Independent Ireland', in *The Reimagining Ireland Reader: Examining Our Past, Shaping Our Future*, edited by Eamon Maher (Oxford: Peter Lang, 2017), 85–104.

A little over a decade later, in 1949, the Republic of Ireland Act (1948) came into effect, grounding in statute Independent Ireland's withdrawal from the British Commonwealth and enabling its re-casting as an autonomous republic. While constitutionally momentous, for Joe Cleary, this represented less a 'fulfilment [than] a terminus – when the [...] state embarked on an alternative strategy of dependent development that would see Ireland increasingly integrated into the global capitalist economy'.[7] In this light, it is perhaps unsurprising that this was the year in which Samuel Beckett completed *En Attendant Godot*, in Paris, and Sean O'Casey's *Cock-a-Doodle Dandy*, written in Devon, premiered at the People's Theatre, Newcastle-upon-Tyne.[8] Beckett's play, a series of parables of people suspended in a condition of stasis, premiered in Paris in 1954, and, as *Waiting for Godot*, in London and Dublin in 1955. O'Casey's own 'favourite play' was promptly banned in Ireland and a Dublin premiere was not to be given for almost thirty years.[9] The central concerns of his sharp satire on the betrayals of the Irish Free State were far from private obsessions, and they returned thematically, if not with commensurate formal inventiveness, in Dublin and Galway, the following year. In April 1950, the Abbey produced *Design for a Headstone*, by Séamus Byrne, while, in December, Taibhdhearc na Gaillimhe staged Siobhán McKenna's *San Siobhán*, her translation of Bernard Shaw's *Saint Joan* (1924). McKenna's decision to stage Shaw's play indicates an appetite for critical examination of the limits imposed by interlocking interests of Church and State on personal freedom to enter and act on history. Pilkington includes Byrne's play among a significant body of Abbey productions in the late-nineteen-forties and early fifties, that 'urge the need for a reassessment of nationalist verities'.[10] Both *San*

---

7 Joe Cleary, *Outrageous Fortune: Capital and Culture in Modern Ireland* (Dublin: Field Day Publications, 2007), 204.
8 Ronald Ayling (ed.), *Seven Plays by Sean O'Casey* (Basingstoke: Macmillan, 1985), xxxvii.
9 It was staged at 'the Abbey Theatre on 11 August 1977' https://www.irishplayography.com/play.aspx?playid=32025#:~:text=Irish%20Premiere%20Notes,Stanley%20and%20Miche%C3%A1l%20%C3%93%20hAonghusa [accessed 12 January 2023].
10 Lionel Pilkington, *Theatre and the State in Twentieth Century Ireland: Cultivating the People* (London: Routledge, 2001), 149.

Siobhán and *Design for a Headstone*, 'the story of a political hunger strike in a prison',[11] draw on Shaw's, and anticipate Brendan Behan's, metaphorical use of carceral settings to critique the ideology of the nation and the political economy of the state.

The first inter-party government collapsed in 1951, enabling the re-elected Taoiseach, Eamon De Valera, no advocate of critical culture, to preside over the inaugural meeting of An Chomhairle Ealaíon / The Arts Council, in December of that year. While he took kudos for an enlightened policy initiative in a fine Georgian townhouse in Merrion Square, Maura Laverty's *Tolka Row* was breaking attendance records across the River Liffey, at the Gate Theatre. *Tolka Row* drew attention to emerging norms of Dublin life among tenants of new local authority housing schemes, into which inner-city families had been decanted from decaying Georgian tenements on the city's Northside. In tune with Byrne's and McKenna's productions, Laverty's play exposed to view the impact of the pressures and desires of encroaching modernity on the constitutional ideal of Irish family life. Laverty's working-class Dubliners are shaped by intimate exchanges between urban Ireland and industrial Britain, setting them at odds with Church hegemony and ethnocentric nationalist pieties. This, Pilkington points out, was a core feature, also, of *Design for a Headstone*, which sought, 'in particular a reassessment of Ireland's antagonistic relationship with Britain'.[12]

As this chapter was being written, the death of Shane MacGowan brought once more into focus, the reality that 'Anglo-Irish ties, distances, absorptions, rejections and misunderstandings are not just matters of politics; they are economic, social, cultural, personal and profoundly emotional'.[13] These inter-relationships shape Laverty's and Byrne's dramatic worlds and are enduring concerns in works by a later 'generation of playwrights', such as Brian Friel's *Translations* (1980), *Faith Healer* (1979), Tom Murphy's *Famine* (1968) and *The Gigli Concert* (1983). Anglo-Irish

---

11   https://irishplayography.com/play.aspx?playid=31242 [accessed 12 January 2023].
12   Pilkington, *Theatre and the State in Twentieth-Century Ireland*, 149.
13   https://www.irishtimes.com/opinion/2023/12/08/diarmaid-ferriter-shane-macgowan-captured-what-it-was-to-struggle-on-the-margins-of-a-place-that-didnt-want-you/ [accessed 12 January 2023].

relations had been central to the nation-building purpose of the national theatre, in early anti-colonial works such as Yeats and Gregory's *Kathleen Ni Houlihan* (1902) and Gregory's *Spreading the News* (1904).[14] They are the explicit concern of a play commissioned and then rejected by Yeats for the Irish National Theatre's inaugural season at the Abbey Theatre (1904), the altogether more nuanced, *John Bull's Other Island* by Bernard Shaw. W. B. Yeats's refusal to stage this play points to a fundamental incompatibility between Shaw's analysis of, and prescriptions for, Ireland and its people, and the perspectives and values of Yeats and his fellow-artists – Synge excepted.[15] To the extent that Yeats, with Augusta Gregory and George Martyn, aspired to interrogating nationalist ideology, they did so on nationalism's idealist terms and produced many significant works of anti-colonial consciousness.

They eschewed direct engagement with material reality, subscribing instead, as Paul Murphy points out, to Standish O'Grady's 'mythopoeic vision of Irish history'.[16] Shaw's internationalist materialism stood in stark contrast to this, seeing 'Irish experience as bound in with modern economies rather than evolving cultural resistance'.[17] Shaw envisaged capitalist political relations as generators of social psychodramas, in which 'impersonal capital is still always inflected through specific socio-cultural – in this case imperialist – relations'.[18] Nelson O'Ceallaigh Ritschel places Shaw's perspective in radical contradistinction to that of Yeats:

> [G]rotesque capitalism was the result of breaking the feudal-like landlord system in Ireland, the truth of rural Ireland in 1904. Shaw was right in that the truth was

14   See Victor Merriman, '"At Me Too Someone Is Looking": Staging Surveillance in Irish Theatre', in *Technology in Irish Literature and Culture*, edited by Margaret Kelleher and James O'Sullivan (Cambridge: Cambridge University Press, 2023), 267–283.
15   See Levitas, 'These Islands' Others', 19–20.
16   Paul Murphy, 'Drama, 1900–1950', in *A History of Irish Working-Class Writing*, edited by Michael Pierse (Cambridge: Cambridge University Press, 2018), 273.
17   Levitas, 'These Islands' Others', 16.
18   Levitas, 'These Islands' Others', 27.

not in Yeats's mystical and nationalistic Kathleen Ni Houlihan, where materialism is shunned in favor of sacrificing one's self for Ireland.[19]

One of Irish theatre's strengths is that its best plays stage heightened human experiences pointed to a sharp critical edge. Kevin Curran refers to William Shakespeare's writings, and the plays in particular, as 'vital thought-worlds that struggle, across time, with foundational questions of metaphysics, ethics, politics, and aesthetics'.[20] Curran argues for reading his dramas as sites of 'ethical encounter',[21] criss-crossed by historical forces competing to expand or restrict social, political and economic participation. This chapter will apply such a perspective across a span of fifty years, to ask in what ways *John Bull's Other Island* (1904) and Brendan Behan's *The Quare Fellow* (1954), separately and in counterpoint, respond to the provocation that a homogenized ideal nation has been constituted at someone's expense.

John Bull's Other Island first saw the light of day in London, at the Royal Court Theatre, and Shaw himself carved out a multivalent career and a gilded reputation in the English capital. Larry Doyle and Tom Broadbent's transnational capital projects embrace both Britain and Ireland, and generate profoundly intimate personal and professional relationships:

> LARRY. It is by living with you and working in double harness with you that I have learnt to live in a real world and not an imaginary one. I owe more to you than to any Irishman.[22]

Act II of *John Bull's Other Island* introduces audiences to the hinterland of Rosscullen, Larry Doyle's fictive West of Ireland home:

> Westward a hillside of granite rock and heather slopes upward across the prospect from south to north. A huge stone stands on it in a naturally impossible place, as if

---

19   Nelson O'Ceallaigh Ritschel, 'Shaw and the Syngean Provocation', in *Shaw* (Penn State University Press, 2010), vol. 30, 87.
20   Kevin Curran, 'Series Editor's Introduction' to *Shakespeare in Hindsight: Counterfactual Thinking and Shakespearean Tragedy*, by Amir Khan (Edinburgh: Edinburgh University Press, 2016), xiii.
21   Curran, 'Series Editor's Introduction', xii.
22   Bernard Shaw, *John Bull's Other Island* (London: Penguin, 1984), 83.

it had been tossed up there by a giant. Over the brow, in the desolate valley beyond, is a round tower. A lonely white road trending a way westward past the tower loses itself at the foot of the far mountains. It is evening; and there are great breadths of silken green in the Irish sky. The sun is setting.[23]

The setting is heavy with mythic elements and contrasts spectacularly with the London chambers of Broadbent and Doyle, Engineers, in which Act I is set. There are three living beings in this landscape, a grasshopper which is engaged in conversation with a defrocked priest, Peter Keegan, and Patsy Farrell, a landless peasant, hidden from view, but privy, to his consternation, to their dialogue. Following a fraught exchange with an exasperated Keegan, in which Patsy reveals his fears of devilry abroad in the world in the shape of a grasshopper, Keegan reminds him forcefully of his duty to attend to Master Larry's arrival:

KEEGAN.   Off widja to the road: you'll be late for the car if you don't make haste [bustling him down the hill]. I can see the dust of it in the gap already.

PATSY.   The Lord save us! [He goes down the hill towards the road like a haunted man].[24]

Patsy's lack of property shapes his abject demeanour, but that masks a versatile repertoire of strategies to proof himself against the worst effects of economic precarity:

> An instinctively acquired air of helplessness and silliness, indicating, not his real character, but a cunning developed by his constant dread of a hostile dominance, which he habitually tries to disarm and tempt into unmasking by pretending to be a much greater fool than he really is.[25]

His station in life fits him only for labouring tasks and, in Act II, he collapses under the weight of 'three men's luggage', which he has been directed to carry by his monied betters, Father Dempsey and Cornelius Doyle. Degraded he may be, and haunted by fears of liquidation by forces

---

23   Shaw, *John Bull's Other Island*, 90.
24   Shaw, *John Bull's Other Island*, 93.
25   Shaw, *John Bull's Other Island*, 93.

of Hell or property, but Patsy himself possesses a spectral symbolic capital of which he is wholly unaware. In Act III, he is as a ghost at the feast of smallholders who have benefited from recent land reform, a retributive shadow on their new acquisitions:

> CORNELIUS. But hwat man in his right senses ever wanted to give land to Patsy Farrll an dhe like o him?[26]

Contradicting his father, Larry makes rhetorical use of the men's fear of Patsy, to talk himself into conflict with their petit-bourgeois acquisitiveness, and out of consideration as their prospective parliamentary candidate for Rosscullen:

> LARRY [to Matt Haffigan] [Y]ou, that are only one little step above [Patsy], would die sooner than let him come up that step; and well you know it.[27]

John Bull's Other Island is a sharp and entertaining critique of the interpenetration of bourgeois interests across Britain and Ireland, which explicitly concerns itself with the predictable consequences of the 'cronyism and incompetence of the political class' in Ireland.[28] Its moral stance is embodied in Peter Keegan, a bearer of second sight; one who knows both the co-ordinates and texture of an Irish utopia and the forces which prevent its emergence. Dispossessed of material possessions and social position, he is radically possessed by 'the dream of a madman [...] a country where the State is the Church and the Church the people [...] in which work is play and play is life: three in one and one in three'.[29] Keegan's ability to contrast unfavourably this vision of a flourishing society with the fine detail of plans for Rosscullen proposed by Broadbent and Doyle's 'syndicate', amazes them both, and they *look quickly at one another; for this* [analysis], *unless the priest is an old financial hand, must be an inspiration.*[30] Ben Levitas argues that

---

26 Shaw, *John Bull's Other Island*, 116.
27 Shaw, *John Bull's Other Island*, 119.
28 Murphy, 'Drama, 1900–1950', 287.
29 Shaw, *John Bull's Other Island*, 163.
30 Shaw, *John Bull's Other Island*, 160.

the dramatic impact of Keegan's grasp of the mendacity of imperialist economics establishes him as 'a voice capable of testifying to Ireland's various resources of insight, and the possibility that a new Ireland might combine revival and radical reform'.[31] Keegan's vision of an earthly heaven, however, rests on a dynamic of triangular relationships against which Ireland's actual condition, and future prospects, take the form of Hell, 'a place of torment [which, should Broadbent prosper in Rosscullen] shall be as clean and orderly as the cleanest and most orderly place I know in Ireland, which is our poetically named Mountjoy prison'.[32]

Brendan Behan's, *The Quare Fellow*,[33] is set in that hellish place, half a century later, on the eve of the execution of the eponymous criminal, in the year that the last judicial hanging took place in Ireland.[34] Both Shaw and Behan are fully alive to the condition of working people under, respectively, imperial and neo-colonial capitalist relations. These plays stage system dynamics as they play out in the detail of everyday life, and point audiences toward a critical perspective on Ireland's circumscribed polity, organized at the expense of individuals and groups denied full social participation. In both plays, England's presence raises sharp questions of the ethics and purpose of the independent state; Shaw interrogating the colonial province's aspiration to sovereignty, and Behan, the successor state's performance as a formally autonomous entity. *The Quare Fellow* transferred from a run in the miniature Pike Theatre, Dublin, to the Theatre Royal, Stratford East, and thence to lucrative runs in London's West End and on Broadway, and a production at the Abbey. Behan's *The Hostage*, which played in its original one-act form as *An Giall*, at Dublin's An Damer theatre, followed the same route, securing international notoriety for its author.

In Act I of *The Quare Fellow*, Behan's prisoners parse the honorific title, 'lag', in terms so replete with references to Erin's other island – 'on

---

31 Levitas, 'These Islands' Others', 31.
32 Shaw, *John Bull's Other Island*, 158.
33 Brendan Behan, *The Quare Fellow* (London: Methuen, 1977).
34 Michael Manning was hanged in Mountjoy prison 'on 20 April 1954', *Capital Punishment in Independent Ireland: A Social, Legal and Political History*, by David M. Doyle and Liam O'Callaghan (Liverpool: Liverpool University Press), 173.

the Moor and at Parkhurst'[35] – as to suggest, as in Laverty's *Tolka Row*, an intimacy between major urban centres on either side of the Irish Sea rivalling that of Broadbent and Doyle. Indeed, Behan's Mountjoy houses an English prisoner, 'on remand [...] over the car smuggling',[36] and, in Act III, foregrounds, 'the most egregious relic of imperialism – the hiring of an Englishman to hang Irish prisoners'.[37] In late 1932, when Fianna Fáil took office as a single-party government, a clemency petitioner wrote to the Minister for Justice, Gerald Boland, expressing the view that 'John Bull's Hangman ought to get a rest in this country'.[38] Despite this, and the rawness of wounds of Civil War atrocities notwithstanding, that government, and subsequent inter-party administrations, made regular use of the services of Albert Pierrepoint, an English hangman.[39] Behan's dialogue sardonically references a historical lack of success in recruiting native executioner:

> GOVERNOR. We advertised for a native hangman during the Economic War. Must be a fluent Irish speaker. Cáilíochtaí de réir Meamram V. a seacht. There were no suitable applicants. [40]

If this suggests that the state's commitment to the practice was viewed unenthusiastically by the population at large, Doyle and O'Callaghan conclude that 'maintaining the death penalty was clearly more desirable than not doing so; an English hangman was better than no hangman at all'.[41]

As the hours run down to the morning of execution, Behan's dramaturgy foregrounds the character and circumstances of the almost exclusively working-class prison population. Dunlavin, a prisoner of an age to qualify as Patsy Farrell's urban doppelgänger, is, *an old man, he has spent most of*

---

35   Behan, *The Quare Fellow*, 36.
36   Behan, *The Quare Fellow*, 16.
37   Doyle and O'Callaghan, *Capital Punishment in Independent Ireland*, 66.
38   NAI, JUS/H234/4684 (Patrick McDermott), Bernard O'Connor to Gerald Boland, 10 December 1932, cited in Doyle and O'Callaghan, *Capital Punishment in Independent Ireland*, 76.
39   Doyle and O'Callaghan, *Capital Punishment in Independent Ireland*, 90–100.
40   Behan, *The Quare Fellow*, 74.
41   Doyle and O'Callaghan, *Capital Punishment in Independent Ireland*, 66.

his life in jail. Unlike most old lags he has not become absolutely dulled by imprisonment.[42] As the play opens, he is discovered preparing his cell for inspection by Holy Healey, a senior civil servant in the Department of Justice. Healey has a double function: as an active member of charitable Catholic organizations and a committee member of the Society of Sick & Indigent Roomkeepers, he has power to recommend a released prisoner as a suitable beneficiary of charitable accommodation. When he arrives, Healey stops at Dunlavin's cell, and remarks:

HEALEY.   Very nice.

DUNLAVIN.   Of course, I do like to keep my little place as homely as I can with the little holy pictures you gave me of Blessed Martin, sir.

[....]

HEALEY.   Yes, yes, but what is it you want?

DUNLAVIN.   I've the chance of a little room up round Buckingham Street, sir, if you could only give me a letter to the Room-Keepers after I go out, for a bit of help with the rent [....] Thank you, sir, and a bed in heaven to you, sir.

HEALEY.   And the same to you. [Goes to next cell.]

DUNLAVIN.   And many of them, and I hope we're all here this time next year (venomously after MR. HEALEY) that it may choke you.[43]

Dunlavin's performative obsequiousness is carefully calibrated to material ends; in this case, securing accommodation on the outside. Like Patsy before him, he deploys cunning against looming precarity, and, though a recidivist of long standing, his grovelling piety appeals to Healey.

Irish theatre returns again and again to members of 'disenfranchised social groups [...] small farmers, landless workers and itinerant labourers'.[44]

42   Behan, *The Quare Fellow*, stage directions, 3.
43   Behan, *The Quare Fellow*, 31.
44   Paul Murphy, 'Drama, 1900–1950', in *A History of Irish Working-Class Writing*, edited by Michael Pierse (Cambridge: Cambridge University Press, 2018), 272.

Despite their degraded or precarious status, Paul Murphy argues, such people 'were nonetheless central to the dramatic and political imaginations of both Irish and Anglo-Irish Ireland'.[45] Though effectively powerless, Shaw reminds us of their capacity to appear monstrous in the imaginations of such as Matt Haffigan, the terms of whose own precarity are exposed by Keegan, at the end of *John Bull's Other Island*:

> BROADBENT. [...] Haffigan's too old. It really doesn't pay now to take on men over forty even for unskilled labour [...]
>
> KEEGAN. Poor lost soul, so cunningly fenced in with invisible bars.
>
> LARRY. Haffigan doesn't matter much. He'll die presently.[46]

Shaw's deployment of a carceral metaphor is telling, anticipating the plight of Dunlavin and his fellow-convicts, dissembling before Catholic state officials, in hope of rescue from destitution. Social conditions testified to by Shaw anticipate continuities in class relations dramatized in Behan, cumulatively providing an ironic rejoinder to the insistence, in the ideology of the national state, on 'the unity of the classes in the common name of Irishman'.[47] Comparing Patsy, a young man in a country anticipating Home Rule, and Dunlavin, his peer, now an elderly denizen of a recently proclaimed Irish Republic, reiterates the question as to whether the political integrity of the capitalist successor state is only ever achievable at someone's expense. As in Behan, and a half-century on from *The Quare Fellow*, the controlled rage of Gerard Mannix Flynn's chronicle of juvenile incarceration, *James X*, suggests the answer to that question is an unequivocal, 'yes'.

The ethical encounters between Patsy and his betters, and between Peter Keegan and Broadbent and Doyle enable *John Bull's Other Island* to

---

45 Murphy, 'Drama, 1900–1950', 272.
46 Behan, *The Quare Fellow*, 157.
47 Fintan O'Toole, *Tom Murphy: The Politics of Magic* (Dublin: New Island, 1994), 37–38.

articulate a desired 'commonwealth', always anticipated and ever at risk of being thwarted. *The Quare Fellow* makes visible the extremes of a *de jure* republic, simultaneously functioning and postponed, in which people disenfranchised by ways of living at odds with norms of nation and capital, live in hope, rather than expectation of a fair share. Their enduring centrality to Ireland's public imagination – dramatic and political – rests on how their compromises and refusals symbolize the fraught tenacity of egalitarian aspirations in an incomplete state. Both Shaw and Behan present disenfranchised persons, functionally essential to the polity, but who are denied a secure stake in a rigged system. Their rights and needs unseen or dismissed by policy makers, their visibility in dramatic worlds creates both a logical paradox and an ethical opportunity. Asserting and validating the existence of a large unintegrated collective confirms the stage as a critical forum for moral questions as to who may enjoy, and who is denied, citizenship, in whose interests and on what ethical grounds. In a further suggestive contradiction, it is Britain now that faces political fragmentation in pursuit of an impossible ethno-nationalist political project, and Irish civil spaces, including theatre, commit to pluralist public deliberation, a non-negotiable feature of any democratic national political project.

ANNE FOGARTY

21 Writing the Unspeakable in Irish Feminist Life-Writing: Emilie Pine's *Notes to Self* and Doireann Ní Ghríofa's *A Ghost in the Throat*

Feminist life-writing has attained fresh prominence in Ireland in recent years, captivating several generations of readers while remoulding the possibilities of this form of self-portrayal. Anne Enright's *Making Babies*, Lia Mills's *In Your Face*, Éilís Ní Dhuibhne's *Twelve Thousand Days*, Sinéad Gleeson's *Constellations*, Kerri Ní Dochartaigh's *Thin Places*, Claire Lynch's *Small: On Motherhoods*, Elizabeth Boyle's *Fierce Appetites*, Kit de Waal's *Without Warning and Only Sometimes* and Clair Wills's *Missing Persons, Or My Grandmother's Secrets* have broached an array of themes that, while not taboo, are still insufficiently explored and customarily held fastidiously at a distance, including illness, bodily stigma, pregnancy, conception and motherhood in all of its many aspects, race, marital discord, and sectarian violence.[1] These variegated and impactful texts connect with signal late twentieth-century feminist autobiographical works,

---

1   Anne Enright, *Making Babies: Stumbling into Motherhood* (London: Jonathan Cape, 2004); Lia Mills, *In Your Face* (Dublin: Penguin Ireland, 2007); Éilís Ní Dhuibhne, *Twelve Thousand Days: A Memoir of Love and Loss* (Newtownards: Blackstaff Press, 2018); Sinéad Gleeson, *Constellations: Reflections from Life* (London: Picador, 2019); Kerri Ní Dochartaigh, *Thin Places* (London: Canongate, 2021); Claire Lynch, *Small: On Motherhoods* (London: Brazen, 2021); Elizabeth Boyle, *Fierce Appetites* (London: Penguin Sandycove, 2022); *Kit de Waal's without Warning and Only Sometimes: Scenes from an Unpredictable Childhood* (London: Tinder Press, 2022) and Clair Wills, *Missing Persons, Or My Grandmother's Secrets* (London: Allen Lane, 2024).

including Edna O' Brien's *Mother Ireland*, Nuala O'Faolain's *Are You Somebody?* and Leland Bardwell's *A Restless Life*.[2]

Yet they conspicuously put a peculiar contemporary stamp on this mode and endow it with a pressing relevancy and artistic piquancy. They have in common a resolute scrutiny of the self and refusal to mitigate or mask painful emotional realities. Stringent self-exploration coincides in these texts with an empathetic but unsparing account of devastating everyday experiences that are usually tacitly endured and rarely publicly articulated. The social decorum silencing a host of subjective experiences is counteracted and overridden in these works. Crucial facets of female subjectification, instead of being masked or dismissed as unspeakable, are drawn into the realm of the discursive and mined to form the very basis of a personalized artistic aesthetic. But they also are open and partial in a manner that departs from earlier practice. In general, the authors, often at an early age, look back at a life phase or connected series of experiences and do not endeavour to furnish us with complete and summative overviews.

The purpose of this essay is to analyse Emilie Pine's *Notes to Self* (2018) and Doireann Ní Ghríofa's *A Ghost in the Throat* (2020) with a view to establishing the ways in which they reinvigorate the interlinked modalities of autobiographical, biographical and non-fictional writing through their fearless depictions of the self as porous, abject and vulnerable and their exacting and venturesome opening up to scrutiny of private experience.[3] These texts assume authority and force through their insistence on a first-person veracity, their parsing of the variegated affects that attend on deep-seated but everyday troubles, their probing of the many facets of embodiment, their limning of the interpersonal and their delineation of the vagaries of female desire. They are further cross-linked because of their concern with examining contradictory facets of motherhood, viewed not as an idealized state or biological given, but as a purposeful personal

---

2   Edna O'Brien, *Mother Ireland* (London: Weidenfeld and Nicolson, 1976); Nuala O'Faolain, *Are You Somebody?: The Life and Times of Nuala O'Faolain* (Dublin: New Island, 1996) and Leland Bardwell, *A Restless Life* (Dublin: Liberties Press, 2008).

3   Emilie Pine, *Notes to Self* (Dublin: Tramp Press, 2018) and Doireann Ní Ghríofa, *A Ghost in the Throat* (Dublin: Tramp Press, 2020).

quest and life choice, an autonomous social role, a considered relationship of care and an arduously negotiated set of corporeal and emotional processes. Above all, these texts are linked in their concern with linguistic precision and their contrivance of artistic designs by which to contour and fathom the self. Subjectivity is inextricably interwoven with affect in these works and mediated by distinctive narrative forms designed to create a fresh idiom and set of vantage points for painful, commonly repressed, personal experience.

Current critical re-investigations of life-writing foreground its hybridity and ability to combine multifarious generic traits. Indeed, Laura Marcus has picked out instability as, not just a defining feature, but the central crux of autobiography as a genre which, as she claims, pits 'postulated opposites between self and world, literature and history, fact and fiction, subject and object' against each other.[4] Above all, autobiographical writings are seen as perilously negotiating the slippery divisions between fact and fiction and navigating the ethical costs and trade-offs entailed in laying bare intricate personal truths and piecing together confessional narratives. The counterpointing but also jarring alternation of impartiality and emotion, overwhelming affect and reasoned political evaluation, self-reflexivity and immersive narration are the conjoint traits, it will be seen, of contemporary expositions of the personal.

The renewed popularity and cultural importance of life-writing and biographical fictions in recent decades have added fuel to debates about the usefulness of available designations for such work. Even though life-writing has generally been adopted as an overall term for this mode of creation, a proliferation of other labels, such as creative non-fiction, self-writing, autobiografiction, auto-ethnography and autofiction, has endeavoured to encapsulate the fresh accents in contemporary writing and to classify its subgenres.[5] At stake, is the desire to provide tools for discriminating between

---

4 Laura Marcus, *Auto/biographical Discourses: Theory, Criticism, Practice* (Manchester: Manchester University Press, 1994), 7.
5 On the history and import of this term, usually attributed to Virginia Woolf, see Zachary Leader (ed.), *On Life-Writing* (Oxford: Oxford University Press, 2015), 1–6; and Hermione Lee, *Biography: A Very Short Introduction* (Oxford: Oxford University Press, 2009), 5.

fictional and verifiable truths while yet acknowledging the numerous modes of hybrid writing that blur these two domains. As Julia Novak has demonstrated, while some critics such as Dorrit Cohn and Michael Lackey insist that factual and fictional histories may be held apart, others such as Gunnþórunn Guðmundsdóttir have validly argued that autobiographies necessarily draw on fictional strategies and that they are an in-built and vital facet of such writing.[6]

Because memoirs blend the creative and the referential, the nature of what Philippe Lejeune has called the 'autobiographical contract' continues to be actively debated and is negotiated afresh by the authors under consideration in this essay.[7] For Lejeune, the author and reader operate in unison and an implicit guarantee ensures an alliance between the author and the narrative voice. Such certainties no longer hold good where contemporary Irish life-writing is concerned. Writers are at pains to foreground the instability of their contract with their readers and the hard-won nature of the textual spaces they commandeer and create and their openness to misconstruction. Further, they exhibit a wariness about the generic frameworks brought to bear on autobiographical writing and find them wanting or inexact, voicing caveats and suggesting provisional lenses by which to view their books. Thus, Emilie Pine quibbles with the use of the term memoir in relation to her work because of its implications of completion and resolved retrospection and indicates by contrast its designedly ragged and tentative qualities.[8] In a similar vein, Doireann Ní Ghríofa stresses the multivalent and unfinished aspects of her book, describing it as a 'liquid novel' and a vessel into which she incorporates many different genres.[9]

---

[6] Julia Novak, 'Experiments in Life-Writing: Introduction', in *Experiments in Life-Writing*, edited by Lucia Boldrini and Julia Novak (London: Palgrave Macmillan, 2017), 3–12.

[7] Philippe Lejeune, *Le pacte autobiographique* (Paris: Seuil, 1975), 26.

[8] See 'Speaking to Emilie Pine', 21 November 2019, https://fivedials.com/interviews/speaking-to-emilie-pine/ [accessed 10 October 2023].

[9] See 'Acts of Repair: Doireann Ní Ghríofa Interviewed by Naheed Phiroze Patel', *Bomb Magazine* 6 January 2022, https://bombmagazine.org/articles/doireann-n%C3%AD-ghr%C3%ADofa-interviewed [accessed 25 September 2023].

Yet, this emphasis on the text as provisional, communal and unfinished is counterposed by a recognition that it aims to foreground and validate the female self who constructs it and is its central subject. A consonance may be found with Annie Ernaux's challenging delineation of her aesthetic in her Nobel speech in December 2022. Outlining her reservations about how her autobiographical fiction has been viewed, Ernaux rejects the aptness of the term autofiction, a neologism coined by the French novelist Serge Doubrovsky, as it masks the truth-telling endeavour of her work and its interactive engagement with its readers.[10] She declares that her aim in writing about her family and personal life was to delve into 'the unspeakable' while also seeking to avenge her working-class origins and her gender by articulating them at large. The goal of unflinchingly depicting facets of life that are routinely censored or debarred from discourse is an over-riding concern of her fictions. Despite the emphasis on the personal, she avers that she uses the first person in them as a tool of exploration and not to autofictionalize the self. Instead, the primary end of her work is to find 'the words that contain both reality and the sensation provided by reality'.[11] Fidelity to lived experience is its core *raison d'être*. Citing Victor Hugo's comment that '[n]ot one of us has the honour of living a life that is only his own', she concludes that for the 'I' in her writing to be effective it must become transparent and transpersonal and include the 'I' of the reader.[12] Hence, far from being narcissistic or self-regarding, the 'I' is transactional and inclusive.

10 On the coinage of this term, see Elizabeth H. Jones, 'Serge Doubrovsky: Life, Writing, Legacy', *L'Esprit Créateur*, 49/3, Serge Doubrovsky: Life, Writing, Legacy (Fall 2009), 1–7. For a discussion of this problematic but widely deployed concept, see Hywel Dix, *Autofiction in English* (London: Palgrave Macmillan, 2018); and Alexandra Effe and Hannie Lawlor (eds), *From Autofiction to the Autofictional* (London: Palgrave Macmillan, 2022). See Annie Ernaux, 'Nobel Lecture by Annie Ernaux' (Svenksa Akademie: La Fondation Nobel, 2022), 1–7, https://www.nobelprize.org/uploads/2022/12/ernaux-lecture-english.pdf [accessed 10 December 2023].
11 Ernaux, 'Nobel Lecture', 4.
12 Ernaux, 'Nobel Lecture', 5. See also Ernaux, 'Towards a Transpersonal I', translated by Dawn M. Cornelio, *RITM* 6 (University of Paris, 1993), X: 219–222,

Ernaux's comments revealingly gloss her singular fictions that document multiple aspects of her life, from her experience of a backstreet abortion as a student to her conflicted relations with her working-class parents and her clandestine love affairs. But they also aptly adumbrate intertwined facets of the very different and distinctive non-fictional works by Pine and Ní Ghríofa. Like Ernaux, these writers share a wariness about generic labels and question the distortions, biases and simplifications to which they may lead. Rather than cleave to a single mode, they strive instead for work that is fluid and formally inventive and hybrid. Akin to Ernaux, they create texts that are unerringly centred on writing the unspeakable through the concretization of female experience. In daring to broach occluded topics, they are committed to veracity and exactitude in their renderings of events usually shamefully repressed. Yet, they counter-balance the overall heuristic quest of their work, with an ethical responsiveness to the viewpoint of Others and a self-reflexive scepticism about the overall power of the authorial self and of texts that are univocal. In what follows, I shall consider each of these texts in turn with a view to taking soundings of the provocative questions that they raise and the formal patterns that they achieve and to probing how they mould their narratives to convey singular experiences from multiple perspectives. My aim is to get a measure of the cultural and political work undertaken by these compelling books and why they have such a purchase on readers in the current moment. The elicitation of visceral and open-ended personal themes is effected, it will be seen, through the depiction of an array of exactingly evoked but also sharply debated images of embodiment.

Emilie Pine's *Notes to Self* consists of six separate essays engaging with varying aspects of feminist body politics and of the author's personal history. They move backwards and forwards in time and collectively constitute a set of non-chronological reflections on critical issues and flashpoints in her life. Even though designed to be read in sequence, they trouble any assumption that a life can be narrativized as a coherent whole or reviewed to

---

https://www.annie-ernaux.org/texts/vers-un-je-transpersonnel-2 [accessed 10 December 2023].

yield definitive evidence of progress and onward development.[13] Instead, they assemble a collection of views and counterviews that alternate between immersing us in searing life moments, encapsulating incisive descriptions of painful emotions and affects and crystallizing thought-provoking political reflections on troubling facets of women's lives and the author's personal history. A movement between engagement and disengagement, detached analysis and emotional involvement patterns these essays and contours the flow of ideas and perceptions they sustain. To this degree, they exhibit the quality that Brian Dillon has dubbed 'essayism', the urge of the essay genre to be 'suspended between its impulses to hazard or adventure and to achieved form, aesthetic integrity'.[14] Pine's essay-like chapters display the riskiness, contradictoriness and impulsiveness of this mode as well as its investment in giving artistic shape to disordered and chaotic processes of reasoning and felt experience.

In her 'Acknowledgements', Pine states that in composing her book she tried 'not to tell anyone else's story'.[15] But, in fact, disentangling her story from that of others proves impossible. The self she depicts is inherently relational and fractured around differing and sometimes conflicting narratives of embodiment. While she fights to claim the right to disinter the buried truths that have impacted most on her physically and emotionally, she is still concerned to probe and assess her bonds with others. But crucially these links are carefully recalibrated and dissevered from assumptions about the endemic or beneficent nature of female empathy. Like all the affects portrayed, it is revealed to consist of many crosscurrents and not to be monovalent. Hence, in the first chapter Pine concludes that tussles about reining in her empathy for her father merely worked to her detriment not his, but in the final essay we learn that, based on supposedly incontrovertible personality assessment tests, she is deemed peculiarly lacking in

---

13 See Samantha Matthews, 'Autobiography', *Oxford Bibliographies*, 24 July 2018, on the processes of personal transformation and concepts of progress that underwrite traditional autobiographies in the Victorian era https://www.oxfordbibliographies.com/display/document/obo-9780199799558/obo-9780199799558-0023.xml [accessed 20 August 2023].

14 Brian Dillon, *Essayism* (London: Fitzcarraldo Editions, 2017), 21–22.

15 Pine, *Notes to Self*, n.p.

this facility anyway. Consistently, emotions are commandingly voiced but also refracted and rendered opaque. In her account of her failed attempts to conceive, Pine declares: 'I was fearful and hopeful and shameful',[16] thus pinpointing how countervailing emotions may coexist and form a complex subtext for confounding everyday experiences that do not lend themselves to smooth narratives. Following what doctors deem a 'missed miscarriage' and ensuing surgery to remove the foetus, she describes her state of mute distress, declaring the experience 'too raw [...] too hard [...] too shameful'.[17] Plangency and the intricacy of unaccommodated emotion go hand in hand.

Just as affects are either overwhelming, in abeyance, unreadable or sites of contradiction, so too the body is multiply perceived as at once over-present, erased or a source of sexist misreading.[18] Provocatively, the volume opens with the searing image of the author's father, fatally ill from the debilitating effects of long-term alcoholism, 'lying in a small pool of his own shit' in a badly managed and chronically understaffed Greek hospital.[19] The father's story and his miraculous recovery after much contention precipitate the instigating crisis, especially when he unrepentantly writes about his alcoholism in a journalistic piece that fails to acknowledge the emotional damage he has caused to his family. Pine's text sets out to wrest writerly authority from him and to address what has been suppressed as unspeakable in a feminist idiom which she concocts afresh. The narratives that emerge about infertility, her parents' hostile separation, her risky resort to drink, drugs and wild living as a teenager in London, and sexual assaults by supposed friends focus on embodied experience and yield many piercing perceptions but few conclusions. Emotional truths are vividly distilled, their exactitude a compelling flexing of the feminist epistemology informing the text: readers are told that 'infertility is a particular kind of loneliness',[20] and that '[w]hen your parents don't speak, you become their go-between'.[21] But telling the story of a female body is not straightforward because of the ways

---

16   Pine, *Notes to Self*, 37.
17   Pine, *Notes to Self*, 54.
18   On the difficulty of counteracting the marginalization of embodiment in discourse, see Chris Shilling, *The Body and Social Theory* (London: Sage, 2012), 209–258.
19   Pine, *Notes to Self*, 5.
20   Pine, *Notes to Self*, 44.
21   Pine, *Notes to Self*, 85.

in which it is overwritten by internalized ideological values and social norms. Thus, Pine observes that women are 'well-rehearsed in rituals of bodily self-appraisal'[22] when it comes to seemingly consensual standards of appearance, and that the traumatic experience of rape led her to separate 'the body and the self' contrary to current thinking that insists on the interfusion of the two.[23]

Self-reflexive analysis of clouded and knotted realities, however, is held in apposition to the concerted articulation of feminist values.[24] Bearing out Theodor Adorno's apprehension that the essay is inherently the realm of intellectual freedom, Pine utilizes her multifaceted descriptions of painful life experiences to reinforce fundamental feminist stances and to endow them with a new-found relevance and contemporary application.[25] In her meditation on her battle with fertility, she castigates the medical establishment which belittled her and withheld information at vital junctures during and after her miscarriage, while in a dissection of the competing pressures at play in professional life she uncovers how sexism operates in academe and how women are forced to side-step into 'a kind of silence',[26] thereby involuntarily upholding the patriarchal status quo.

Political analysis is linked too with the tracking of elusive and repressed facets of women's lives in Doireann Ní Ghríofa's *A Ghost in the Throat*, a text which unites and crosses over biography and self-writing and blends elements of the essay, elegy, history, lyric and novel. In so doing, though, it concocts a deconstructed, abyssal text seamed with evocative images and acts of conjuration. Its reigning metaphors stem from the two opposing terrains of the ghostly and somatic which it overlaps throughout. At its kernel is *The Lament for Art Ó Laoghaire* by Eibhlín Dubh Ní Chonaill, who performed it for her

22   Pine, *Notes to Self*, 209.
23   Pine, *Notes to Self*, 145.
24   On the dialogic aspects of Pine's work, see María Amor Barros-del Río, and Melania Terrazas Gallego, 'Irish Women's Confessional Writing: Identity, Textuality and the Body', *Life Writing*, 20/3 (2023), 473–490.
25   Theodor Adorno, 'The Essay as Form', *Notes to Literature*, translated by Sherry Weber Nicholsen (New York: Columbia University Press, 1991), vol. 1, 3–23. On the emancipatory potential of the feminist essay, see *The Politics of the Essay: Feminist Perspectives*, edited by Ruth-Ellen Boetcher Joeres and Elizabeth Mittman (Bloomington: Indiana University Press, 1993), 12–20.
26   Pine, *Notes to Self*, 166.

husband after his murder on 4 May 1773 near Carraig an Ime (Carriganimmy), County Cork.[27] The poem titled *Caoineadh Airt Uí Laoghaire* counts as the most accomplished composition of the eighteenth century. Dispersed fragments survive as well as two longer versions, written down several decades after Eibhlín Dubh's performance. It is the most translated and anthologized poem in the Irish language, but until recently the leading translations were by male writers. Ní Ghríofa's translation joins recent versions by Angela Bourke and by the poet Vona Groarke and forms the Afterword to her exploration.[28]

Yet, it is not its ultimate destination or apogee. Instead, Eibhlín Dubh's work along with other sources is forensically sifted through to provide clues to her life. Quotations from the lament interleave the text furnishing the epigraphs to most of the chapters and acting as spectral signposts to her elusive presence. The *caoineadh* encodes and entombs the woman who composed and performed it, and this is the conundrum Ní Ghríofa faces. Early in her meditation on her wholehearted involvement in motherhood and on her concomitant obsession with *Caoineadh Airt Uí Laoghaire*, she completes her pain-staking translation of it only to conclude that '[m]y document doesn't hold her voice'.[29] What is missing is the author who is a ghostly absence sequestered in an unreachable zone with the other female voices of the oral tradition.[30] To counter this absence, Ní Ghríofa ranges beyond the words on the page discerning a 'female breath' in them and confides that her favourite element is 'the untranslatable

---

27   For the best-known edition of the work, see Eileen O'Connell, *Caoineadh Airt Uí Laoghaire*, edited and translated by Séan Ó Tuama (Dublin: An Clóchomhar, 1961). For a less widely circulated version, see Angela Bourke, 'Lamenting the Dead: Eibhlín Dubh Ní Chonaill (c.1743–c.1800), From Ferriter MS No. 1, University College Dublin', Angela Bourke, Siobhán Kilfeather et al. (eds), *The Field Day Anthology of Irish Writing, Volume IV: Irish Women's Writings and Traditions* (Cork: Cork University Press in association with Field Day, 2002), 1372–1384.

28   Vona Groarke, *Lament for Art O'Leary from the Irish of Eibhlín Dubh Ní Chonaill* (Loughcrew: Gallery Press, 2008).

29   Ní Ghríofa, *A Ghost in the Throat*, 41.

30   On the oral and performative status of Eibhlín Dubh's *caoineadh* which has regularly been elided, see Angela Bourke, 'Performing, Not Writing: The Reception of an Irish Woman's Lament', in *Dwelling in Possibility: Women Poets and Critics on Poetry*, edited by Yopie Pins and Maeera Shreiber (Ithaca, NY: Cornell University Press, 1997), 132–146.

pale space between stanzas'.[31] It is this pale space that she conjures up for us, interweaving metaphors of ghostliness and of maternal embodiment. As she notes, works composed by women ended up not in physical books but in female bodies which served as 'living repositories'.[32]

Her text has the ambition of undoing the erasures of literary history and rescuing Eibhlín Dubh from the 'masculine shadow',[33] in which scholars routinely place her. A central conceit of Ní Ghríofa's creation is that she gives birth to and gestates her subject, cross-connecting the labour of reconstructing her life with the activities of mothering, above all breastfeeding, and the routine household chores or 'drudge-work'[34] that feature on her hypnotic daily to-do lists. Her objective is to find material traces of Eibhlín Dubh that allow her to outline micro-narratives about her life. Juxtaposed with these evocatively delineated projections of her childhood, two marriages and anguish when Art O'Leary is shot is Ní Ghríofa's metacommentary on her feverish reading, and visits to archives, libraries and the redolent sites of her 'beloved ghost's life',[35] primarily the houses and environs in which she lived, primarily Derrynane where she grew up and Raleigh House, where she lived with her second spouse. Interlaced with this increasingly frustrated biographical quest, she describes vivid scenes from her own daily existence and renders emotional flashpoints such as the birth by caesarean of her daughter and her struggle to feed her, her mental health problems and suicidal feelings as a pre-medical student in University College Cork, the harrowing impact of performing a dissection on the body of a stranger in an anatomy theatre and her disputes with her husband who elects to undergo a vasectomy in order to free her from 'the drug of birth' [36] and the exhaustion of motherhood and 'milk-broken sleep',[37] a rescue measure which she resists.

---

31   Ní Ghríofa, *A Ghost in the Throat*, 42.
32   Ní Ghríofa, *A Ghost in the Throat*, 74.
33   Ní Ghríofa, *A Ghost in the Throat*, 70.
34   Ní Ghríofa, *A Ghost in the Throat*, 6.
35   Ní Ghríofa, *A Ghost in the Throat*, 182.
36   Ní Ghríofa, *A Ghost in the Throat*, 275.
37   Ní Ghríofa, *A Ghost in the Throat*, 275.

The opening chapter of *A Ghost in the Throat* repeats the mantra, 'This is a female text', five times and the text overall circles back to it at the end.[38] This pronouncement operates as an incantation and an index to the many female texts both embodied and spectral with which the work concerns itself. Female desire is linked by Ní Ghríofa not just with sexuality but with the joy of breastfeeding her children, the painful pleasure of expressing milk to donate to a milk bank, and the drivenness of her need to write and engage with the past. Unfashionably in a culture that prizes individualism, she declares her delight in being subsumed 'in the need of others'.[39] Myra I. Hird has contended that pregnancy and breastfeeding may be seen as acts of 'corporeal generosity' that resist 'liberal notions of a closed economy'.[40] Ní Ghríofa similarly envisages pregnancy as binding a woman's body to 'altruism as instinctively as to hunger'.[41] Imagining a female text is a further action that she adds to this alternative altruistic structure of feelings and aesthetic. In a crucial scene at a symbolic mid-point in her own text, she speculates about the identity of the unnamed 'old hag',[42] who stands sentinel near Art O'Leary's body and concludes that this 'stranger holds all of us'.[43] She is Eibhlín Dubh's 'older self ... She is also you, and she is me'.[44] The act of imagining here is thought of as a commingling of author, subject and reader and as a vital act of reciprocity. Chiming with Annie Ernaux's carefully enunciated distinctions, it is much more the domain of the transpersonal than the personal.

Moreover, in keeping with this non-possessive logic, albeit reluctantly, Ní Ghríofa decides to set Eibhlín Dubh free towards the end of her work, especially as she fails time and again to find any traces of her existence after the death of

---

38   For a discussion of the resonance of this phrase and especially its connection with Hélène Cixous' notion of écriture féminine, see Sarah Nolan, 'This Is a Female Text, I Think': 'New Words' and Franco-Gaelic Sources in Doireann Ní Ghríofa *A Ghost in the Throat*', in *New Beginnings: Perspectives from France and Ireland*, edited by Máirtín Mac Con Iomaire and Eamon Maher (Oxford: Peter Lang, 2020), 181–196.
39   Ní Ghríofa, *A Ghost in the Throat*, 33.
40   Myra I. Hird, 'The Corporeal Generosity of Maternity', *Body and Society*, 13/1 (2007), 1–20, 14.
41   Ní Ghríofa, *A Ghost in the Throat*, 35.
42   Ní Ghríofa, *A Ghost in the Throat*, 150.
43   Ní Ghríofa, *A Ghost in the Throat*, 151.
44   Ní Ghríofa, *A Ghost in the Throat*, 151.

Art. Her sons' and grandson's lives can be pieced together, but she continues to be an absent presence, a life without a chronology and a body without a grave. In place of a fully rounded story, the text furnishes us with a narrative that abounds in gaps, silences, tangents and dissonances as well as material evocations of female texts and bodies. Ironically, the unspeakable in this text centres both on the female body and the oral performance of a woman keener.

Two visits to Kilcrea Abbey bookend Ní Ghríofa's quest for Eibhlín Dubh: the first outlined in chapter five takes place sometime after the birth of her daughter, her fourth child. While there, she muses on the fact that *Caoineadh Airt Uí Laoghaire* entwines the strands of several female voices; it is an oral composition jointly created rather than the product of a single author. In line with this oral provenance, she recites the text aloud and hears it reverberate in the ruins. In so doing she locates the first material echo of Eibhlín Dubh. Despite this early promise, she decides in her final visit to Kilcrea with her daughter in the closing pages of the book that the gaps she has discovered are more important even than the palpable echoes. She thanks Eibhlín Dubh and senses her words floating away from her into the 'disarticulated dark'.[45] Fittingly, as Sonja Lawrenson has contended, Ní Ghríofa has created a form of oral textuality in homage to Eibhlín Dubh and eschewed the fixities of written words.[46] In keeping with the evanescence, fluidity and intangibility of the oral, the text ends with her soothing her daughter who wants to continue playing in Kilcrea graveyard and planning to find more space for her writing in her daily life, beyond the tyranny of domestic to-do lists. The final invocation, at once a rallying cry, an intertextual echo and a refrain stitching the book together, *This is a female text*, serves as a renewed endorsement of a shared feminist impetus that links women keeners from the eighteenth century and earlier with the twenty-first century poet.

Jennifer Cooke has christened the feminist life-writing that has emerged in the UK and the US in recent years the 'new audacity'.[47] Her finding is equally applicable to contemporary feminist life-writing in Ireland, and it is striking that

---

45 Ní Ghríofa, *A Ghost in the Throat*, 281.
46 Sonja Lawrenson, 'Oral Textuality, Gender and the Gothic in Doireann Ní Ghríofa's *A Ghost in the Throat*', *Estudios Irlandeses*, Special Issue, 18/2 (2023), 28–42.
47 Jennifer Cooke, *Contemporary Feminist Life-Writing: The New Audacity* (Cambridge: Cambridge University Press, 2020).

autobiography is no longer tied to what Liam Harte has argued is its 'master trope', 'the symbolic refraction of the life of the individual through the lens of the nation and society'.[48] As Cooke points out, women who questioned norms and challenged conventions were routinely accused of audacity. This new mode of life-writing, however, turns such daring into a radical and uncompromising aesthetic. Emilie Pine's *Notes to Self* and Doireann Ní Ghríofa's *A Ghost in the Throat* are audacious and original in providing us with uniquely intimate and revelatory studies of women's lives that we have never had before. They foreground topics normally held to be unspeakable, such as infertility, miscarriage, rape, breastfeeding, suicide, self-harm and widowhood, and investigate them in and through central grounding metaphors of the female body. Their works invoke and reinvigorate key tenets of feminist politics and call out aspects of patriarchy, family structures, the neoliberal underpinnings of professional life and the obtuse maltreatment of women by the medical system. Prominently, they creatively remould the premises, contours and forms of autobiographical writing and dislodge expectations that lives can be made fit into neatly coherent and linear patterns. In utilizing and splicing together multiple forms, they create hybrid texts that unsparingly confront us with and immerse us in affective events that do not permit of easy resolution and that remain provisional and open-ended. Above all, their daring, suggestive and interrogatory representations of personal experience are designed to include readers and to invite involvement and emotional cross-connection. The personal is rendered not as a place apart but as a transpersonal space in which readers and authors can coincide and debate what counts as unspeakable and consider the tacit principles governing the politics of everyday life in which we are all enmeshed.

---

48 Liam Harte, 'Introduction: Autobiography and the Irish Cultural Moment', in *Modern Irish Autobiography: Self, Nation and Society*, edited by Liam Harte (London: Palgrave Macmillan, 2007), 1–13, 7.

SARAH NOLAN

22 Re[p]laying Voices in Translation: Peter Sirr and the Troubadours of Twelfth-Century France

Poetry is often located on the margins, skirting the more popular centre of prose. Peter Sirr, a prize-winning Irish poet, critic, translator, playwright and editor, has always been connected to the elsewhere in the various and interconnected fields of his output, bringing an internationalism and transnationalism to Irish poetry, challenging conceptions of what is of central or marginal influence on the Irish poetic tradition.[1] His collections have, over time, delineated Dublin and other cities in which he has lived. Increasingly, these collections have incorporated lines of, and written out to, other poets' material, such as Borges, Breton, Catullus and Sapho, among many others, resulting in highly intertextual collections. These collections have involved travel across Europe and explicit engagements with the work of European, Asian and South American poets, and they fit with his ideals on the international rather than national status of the poet or poetry.

Sirr, in his final editorial of *Poetry Ireland Review* in 2007 (having edited fifteen publications), entitled 'This is Not an Editorial', urged an engagement with the 'internationalism that is the lifeblood of poetry'.[2] This chapter will consider this statement in terms of Sirr's poetic practice, which brings him to intertextuality – *to* writers – and through them to places and spaces which foster multiplicity of voice and perspective. Sirr's ninth collection, *Sway* [2016], which will be examined a little further on,

---

1   Peter Sirr is a winner of the Patrick Kavanagh Award [1982], the O'Shaughnessy Award [1998] and the Michael Hartnett Award [2011]. He is a member of Aosdána.
2   Peter Sirr, *Sway*: *Versions of Poems from the Troubadour Tradition* (Oldcastle: Gallery Press, 2016) 'Afterword', 91 https://thehighwindowpress.com/2016/09/01/peter-sirr-under-the-sway-of-the-troubadours/afterword [accessed 12 January 2024].

gives itself over to this project more fully than any of his previous publications. The works of twelfth-century troubadours from southern France are centrally placed and are the basis for the whole collection of new versions ('interpretive versioning') which references / credits the relevant poet at the end of each poem.[3]

In email correspondence relating to *Sway* I asked Sirr whether he enjoyed 'taking on the voice of another time', 'or did you feel that your approach was more about bringing that poetry into your voice?' He replied:

> I did also end up making new poems inspired by the material, but they're clearly distinguished from the others. Even there I think I was trying to find a different voice, it wasn't about fitting it into my own voice, whatever that is. I'm a bit suspicious about the notion of voice in poetry, of poets having a single identifiable voice. [I] prefer to think in terms of multiple voices, multiple identities.[4]

T. S. Eliot concluded his essay 'The Perfect Critic' thus: 'it is to be expected that the critic and the creative artist should frequently be the same person.'[5] Like the critic, the poet / critic / editor must not, or cannot, confine themselves to the celebratory. As Sirr puts it: '[I]f you haven't made enough enemies in life, then you need a spell in an editor's chair to set the balance right. The stock in trade of editing is disappointment.'[6] At the same time, Eliot argued that

---

[3] Email: 21 May 2019. My reason, in this instance, for sending questions to Sirr, to which he always generously replied, was that while I was due to present on *Sway* at an AFIS (Association of Franco-Irish Studies) conference in Lille, I was missing an International Literature Festival Dublin event, 'Talking Translation: Eiléan Ní Chuilleanáin: Poetry and Translation', at which Peter Sirr was to be in conversation with Professor Emeritus of Trinity College Dublin and the then Ireland Chair of Poetry, Eiléan Ní Chuilleanáin [Thursday 23 May]. The conversation would address questions such as 'Why do poets choose to translate each other? Is their creative work then influenced by the act of translation?' https://ilfdublin.com/archive/talking-translation-eilean-ni-chuilleanain-poetry-and-translation/ [accessed 12 January 2024].

[4] Email: 21 May 2019.

[5] T. S. Eliot, *The Sacred Wood* (London: Faber, 1921), 13.

[6] Peter Sirr, 'This is not an Editorial', *Poetry Ireland*, November/December 2007, https://www.poetryireland.ie/site/search?keywords=peter+sirr%2C+%27this+is+not+an+editorial%27 [accessed 12 January 2024].

the progress of an artist is a continual self-sacrifice, a continual extinction of personality [...] poetry is not a turning loose of emotion, but an escape from it; it is not the expression of personality, but an escape from personality. But, of course, only those who have personality and emotions know what it means to want to escape from these things.[7]

Sirr has commented in correspondence in a similar vein:

> Writing poetry is all about exploration, and so it's necessarily a journey of self-discovery. But it's also an escape from self. I'm not that interested in whoever or whatever Peter Sirr is, but am much more interested in finding the deeper resonances of things, or in connecting my own experiences with a greater current of energy. The confessional or anecdotal doesn't hold much interest for me, although poems do very often come from personal experience.[8]

A substantial body of Sirr's poetry concerns itself with engagements with the elsewhere, and other voices – with this 'greater current of energy' – and the reader of contemporary Irish poetry in general, I think, no longer expects the same themes or locations to hold as they did a century or even a few decades ago. Sirr's time teaching, editing and translating texts from various languages (which included getting into the 'verbal music' of Old Occitan) means that his material moves between the Hiberno and the European – and beyond.[9]

As editor of *Poetry Ireland Review*, his choices could affect perceptions of the state of Irish poetry – definitions of Irish poetry – through his placement of poetry in translation alongside those written in Irish or English. In 'How things begin to happen: Notes on Eiléan Ní Chuilleanáin and Medbh McGuckian', while praising these poets (Ní Chuilleanáin followed Sirr as editor of *PIR*), Sirr argued that: 'Given the full range of what has been possible in verse in our century, Irish poetry is essentially conservative. It tends to avoid formal experiment, jealously hoards its clarities, its logic,

---

[7] T. S. Eliot, 'Tradition and the Individual Talent', *Selected Essays* (London: Faber, 1932), 17, 21.
[8] Email: 21 May 2019.
[9] Email: 21 May 2019.

its trove of paraphrasable content.'[10] This statement and his final editorial can be read as part of a continuum of charting and defining Irish poetry:

> Editing a magazine is a strange business [...] Vague ideas slide around the back of the mind [...] What about Wales? Afghanistan? What about Mangan, MacNeice, Mandelstam? [...] and here comes some good old bias – a large part of me thinks that the whole notion of Irish poetry is fairly boring, a kind of branding exercise for a product few, if put to it, could really define. The currents of poetic influence flow across continents and languages and few poets would seek to confine themselves within national boundaries, or to measure themselves against a set of 'national' criteria. The dismaying parochiality of so much of Irish critical and cultural discourse – not least the flawed concept of 'Irish Studies' – shouldn't blind us to the internationalism that is the lifeblood of poetry.[11]

He also warns against closed lines of inquiry:

> Those who assume the exceptionality of Irish poetry will witter on about the lines of influence from Yeats to Heaney to Muldoon and ignore the fact that Montale, Pessoa, Celan, Bonnefoy, Lowell, Murray and a host of other unacknowledged legislators have long since gatecrashed the party.[12]

Internationalism can be understood from various perspectives, including geographic and scopic, and in terms of reception, breakthrough, readership, content or context – and Sirr concedes, 'I actually don't know any serious practitioners who don't have an ear cocked to the news from elsewhere, and aren't excited by what they discover from one end of the planet to the other.'[13] Perhaps it is also that now there are new ways of reading and listening to poetry – such as with the rise of the audiobook and the video poem, and the fact that readers can, more quickly than ever, inform themselves of the context of a writer and the time or location in which they were writing. Edna Longley takes aim at the term: 'I want to

---

10 Peter Sirr, '"How things begin to happen": Notes on Eiléan Ní Chuilleanáin', *Southern Review*, 31/1 (Summer 1995), Non-Fiction, 450, https://thesouthernreview.org/issues/detail/Summer-1995/99/ [accessed 12 January 2024].
11 Sirr, 'This Is Not an Editorial'.
12 Sirr, 'This Is Not an Editorial'.
13 Sirr, 'This Is Not an Editorial'.

complain about fuzzy uses of the word "international" in criticism of Irish poetry.'[14] She lists various anthologies and collections which present this outward-looking perspective as new, noting that Irish poetry, like Irish society, is often congratulated on having become more outward-looking. Longley quotes Seamus Deane's 1985 *Celtic Revivals*, 'Many Irish writers, sensitive to the threat of provincialism, have tried to compensate for it by being as cosmopolitan as possible. In consequence, they became citizens of the world by profession', noting that '[h]ere Deane sees "trying to be cosmopolitan" as denial of Ireland'.[15] Conversely, John McAuliffe noted in a more recent 2019 *Irish Times* article entitled 'Internationalism looms large in new poetry collections', that 'cosmopolitanism [...] may now be as much a set part of Irish poetry's repertoire as our vaunted "poetry of (one) place"'.[16]

Longley energetically engages with the debate:

> A spoof blurb I once wrote may serve as epigraph: X is one of Ireland's internationally minded young European poets. The sly postmodern subversiveness of the poems reflects his / her spell in Amsterdam's sex-industry, the ideas of Baudrillard and the mood of German politics after die Wende. X currently works in an Irish pub in Prague.[17]

On a more serious note, she considers the processes that a poem can undergo: 'One measure of transcultural trace-elements is translation. Yet translation can be a one-way street. [....] Only rarely, perhaps, does translation, in either its strict or loose sense, become a two-way transaction mutually extending horizons of expectation.'[18] Sirr's poetic practice of both translation and intertextuality more than rise to this challenge, and play out in the poetic and also professional fields with his teaching

---

14　Edna Longley, 'Irish Poetry and "Internationalism"': Variations on a Critical Theme', *The Irish Review*, 30 (Spring–Summer 2003), 48–61, 48.
15　Seamus Deane, *Celtic Revivals* (London: Faber, 1985), 156.
16　John McAuliffe, 'Internationalism Looms Large in New Poetry Collections', *Irish Times*, Saturday 4 May 2019, https://www.irishtimes.com/culture/books/internationalism-looms-large-in-new-poetry-collections-1.3874284 [accessed 12 January 2024].
17　Edna Longley, 'Irish Poetry and "Internationalism"', 48.
18　Longley, 'Irish Poetry and "Internationalism"', 53.

of literary translation in TCD, Dublin. In the 'Afterword' to *Sway* [2016] Sirr explains how and why he embarked on this collection of poetry which brings the content and song of the troubadours of southern France to contemporary readers. 'While looking for something else, I happened on lines from Guilhem de Peiteus in contrasting versions by Paul Blackburn and W. D. Snodgrass [...] one relatively smooth and straightforward, the other more broken, jumpy and contemporary'.[19] In correspondence he remarked: 'It all happened pretty organically, in the sense that I translated one poem, "*Farai un vers de dreyt nien...*" because I was very taken with it, it's knowingness, its flourish.'[20] As he was further drawn to the troubadour verse, he began learning Old Occitan, 'paying close attention to the originals, listening to the music where that existed, trying to get a sense of the verbal music of the poems themselves'.[21]

The troubadours of the first half of the twelfth century were, after all, singer-poet-composers, and Sirr endeavours to go back to that music in order to bring it forth, for the reader: 'I wanted, as much as possible, to work from the originals; to have that primal relationship with their forms and music. My aim was to find a matching music in English, to make poems as close as I could manage to the spirit of the original.'[22] He is of course limited by restraints in accessing this material, and the selection he chooses is dictated to some degree by the anthologies that are available and the recordings of the sung poems to which he is drawn. He does go at things with a dictionary though, 'numerous dictionaries', trying 'to decipher the original texts'.[23] The reader of *Sway* is presented with a smaller selection again – those lines and poems which spoke or sang to Sirr – which roused his textual and intertextual desire as he listened, mouthed, played and then relayed them. His 'Afterword' is followed by 'Notes on the Poets', and so the reader, if they choose, can get an idea about the original troubadours' lives and times, decide to research further, or disregard altogether the details behind, or indeed the original language and voice of those men – and

19   Sirr, *Sway*, 'Afterword', 91.
20   Email: 21 May 2019.
21   Email: 21 May 2019.
22   Sirr, *Sway*, 'Afterword', 91.
23   Sirr, *Sway*, 'Afterword', 91.

women (*troubairitz*), predominantly from the twelfth century (spanning the eleventh to the fourteenth), whose words and ideas are re[p]layed in *Sway*.

The word troubadour is derived, through French, from the Occitanian *trobar* – 'to find', or 'to invent'. Confined initially to southern France, the troubadour tradition of using the canso form, which consisted of five or six stanzas followed by an envoi, written and sung in the *langue d'oc*, later took hold and was further developed by the trouvères of northern France writing in the *langue d'oïl* in the twelfth and thirteenth centuries. Haines posits that the 'variety and number of extant sources bear witness to this complex and lively transmission process. Over 2,500 poems in Old Occitan survive in some thirty primary manuscripts'.[24] Sirr expresses admiration for Guilhem (William) VII count of Poitiers (Guilhem de Peiteus) IX duke of Aquitaine (1071–1126), whose poems in Old Occitan have survived, while noting that there's 'something contradictory about Guilhem's poems – he is credited with being the first troubadour, yet the swagger and sophistication suggests more the pinnacle of an already achieved tradition than a raw beginning'.[25] Haines' text confirms this, adding that it is 'unfortunately typical of early troubadour song transmission that none of Guilhem's melodies has survived', charting the increased preservation, as time passed, of the poems and melodies: 'Whereas only roughly 10 per cent of troubadour poems survive with a melody, most trouvère poems have music.'[26]

While there have been many readings, allegorical, historical, theoretical (see Kristeva, Lacan and Žižek, for example) and otherwise, of the love songs of the troubadours, and of the *fin'amor* / amour courtois / courtly love which focused on chivalry and nobility, centring on a married woman, Lazar argues that 'the mode of *fin'amor* extolled by the troubadours is conceived in a purely secular framework. When they invoke God and the saints it is never to confess sin or remorse; instead it is generally to ask for assistance in obtaining the ladies' favour.'[27] In contrast to the biblical or

---

24   John Haines, *Eight Centuries of Troubadours and Trouvères: The Changing Identity of Medieval Music* (Cambridge: Cambridge University Press, 2004), 20.
25   Sirr, *Sway*, 'Afterword', 91.
26   Haines, *Eight Centuries of Troubadours and Trouvères*, 20.
27   F. R. P. Akehurst and Judith M. Davis (eds) *A Handbook of the Troubadours* (Berkeley: University of California Press, 1995), 74.

societal roles of the time, Burns argues that '[c]ourtly love offers a number of amorous scenarios that represent gender in more unpredictable terms, staging complex love relations that push productively against the boundaries and expectations of normative heterosexuality'.[28] Sirr acknowledges perceptions that the 'abstract seeming courtly love sometimes resolves itself into a slightly cartoonish image of lovelorn poets and idealized love, a sort of medieval Hallmark of romantic gestures.'[29]

Sirr's translations present a selection of poems which deal with the interplay of desire, the erotic, status and jealousy within a feudal system, and even war. Referencing Bertran de Born's canso, '*Bem platz lo gais temps de pascor*', beneath his own title, 'Joys of Spring', the speaker in Sirr's version declares, 'I love the song / of trenches [...] Tanks and guns.' The envoi sings 'My heart is full: it's time at last / to put an end to peace'.[30] Those few words in Occitan which sub-head each poem are the reader's invitation to the original language, the original shape – and to the many other translations which exist. '*Estai ai en greu cossirier*', by the troubairitz Beatriz de Dia, Sirr's 'How I'd like him...', is among the most explicit and goes further than most of those by the male poets:

> My tender cavalier
>
> when will I have you for myself?
>
> For one night only
>
> naked in your arms
>
> If you could only take
>
> My husband's place
>
> and swear to me you'll answer
>
> when I call, and heed my desire.[31]

---

28 E. Jane Burns, 'Courtly Love: Who Needs It? Recent Feminist Work in the Medieval French Tradition', *Signs*, 27/1 (2001), 23–57, 25.
29 Sirr, Sway, 'Afterword', 92.
30 Sirr, *Sway*, 'Joys of Spring', 53–54.
31 Sirr, Sway, 'How I'd like him [...]', 27.

Re[p]laying Voices in Translation   311

From the above stanzas, the final two of the poem, it looks like Sirr is writing consistently in quatrains, but in this poem, even more than in others, he is flexible with the form and in making it his own, leaving standalone lines and additional spacing, such as at the beginning:

How I'd like him

    oh

how I would like him   my

cavalier.[32]

The collection begins with an epigraph from Cercamon, one of the earliest troubadours from Gascogne: '*Ist trobador, entre ver e mentir, / Afollon drutz e molhers et espos...*' (These troubadours, between truth and lies, corrupt lovers, women and husbands...) – and how apt is this in-between when Sirr's collection is such – between women and husbands (reflecting the Occitan and French language to come), between then and now, and between the here and there of the poems, the distances local and inherent to the poetry.

In *Lark in the Morning: The Verses of the Troubadours*, which features translations by Pound and Snodgrass, Kehew notes that Blackburn inserts 'dockside taverns' into his translation of Peire Vidal's '*Ab l'alen tir vas me l'aire*' in order to satisfy contemporary readers' craving for an immediate and concrete setting.[33] I asked Sirr about place, which features heavily in his other collections – cities and streets, named or not, and even internal spaces, as in *The Rooms* [2014] – whether it was a challenge working with material which was placeless in terms of any specifics – except for the 'here' and 'there' of a missed or desired one. Did the focus on time locate it for him, the past or present or future of a love or loved one? Regarding a place

---

32   Sirr, *Sway*, 'How I'd like him [...]', 27.
33   Robert Kehew (ed.), *Lark in the Morning: The Verses of the Troubadours*, bilingual edition, translated by Ezra Pound, W. D. Snodgrass, and Robert Kehew (Chicago: University of Chicago Press, 2005) [see 108. of *Proensa*].

and time, he identified the Occitan-speaking areas of southern France but also 'its cultural continuity into Italy, Spain, Catalonia, Portugal', noting:

> So there's a particular landscape and seasonality which I made use of. But as you say there's also the identifiable linguistic and erotic atmosphere of these poems of stylised desire, which unifies them and makes them part of a single impulse and that's also what I was exploring [..] trying to get through to the real feeling behind all the clever devices the poets wrapped around themselves.[34]

In the 'Afterword', Sirr considers the impact a poet's language choices can have – 'Dante, like many Italian poets of his era, considered writing in Occitan before plumping for Italian' – and how their play with language, as well as changing trends in and uses of language, can be the very substance of the poetry which follows. 'In the *Purgatorio* he meets the original "*miglior fabbro*", Arnaut Daniel, who addresses him in Old Occitan: *'Ieu sui Arnaut, que plor e vau cantan*' ('I am Arnaut, who weeps and goes singing')'.[35] Sirr gives renewed voice to these tongues, which he has also followed through Petrarch, Pound, Eliot and Dante, and does so with his own understanding of courtly love, with his ear cocked for the music and possibility of a vernacular poetry.[36]

Here is one of the final stanzas from the poem '*Farai un vers de dreyt nien*' by Guilhem de Peiteus. As mentioned, this was the initial troubadour poem which caught Sirr's eye, and the playful title translates as 'I'll Make a Verse / Song out of Nothing at all'. It can be compared across several versions below in terms of the combination of long and short lines, line number, lexical choice, tone and rhyme:

Anc non la vi et am la fort,

Anc no n'aic dreyt ni no'm fes tort;

Quan non la vey, be m'en deport,

---

34 Email: 21 May 2019.
35 Sirr, *Sway*, 'Afterword', 91–92.
36 Sirr mentions Pound's role in reviving the troubadours, while noting Pound's 'oddly archaizing versions', 'complicated by the intersection of the troubadours with the heights of Modernism'. Sirr, *Sway*, 'Afterword', 93.

No'm pretz un jau
Qu'ie'n sai gensor e bellazor,
E que mais vau.[37]

The rhyming scheme is often slightly more varied than the abab of this stanza, with examples of typical canso rhyming schemes being AABCBC / BBCACA. Kehew discusses the challenges of translation:

> Poems in Old Occitan adhere to strict patterns regarding the number of syllables per line. Most traditional English poetry [...] is accentual syllabic [...] count stresses and syllables. [...] leads to greater flexibility. Old Occitan, like other Romance languages and in contrast to English, is rich in words that rhyme. This [...] allowed the Occitanian poets to construct ever more intricately rhymed poetic edifices. As a translator, Pound was drawn to the formalistic pyrotechnics of Arnaut Daniel.[38]

As Pound would note, 'I have proved that the Provençal rhyme schemes are not *impossible* in English. They are probably *inadvisable*.' Kehew remarks that Pound 'outgrew his early, fin-de-siecle love of archaisms – what he later called 'the crust of dead English' and found a more living voice'.[39] W. D. Snodgrass observes changing ideas about the troubadours, having concentrated on their material as song lyric and composition: '[G]one is the wistful figure singing sweetly ... to a far-off idealized lady [....] By now, we are almost ready to say that Troubadour songs have only two subjects: one, let's go crusading and kill lots of Moors; two, let's go get in the boss's wife.'[40] Below is Snodgrass' translation of the de Peiteus stanza above:

> Though I've not seen her, my love's strong;
>
> Not seeing her, I'm scarce undone;
>
> She never did me right or wrong

---

37   Guilhem de Peiteus, 'Farai un vers de dreyt nien', in *Lark in the Morning: The Verses of the Troubadours*, 24–26.
38   Kehew, *Lark in the Morning*, xiv.
39   Kehew, *Lark in the Morning*, xvi.
40   Kehew, *Lark in the Morning*, xvi.

> And who cares, for
>
> I know a nicer, fairer one
>
> Who's worth lots more.[41]

Here Snodgrass has produced an abacbc rhyming scheme which takes us through the turn in the stanza from love of 'her' to a 'fairer one'. The next translation is by Paul Blackburn, who claimed to turn to translating when going through dry periods in his own writing: 'In a very real way I use translations to fill in that time, because I do enjoy translating, getting into other people's heads. Thass [*sic*] right … This is one motivation for translation. Are there others? There must be.'[42] Blackburn's version does not just mention the 'other one', who is worth more, but comments negatively on the first 'friend', who is 'not worth a rooster':

> Never saw her and I love her
>
> very much. It doesn't matter if
>
> she treats me straight or not, for I
>
> do very well without her,
>
> and besides, I know another who is
>
> prettier and such.
>
> Why, she is not worth a rooster, and
>
> this other one is rich![43]

But what of these different versions of troubadour verse – and how does the contemporary reader gather their spatio-temporal bearings – how is song brought out from the page? For Sirr the 'original stays put

---

41 Kehew, *Lark in the Morning*, 25–27.
42 Paul Blackburn, *New York Quarterly Questionnaire*, conducted by Marina Roscher, quoted in George Economou, 'Introduction', in *Proensa: An Anthology of Troubadour Poetry*, selected and translated by Paul Blackburn (New York: New York Review Books, 2016), xvii.
43 Blackburn, *Proensa: An Anthology of Troubadour Poetry*, 8.

while the translators sit in the booth of their moment and broadcast their short-range FM signals. Translation is never fixed or finished.'[44] In Sirr's version we see inventions and innovation of approach:

> I never saw her, still I love her.
>
> Do I contradict myself?
>
> Don't worry,
>
> judge and jury have left the room.
>
> The thing is
>
> I love another: nicer, prettier. I love her more.[45]

In this stanza there is a lot more punctuation than in many of Sirr's versions, and unlike any of the other poets' translations seen above, he ends that first line with a full stop. The first lines of this stanza, in the original and in the versions above, reference '*am*' / 'love'. Both Snodgrass and Blackburn mention the worth of the other in the final lines, while Sirr mentions love again, reinforcing the feeling, where even Guilhem de Peiteus steers towards value.

Sirr poses a question that the others do not. He mentioned that there was 'something contradictory' about Guilhem's verse, his coming seemingly at the beginning of a literary and musical movement, and yet full of 'swagger and sophistication'.[46] But this question asks another question too, with regard to the intertext, which the reader is alert to, or not, depending on their marginal or mainstream poetic interests. After more than 1,000 lines, in the fifty-first section, the second-last canto of Whitman's 'Song of Myself', is a line that lodges in the reader's mind, arguably, after just one reading – and it is a question: 'Do I contradict myself?' Whitman continues, 'Very well then I contradict myself / (I am large, I contain multitudes.).'[47] Here, and surely wittingly, Sirr poses

---

44   Sirr, *Sway*, 'Afterword', 92.
45   Sirr, *Sway*, 'Nothing Song', 11–12.
46   Sirr, *Sway*, 'Afterword', 91.
47   Walt Whitman, *Song of Myself and Other Poems*, Introduction by Robert Haas (Berkeley: Counterpoint Press, 2010), 69.

the same question, bringing the reader in and out of the intertexts that have become part of his vernacular of the poetic. Like the self-awareness and large embrace of Whitman's original question and answer, Sirr's knowing play with text and intertext brings the reader closer, taking any pressure off speaker and reader / listener alike, as he steps into the vernacular with his answer – 'Don't worry'. Since 'judge and jury have left the room', logic and consequence are more loosely perceived, if at all. What is in play is 'another: nicer, prettier'.[48] Sirr, in the next line, which hangs and takes its time, 'The thing is /', calls forth another intertext, his 2009 collection of the same title, *The Thing Is*, bringing a whole other swathe of material into the space between.

Other collections of Sirr's have described contemporary relationships – the 'trashy grief / of airports, train stations' – so what of his stepping into the 'linguistic and erotic atmosphere of the troubadour poems', what will this reworking or restaging bring?[49] A musical example, given the lyrical foundations of the troubadours, and the possibility to transpose, comes to mind. If you are familiar with Vivaldi's *The Four Seasons* (published in 1725, with four accompanying sonnets, one for each season), you have possibly come across Nigel Kennedy's 1989 version, *Vivaldi: The Four Seasons – Nigel Kennedy*, termed 'affectionate and irreverent in equal measure' by one reviewer.[50] Another notes that Kennedy 'brings the full range of violin techniques – ancient and modern – to Vivaldi's work, creating the unequivocal ba-rock version – exhilarating and exuberant'.[51] Max Richter's *Recomposed by Max Richter: Vivaldi The Four Seasons* (2012/2022) brings him back twice to this work, and as he says in an interview, it is like 'seeing a sculpture

---

48 Sirr, 'Nothing Song', Sway, 11–12.
49 Sirr, 'Postscript', *Talk, Talk* (Oldcastle: Gallery Press, 1987), 37.
50 Erica Jeal, 'Nigel Kennedy: The New Four Seasons CD review', *The Guardian*, 29 October 2015, https://www.theguardian.com/music/2015/oct/29/nigel-kennedy-the-new-four-seasons-cd-review-orchestra-of-life?CMP=share_btn_gp [accessed 12 January 2024].
51 https://www.classicfm.com/composers/vivaldi/album-reviews/four-seasons-nigel-kennedy/ [accessed 12 January 2024].

from a different angle'.[52] Described as 'a radical reinterpretation', Richter describes part of the process as follows: '[S]ome of the time, I'm taking the original and subverting or recontextualizing it.'[53] If one has only heard these, and not the original, what of Vivaldi has one absorbed – or does one even pause to wonder what change has come about through distance, or time or alteration? If the mood or mode changes in its replaying, does the listener, perhaps particularly one who knows the original, experience an augmentation of that original, and not a lack?

For Sirr, the musical aspect of the troubadour texts / songs was a vital element, explaining in correspondence: 'I came across a video that had the music of the Guilhem de Peiteus poem [...] and I was hooked. It was as if a door opened into that whole world, and I just immersed myself in all of it. It really was pretty obsessive.'[54] What has been termed, among other things, recomposition, as above, is a process which Sirr has also defined and named: 'I feel the need to keep forging conversations with the past, and so translation or *interpretive versioning* becomes part of the whole aesthetic. [...] Translation and creation are, for me, part of the same continuum.'[55] His position on translating and on texts in translation, particularly in light of his choices as editor of the *Poetry Ireland Review*, are part of a larger picture regarding the engagement of poets through time and across language. Sirr, in reference to the troubadours, calls it 'a continuous wave of influence that washed up on or own shores too' and, arguably, a reengagement with this influence is fruitful for poet and reader alike.[56] His own poems join those of the troubadours in a six-page 'Coda' to the collection entitled 'Road Songs',

52 Max Richter, 'Like seeing a sculpture from a different angle': Max Richter on rewriting The Four Seasons – for the second time', *The Guardian*, 10 June 2022, https://www.theguardian.com/music/2022/jun/10/like-seeing-a-sculpture-from-a-different-angle-max-richter-on-rewriting-the-four-seasons-for-the-second-time [accessed 12 January 2024].
53 'I Fell in Love with the Original Again': Max Richter on Recomposing Vivaldi's 'Four Seasons', 31 August 2021, https://www.udiscovermusic.com/classical-featu res/max-richter-recomposed-vivaldi-four-seasons/ [accessed 12 January 2024].
54 Email: 21 May 2019.
55 Email: 21 May 2019.
56 Email: 21 May 2019.

with a final line that very fittingly hands his translations, his interpretations, his creations to [...] you!

> pouring from shop window and café
>
> where *cansos* crumble, *coplas* collapse
>
> the singers, stumblers and I myself
>
> fall out of the lines, and into your arms. [...]
>
> boreen to mountain
>
> dunegrass to sea
>
> my geography of desire
>
> the poem steps before me [...]
>
> On its way to you.[57]

---

57   Sirr, *Sway*, 'Road Songs', 88.

BARRY HOULIHAN

23 'The Fear of Speaking Plainly': Translating John McGahern and the Letters of Alain Delahaye

Writing to Madeline McGahern in April 2006, the French writer and translator Alain Delahaye (1944–2020) wrote in *The Wake of Death* about John McGahern, stating that 'Life is definitely harder without John's presence, and every day I have memories of him coming back to me, good memories of course, of a writer who was a wonderful mixture of kindness and intelligence [...] He left us his books, a presence and a voice which can never be altered'.[1]

Among 1,500 letters sent to John McGahern over his lifetime and which are collected today within his archive at University of Galway is a large file from his long-time French translator, Alain Delahaye. The Delahaye letters comprise one of the single biggest collections of literary letters from a single individual in the McGahern archive.[2] Delahaye translated a number of Irish literary works into French, from Oscar Wilde to McGahern,[3] but

---

1   Letter from Alain Delahaye to Madeline McGahern, April 2006. McGahern Archive, University of Galway.
2   There are significant collections of letters between McGahern and Patrick Gregory, editor at Knopf Publishers in New York and also with Niall Walsh, an oncologist based at Ballinasloe Hospital in Co. Galway, who along with his wife were close friends of John and Madeline McGahern.
3   In a letter to John McGahern from Brian Friel, Friel noted his hope that Delahaye would translate plays of his into French, namely *Faith Healer*. 'I still hope that Delahaye will look at the text [of Faith Healer] [...] I do hope we can proceed with your man.' In other letters Friel discusses 'confusion' and issues around Delahaye's interest. This confusion is perhaps due to Delahaye writing to McGahern, congratulating him on the text of *Faith Healer*, not realizing the play was in fact written by Brian Friel, adding that he [Delahaye] had not heard of Friel until McGahern corrected him and told him that he did not write *Faith Healer*. P71/1642 Letters from Brian Friel to McGahern, McGahern Archive, University of Galway.

it was translating McGahern's books into French (including *The* Dark, *The Pornographer, Getting Though* and *Amongst Women*) that occupied the bulk of Delahaye's output from the late 1970s through the 1990s. The work of translation, through Delahaye, and the established relationship between translator, author, and text, played an important role in the wide readership and warm critical reception McGahern received in France throughout his lifetime.

The deep connections between Irish and French literature and culture have long been explored by Eamon Maher, among others, in a wide-ranging body of scholarship. Denis Sampson traces the early influences and interests of French culture on the young McGahern. Among established classic French writers from Marcel Proust, Gustave Flaubert, Charles Baudelaire, and François-René Chateaubriand, all of whom McGahern read, Sampson adds that 'McGahern's interest in French films is an indication that he was already becoming a Francophile'.[4] In a chapter exploring the similarities in the writing and treatment of sexuality by McGahern and French Nobel laureate François Mauriac, Maher identifies a neglected overlap in literary form and theme of both writers:

> They were both exposed to a puritanical form of Catholicism during their youth which emphasised the sinfulness of the human body [...] in the fiction of the two writers many characters feel obliged to repress their sexual urges, a decision that can have severe psychological consequences.[5]

The connections in particular between McGahern and the influence of and symmetries with French literature have been particularly important and influential in the field of McGahern studies. From 'the local to the universal', to draw on the title of Maher's monograph situating McGahern's writing within world-writing, linking McGahern's Ireland to the international, to later consideration of the reading of Marcel Proust by McGahern, have provided critical interventions in the reading,

---

4   Denis Sampson, *Young John McGahern: Becoming A Novelist* (Oxford: Oxford University Press, 2012), 55.
5   Eamon Maher, 'Sins of the Flesh, Problematic Sexuality in McGahern and François Mauriac', in *Essays on John McGahern: Assessing a Literary Legacy*, edited by Derek Hand and Eamon Maher (Cork: Cork University Press, 2019), 182.

appreciation, and intercultural synergies in McGahern's writing, and between Ireland and France in particular.

A site of influence: France, Ireland, and McGahern

The form and tone of Marcel Proust's writing was undoubtedly an influence on McGahern. Proust's style of memory writing and recall through extensive streams of sentences and paragraphs was arguably less of a stylistic influence. McGahern was a stylist of a kind which utilized a more compact form of structure and syntax. The impact of recall of memory was more powerfully deployed by McGahern in a single line than by extensive exposition or narrative. As Maher has noted: 'It is the use of involuntary memory, a technique that allows episodes from the past to be relived in the present thanks to the activation of certain triggers, that is the most salient intersection between the two writers.'[6]

In navigating a plane of memory that oscillates between past and present, a liveness is brought to what is recalled by McGahern through place and language. As Maher explains by comparing McGahern's experience of memory to that of Proust: 'McGahern experienced something similar [to Proust's experience of recall] when strolling through the lanes of Leitrim in his later years, where he sporadically felt as though he was once more walking along these same lanes hand in hand with his beloved mother on their way to school. The effect was "an extraordinary sense of security, a deep peace", the conviction that he could live for ever.'[7]

Within the extensive correspondence collected over three decades between John McGahern and Alain Delahaye is an exchange of letters that documents the development of a literary relationship, one that placed

---

[6] Eamon Maher, 'In "memory" of Marcel Proust: Madeleines, Leitrim lanes and John McGahern (1871–1922)', *Irish Times*, 27 October 2022. DOI: 10.21427/KPMA-T563.

[7] Maher, 'In "memory" of Marcel Proust', 27 October 2022, DOI: 10.21427/KPMA-T563.

McGahern at the forefront of the modern Irish writing in French translation. Through detailed files of press cuttings, interviews, and documents from wider French media and official circles, all collected within the McGahern Archive, further evidence is gathered of the esteemed regard McGahern was received in French culture. This chapter will explore in detail the establishment, development, and impact of the literary relationship of John McGahern and Alain Delahaye, as well as expand on archival evidence of the literary process of translation employed by Delahaye on works by John McGahern.

Translating *The Dark* and making of *L'Obscur*

The first letter by John McGahern to Alain Delahey that is recorded within *The Letters of John* McGahern is dated 14 May 1980. This comes at the latter period of translation work by Delahaye on McGahern's second novel, *The Dark*, published by Faber and Faber in 1965. McGahern clarified questions from Delahaye on the text and meaning of words and phrases in *The Dark*. The help on translating meaning and context sought by Delahaye was primarily in relation to local places and essences of rural Irish life. These clarifications from McGahern included: 'The post office would be the only shop [in a rural village], keeping all sorts of goods – newspapers, tea, butter, chocolate, lemonade etc. Even if it was a Sunday, people would still knock on the back door.' Also noted by McGahern in response to Delahaye was 'E.S.B. – Electricity Supply Board, a semi-state body. Quiet office job'.[8] This point in particular is a key translation to one theme of the book – the quandary of the young Mahony in leaving a university education to enter a secure and stable if also relatively unstimulating job in a semi-state body. Delahaye outlined his own similarities to the protagonist of McGahern's book, noting he too studied Latin and

---

[8] Letter from John McGahern to Alain Delahaye, *The Collected Letters of John McGahern*, edited by Frank Shovlin (London: Faber and Faber, 2022), 510.

Greek and 'like the young Mahony in *The Dark* I didn't have the nerve to finish my studies'.[9]

By mid-1980 Delahaye was finishing his translation of *The* Dark, a work that became *L'Obscur* in its French translation. At this time Delahaye was writing primarily from his home in Valenciennes, a small town about 60km from Lille. In June 1980 he wrote to McGahern seeking clarification on aspects of the novel's language, namely select terms and place names that carry unique resonances beyond literal translation. Such points include:

> What is Ireland's Own – the answer will enable me to know as well what kind of shop is Flynn's.
>
> Girls from Cathal Brugha: Is this the name of a suburb in Dublin? Or a company where the girls are employed?[10]

McGahern replied to Delahaye to clarify these points of translation. 'Ireland's Own,' McGahern outlined, 'is a peasant magazine, horoscopes, lonely hearts, serials, with a green cover. Cathal Brugha – school where young girls are taught "Domestic Science", cookery, nutrition, hotel management'.[11] These two points as discussed by author and translator reveal McGahern's choices of references within the novel, of both popular magazines read in rural Ireland, like *Ireland's Own*, and how he considered them 'peasant magazines'.

Delahaye's discussion around language and of the intended meaning of words and phrases by McGahern to convey sexual matters and their effects on the body, is answered by McGahern in relation to *The Dark*. One word, 'interfere', is queried by Delahaye as to its meaning and intent regarding sexual harm. He wrote to McGahern on 2 July 1980 when in the final stages of translating *The Dark*. He thanks McGahern for his clarification around the language of sexual abuse in the book. McGahern clarified the use and resonance of the word in an Irish social context:

---

9   Letter from Delahaye to McGahern, 2 July 1980. McGahern Archive, University of Galway.
10 Letter from Delahaye to McGahern, June 1980. McGahern Archive University of Galway.
11 Letter from McGahern to Delahey, *The Collected Letters*, 513.

> Interfere is very vague, implying the father's fear of sex; attempted rape is even too strong. It's almost legalistic or doctrinal. Inflict himself sexually on her in any way. Harm vague again. Did he hurt her, have intercourse and – worst fear – get her pregnant? The vagueness or timidity goes hand in hand with the violence. If he had, it might be cause of murder.[12]

Delahaye responds in thanks to McGahern and expands on the Irish context of silence in society regarding matters of sexual abuse and the family:

> I now understand how I was wrong to take 'interfere' in the legal sense of the word, while you meant only very imprecise ways of bothering a young girl sexually. I am also grateful to you for saying that the word 'interfere' is used because of the fear of speaking plainly of sexual matters. This vagueness combined with a kind of shyness will be somewhat delicate to the reader in French, but you can be sure I will do my best to keep as near as possible to your intentions in the original.[13]

The French edition of *L'Obscur* was published by Éditions de la Sphére in 1980. By November, Delahaye is disappointed with the published text of *L'Obscur*, citing that the publisher did not include his last corrections. Further proofing errors were less serious and detrimental to the published translated text but enough to warrant Delahaye to add, 'What a pity, after all this work, which really was a labour of love.'[14]

In December 1980 Delahaye updates McGahern that he has received a grant of 4,500fr from the Centre National des Lettres in support of his work on translation of McGahern into French and which Delahaye planned to use for a trip to Ireland to meet with McGahern and work on translation is closer dialogue with the author. The financial award was a significant sign of French national recognition and appreciation for McGahern, and also of the impact of Delahaye's translations in bringing McGahern's writing to a French readership in translation. He wrote McGahern:

---

[12] Letter from McGahern to Delahaye 2 July 1980, *The Collected Letters*, 513.
[13] Letter from Delahaye to McGahern, McGahern Archive, University of Galway.
[14] Letter from Delahaye to McGahern, 6 November 1980. McGahern Archive, University of Galway.

This means also that our 'cultural authorities' (!) have at last recognised you as a major writer – because the quality of the book itself plays an important role in the decision to give or not give the grant.[15]

Delahaye mentions at this time that he is also currently working on translating McGahern's 1979 novel, *The Pornographer* and that he will have finished working on it the coming months. By July 1981 Delahaye's translation is published as *Le Pornograph* by Prèsses de la Renaissance. Delahaye outlines to McGahern that public and critical notices about the novel were slow in coming but that reputation and reception of the novel was circulating: 'Several signs tell me that your novel will not go unnoticed.'[16]

By December 1981 *Le Pornograph* has sold an impressive 2,500 copies.[17] Tony Cortero (noted by Delahaye as being 'a very gifted novelist') has by this time become editor of Prèsses de la Renaissance in Paris and wrote to Delahaye to say he would be interested in publishing more work by McGahern. Delahaye suggests the short story collections of *Getting Through* or *Nightlines* and of the novels he suggests *The Barracks* or *The Leavetaking*. Delahaye adds that he would also consider translating *The Barracks* but with the caveat that it would be 'a rather hard experience mainly because of the very accurate description of cancer in evolution, but I feel ready to undertake it'.[18] Both novels, he feels, would leave a strong impact on French readers.

By November 1982 Delahaye confirms that Prèsses de la Renaissance has asked Delahaye to translate *The Leavetaking*.[19] In his preface to the revised edition of *The Leavetaking*, published a decade after the original novel text was published in 1974, McGahern reminds us that he returned to the

---

15   Letter from Delahaye to McGahern, 20 December 1980. McGahern Archive, University of Galway.
16   Letter from Delahaye to McGahern, 15 July 1981. McGahern Archive, University of Galway.
17   Letter from Delahaye to McGahern, 16 December 1981. McGahern Archive, University of Galway.
18   *The Barracks* was published in French in 1986 by a different translator, Georges-Michel Sarotte, published by French publisher, Belfond.
19   Letter from Delahaye to McGahern, 19 November 1982. McGahern Archive, University of Galway.

book, reviewing it with Alain Delahaye, who was then translating the text for the French edition. 'The more I saw of it, the more sure I was it had to be changed', McGahern wrote. 'The crudity I was attempting to portray, the irredeemable imprisonment of the beloved in the reportage, had itself become blatant. I had been too close to the "Idea", and the work lacked the distance, that inner formality or calm, that all writing, no matter what it is attempting, must possess.'[20] The novel incorporated numerous changes, many of which were a product of Delahaye's interventions.

As with previous works of translation, the letters show how Delahaye had built up a vocabulary of McGahern language since 1980 and the publication of *L'Obscur*. He notes that he was struggling with some words such as 'pull-ups' – items worn on the trousers when riding a bicycle or what form of Irish was 'the modh-muinte'. 'Usually', Delahaye queried, 'I can guess rather easily the meaning of the Irish phrases, but here I have a problem.'[21]

One further example relates to the understanding of the language and writing of the close relationship between seasons, nature, and the passage of time, as seen in so much of McGahern's writing. Delahaye queries with McGahern an early section of *The Leavetaking*, where the mother tells the child to count the seconds between the thunder and the lighting in order to reassure and calm the child that the storm was still some distance away and not a threat. 'In France', Delahaye states, 'we all learned to guess the distance of a storm by counting the seconds between 1. Lighting and 2. Thunder, since the speed of light is much faster than the speed of sound'.[22] This point further links the shared experience of Irish and French folk customs with regard to the experience of nature within the family. This change was incorporated into the revised edition of *The Leavetaking* by McGahern and which was published by Faber and Faber in 1984. Delahaye's translation of the novel was published in French as *Journée d'Adieu* by Prèsses de la Renaissance, in 1983.

20   John McGahern, *Love of the World: Essays* (London: Faber and Faber, 2009), 277.
21   Letter from Delahaye to McGahern, 9 April 1983. McGahern Archive, University of Galway.
22   Letter from Delahaye to McGahern, 11 April 1983. McGahern Archive, University of Galway.

Following this and by September 1985, Delahaye writes to McGahern that he is reading *High Ground*, McGahern's collection of stories from 1985, first published by Faber and Faber, but owing to pressures and job struggles he will have to end his work on translating. This includes abandoning the ongoing work to translate McGahern's first novel, *The Barracks*, and instead seek out more stable employment.

McGahern, Delahaye, and translating funeral practices and Irish rural pastoral

Stories and scenes that depicted funeral practices and the act of coming together at times of grief and loss in McGahern's writings particularly fascinated Delahaye. He often cited McGahern's short story, *The Country Funeral* as a favourite of his. He also picked up on the scene of preparing and laying out of the corpse within McGahern's last novel, *That They May Face The Rising Sun*. McGahern described the original event that inspired that scene and which he experienced in reality:

> Francie, the man across the lake, his brother came from England 2 weeks ago and died. I and a crazy chemist from Dublin had to lay him out. He, the chemist, kept adjusting the mouth. 'You'll never get it any better than that', I said after the 16th attempt. 'They're wondering already what's keeping us. This is your very last chance'. I knew the pursuit of perfection would go on all night. The murmurs outside the door were rising. People restless to start drinking which they couldn't do decently until they had viewed the Departed. 'O we'll have our critics. Never you mind', he said resentfully. 'We'll have our critics'.[23]

Similarly, the French writer Michel Déon (who lived primarily in Ireland since 1968) wrote to McGahern in 1996, discussing the selection of short stories in the French edition of McGahern's *Les Créatures de la Terres et Autres Nouvelles*, translated by Alain Delahaye. Déon lamented that the stories *My Love, My Umbrella* and *Bank Holiday* were not included

23   Letter from John McGahern to Alain Delahaye, *The Collected Letters*, 532.

before adding *The Country Funeral* meant most to him from living in rural Ireland where 'these gatherings [funerals] are so genuine, so opened [sic] that they are mostly an occasion to break the stillness of country life'.[24]

In further exchanges McGahern writes to Delahaye relaying the news of everyday life in Leitrim, with updates of farm life, patterns of nature, and again, news of local deaths, all of which is tinged with news of Religious ritual:

> Not much news in Foxfield. The cow had a bull calf the colour of café au lait on Good Friday. The early plum tree is in white blossom. There's fine weather, frost at night. The old woman up the lane – I was mowing her meadow when you were here – died in Sligo last Thursday, was buried in Fenagh on Sunday. She broke her hip and died of homesickness. The postman scolded me and a few locals for standing on neighbouring tulips as we started to fill the grave.[25]

The later years: Translating 'unforgettable presences'

By July 1990 Delahaye is completing his translation of McGahern's *Amongst Women*, published as *Entre Toutes Les Femmes*. Delahaye outlines how the characters in the book came alive to him during translation, even more so than through the act of reading, signifying an active practice of translation, embodying an empathetic response to character development within the book, even towards the protagonist of Moran: 'By the intensity of presence of Moran and all of the characters [...] and somewhat like the girls, despite his monstrous violence, I had started to like him.'[26]

24 Barry Houlihan, '"Dear John": New archive of letters to John McGahern opens a window into his world', *Irish Times*, 1 September 2022, https://www.irishtimes.com/culture/books/2022/09/01/dear-john-new-archive-of-letters-to-john-mcgahern-opens-a-window-into-his-world/ [accessed 3 January 2024].
25 Letter from McGahern to Alain Delahaye, 14 April 1982, *The Collected Letters*, 541.
26 Letter from Delahaye to McGahern, 5 July 1990. McGahern Archive, University of Galway.

In the latter part of 1990 Delahaye was preoccupied with translating McGahern's stage play, *The Power of Darkness*. He writes from Paris that he has received the reworked script of McGahern's from the BBC, which includes McGahern's revisions and edits, to which Delahaye commented: 'All changes were real improvements. The play has acquired still more density, more dramatic power, and the beginning is much stronger.'[27] In this letter Delahaye outlines to McGahern the connection to and relation with Simone Gallimard, owner of Mercure de France. She commissioned Delahaye to translate the complete works of Oscar Wilde into French, a project which took him a number of years to complete and which was published in 1992 by Mercure de France (owned by Gallimard) as *Oeuvres Complètes*.

Gallimard published Delahaye's first book of poems under Mercure de France in 1971, entitled *L'Éveil des Traversées*. Delahaye gifted McGahern a copy of his book of poems and also in later years he gifted McGahern editions of the journals of Eugène Delacroix. Also in 1971, Gallimard published the French translation of McGahern's *Nightlines* (*Lignes de Fond*) translated by Pierre Leyris. Further evidencing the firm regard of McGahern by France's leading publishers, Delahaye writes in a letter that 'She [Simone Gallimard] deeply regrets not to have published your other works, and she would be very happy if she could publish your future writings, starting with your play.'[28]

By early March 1991, Delahaye sees that *Entre Toutes Les Femmes* is selling well in French bookshops and is being 'talked about with admiration' while he is also being contacted by other French publishers seeking new and future work by McGahern to publish in France. At this time he also outlines that he has begun translating *Getting Through*, McGahern's 1978 collection of short stories for Prèsses de la Renaissance. Delahaye struggles to construct a meaning for the title that he will use for *Getting Through* in French and questions McGahern about this, querying if it is intended to mean:

27   Letter from Delahaye to McGahern, 18 October 1990. McGahern Archive, University of Galway.
28   Letter from Delahaye to McGahern, 18 October 1990, McGahern Archive, University of Galway.

(a) to succeed (in meeting someone or in searching something)

(b) to complete or to finish

(c) to make oneself understood?

(d) Or is it simply like the French 'Traverser' (which would be a good title)?[29]

In a letter dated 31 March 1992, Delahaye adds that the title of the book will be *Les Huîtres de Tchekhov* and that it has just recently been published and declaring that Tony Cortero, Head of Prèsses de la Renaissance, found that title 'better' than *Getting Through* [...] I only know it is an extraordinarily deep and moving book, full of humanity, of unforgettable presences (the priest remembering his 'external moments' before dying'), and written with a rare accurateness'.[30]

Conclusion

As the letters and exchange between Delahaye and McGahern continues through the years it extends to a warm and firm friendship, rooted through family as much as in a literary nature. Delahaye and his family visited and stayed with the McGaherns in Leitrim in 1980. A year later, in August 1981, Delahaye writes from Del at Buire le Sec (where he had bought a new house and moved to with his family) with fond memories of his time in Leitrim and being close to the wellspring of McGahern's imagination. He writes with clear warmth of his connection to the rhythms and patterns of rural Irish life that he saw and was part of that summer in Leitrim in 1980. 'I remember vividly the morning we did the hay together last year, with the tractor and forks, and the wonderful smell in the field.'[31]

29   Letter from Delahaye to McGahern, 9 March 1991, McGahern Archive, University of Galway.
30   Letter from Delahaye to McGahern, 31 March 1992, McGahern Archive, University of Galway.
31   Letter from Delahaye to McGahern, 26 August 1981. McGahern Archive, University of Galway.

News of Delahaye's wife and young daughter, Pascale, are shared in nearly all letters, as is Delahaye's regard and best wishes to Madeline McGahern. The vision of caring and loving parenthood offered by the Delahayes strikes a deep chord with McGahern. He recognized and appreciated the love of the father-child relationship between Alain and Pascale, despite the stresses of various house moves and the precarity of translation work undertaken by Delahaye. In a letter of reply in August 1981, McGahern writes to Delahaye adding: 'Give our congratulations to Pascale [Delahaye's daughter]. Her parents seem the sort of parents everybody should have – my old peach in the graveyard would look on such generosity as positively subversive.'[32]

In his interview with John McGahern in 2002, Eamon Maher asked McGahern what his next writing plans would be. In a brilliantly typical McGahern answer he replied: 'No great plans. I'm beginning to work again. What it will become I have no idea at this stage, and it may not become anything at all.'[33] That answer was handwritten by McGahern onto the transcript of the interview, which he kept within his archive, now at University of Galway. The interview transcript was painstakingly reread and edited by McGahern, adding further comments and thoughts to already intriguing answers to an invaluable interview with Maher. The sign-off and final comments by McGahern are revealing towards the gestation of ideas, of literary image and form that dominates the development of McGahern's writings. A similar process was employed by Delahaye in crafting an interpretation and new form through which McGahern's writing was encountered by French readers.

The precise skill and focus of the translator, as exemplified in the letters from Delahaye, reveal an important cultural and transnational recognition of McGahern's writing through the French critical and public reception of the works of John McGahern. The letters document the input and impacts of French publishers in making work by McGahern available to the French public. As Delahaye stated, one legacy of McGahern is that he

---

32   Letter from McGahern to Delahaye, *The Collected Letters*, 513.
33   P71/1715, Transcript of Interview by Eamon Maher with John McGahern, 25 August 2002, McGahern Archive, University of Galway.

left behind 'a voice which can never be altered', and the act of a translator and the important and lasting work of Delahaye as McGahern's French translator becomes all the clearer. Delahaye became a medium and an interpreter of the words, tone, style, and vision of McGahern, creating a linguistic access point to the characters, thoughts, feelings, and places of McGahern Country.

JOHN LITTLETON

24 The Changed Reality of Being a Catholic Priest in Today's Ireland

Setting the scene

I was ordained a Catholic priest on 8 June 1986. That is nearly forty years ago, indeed probably half my lifetime. Over the decades since then, my personal reflections along with my conversations with family members, colleagues and parishioners have persuaded me that the experience of being a priest in Ireland in 2022 differs greatly from that of the 1980s and earlier times.

It is frequently said that change in the hierarchical Church happens incredibly slowly, usually occurring over centuries as the Church trundles along rather like a huge millwheel moving almost undetectably. But irrespective of the pace of change within the Church, the past half-century has witnessed a major transformation in how the institutional Church in particular – and Catholicism in general – are perceived in Ireland where the reality is that contemporary Irish society, similar to other Western democracies, is becoming increasingly secular, individualistic and materialistic.

Anecdotal testimony

One of my abiding memories is that, within a few weeks of ordination, I was asked to help with the hearing of confessions at one of the large Redemptorist novenas (nine consecutive days of prayer) in honour of Our Lady of Perpetual Help that were common at that time in various locations around the country.[1] The availability of confession (the sacrament of reconciliation) for novena attendees, which was provided by a sizeable team of confessors, was a noteworthy part of each novena session and participants were encouraged to use that opportunity to express repentance for their sins, receive God's forgiveness and renew their commitment to the principles and values of the Gospel. A recurring phrase in the standard list of novena announcements each day was: 'Confessions are being heard before, during and after each session!'[2]

What astonished me most during my first experience of hearing confessions was the large number of people who specifically asked how they should vote in the upcoming referendum on 26 June 1986 which would propose an amendment to remove the prohibition on divorce from *Bunreacht na hÉireann* (*Constitution of Ireland*). Some of them did not desire the sacrament; they simply wanted to be told how to vote. Many of them were well educated and worked in professional settings where they made important daily decisions that had serious consequences for business, finance and people. Yet when it came to deciding how to vote on an issue that had significant moral and social implications, they abdicated their responsibility as citizens in a democracy and expected the priest to tell them what to do. It was as though their faith development had ceased at the end of their secondary schooling, although their expertise and competence in other capacities had continued to develop according to their chosen career paths.

Thankfully, although inexperienced, I had sufficient common sense to refuse to tell them how to vote. I told them that they needed to vote in accordance with their conscience and that I would answer any questions about the Church's teaching on conscience, marriage and divorce, but that it would be wrong for me to tell them how to vote. Some penitents were displeased with my stance and threatened to complain about me to the

---

1   These novenas were popularly known as 'festivals of faith' because they attracted large crowds of Catholics whose faith was enlivened, encouraged and challenged in a festive atmosphere of prayer, singing and preaching – all of which were incorporated in the celebration of Mass lasting less than one hour.
2   The phrase was modified in later years to 'Confessions are being heard before and after each session' because it was recognized that hearing confessions during the celebration of Mass was not correct liturgically.

priest-in-charge. Nevertheless, I insisted that it would be improper for me to tell them how to vote.[3] Afterwards, I discovered that the other confessors on the team had much the same experience as me. This demonstrated to me that there was a perception among Catholics that priests – in addition to bishops – had the right and the duty to inform people how they should act in fundamentally important areas of life.

About thirty years later, following the 1986 unsuccessful referendum to remove the prohibition on divorce from the Constitution, my experience was that the perception of priests' rights and duties had changed completely especially in the lead-up to more recent referenda. In the 2015 'Marriage Equality' referendum, the proposal was that marriage between two people be recognized regardless of the sex of the partners.[4] Then three years later, in 2018, the 'Repeal the Eighth' referendum proposed that the 1983 Eighth Amendment to the Constitution, which had recognized the equal right to life of the mother and of her unborn child, be repealed.[5] The Catholic Church is unambiguous in its teaching on of these matters.[6]

Quite apart from the fact that there has been a vast decline in the number of Catholics going to confession in the past few decades, it is no exaggeration to state that not one person asked me how to vote in either of those referenda. Neither were any of my colleagues asked by parishioners or penitents how they should vote. In summary, comparing my first experience of hearing confessions in 1986 to the absence of any discussions with people before the 2015 and 2018 referenda provides convincing anecdotal evidence of the seismic shift in opinion that has occurred regarding the

---

[3] The proposed amendment was rejected by 63–37 per cent of the voters. In a subsequent referendum on 24 November 1995 the amendment was approved and divorce was legalized in Ireland on 17 June 1996.

[4] The referendum was on 22 May 2015 and the proposed amendment was approved by 62.07–37.93 per cent. Same-sex marriage was subsequently legalized. Ireland was the first country to introduce same-sex marriage through a popular vote.

[5] The referendum was on 25 May 2018, the proposal being approved by 66.4–33.6 per cent.

[6] See *Catechism of the Catholic Church*, nn. 1778–1794 (regarding conscience), nn. 1601–1624 (with reference to marriage) and nn. 2270–2275 (concerning abortion).

role and influence of the Catholic Church in Ireland and also in people's perceptions of priests.

Another remarkable memory from my teenage years, in the early 1970s, is that the parish priest in the town where I was reared, always dressed in a red-buttoned soutane and wearing a red-tasselled biretta, visited the Garda station every morning to enquire if there had been any incidents or disruptions around the town since the previous day. He then went to the local hotel and read the guest register to check the names of those who had stayed in the hotel overnight. Nobody thought it strange. It was simply accepted that the parish priest acted in this way. In fairness, I presume that he genuinely believed he was exercising his duty of pastoral care as the spiritual father to the parishioners.

Nevertheless, on reflection no priest could act in such a presumptuous way in 2022. Even if there were no GDPR (General Data Protection Regulation) restrictions applicable, no person without proper authorization from the appropriate statutory or civil authority could expect to gain access to privileged information. Likewise, it would be unprofessional and unacceptable to provide such information.

This reminiscence provides further anecdotal corroboration of the transformed perception of priests in Ireland. Nowadays, the priest is considered just another man in the crowd. And that is how it ought to be, unless reference is being made to the priest's unique function within the believing, worshipping, Christian community.

A changed reality

An obvious and dominant reason for the changed perception of priests is the ongoing series of revelations about sexual abuse scandals involving clergy. Understandably, the scandals have undermined people's faith in the Church as an institution and largely destroyed their trust in priests – although it must be acknowledged that most parishioners continue to hold their local priest(s) in high regard. Whereas every institution, both secular and religious, besides members of all professions have a moral and legal obligation to behave honourably and to respect the dignity of all those with whom they work and for whom they care, members of the general public correctly expect more from the Church and from clergy, and they are entitled to do so.

After all, at the heart of the Church's message is the conviction that all people are made in the image and likeness of God (Genesis 1:27) and that everyone has an innate human dignity which must be respected and cherished. What disturbed people even more than the scandals themselves was the 'cover up', lack of transparency and obfuscation by bishops and other religious superiors in dealing with them. The logical conclusion was that the Church was corrupt and that there was structural sin at its core.

I remember a pastoral visit to the home of an elderly woman sometime after the well-publicized 2018 conviction of Australian Cardinal George Pell on five counts of sexual abuse against two boys and the 2019 conviction of French Cardinal Philippe Barbarin for covering up child sexual abuse.[7] She challenged me by asking: 'How can cardinals [and priests] say Mass the next day, after behaving so shamefully and sinfully, while lay people like me do not think ourselves worthy to receive Holy Communion unless we have first been to confession? Do these men not know that they have committed grave sins as well as serious crimes?'

The only answer I could offer was that, as a priest, I too was disgusted, confused and ashamed by such evil behaviour. I could not think of a satisfactory explanation. At that moment, it seemed pointless trying to explain to her the theological nuance that the Church's membership includes both saints and sinners and that the dreadful behaviour of its sinful members often overshadows completely the good work done by its saintly members – and that, anyway, most people simultaneously exhibit a blend of saintly and sinful characteristics. The visit to the elderly woman reminded me yet again that my experience of being a priest had changed considerably since ordination in 1986. Back then I was so idealistic that I would have found it

---

7   Cardinal George Pell was convicted on 11 December 2018. Having spent 404 days in prison, his conviction was subsequently quashed on appeal to the High Court of Australia on 7 April 2020. Cardinal Philippe Barbarin was convicted in March 2019 and received a six-month suspended sentence.

unimaginable that clergy would sexually abuse children, whereas by 2020 I did not doubt this reality. What a metamorphosis!

Not surprisingly, parents and guardians no longer leave their children unsupervised in the presence of priests.[8] Similarly, for their own protection, priests are unwilling to be alone with children (e.g. Mass servers) without other suitably trained and designated adults being present. Consequently, the safeguarding of children and vulnerable adults is now a major focus in the Church's various pastoral apostolates. Sadly, the child sexual abuse scandals have caused incalculable damage and permanently affected the interactions between priests and people.

But the abuse scandals are not the sole reason for people's changed perceptions of the Church and priests. There are several other reasons why the influence of the Catholic Church in Ireland has waned and why the experience of being a priest has altered radically over the years. There is no need to rehearse them in detail because the facts are self-evident.

The Catholic Church in Ireland currently influences people's lives far less than in the past. The numerous reasons, apart from the sexual abuse scandals, can be summarized as follows: The reality is that most forms of organized religion are in decline. This is true not only within the Catholic Church and in the Irish context. It is a universal phenomenon closely associated with the emerging trend of 'believing but not belonging' which describes the experience of many people who claim to be spiritual but not religious in the sense of belonging to a recognized community. Such people are quite happy to engage with the transcendent without relying on official religious structures and rituals.

All the surveys and statistics – and, indeed, a casual glance around churches during liturgical celebrations – indicate that fewer people are practising their faith, at least in the traditional ways, and that the majority of church-goers are elderly. Mass attendance is no longer the yardstick by which people's engagement with the Church can be measured.

---

[8] Lest there be any misunderstanding that parents only worry about their children's safety with priests, their concern also applies to any unsupervised adult. It seems to me that the default position should be that parents trust nobody with their children.

Neither can it be claimed, as in the past, that being Irish is synonymous with being Catholic and vice versa.[9] At best, many people perceive the Catholic Church to be just another lobby group in society which may have some limited usefulness. At worst, an increasing number of people are deciding that the Church is irrelevant and have disengaged from it. While this might be expected in the case of teenagers and young adults, who judge much of the Church's teaching to be outdated and meaningless, it is also occurring among middle-aged and older people who have become disillusioned. In the midst of all this are priests like me who are trying to make sense of the changes that have turned much of what we had taken for granted upside down. Then there are the much fewer recently ordained priests for whom ministry in this fast-changing society is their only experience of being a priest. They may not even have been born when the Church's influence dominated so many aspects of Irish society. So how do priests cope with the upheaval that has brought about such change?

Happy in irrelevancy

Several years ago, I attended a day of prayer and reflection with about thirty other priests from around the country. During one of the discussion sessions, I was captivated by the phrase of one speaker who said: 'Priests need to learn to be happy in their irrelevance.' On reflection, this priest was astute in reading of the signs of the times and he was offering wise advice.

In previous decades, there was no shortage of priests. Actually, many priests trained in Irish seminaries went abroad after ordination because there was no place for them in Irish dioceses. Here in Ireland, priests were routinely placed on pedestals by the laity – albeit that at least some priests did

[9] I have discussed this at length elsewhere. See John Littleton, 'Catholic Identity in the Irish Context', *Irish and Catholic? Towards an Understanding of Identity*, edited by in Louise Fuller, John Littleton and Eamon Maher (Dublin: The Columba Press, 2006), 12–30.

not wish for that. The vast majority of people had tremendous respect and reverence for priests. They were in awe of them. But there were, of course, exceptions if a particular priest was bad-tempered or rude, or if a lay person had an unpleasant experience when dealing with a priest. Unfortunately, such instances usually instilled fear instead of respect. Generally, however, priests were perceived as holy men, men of prayer who had sacrificed their lives for the Kingdom of God and the service of God's people in the Church.

Priests, in addition to being spiritual leaders, were considered to be key figures in other areas of community life. Thus they were regularly appointed to the office of president of the local golf club and/or the local GAA (Gaelic Athletic Association) club. They were automatically given honorary positions on community councils in addition to their *ex officio* roles on parish committees. The outcome was that, on several evenings each week, there were meetings to be attended. At these meetings, their advice was sought on all kinds of matters and there was great deference shown to them. Parishioners were delighted to welcome priests to their homes. All of this meant that enormous trust was given to priests. I experienced that myself during the early years after my ordination.

However, over time all that began to change. Initially, the change was gradual but after a while it happened more quickly. Many commentators claim that the estrangement of the people from the Church and the formal beginning of the separation of Church and State began in the aftermath of the news media publicizing the Bishop Casey scandal in 1992.[10] Personally, I disagree with that opinion. Although the Casey / Murphy scandal contributed to the weakening of the Church's position of power and influence in Ireland, it was part of a series of happenings that was already gathering momentum. And, of course, much worse in terms of the dysfunctional behaviour of clergy was to be disclosed over the following years.

Nonetheless, I still remember clearly the day that the Casey scandal broke. At that time I was teaching theology in the seminary and I used to

10 Eamonn Casey, who in 1992 was Bishop of Galway, had previously had an affair with American woman Annie Murphy while he was Bishop of Kerry. The affair resulted in the birth of a son in 1974. To avoid any scandal for himself and the Church, Casey made secret maintenance payments and refused to develop a relationship with his son.

celebrate early morning Mass in a nearby convent. I was driving back to the seminary after Mass and listening to the 8.00 am RTÉ (Raidió Teilifís Éireann) news on the car radio. I was dumbfounded when I heard the report that Eamonn Casey had resigned as Bishop of Galway because he had previously had an affair with an American woman and had fathered a child. When I spoke to my priest colleagues in the seminary, they were as shocked as me. It certainly felt surreal teaching theology to the seminarians that morning. They were just as astonished as me on hearing the news. Consider that among the main purposes of seminary formation is the preparation of men for ordained ministry to God's people while living a celibate life.

The recommendation that priests should learn to be happy in their irrelevancy is helpful guidance. This is because priests have in many instances become redundant. Yet they need to remain convinced that they have an important and necessary role to play in the Church's mission and in the overall good of society. For the reasons already outlined – including but not confined to the sexual abuse scandals – priests have lost people's trust because it has been repeatedly violated by a small number of priests. Furthermore, many couples are choosing to get married civilly rather than have a church ceremony. There is an increase in humanist funeral ceremonies and fewer parents are having their children baptized.

Even when children receive the sacraments, most of them cease any involvement with the Church after they celebrate the sacrament of confirmation. After that, there is the possibility that, as adults, they may occasionally attend church again for baptisms, weddings, funerals and anniversary Masses. But they have no real attachment to the Church. They are effectively nonreligious and are more accurately described as cultural Catholics.

This can cause great dilemmas for priests who do their best to be pastorally sensitive in situations where those requesting their service have no adherence to any of the Church's core beliefs and who especially have no appreciation of Catholic theology's essential understanding that, despite his human imperfections, at ordination to the priesthood the man is conformed to Christ. Thereafter, whenever exercising his priestly ministry, he acts *in person Christi* (in the person of Christ) and is *alter Christus* (another Christ).

Then there is the reality that there are far fewer priests. The average age of priests is increasing and priests are expected to take on heavier workloads. Lay people are being trained to preside at burial services when priests are unavailable. What a change from the 1980s when there was an abundance of priests.

Finally, in more recent times, there is a restructuring of parishes taking place in most dioceses – again due to the shortage of priests. Parishes are being grouped in clusters, families[11] or pastoral units.[12] Such reorganization brings with it serious challenges for the priests involved as well as for parishioners. In addition, there is the current task of encouraging people to return to the celebration of Sunday Mass after the protracted COVID-19 pandemic.[13] It is no wonder that, at times, priests can think that they are being left behind and feel irrelevant. That is why they need to cultivate a sense of happiness in their irrelevancy.

Signs of hope

However, the situation is not totally pessimistic. There are positive signs of hope coming from the prophetic voices of several priests in Ireland

---

[11] See statement from Fintan Gavin, Bishop of Cork and Ross, dated 3 August 2022, in which he details how priests will minister in parishes in the future https://www.Catholicbishops.ie/2022/08/02/bishop-fintan-gavin-publishes-pastoral-letter-transforming-parishes-in-cork-ross-into-mission-centred-faith-communities/ [accessed 12 December 2023].

[12] See letter to the people of the Archdiocese of Cashel and Emly from Kieran O'Reilly SMA, Archbishop of Cashel and Emly, to be read at all Masses on weekend of 23/24 July 2022, in which he outlines a new way of bring Church in Ireland https://efaidnbmnnnibpcajpcglclefindmkaj/https://cashel-emly.ie/wp-content/uploads/2022/07/Archbishops-letter-to-people-of-Cashel-Emly.pdf [accessed 12 December 2023].

[13] This is not just a problem for the Church and for priests. Recently, I heard a representative of the Licensed Vintners Association being interviewed on radio about the challenge for publicans to get customers to return to their premises.

who are courageous enough to think outside the box in their appraisals of the institutional Church and in promoting ideas for discussion among priests. Among these are Seán Fagan SM, Tony Flannery CSsR, Brendan Hoban, Gerry O'Hanlon SJ, Vincent Twomey SVD and Willie Walsh.[14] They also offer suggestions about renewal in the Church. One does not necessarily have to agree with all of what they are writing or saying. But it does no harm to have the mind and soul challenged to look at the bigger picture in an attempt to make sense of the signs of the times and to chart a way forward for those of us for whom the reality of being a Catholic priest in Ireland has changed significantly over the past few decades.[15]

---

14 For further information and discussion see, for example, Tony Flannery, *A Question of Conscience* (Dublin: Londubh Press, 2013); *From the Outside: Rethinking Church Doctrine* (Dublin: Red Stripe Press, 2020); Gerry O'Hanlon, *A New Vision for the Catholic Church: A View from Ireland* (Dublin: The Columba Press, 2011); Angela Hanley, *What Happened to Fr Seán Fagan?* (Dublin: Columba Books, 2019); D. Vincent Twomey, *The End of Irish Catholicism?* (Dublin: Veritas Publications, 2003); and Willie Walsh, *No Crusader* (Dublin: The Columba Press, 2016).

15 This chapter was previously published as an article in *Studies*, 111/443 (Autumn 2022).

Notes on Contributors

ANDREW J. AUGE is Professor Emeritus of English at Loras College in Dubuque, Iowa. He has published essays on a number of contemporary Irish poets. His book, *A Chastened Communion: Catholicism and Modern Irish Poetry*, was published in 2013 by Syracuse University. He co-edited with Eugene O'Brien, *Contemporary Irish Poetry and the Climate Crisis* (Routledge, 2021) in which his essay, 'Reading Heaney's Bog Poem in the Anthropocene' appeared.

PAUL BUTLER is a documentary photographer who lives with his family in Farnaght, County Leitrim. Documenting the ordinary and exploring the north-west of Ireland is his passion and Paul has held various photographic exhibitions, presented papers and webinars particularly around the theme, 'sense of place'. He is a graduate of Technical Photography from Kevin Street, and he also holds a Master of Arts by Research from TU Dublin. His book, *A Deep Well of Want – Visualising the World of John McGahern* was published in July 2023 by Peter Lang. Paul works as part of the Marketing and Communications Department for The Technological University of Dublin.

BERTRAND CARDIN, Professor of Irish Literature at the *Université de Caen Normandie* (France), has published many articles and several books about contemporary Irish novelists and short-story writers: *Neil Jordan, Author and Screenwriter. The Imagination of Transgression* (Oxford: Peter Lang, 2023), *Colum McCann's Intertexts: 'Books Talk to One Another'* (Cork University Press, 2016), *Lectures d'un texte étoilé. 'Corée' de John McGahern* (Paris: L'Harmattan, 2009) and *Miroirs de la filiation. Parcours dans huit romans irlandais contemporains* (PUC, 2005). In 2014, he was the guest editor of a special issue of the *Journal of the Short Story in English* on 'The 21st Century Irish Short Story' (Presses de l'Université d'Angers, 2014). He co-edited *Ecrivaines irlandaises / Irish Women Writers* with Professor Mikowski (Presses Universitaires de Caen, 2014) and *Irlande, écritures et réécritures de la Famine* with Professor Fierobe (Presses Universitaires de Caen, 2007).

MICHAEL CRONIN is 1776 Professor of French and Director of the Centre for Literary and Cultural Translation at Trinity College Dublin. Among his published titles are *Translating Ireland: Translation, Languages and Identity* (1996); *Across the Lines: Travel, Language, Translation* (2000); *Translation and Globalization* (2003); *Irish in the New Century / An Ghaeilge san Aois Nua*; *Translation and Identity* (2006); *Translation goes to the Movies* (2009), *Translation in the Digital Age* (2013); *Eco-Translation: Translation and Ecology in the Age of the Anthropocene* (2017) and *Irish and Ecology: An Ghaeilge agus an Éiceolaíocht* (2019). He is an elected Member of the Royal Irish Academy and the Academia Europaea, an Officier in the Ordre des Palmes Académiques and a Fellow of Trinity College Dublin.

ANNE FOGARTY is Professor Emerita of James Joyce Studies at University College Dublin. She was Associate Director of the Yeats International Summer School 1995–1997 and Director of the Dublin James Joyce Summer School 2017–2023. She was editor of the *Irish University Review* 2002–2009 and is co-editor with Luca Crispi of the *Dublin James Joyce Journal*. Currently, she is the editor for the Irish Writers series for Bucknell University Press. She has co-edited several collections of essays on Joyce and recently co-edited with Marisol Morales-Ladrón, *Deirdre Madden: New Critical Perspectives* (2022) and with Tina O'Toole, *Reading Gender and Space* (2023). She has published widely on aspects of twentieth- and twenty-first-century Irish writing, especially on the Revival period and on women authors. Her new edition of *Dubliners* is forthcoming from Penguin in 2024 as is a collection co-edited with Eugene O'Brien, *The Routledge Companion to Twenty-First Century Irish Writing*.

ANNE GOARZIN is Professor of Irish Literature and Culture at the University of Rennes 2, France. Her research focuses on the intersections between literature, visual studies and twenty-first-century critical theories. She is director of GIS E.I.R.E. (*Etudes irlandaises: réseaux et enjeux*), a research network for Irish studies supported by the Irish Embassy in France and DFAT. She is Dean of Graduate Studies for Arts, Languages and Literature (ED ALL Bretagne), and she is involved in a transdisciplinary Graduate School programme on 'Creative Arts in Public Space' based in Rennes. Her recent publications include: *New Readings of Louis MacNeice*, edited by A. Goarzin and Clíona Ní Ríordain (Rennes: PUR, 2018); *New Cartographies, Nomadic Methodologies: Contemporary Arts, Culture and Politics in Ireland*, edited by A. Goarzin and Parsons Maria (London: Peter Lang, 2020); *Irish Arts: New Contexts*, edited by A. Goarzin, Morisson Valérie and Staunton Mathew; and *Etudes Irlandaises*, 45/1 (Spring 2020).

DEREK HAND is Professor and Head of the School of English at Dublin City University. The Liffey Press published his book *John Banville: Exploring Fictions* in 2002. He edited a special edition of the *Irish University Review* on John Banville in 2006. His *A History of the Irish Novel: 1665 to the present* was published by Cambridge University Press in 2011. He is also the co-editor of a collection of essays on John McGahern entitled *Essays on John McGahern: Assessing a Literary Legacy*, published by Cork University Press in 2019.

BARRY HOULIHAN is an archivist at NUI Galway and teaches Theatre History and Archives, Digital Cultures as well as working on various archive and digitization projects. His recent books include the monograph *Theatre and Archival Memory: Politics, Social Change and Modernising Ireland* (Palgrave MacMillan, 2021) and the edited collection of essays, *Navigating Ireland's Theatre Archive: Theory, Practice, Performance* (Peter Lang, 2019). He has co-curated recent touring exhibitions such as *Judging Shaw* with the Royal Irish Academy (2019), *Yeats and the West* (2015) and *A University in Wartime and Revolution: The Galway Experience* (2016). Barry is the co-editor of the SHAW journal issue *Shaw and Legacy, the Journal of Bernard Shaw Studies* (2020).

PIERRE JOANNON, Doctor of Law, historian, and one of the foremost specialists in France on the subject of Ireland, is the author of many books including *Histoire de l'Irlande et des Irlandais* (2006 and 2009), and of the only French biographies of Michael Collins and John Hume. Founder of the Ireland Fund of France, he has been Honorary Consul General of Ireland in the South of France since 1973. Awarded Honorary Doctorates by the National University of Ireland and by the University of Ulster, he received one of the first annual Presidential Distinguished Service Awards for the Irish Abroad in 2012 and was elected Member of the Royal Irish Academy in 2021.

JOHN LITTLETON is a priest of the Archdiocese of Cashel and Emly. He is Director of the Priory Institute, a Dominican centre for theological studies, in Tallaght, Dublin. He served as President of the National Conference of Priests of Ireland (NCPI) from 2001 until 2007. He has co-edited with Eamon Maher several books dealing with various aspects of Catholicism and, in particular, Irish Catholicism.

MÁIRTÍN MAC CON IOMAIRE is a senior lecturer in the School of Culinary Arts and Food Technology at Technological University Dublin. He is the co-founder and chair of the biennial Dublin Gastronomy Symposium and is a trustee of the Oxford Symposium on Food and Cookery. He is chair of the Masters in Gastronomy and Food Studies in TU Dublin, the first such programme in Ireland. He is co-editor with Eamon Maher of *'Tickling the Palate': Gastronomy in Irish Literature and Culture* (Peter Lang, 2014) and with Rhona Richman Kenneally on 'The Food Issue' of *The Canadian Journal of Irish Studies* (2018). He has published widely in peer-reviewed journals and is a regular contributor on food in the media. In 2018, he presented an eight-part television series for TG4 called *Blasta* celebrating Ireland's food heritage. Along with Michelle Share and Dorothy Cashman, he is co-editor of the new *European Journal of Food, Drink and Society*.

DR ALEXANDRA MACLENNAN is an associate professor at the University of Caen Normandy where she teaches British, Irish and South African civilization. She is half-South African but has been associated with Irish Studies for twenty-five years, since she spent two years in Trinity College Dublin as a teaching assistant. She has published books and articles on aspects of Irish cultural policy and religious history. She published *L'Etat et la culture en Irlande* (2010) prefaced by Michael D. Higgins. She is a former editor of *Etudes irlandaises* (2011–2017) and was commissioned to write *an Histoire de l'Irlande de 1912 à nos jours* (*2016, 2021*). She is now writing the first biography of Cardinal Owen McCann. She defended her Habilitation à Diriger des Recherches (HDR) in September 2023, and was awarded two research fellowships in 2023–2024: Chercheur Résident at the Ecole Française de Rome (October–December 2023) and Research Fellowship at the Arts and Humanities Institute, Maynooth (Spring 2004). She is also vice-president of the SOFEIR for international affairs, and the French delegate to EFACIS.

CATHERINE MAIGNANT is Professor of Irish Studies at the University of Lille (France) where she was the head of a research group in Irish Studies for over 20 years. She was President of the French Association of Irish Studies (SOFEIR) and of the European Federation of Associations and Centres of Irish Studies (EFACIS) for a number of years. After writing a PhD on early medieval Irish Christianity, she now specializes in contemporary Irish religious history. Her research interests include the New Religious Movement, the response of the Catholic Church to secularization, interreligious dialogue, Celtic Christianity and the religious aspects of globalization. She has widely published in all these areas.

PATRICIA MEDCALF is a senior lecturer in Advertising and Marketing at TU Dublin. In 2018, she completed her PhD thesis under the supervision of NCFIS President, Dr Eamon Maher. Her research analysed five decades of Guinness advertising in Ireland and explored the extent to which it responded to or initiated social and cultural change between 1959 and 2010. In 2020, she published *Advertising the Black Stuff in Ireland 1959–1999: Increments of Change*, volume 95 in the Reimagining Ireland series. Other recent publications in this area include a chapter on Irish cultural heritage through the prism of Guinness's ads in the 1980s in *Patriomoine / Cultural Heritage in France and Ireland* (2019); a piece on advertising in *Recalling the Celtic Tiger* (2019); and a chapter on sport and national and brand identities in *Voyage between France and Ireland* (2017). In 2004, her textbook *Marketing Communications: An Irish Perspective* was published. Before joining TU Dublin, she was Project Director with branding specialists The Identity Business (renamed Brand Union) and Marketing Consultant with Siemens.

VICTOR MERRIMAN is Professor of Critical Studies in Drama at Edge Hill University, and author of *Because We Are Poor: Irish Theatre in the 1990s* (2011) and *Austerity and the Public Role of Drama: performing lives-in-common* (2019). He has edited four special issues of the journal, *Kritika Kultura* and publishes and lectures regularly on public policy, Irish theatre and postcolonial critical thought. A co-founder of One Hour Theatre Company (2016), his most recent directing credits include David Lloyd's *The Pact* (Rose Theatre Studio, Edge Hill University, July 2023) *Lear in Brexitland* by Tim Prentki (Shakespeare North Playhouse Studio, 2023), and *Bartleby the Scrivener*, by Tom Hall (WoWFest online, 2021). He was appointed a member of An Chomhairle Ealaíon (1993–1998) by Michael D Higgins, then Minister for Arts, Culture, and the Gaeltacht, and has served on the boards of Liverpool Irish Festival and the British Association of Irish Studies.

SYLVIE MIKOWSKI is Professor of Irish and English Studies at the University of Reims-Champagne-Ardenne (France). Her main interests are the contemporary Irish novel and popular culture. She completed her PhD on the novels of John McGahern in 1995, and defended her *habilitation* dissertation in 2003 on 'The Invention of a Tradition in the Irish contemporary Novel'. Her main publications include *Le Roman irlandais Contemporain*; *The Book in Ireland*; *Memory and History in France and Ireland*; *Irish Women Writers*; *Ireland and Popular Culture*; *Popular Culture Today* and *The Circulation of Popular Culture between Ireland and the USA*. She has also published numerous book chapters and articles on various contemporary Irish writers, such as John McGahern, William Trevor, Colum McCann, Patrick McCabe, Roddy Doyle, Deirdre Madden, and Sebastian Barry. She served as literary editor of the French journal of Irish Studies, *Etudes irlandaises*, and is currently President of the SOFEIR, the French Society of Irish Studies, as well as President of the steering committee of GIS E.I.R.E., a scientific grouping of universities. She is also review editor for *RISE (Review of Irish Studies in Europe)*.

MARISOL MORALES-LADRÓN is full Professor of English and Irish Literature at the University of Alcalá where she has been teaching since 1994. She holds degrees in English, Spanish and Psychology, and her research focuses on contemporary Irish literature, gender studies and cultural memory. Her publications include the books *Breve introducción a la literatura comparada* (1999) and *Las poéticas de James Joyce y Luis Martín-Santos* (2005). She has edited the monographs *Postcolonial and Gender Perspectives in Irish Studies* (2007), *Family and Dysfunction in Contemporary Irish Narrative and Film* (2016) and has co-edited *Glocal Ireland: Current Perspectives on Literature and the Visual Art* (2011), as well as two studies on feminist criticism. Her most recent publication is *Deirdre Madden: New Critical Perspectives* (2022), co-edited with Anne Fogarty. She is currently Head of the EFACIS research Centre for Irish Studies 'Alka-Éire', based at the University of Alcalá.

BRIAN MURPHY is a Senior Lecturer in the School of Culinary Arts and Food Technology at the Technological University Dublin (TU Dublin) where he lectures on food and drink studies. He has a particular interest in gastronomic research and is keen to explore the role that place and story play in perceptions of food and drink. He has published a number of articles in this and related areas. A co-founder of the Dublin Gastronomy Symposium, he is also an active member of the National Centre for Franco-Irish Studies, which is also based in TU Dublin. In recent years, he has sought to expand the Centre's research remit to include strong elements of gastronomic culture.

GRACE NEVILLE is a graduate of University College Cork (BA in French and Irish), Caen (maîtrise) and Lille (DEA / Diplôme d'Etudes Approfondies and Doctorate). She is an emeritus Professor of French at UCC where she was also Vice-President for Teaching and Learning (2008–2012). Since retiring from UCC in 2012, she has been a member of numerous committees on aspects of French higher education reform at the ANR / Agence National de la Recherche, the French Ministry of Education, the Sorbonne, the HCERES and the CRI in Paris, as well as in the universities of Aix-Marseille, Rennes, Cergy-Pontoise, Ljubljana and the European Commission. Her research focuses especially on

Franco-Irish links from medieval to modern times. She holds the Palmes Académiques and the Légion d'honneur.

SARAH NOLAN is the current President of AFIS (Association of Franco-Irish Studies) and programme chair in the Department of Humanities and Arts Management in IADT (Institute of Art, Design and Technology, Dun Laoghaire) where she lectures on Urban, American, and Contemporary Anglophone and Irish Literature. She was awarded a research fellowship at the National Centre for Franco-Irish Studies in TU Dublin, where she completed a doctoral thesis which analysed interconnections between the works of several city poets including Charles Baudelaire, Fernando Pessoa, T. S. Eliot and contemporary Irish poet Peter Sirr. A particular focus was on the role of woman or other within the city space. Sarah has published a number of chapters on these and other poets, including Paula Meehan and Doireann Ní Ghríofa, and has co-edited a collection, *Sounding the Margins*, in the *Studies in Franco-Irish Relations* series.

EUGENE O'BRIEN is Professor of English Literature and Theory, and Head of the Department of English Language and Literature in Mary Immaculate College, University of Limerick, and is also the Director of the Mary Immaculate Institute for Irish Studies. He is the editor for the *Oxford University Press Online Bibliography* project in literary theory, and of the *Routledge Studies in Irish Literature* series. His more recent books include *Seamus Heaney as Aesthetic Thinker* (Syracuse University Press); *The Soul Exceeds its Circumstances*: *The Later Poetry of Seamus Heaney* (Notre Dame University Press); *Recalling the Celtic Tiger*, with Eamon Maher and Brian Lucey (Peter Lang) and *Representations of Loss in Irish Literature*, with Deirdre Flynn (Palgrave). His latest book, *Reading Paul Howard*: *The Art of Ross O'Carroll-Kelly*, is published by Routledge in 2023, and he is co-editing a book entitled *The Frontier of Writing*: *A Study of Seamus Heaney's Prose*, with Ian Hickey, to be published by Routledge in 2024. He is currently working on a monograph entitled *Reading Michael O'Siadhail*: *The Gift of Tongues* (Routledge) and *A Companion to 21st Century Irish Writing*, with Anne Fogarty (Routledge).

MARÍA ELENA JAIME DE PABLOS is a Senior Lecturer at the University of Almería, Spain, where she teaches English Literature. Her major research interest is Irish literature, with a special focus on women writers and gender issues, and literary translation. She is the author of nearly sixty essays (articles and book chapters) and the author, editor or co-editor of nineteen books published by prestigious national and international presses. Among the most recent ones: Giving Shape to the Moment: The Art of Mary O'Donnell, Poet, Novelist and Short-Story Writer (Oxford: Peter Lang, 2018), Mujeres, feminismo y género en el siglo XXI (Sevilla: Arcibel Editores, 2018), Remaking the Literary Canon in English: Women Writers, 1880–1920 (Granada: Comares, 2018). She is currently the Associate Editor of Raudem, Revista de Estudios de las Mujeres, an online journal on Women's Studies, the manager of the research group: 'Women, Literature and Society' ('Women, Literature and Society') and the Secretary of the Communication and Society Research Centre (CySOC) based at the University of Almería.

MARY PIERSE has taught a range of English literature modules at University College, Cork, where she also gave courses on Irish feminisms for the MA programme in Women's studies. Instigator of the George Moore international conference series, she has edited and co-edited several volumes on Moore's works, including *George Moore: Artistic Visions and Literary Worlds* (2006). She has published on the writings of Kate Chopin, Antonio Fogazzaro, Katherine Cecil Thurston, and of contemporary Irish poets Dennis O'Driscoll and Cathal Ó Searcaigh. She edited and compiled the five-volume collection, *Irish Feminisms 1810–1930* (Routledge, 2010). Her ongoing research focuses on the often-intersecting topics of Moore's writings, on Franco-Irish artistic connections in visual art and music, and on Irish women writers at the *fin-de-siècle* period. A board member at the National Centre for Franco-Irish Studies, she also serves on editorial boards / scientific committees for publications in France and Spain.

PILAR VILLAR-ARGÁIZ is a Senior Lecturer of British and Irish Literatures in the Department of English and the Director of the Circle of Irish Studies at the University of Granada. She is the author of the books *Eavan Boland's Evolution as an Irish Woman Poet: An Outsider within an Outsider's Culture* (Edwin Mellen Press, 2007) and *The Poetry of Eavan Boland: A Postcolonial Reading* (Academica Press, 2008), and has been for a period of 8 years the General Editor of the major series 'Studies in Irish Literature, Cinema and Culture' in Edward Everett Root Publishers. Villar-Argáiz has published extensively on contemporary Irish poetry and fiction, in relation to questions of gender, race, migration and interculturality. Her edited collections include *Literary Visions of Multicultural Ireland: The Immigrant in Contemporary Irish Literature* (Manchester University Press, 2014), *Irishness on the Margins: Minority and Dissident Identities* (Palgrave Macmillan, 2018), *Secrecy and Community in 21st-Century Fiction* (Bloomsbury, 2021), the special issue of *Irish Studies Review* (entitled 'Irish Multiculturalism in Crisis', co-edited with Jason King, 2015), and the special issue of *Nordic Irish Studies* (entitled 'Discourses of Inclusion and Exclusion: Artistic Renderings of Marginal Identities in Ireland', 2016). Villar-Argáiz is currently the Chairperson of AEDEI (the Spanish Association for Irish Studies) and Member of the Executive Board of EFACIS (the European Federation of Associations and Centres of Irish Studies).

EAMONN WALL is a professor of Global Studies and English at the University of Missouri-St. Louis. A past-president of the American Conference for Irish Studies, he is also the author of *From Oven Lane to Sun Prairie: In Search of Irish America* (Arlen House, 2019); *Writing the Irish West: Ecologies and Traditions* (Notre Dame 2011) and *From the Sin-e Cafe to the Black Hills: Notes on the New Irish* (Wisconsin 2000), as well as many essays, articles, and reviews. His most recent collection of poetry is *Junction City: New and Selected Poems 1990–2015* (Salmon Poetry, 2015). A native of Co. Wexford, he has lived in the US since 1982.

HARRY WHITE is Professor of Music at University College Dublin and a Fellow of the Royal Irish Academy of Music. His recent publications include *Music, Migration and European Culture*, co-edited with Ivano Cavallini and Jolanta Guzy-Pasiak (Zagreb: Croatian Musicological Society, 2020) and *The Musical Discourse of Servitude* (New York: Oxford University Press, 2020). His current research is concerned with the conceptual prowess of the musical work in Irish cultural history, and with representations of privacy in early eighteenth-century music. He was elected to the Royal Irish Academy in 2006 and to the Croatian Academy of Sciences and Arts in 2018.

Reimagining Ireland

Series Editor: Dr Eamon Maher, Technological University Dublin

The concepts of Ireland and 'Irishness' are in constant flux in the wake of an ever-increasing reappraisal of the notion of cultural and national specificity in a world assailed from all angles by the forces of globalisation and uniformity. Reimagining Ireland interrogates Ireland's past and present and suggests possibilities for the future by looking at Ireland's literature, culture and history and subjecting them to the most up-to-date critical appraisals associated with sociology, literary theory, historiography, political science and theology.

Some of the pertinent issues include, but are not confined to, Irish writing in English and Irish, Nationalism, Unionism, the Northern 'Troubles', the Peace Process, economic development in Ireland, the impact and decline of the Celtic Tiger, Irish spirituality, the rise and fall of organised religion, the visual arts, popular cultures, sport, Irish music and dance, emigration and the Irish diaspora, immigration and multiculturalism, marginalisation, globalisation, modernity/postmodernity and postcolonialism. The series publishes monographs, comparative studies, interdisciplinary projects, conference proceedings and edited books. Proposals should be sent either to Dr Eamon Maher at eamon.maher@ittdublin.ie or to ireland@peterlang.com.

Vol. 1   Eugene O'Brien: 'Kicking Bishop Brennan up the Arse': Negotiating Texts and Contexts in Contemporary Irish Studies
ISBN 978-3-03911-539-6. 219 pages. 2009.

Vol. 2   James P.Byrne, Padraig Kirwan and Michael O'Sullivan (eds): Affecting Irishness: Negotiating Cultural Identity Within and Beyond the Nation
ISBN 978-3-03911-830-4. 334 pages. 2009.

Vol. 3   Irene Lucchitti: The Islandman: The Hidden Life of Tomás O'Crohan
ISBN 978-3-03911-837-3. 232 pages. 2009.

Vol. 4   Paddy Lyons and Alison O'Malley-Younger (eds): No Country for Old Men: Fresh Perspectives on Irish Literature
ISBN 978-3-03911-841-0. 289 pages. 2009.

Vol. 5   Eamon Maher (ed.): Cultural Perspectives on Globalisation and Ireland
ISBN 978-3-03911-851-9. 256 pages. 2009.

Vol. 6   Lynn Brunet: 'A Course of Severe and Arduous Trials': Bacon, Beckett and Spurious Freemasonry in Early Twentieth-Century Ireland
ISBN 978-3-03911-854-0. 218 pages. 2009.

Vol. 7   Claire Lynch: Irish Autobiography: Stories of Self in the Narrative of a Nation
ISBN 978-3-03911-856-4. 234 pages. 2009.

Vol. 8   Victoria O'Brien: A History of Irish Ballet from 1927 to 1963
ISBN 978-3-03911-873-1. 208 pages. 2011.

Vol. 9   Irene Gilsenan Nordin and Elin Holmsten (eds): Liminal Borderlands in Irish Literature and Culture
ISBN 978-3-03911-859-5. 208 pages. 2009.

Vol. 10   Claire Nally: Envisioning Ireland: W. B. Yeats's Occult Nationalism
ISBN 978-3-03911-882-3. 320 pages. 2010.

Vol. 11   Raita Merivirta: The Gun and Irish Politics: Examining National History in Neil Jordan's *Michael Collins*
ISBN 978-3-03911-888-5. 202 pages. 2009.

Vol. 12   John Strachan and Alison O'Malley-Younger (eds): Ireland: Revolution and Evolution
ISBN 978-3-03911-881-6. 248 pages. 2010.

Vol. 13   Barbara Hughes: Between Literature and History: The Diaries and Memoirs of Mary Leadbeater and Dorothea Herbert
ISBN 978-3-03911-889-2. 255 pages. 2010.

Vol. 14   Edwina Keown and Carol Taaffe (eds): Irish Modernism: Origins, Contexts, Publics
ISBN 978-3-03911-894-6. 256 pages. 2010.

Vol. 15   John Walsh: Contests and Contexts: The Irish Language and Ireland's Socio-Economic Development
ISBN 978-3-03911-914-1. 492 pages. 2011.

Vol. 16   Zélie Asava: The Black Irish Onscreen: Representing Black and Mixed-Race Identities on Irish Film and Television
ISBN 978-3-0343-0839-7. 213 pages. 2013.

Vol. 17   Susan Cahill and Eóin Flannery (eds): This Side of Brightness: Essays on the Fiction of Colum McCann
ISBN 978-3-03911-935-6. 189 pages. 2012.

Vol. 18   Brian Arkins: The Thought of W. B. Yeats
ISBN 978-3-03911-939-4. 204 pages. 2010.

Vol. 19   Maureen O'Connor: The Female and the Species: The Animal in Irish Women's Writing
ISBN 978-3-03911-959-2. 203 pages. 2010.

Vol. 20   Rhona Trench: Bloody Living: The Loss of Selfhood in the Plays of Marina Carr
ISBN 978-3-03911-964-6. 327 pages. 2010.

Vol. 21   Jeannine Woods: Visions of Empire and Other Imaginings: Cinema, Ireland and India, 1910–1962
ISBN 978-3-03911-974-5. 230 pages. 2011.

Vol. 22   Neil O'Boyle: New Vocabularies, Old Ideas: Culture, Irishness and the Advertising Industry
ISBN 978-3-03911-978-3. 233 pages. 2011.

Vol. 23   Dermot McCarthy: John McGahern and the Art of Memory
ISBN 978-3-0343-0100-8. 344 pages. 2010.

Vol. 24   Francesca Benatti, Sean Ryder and Justin Tonra (eds): Thomas Moore: Texts, Contexts, Hypertexts
ISBN 978-3-0343-0900-4. 220 pages. 2013.

Vol. 25   Sarah O'Connor: No Man's Land: Irish Women and the Cultural Present
ISBN 978-3-0343-0111-4. 230 pages. 2011.

Vol. 26   Caroline Magennis: Sons of Ulster: Masculinities in the Contemporary Northern Irish Novel
ISBN 978-3-0343-0110-7. 192 pages. 2010.

Vol. 27   Dawn Duncan: Irish Myth, Lore and Legend on Film
           ISBN 978-3-0343-0140-4. 181 pages. 2013.

Vol. 28   Eamon Maher and Catherine Maignant (eds): Franco-Irish
           Connections in Space and Time: Peregrinations and Ruminations
           ISBN 978-3-0343-0870-0. 295 pages. 2012.

Vol. 29   Holly Maples: Culture War: Conflict, Commemoration and the
           Contemporary Abbey Theatre
           ISBN 978-3-0343-0137-4. 294 pages. 2011.

Vol. 30   Maureen O'Connor (ed.): Back to the Future of Irish
           Studies: Festschrift for Tadhg Foley
           ISBN 978-3-0343-0141-1. 359 pages. 2010.

Vol. 31   Eva Urban: Community Politics and the Peace Process in
           Contemporary Northern Irish Drama
           ISBN 978-3-0343-0143-5. 303 pages. 2011.

Vol. 32   Mairéad Conneely: Between Two Shores/*Idir Dhá Chladach*: Writing
           the Aran Islands, 1890–1980
           ISBN 978-3-0343-0144-2. 299 pages. 2011.

Vol. 33   Gerald Morgan and Gavin Hughes (eds): Southern Ireland and the
           Liberation of France: New Perspectives
           ISBN 978-3-0343-0190-9. 250 pages. 2011.

Vol. 34   Anne MacCarthy: Definitions of Irishness in the 'Library of
           Ireland' Literary Anthologies
           ISBN 978-3-0343-0194-7. 271 pages. 2012.

Vol. 35   Irene Lucchitti: Peig Sayers: In Her Own Write
           ISBN 978-3-0343-0253-1. Forthcoming.

Vol. 36   Eamon Maher and Eugene O'Brien (eds): Breaking the
           Mould: Literary Representations of Irish Catholicism
           ISBN 978-3-0343-0232-6. 249 pages. 2011.

Vol. 37   Mícheál Ó hAodha and John O'Callaghan (eds): Narratives of the
           Occluded Irish Diaspora: Subversive Voices
           ISBN 978-3-0343-0248-7. 227 pages. 2012.

Vol. 38	Willy Maley and Alison O'Malley-Younger (eds): Celtic Connections: Irish–Scottish Relations and the Politics of Culture ISBN 978-3-0343-0214-2. 247 pages. 2013.
Vol. 39	Sabine Egger and John McDonagh (eds): Polish–Irish Encounters in the Old and New Europe ISBN 978-3-0343-0253-1. 322 pages. 2011.
Vol. 40	Elke D'hoker, Raphaël Ingelbien and Hedwig Schwall (eds): Irish Women Writers: New Critical Perspectives ISBN 978-3-0343-0249-4. 318 pages. 2011.
Vol. 41	Peter James Harris: From Stage to Page: Critical Reception of Irish Plays in the London Theatre, 1925–1996 ISBN 978-3-0343-0266-1. 311 pages. 2011.
Vol. 42	Hedda Friberg-Harnesk, Gerald Porter and Joakim Wrethed (eds): Beyond Ireland: Encounters Across Cultures ISBN 978-3-0343-0270-8. 342 pages. 2011.
Vol. 43	Irene Gilsenan Nordin and Carmen Zamorano Llena (eds): Urban and Rural Landscapes in Modern Ireland: Language, Literature and Culture ISBN 978-3-0343-0279-1. 238 pages. 2012.
Vol. 44	Kathleen Costello-Sullivan: Mother/Country: Politics of the Personal in the Fiction of Colm Tóibín ISBN 978-3-0343-0753-6. 247 pages. 2012.
Vol. 45	Lesley Lelourec and Gráinne O'Keeffe-Vigneron (eds): Ireland and Victims: Confronting the Past, Forging the Future ISBN 978-3-0343-0792-5. 331 pages. 2012.
Vol. 46	Gerald Dawe, Darryl Jones and Nora Pelizzari (eds): Beautiful Strangers: Ireland and the World of the 1950s ISBN 978-3-0343-0801-4. 207 pages. 2013.
	:ffe and Claudia Reese (eds): New Voices, Inherited y and Cultural Representations of the Irish Family 343-0799-4. 238 pages. 2013.

Vol. 48   Justin Carville (ed.): Visualizing Dublin: Visual Culture, Modernity and the Representation of Urban Space
ISBN 978-3-0343-0802-1. 326 pages. 2014.

Vol. 49   Gerald Power and Ondřej Pilný (eds): Ireland and the Czech Lands: Contacts and Comparisons in History and Culture
ISBN 978-3-0343-1701-6. 243 pages. 2014.

Vol. 50   Eoghan Smith: John Banville: Art and Authenticity
ISBN 978-3-0343-0852-6. 199 pages. 2014.

Vol. 51   María Elena Jaime de Pablos and Mary Pierse (eds): George Moore and the Quirks of Human Nature
ISBN 978-3-0343-1752-8. 283 pages. 2014.

Vol. 52   Aidan O'Malley and Eve Patten (eds): Ireland, West to East: Irish Cultural Connections with Central and Eastern Europe
ISBN 978-3-0343-0913-4. 307 pages. 2014.

Vol. 53   Ruben Moi, Brynhildur Boyce and Charles I. Armstrong (eds): The Crossings of Art in Ireland
ISBN 978-3-0343-0983-7. 319 pages. 2014.

Vol. 54   Sylvie Mikowski (ed.): Ireland and Popular Culture
ISBN 978-3-0343-1717-7. 257 pages. 2014.

Vol. 55   Benjamin Keatinge and Mary Pierse (eds): France and Ireland in the Public Imagination
ISBN 978-3-0343-1747-4. 279 pages. 2014.

Vol. 56   Raymond Mullen, Adam Bargroff and Jennifer Mullen (eds): John McGahern: Critical Essays
ISBN 978-3-0343-1755-9. 253 pages. 2014.

Vol. 57   Máirtín Mac Con Iomaire and Eamon Maher (eds): 'Tickling the Palate': Gastronomy in Irish Literature and Culture
ISBN 978-3-0343-1769-6. 253 pages. 2014.

Vol. 58   Heidi Hansson and James H. Murphy (eds): Fictions of the Irish Land War
ISBN 978-3-0343-0999-8. 237 pages. 2014.

Vol. 59　Fiona McCann: A Poetics of Dissensus: Confronting Violence in Contemporary Prose Writing from the North of Ireland
ISBN 978-3-0343-0979-0. 238 pages. 2014.

Vol. 60　Marguérite Corporaal, Christopher Cusack, Lindsay Janssen and Ruud van den Beuken (eds): Global Legacies of the Great Irish Famine: Transnational and Interdisciplinary Perspectives
ISBN 978-3-0343-0903-5. 357 pages. 2014.

Vol. 61　Katarzyna Ojrzyn'ska: 'Dancing As If Language No Longer Existed': Dance in Contemporary Irish Drama
ISBN 978-3-0343-1813-6. 318 pages. 2015.

Vol. 62　Whitney Standlee: 'Power to Observe': Irish Women Novelists in Britain, 1890–1916
ISBN 978-3-0343-1837-2. 288 pages. 2015.

Vol. 63　Elke D'hoker and Stephanie Eggermont (eds): The Irish Short Story: Traditions and Trends
ISBN 978-3-0343-1753-5. 330 pages. 2015.

Vol. 64　Radvan Markus: Echoes of the Rebellion: The Year 1798 in Twentieth-Century Irish Fiction and Drama
ISBN 978-3-0343-1832-7. 248 pages. 2015.

Vol. 65　B. Mairéad Pratschke: Visions of Ireland: Gael Linn's *Amharc Éireann* Film Series, 1956–1964
ISBN 978-3-0343-1872-3. 301 pages. 2015.

Vol. 66　Una Hunt and Mary Pierse (eds): France and Ireland: Notes and Narratives
ISBN 978-3-0343-1914-0. 272 pages. 2015.

Vol. 67　John Lynch and Katherina Dodou (eds): The Leaving of Ireland: Migration and Belonging in Irish Literature and Film
ISBN 978-3-0343-1896-9. 313 pages. 2015.

Vol. 68　Anne Goarzin (ed.): New Critical Perspectives on Franco-Irish Relations
ISBN 978-3-0343-1781-8. 271 pages. 2015.

Vol. 69   Michel Brunet, Fabienne Gaspari and Mary Pierse (eds): George Moore's Paris and His Ongoing French Connections
ISBN 978-3-0343-1973-7. 279 pages. 2015.

Vol. 70   Carine Berbéri and Martine Pelletier (eds): Ireland: Authority and Crisis
ISBN 978-3-0343-1939-3. 296 pages. 2015.

Vol. 71   David Doolin: Transnational Revolutionaries: The Fenian Invasion of Canada, 1866
ISBN 978-3-0343-1922-5. 348 pages. 2016.

Vol. 72   Terry Phillips: Irish Literature and the First World War: Culture, Identity and Memory
ISBN 978-3-0343-1969-0. 297 pages. 2015.

Vol. 73   Carmen Zamorano Llena and Billy Gray (eds): Authority and Wisdom in the New Ireland: Studies in Literature and Culture
ISBN 978-3-0343-1833-4. 263 pages. 2016.

Vol. 74   Flore Coulouma (ed.): New Perspectives on Irish TV Series: Identity and Nostalgia on the Small Screen
ISBN 978-3-0343-1977-5. 222 pages. 2016.

Vol. 75   Fergal Lenehan: Stereotypes, Ideology and Foreign Correspondents: German Media Representations of Ireland, 1946–2010
ISBN 978-3-0343-2222-5. 306 pages. 2016.

Vol. 76   Jarlath Killeen and Valeria Cavalli (eds): 'Inspiring a Mysterious Terror': 200 Years of Joseph Sheridan Le Fanu
ISBN 978-3-0343-2223-2. 260 pages. 2016.

Vol. 77   Anne Karhio: 'Slight Return': Paul Muldoon's Poetics of Place
ISBN 978-3-0343-1986-7. 272 pages. 2017.

Vol. 78   Margaret Eaton: Frank Confessions: Performance in the Life-Writings of Frank McCourt
ISBN 978-1-906165-61-1. 294 pages. 2017.

Vol. 79　Marguérite Corporaal, Christopher Cusack and Ruud van den Beuken (eds): Irish Studies and the Dynamics of Memory: Transitions and Transformations
ISBN 978-3-0343-2236-2. 360 pages. 2017.

Vol. 80　Conor Caldwell and Eamon Byers (eds): New Crops, Old Fields: Reimagining Irish Folklore
ISBN 978-3-0343-1912-6. 200 pages. 2017.

Vol. 81　Sinéad Wall: Irish Diasporic Narratives in Argentina: A Reconsideration of Home, Identity and Belonging
ISBN 978-1-906165-66-6. 282 pages. 2017.

Vol. 82　Ute Anna Mittermaier: Images of Spain in Irish Literature, 1922–1975
ISBN 978-3-0343-1993-5. 386 pages. 2017.

Vol. 83　Lauren Clark: Consuming Irish Children: Advertising and the Art of Independence, 1860–1921
ISBN 978-3-0343-1989-8. 288 pages. 2017.

Vol. 84　Lisa FitzGerald: Re-Place: Irish Theatre Environments
ISBN 978-1-78707-359-3. 222 pages. 2017.

Vol. 85　Joseph Greenwood: 'Hear My Song': Irish Theatre and Popular Song in the 1950s and 1960s
ISBN 978-3-0343-1915-7. 320 pages. 2017.

Vol. 86　Nils Beese: Writing Slums: Dublin, Dirt and Literature
ISBN 978-1-78707-959-5. 250 pages. 2018.

Vol. 87　Barry Houlihan (ed.): Navigating Ireland's Theatre Archive: Theory, Practice, Performance
ISBN 978-1-78707-372-2. 306 pages. 2019.

Vol. 88　María Elena Jaime de Pablos (ed.): Giving Shape to the Moment: The Art of Mary O'Donnell: Poet, Novelist and Short Story Writer
ISBN 978-1-78874-403-4. 228 pages. 2018.

Vol. 89　　Marguérite Corporaal and Peter Gray (eds): The Great Irish Famine and Social Class: Conflicts, Responsibilities, Representations
ISBN 978-1-78874-166-8. 330 pages. 2019.

Vol. 90　　Patrick Speight: Irish-Argentine Identity in an Age of Political Challenge and Change, 1875–1983
ISBN 978-1-78874-417-1. 360 pages. 2020.

Vol. 91　　Fionna Barber, Heidi Hansson, and Sara Dybris McQuaid (eds): Ireland and the North
ISBN 978-1-78874-289-4. 338 pages. 2019.

Vol. 92　　Ruth Sheehy: The Life and Work of Richard King: Religion, Nationalism and Modernism
ISBN 978-1-78707-246-6. 482 pages. 2019.

Vol. 93　　Brian Lucey, Eamon Maher and Eugene O'Brien (eds): Recalling the Celtic Tiger
ISBN 978-1-78997-286-3. 386 pages. 2019.

Vol. 94　　Melania Terrazas Gallego (ed.): Trauma and Identity in Contemporary Irish Culture
ISBN 978-1-78997-557-4. 302 pages. 2020.

Vol. 95　　Patricia Medcalf: Advertising the Black Stuff in Ireland 1959–1999: Increments of Change
ISBN 978-1-78997-345-7. 218 pages. 2020.

Vol. 96　　Anne Goarzin and Maria Parsons (eds): New Cartographies, Nomadic Methologies: Contemporary Arts, Culture and Politics in Ireland
ISBN 978-1-78874-651-9. 204 pages. 2020.

Vol. 97　　Hiroko Ikeda and Kazuo Yokouchi (eds): Irish Literature in the British Context and Beyond: New Perspectives from Kyoto
ISBN 978-1-78997-566-6. 250 pages. 2020.

Vol. 98　　Catherine Nealy Judd: Travel Narratives of the Irish Famine: Politics, Tourism, and Scandal, 1845–1853
ISBN 978-1-80079-084-1. 468 pages. 2020.

Vol. 99 Lesley Lelourec and Gráinne O'Keeffe-Vigneron (eds): Northern Ireland after the Good Friday Agreement: Building a Shared Future from a Troubled Past?
ISBN 978-1-78997-746-2. 262 pages. 2021.

Vol. 100 Eamon Maher and Eugene O'Brien (eds): Reimagining Irish Studies for the Twenty-First Century
ISBN 978-1-80079-191-6. 384 pages. 2021.

Vol. 101 Nathalie Sebbane: Memorialising the Magdalene Laundries: From Story to History
ISBN 978-1-78707-589-4. 334 pages. 2021.

Vol. 102 Roz Goldie: A Dangerous Pursuit: The Anti-Sectarian Work of Counteract
ISBN 978-1-80079-187-9. 268 pages. 2021.

Vol. 103 Ann Wilson: The Picture Postcard: A New Window into Edwardian Ireland
ISBN 978-1-78874-079-1. 282 pages. 2021.

Vol. 104 Anna Charczun: Irish Lesbian Writing Across Time: A New Framework for Rethinking Love Between Women
ISBN 978-1-78997-864-3. 320 pages. 2022.

Vol. 105 Olivier Coquelin, Brigitte Bastiat and Frank Healy (eds): Northern Ireland: Challenges of Peace and Reconciliation Since the Good Friday Agreement
ISBN 978-1-78997-817-9. 298 pages. 2022.

Vol. 106 Jo Murphy-Lawless and Laury Oaks (eds): The Salley Gardens: Women, Sex, and Motherhood in Ireland
ISBN 978-1-80079-417-7. 338 pages. 2022.

Vol. 107 Mercedes del Campo: Voices from the Margins: Gender and the Everyday in Women's Pre- and Post-Agreement Troubles Short Fiction
ISBN 978-1-78874-330-3. 324 pages. 2022.

Vol. 108 Sean McGraw and Jonathan Tiernan: The Politics of Irish Primary Education: Reform in an Era of Secularisation
ISBN 978-1-80079-709-3. 532 pages. 2022.

Vol. 109   Gerald Dawe: Northern Windows/Southern Stars: Selected Early
          Essays 1983–1994
          ISBN 978-1-80079-652-2. 180 pages. 2022.

Vol. 110   John Fanning: The Mandarin, the Musician and the Mage:
          T. K. Whitaker, Seán Ó Riada, Thomas Kinsella and the Lessons of
          Ireland's Mid-Twentieth-Century Revival
          ISBN 978-1-80079-599-0. 296 pages. 2022.

Vol. 111   Gerald Dawe: Dreaming of Home: Seven Irish Writers
          ISBN 978-1-80079-655-3. 108 pages. 2022.

Vol. 112   John Walsh: One Hundred Years of Irish Language Policy, 1922–2022
          ISBN 978-1-78997-892-6. 394 pages. 2022.

Vol. 113   Bertrand Cardin: Neil Jordan, Author and Screenwriter: The
          Imagination of Transgression
          ISBN 978-1-80079-923-3. XXX pages. 2023.

Vol. 114   David Clark: Dark Green: Irish Crime Fiction 1665–2000
          ISBN 978-1-80079-826-7. 450 pages. 2022.

Vol. 115   Aida Rosende-Pérez and Rubén Jarazo-Álvarez (eds): The Cultural
          Politics of In/Difference: Irish Texts and Contexts
          ISBN 978-1-80079-727-7. 274 pages. 2022.

Vol. 116   Tara McConnell: "Honest Claret": The Social Meaning of Georgian
          Ireland's Favourite Wine
          ISBN 978-1-80079-790-1. 346 pages. 2022.

Vol. 117   M. Teresa Caneda-Cabrera (ed.): Telling Truths: Evelyn Conlon and
          the Task of Writing
          ISBN 978-1-80079-481-8. 228 pages. 2023.

Vol. 118   Alexandra Maclennan (ed.): The Irish Catholic Diaspora: Five
          Centuries of Global Presence
          ISBN 978-1-80079-516-7. 264 pages. 2023.

Vol. 119   Brian J. Murphy: Beyond Sustenance: An Exploration of Food and
          Drink Culture in Ireland
          ISBN 978-1-80079-956-1. 328 pages. 2023.

Vol. 120	Fintan Cullen (ed.): Ireland and the British Empire: Essays on Art and Visuality ISBN 978-1-78874-299-3. 264 pages. 2023.
Vol. 121	Natalie Wynn and Zuleika Rodgers (eds): Reimagining the Jews of Ireland: Historiography, Identity and Representation ISBN 978-1-80079-083-4. 308 pages. 2023.
Vol. 122	Paul Butler: A Deep Well of Want: Visualising the World of John McGahern ISBN 978-1-80079-810-6. 244 pages. 2023.
Vol. 123	Carlos Menéndez Otero: The Great Pretenders: Genre, Form, and Style in the Film Musicals of John Carney ISBN 978-1-80374-135-2. 258 pages. 2023.
Vol. 124	Gerald Dawe: Politic Words: Writing Women	Writing History ISBN 978-1-80374-259-5. 208 pages. 2023.
Vol. 125	Marjan Shokouhi: From Landscapes to Cityscapes: Towards a Poetics of Dwelling in Modern Irish Verse ISBN 978-1-80079-870-0. 260 pages. 2023.
Vol. 126	Pat O'Connor: A 'proper' woman? One woman's story of success and failure in academia ISBN 978-1-80374-305-9. 248 pages. 2023.
Vol. 127	Natalie Wynn: Community, Identity, Conflict: The Jewish Experience in Ireland, 1881–1914 ISBN 978-1-78707-483-5. 338 pages. 2024.
Vol. 128	Marie-Violaine Louvet: The Irish Against the War: Post-Colonial Identity & Political Activism in Contemporary Ireland ISBN 978-1-80079-998-1. 296 pages. 2024.
Vol. 129	Anne Rainey: Hiberno-English, Ulster Scots and Belfast Banter: Ciaran Carson's Translations of Dante and Rimbaud ISBN 978-1-80374-070-6. 338 pages. 2024.
Vol. 130	Nicole Volmering, Claire M. Dunne, John Walsh and Noel Ó Murchadha (eds): Irish in Outlook: A Hundred Years of Irish Education ISBN 978-1-80374-090-4. *Forthcoming*. 2024.

Vol. 131 Grace Neville, Sarah Nolan and Eugene O'Brien (eds): 'Getting the Words Right': A *Festschrift* in Honour of Eamon Maher
ISBN 978-1-80374-144-4. 382 pages. 2024.

9 781803 741444

Milton Keynes UK
Ingram Content Group UK Ltd.
UKHW020751061024
449258UK00009B/179